Speed Reading
for Faster,
More Efficient Comprehension

Mabel Y. Laughter

East Carolina University

Charles E. Merrill Publishing Company
A Bell & Howell Company
Columbus   Toronto   London   Sydney

Published by
Charles E. Merrill Publishing Co.
A Bell & Howell Company
Columbus, Ohio 43216

This book was set in Times Roman and Helvetica.
Production Editor: Lucinda Ann Peck.
Text Designer: Lucinda Ann Peck.

Acknowledgments for reading selections and other quoted material are included on pages 347–350 at the end of the book. These pages are an extension of the copyright page.

Library of Congress Catalog Card Number: 81-85123
International Standard Book Number: 0–675–09877–7
Printed in the United States of America
1 2 3 4 5 6 7 8 9 10—86 85 84 83 82

To
Joe, Tara, and Alex
With Love

Contents

Preface

Speed Reading for Faster, More Efficient Comprehension is designed to help instructors in developmental reading programs who need a core reading program to which other activities may be added. This text provides that core in a series of units, each of which is completely independent of all others. It is designed to promote mastery learning of specific related skills. Supplementary reading selections are provided for skills that the student is likely to find difficult, thus eliminating the instructor's need to search for appropriate exercises from other sources.

A search of the literature in developmental reading for upper level students yielded specific skills and sequences for their development. Thus, in this text, units 1, 2, 3, 4, and 6, when used sequentially, develop high-powered speed skills and efficient comprehension. Units 1, 2, 3, 5, and 7, when combined, help develop effective study reading skills for use in highly technical materials. If the entire text is used and all units are completed, students will also gain reading flexibility, acquiring skills that help them adjust their speed and reading strategies according to the difficulty of the material and their purpose for the reading.

In other types of developmental reading programs, instructors need to personalize their students' reading training without employing dozens of separate reading materials. Upper level students need a reading program that contains varied activities and materials. Creating this type of program, however, is often impractical. Individualizing the programs of 100 to 200 students is difficult and time-consuming because of the logistics involved in selection, distribution, collection, and storage of materials. *Speed Reading for Faster, More Efficient Comprehension* provides numerous supplementary reading selections and activities. (See, for example, pages 67–114 and 293–98.) And, because each unit is independent of the others, instructors can easily tailor a reading program to a student's individual needs by assigning appropriate units and supplementary selections. Exercises and reading selections designed to strengthen the following skills are presented in this text:

1. Using high-powered speed for pleasure reading
2. Using efficient study reading rates

3. Developing flexible reading rates depending on the purpose of the reading
4. Analyzing word meaning
5. Previewing
6. Phrase reading
7. Recognizing keys to meaning in the organization of a selection
8. Skimming
9. Scanning
10. Identifying key words
11. Heeding "speed signals" in reading

Many students, particularly those who have been required to pursue reading improvement training, approach programmed instructional materials reluctantly. *Speed Reading for Faster, More Efficient Comprehension* offers exercises in building vocabulary, comprehension, and speed in a way that intrigues reluctant upper level readers. The reading selections are taken from current, relevant books, magazines,and newspaper articles. The exercises have been constructed and adapted from these same sources to stimulate the interest of the students.

The text introduces students to a skill and proceeds step by step until the students can apply that skill while reading. At all times, increased comprehension is stressed, regardless of what speed or technique is used. If efficient comprehension usually develops more slowly than the acquisition of the specific skill or technique, the text alerts the students to this and urges them to continue the practice at home and in all reading until they reach the desired level of comprehension.

An *Instructor's Manual* is also available from the publisher. It provides help for instructors in writing individualized reading programs and gives alternatives for teaching students who are having difficulty with a particular skill or unit. The readability levels are given for all full length reading selections, including supplementary readings. Additional activity suggestions are given for students who advance rapidly through the learning sequences. Recommendations are also provided for the diagnostic evaluation and counseling of developmental reading students.

Mabel Y. Laughter
Director, Developmental Reading
Program for University Students
East Carolina University
Greenville, North Carolina

To the Student

As a mature reader, you have already developed many sets of good reading skills. Word recognition, comprehension or meaning-getting skills as well as study skills help you easily complete your study assignments and pleasure reading. But what about the time it takes you to complete those reading tasks? Do you ever complain about the length of a reading assignment? Do you often not retain as much information about the reading as you would like? If so, perhaps your speed reading skills are not as fully developed as the other techniques you have already mastered. Being able to read quickly and remember what you have read is an important characteristic of a good reader.

You are now ready to begin one of the most important ventures in your quest for better reading skills—development of speed reading techniques. *Speed Reading for Faster, More Efficient Comprehension* will help you develop greater vocabulary power, faster rates of reading, and techniques for deeper understanding of the material read. As you will see, just being able to read faster is no good unless you can retain what you have read.

As you work through the text, you will find "Comprehension Checks" following each selection that test how well you remember the content of the readings. You will also work on several exercises that will help develop techniques such as previewing, phrase reading, scanning, and skimming that are crucial for efficient, fast reading. The selections are varied so you can apply your newly developed skills to both pleasure reading and study assignments.

UNIT 1

Becoming a Flexible Reader

The most important quality you develop as a speed reader is *flexibility*,[1] the skill to select the most appropriate speed to use with your reading material. Just as a race car driver gears up for speed on the straight way or slows down when the caution flag is up, so should you, the speed reader, adjust your reading rate. Easy materials are meant to be read quickly because the reader does not need to remember every word or event. However, in study reading, you must use a slower speed because of the importance of the information. You can use faster speeds for studying once you learn techniques for becoming thoroughly familiar with the material *before* you begin to read.[2] These techniques, presented in Unit 2, will teach you to preview a selection so when you do begin to read, you will be able to organize quickly and comprehend the ideas. Therefore, you can read even study materials much faster and yet remember what you have read.

WHAT ARE YOUR PRESENT RATES OF READING?

Before you begin to master techniques for improving your speeds of reading, you will need to answer three questions: What are your current reading rates? What is your accuracy in comprehending what you have read? Are you a flexible reader? To help you answer these questions, here are three reading selections for you to read. Before beginning, carefully examine the directions. Determine how you are to read the selection, and then begin reading. You will need a watch with a second hand for recording the time.

Selection 1 is to be read just for fun. It is easy, narrative material. Read as you normally do. Using your watch, record the hour, minute, and second of both your beginning time and ending time in the space provided in the margin of the selection.

Ready? Begin!

Selection 1: Car Rentals

Beginning Time:

_____

Total Words: 1178

For most of us, vacation is all too brief—just a couple of weeks and it's over. And that raises a question: Should you take your car? You'd probably save dollars that way, but you may squander precious vacation days driving hundreds of miles just to get to where the fun begins.

It might make more sense to fly to a city near the places you plan to visit and rent a car there. You'll stretch your vacation, do more sight-seeing, and cover more ground where it counts.

Unfortunately, you can't always assume that you'll automatically get the best or lowest car rental rate for your needs. The rate structure is a complicated maze that varies according to size and type of car, where and when you rent it, how far you drive it, how long you keep it, where you return it, and whether you decide on a national or local rental firm.

People in the reservations offices are also under great pressure to get you to reserve a car—any car—and then get you off the line. Why? Because call volume is almost always heavy, and because some firms rate individual job performance by the number of calls handled. So, when you call seeking full information and comparison prices, you may find yourself in an adversary position with the person answering the phone. The industry is beginning to correct this situation, but it will take time. Meanwhile, the best way to get the best deal is to understand some basic facts about rental rates and know the right questions to ask—persistently.

Here are some of the key factors that influence rental rates:

Car size. Understandably, it will cost more to rent a Cadillac than a Pinto.

Where you rent the car. Not all cars are available in all cities all the time. And not all rates are available everywhere. As a general rule, both luxury and economy cars become increasingly scarce in smaller towns. They seldom offer the special or vacation rates that you're likely to find in larger cities.

Where you return the car. In many cases, money-saving rates and special deals are available only if you return the car to the city where you rent it. There are exceptions to this. In California, for example, a car rented from one of the major rental firms can be dropped off almost anywhere.

How long you keep it. Generally, the longer you keep the car, the less it costs per day.

A car rental company's brochure may list dozens of different rates, depending on the above factors and the type of rate involved, but basically there are four kinds of rates:

Wet rates. A wet rate is one in which the rental company reimburses you for gas. Charges are based on so many dollars a day and so many cents a mile. But note carefully: The term ''day'' may mean anything from eight to 24 hours, depending on which company you choose.

The wet rate is most practical for business trips that don't entail much driving. Business discounts usually apply.

Dry rates. A dry rate simply means that you buy your own gas. Most basic car rental rates are dry rates, although major rental companies will quote both wet and dry rates. In many cases, to get a dry rate you must return the car to the city in which you rent it, and you may have to rent a particular type or size of car. Regular dry rates are based on so many dollars a day and so many cents a mile, as are wet rates; the difference is the price of the gas, which you furnish. Business discounts normally don't apply.

Holiday and weekend rates. These are reduced dry (buy-your-own-gas) rates. There are several versions, but normally the rates are offered only in large cities where business is slack on holidays and weekends. In New York City where business is never slack, these rates won't apply. Generally, you have to return the car to the city in which you rent it and be willing to take whatever size car is available.

Unlimited mileage rate. This is a dry rate in which you pay a flat fee. Thus, it's most practical for long-distance driving. The rate is available primarily in larger cities, and again you normally have to return the car to the same city in order to get the rate. As mentioned earlier, there are exceptions to this in some states. The top three rental firms require you to keep the car a minimum number of days, ranging from three to seven. Other firms have unlimited mileage plans of shorter duration.

Vacationers almost always save money by using the unlimited mileage rate.

Now that you know generally how the rates apply, you need to know exact rates for your particular plans. The best way to get them is to provide the rental agent with the information he or she needs. Begin the conversation by stating what size car you'll need, where you'll rent and return it, and how long you'll keep it.

Be sure to allow yourself some leeway. Before you call, check your map for a couple of alternative rent-and-travel plans.

Finally, keep these tips in mind:

Find out how the rental company defines a "day." The cost difference between an eight-hour "day" and a 24-hour one can be considerable.

Always ask about the contingencies that may apply to the rates quoted you. Do you have to return the car to the same city? Will the rates be different if you keep the car a certain number of days?

Don't ask for only one kind of rate. Even if you think you know which will be best, or a computer has preselected a probably "best" rate for you, ask about all four types. For instance, you may be employed by a company that gets a discount from a car rental company. Or, perhaps you're not driving too far, and thus might save by taking the wet rate. At the same time, don't automatically reserve with the company where your business rents cars. The discounts commonly offered might mean a smaller savings than a non-discounted rental from a company that simply has lower rates.

Ask about a discount even if you don't think you qualify for one. Rental agencies in many areas routinely extend courtesy discounts to firemen, librarians, and people they happen to like. A reservationist in one office said, "If they're wearing a suit and they ask, we give them a discount."

Ending Time:

_____

WPM: _____

Did you record your ending time?

Now check your comprehension accuracy by answering the following questions without looking back at the story.

Comprehension Check: Car Rentals

Directions: Complete each of the following statements by writing in or circling the correct answer.

1. The author is writing principally for

    a. business executives.
    b. vacationers.
    c. large families who plan to travel.

2. Renting a car in the town of your destination

    a. is most desirable when only so many days are available and driving time would consume most of these.
    b. is uneconomical since rates are more reasonable if the car is rented and returned to your hometown.
    c. is very unwise as there is no guarantee that one will be available.

3. *Wet rates* refer to

    a. the rental company's reimbursing you for the gasoline use.
    b. your buying your own gasoline in addition to paying a set amount per mile traveled.
    c. your paying a flat fee that includes mileage and gasoline.

4. What procedure does the author suggest you use when seeking information from those people working at the car rental agency's reservation desk?

    _____

    _____

Comprehension Accuracy:

5. When renting a car, your personal appeal has nothing to do with the service you receive.

    True   False

_____

You can now begin answering the three questions about your present speed reading skills. First of all, what is your present speed of reading? Table 1.1 outlines the steps to follow to determine this rate.

Table 1.1   *Determining Your Rate of Reading*

1. Subtract your beginning time from your finishing time.

       9:48 Ending Time
    − 9:45 Beginning Time
         3 Minutes Total

2. Now find the number of seconds it took to read the article by multiplying sixty times the number of minutes it took for you to read the selection.

       60 Seconds
    × 3 Minutes Total
     180 Seconds

_____

SOURCE: Nila Banton Smith, *Read Faster and Get More From Your Reading* (Englewood Cliffs, N.J.: Prentice-Hall, Inc., 1958), p. 8. Used by permission.

3. Divide the total number of words in the selection by the number of seconds that it took you to read the selection. Be sure to use two decimal places.

$$180 \text{ secs.} \overline{\smash{\big)}\ .00 \text{ words}}$$

4. Multiply the answer times sixty (seconds). The net total is the number of words per minute (WPM) that you read.

Let's apply Nila Smith's procedure to "Car Rentals."

1. Suppose you began the selection at 2:40 and finished it at 2:44. That's a total of four minutes reading time.

$$
\begin{array}{rl}
2{:}44 & \text{Ending Time} \\
-\ 2{:}40 & \text{Beginning Time} \\
\hline
4 & \text{Minutes Total}
\end{array}
$$

2. Now multiply sixty times the total number of minutes:

$$
\begin{array}{rl}
60 & \text{Seconds} \\
\times\ \ 4 & \text{Minutes Total} \\
\hline
240 & \text{Seconds}
\end{array}
$$

3. Divide the total number of words in the selection (1178) by the number of seconds it took you to read the selection (240).

$$
\begin{array}{r}
4.90 \\
240\ \overline{\smash{\big)}\ 1178.00} \\
\underline{960}\qquad \\
2180 \\
\underline{2160}\ \\
200
\end{array}
$$

(Be sure to carry out the division to two decimal places.)

4. Multiply the answer times sixty for the total number of words per minute.

$$
\begin{array}{rl}
60 & \text{Seconds} \\
\times 4.9 & \\
\hline
294 & \text{Words Per Minute (WPM)}
\end{array}
$$

HOW ACCURATE IS YOUR COMPREHENSION?

The second question in evaluating your present reading rate is how efficiently you read. To determine accuracy in comprehension, first decide how many points each question is worth. This figure can be found by dividing the number of questions into 100 (because scores are based on 100 percent accuracy). The number of correct answers, multiplied by the number of points each question is worth, equals the comprehension accuracy.

Now you are ready to determine your comprehension accuracy for the questions at the end of Selection 1, "Car Rentals." First, to find out how many points each of the five questions is worth, divide five into 100. Each correct

Sample Reading Progress Chart

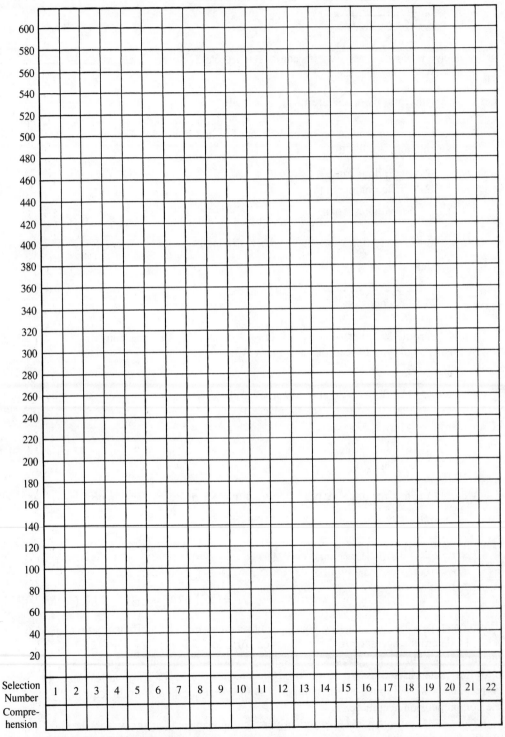

Goal for High-Powered Speed: _____

Goal for Efficient Study: _____

answer is thus worth twenty points. Then look at the Answer Key at the end of Unit 1. How many correct answers did you get? Multiply the number of correct answers by twenty. This procedure yields your comprehension score.

Charting Your Scores

To chart your scores for Selection 1, turn to the Sample Reading Progress Chart on p. 6. Below the box numbered 1 in the line marked "Comprehension," record your comprehension accuracy score. Then move vertically up the column until you find the number of words per minute (WPM) that is nearest your reading rate for the first selection. Place a dot in the first column for Selection 1 at that point.

As you work through each selection and comprehension check in *Speed Reading*, turn to the reading Progress Chart at the end of each chapter and chart your scores.

Before considering the third question in evaluating your present reading rate, whether you are a flexible reader, read the two selections that follow and chart your scores for each. Now proceed to Selection 2.

Reading this article will help you check your rate of reading and comprehension of interesting, informative materials. Read at your normal pace. Record your time in hours, minutes, and seconds both at the beginning and ending of your reading. When you have finished, answer the comprehension questions without looking back at the story. Check your answers in the Answer Key at the end of Unit 1.

Selection 2: Look Out—Your Punctuation Is Showing! ━━━━━

Beginning Time:

_____

Total Words: 570

Did you ever think of people as resembling punctuation marks?

There is the period person, for instance. His judgments are decisive. His pronouncements final. There's simply no use arguing with him, period. He always has the last word.

Or take the quotation marks personality, who carries on almost his entire life's conversation in quotes. Impressed by his vast reading background and the rich storehouse into which his retentive memory can dip, you seldom stop to think that he produces almost no ideas of his own.

The comma person is hesitant, meek, and a trifle pedantic. Careful pauses mark his sentences, as if compelled neatly to hook each thought before proceeding.

The colon and semicolon type is first cousin to the common comma, though a bit bigger, broader, often trailing an advanced degree and a Phi Beta Kappa key. His pauses are less those of the uncertain and tentative than of the organized thinker who lovingly groups his often complex ideas. No mad rush of words for him; you can almost see the structure of his concepts impressively laid out.

The CAPITAL LETTER individual Thinks Big, Talks Big. He is a name dropper, and the bigger the Name the better. Yet he is robust and entertaining, for everything he describes is Epic in scope. He can make a trip to the market to buy a pound of liver sound like an African safari; or if female, a polite thank you to the man who picks up her gloves on a bus, the beginning of a mad romance with a VIP.

No use trying to relate your adventures to the Capital Letter Kids. They're simply too enthralled with their own, you don't stand a chance. But they can be fascinating.

Then there is the species of human being whose entire approach to life seems to be shaped like a question mark. He concludes his simplest statements with, "Isn't that so?" "How about it?" "Wouldn't you say?" He doesn't converse with you, he tests his ideas on you in a kind of earnest interview. Which can be flattering, of course, but also disconcerting.

The no punctuation at all personality talks a blue streak racing from subject to subject without pausing to breathe and seems to have been born talking and will die talking and is hard to get away from especially on the phone but he's often warmhearted and wonderful.

His (or more often her) next of kin is the parenthesis person, who eventually gets back to the original idea, but only after wandering down a bewildering labyrinth of side trails. "This was when Arnold was five years old (Arnold, by the way, was my husband's little brother, who'd been adopted by his stepmother, his stepmother was one of the Flying Filberts—did I ever tell you about their act?). Well, it seems—" And eventually, "Now where was I? Oh, yes, Arnold—"

My favorites are those people whose whole approach to life is best expressed by an exclamation point! They have the gift of enthusiasm. To them everything is vital, exciting, stimulating. They are vigorous, not only in their own speech, but the manner in which they listen. They are not afraid to exclaim.

"An exclamation point in writing," said F. Scott Fitzgerald, "is like laughing at your own jokes." Well, me, I like people who laugh at their own jokes. And at other people's. Who aren't ashamed of their own emotions or unwilling to share yours.

Exclamation mark people! Give us more of them!

Ending Time:

_____

WPM: _____

Comprehension Check: Look Out. . . .

Directions: Complete each of the following statements by writing in or circling the correct answer.

1. Comparing people to punctuation marks was the author's method

   a.   of securing and holding your attention.
   b.   of showing his sarcasm for human beings.
   c.   of alerting the reader to the dangers of being overly trustful.

2. The "name dropper" person who talks big is considered to be

   a.   a colon person.
   b.   a comma person.
   c.   a capital letter person.

3. The author was most partial to the

   a.   period person.
   b.   capital letter person.
   c.   exclamation person.

4. The "no punctuation person" talks like a blue streak and yet is a warm person.

   True   False

5. Which of the following punctuation marks was not used in the comparisons? Check (✔) one.

  period   question mark   semicolon   parentheses
  colon   apostrophe   exclamation mark   comma

Comprehension Accuracy:
_____

Refer to pages 4 and 5 if you need help computing your reading rate or comprehension accuracy scores. Chart your scores for Selection 2, "Look Out—Your Punctuation Is Showing," on the Sample Reading Process Chart on p. 6.

You are now ready to determine your rate when reading a more difficult selection. Read as if this was one of your study assignments.

Selection 3: Images of Nature ━━━━━━━━━

Beginning Time:
_____

Total Words: 1065

"Almost every Englishman," Kenneth Clark once said, "if asked what he meant by 'beauty,' would begin to describe a landscape. . . ." The same might be said of a Japanese, or an American, or, in fact, almost any citizen of a modern society. To the average man, the art of painting is often identified with the landscape—this despite the fact that landscape painting is a vanishing species in the world of art.

This popular conception of art is continually reinforced by the endless number of reproductions of landscape paintings sold in department stores for the decoration of American living rooms. Perhaps the proliferation of these images in our culture has led to their self-cheapening and has reduced them to little more than pleasant ornaments. If this is so, it obscures the fact that landscape painting is a sophisticated product of art and human consciousness. It is the result of a long evolution of artistic changes linked to a history of changing human attitudes toward the natural environment. Varieties of human and cultural relationships to nature and their corresponding representations in art (not only in terms of landscape) are the subjects of this chapter.

Paleolithic Painting. Animals appear to have been the very first subject matter of art. So far as we know, the earliest image makers were members of a hunter-warrior society that existed more than fifteen thousand years ago. The Paleolithic (Old Stone Age) culture left in its painting and sculpture an artistic record of all the larger fauna—mammoths, bison, horses, rhinoceroses, boars, wolves, and reindeer—that inhabited Europe at the time. Ever since the discovery of this art around a century ago, observers have been impressed by the evidence it provides of an extraordinary level of artistic observation and image-forming ability.

Although some of the species painted on the walls of the caves near Lascaux in southern France may no longer exist, the hunter-artists made their images so vivid that we have no trouble recognizing them as various types of grazing animals. The outlines and proportions seem to have been based on fairly accurate observations of the profile views of real beasts. Shown in a variety of lifelike postures, many of the images give the appearance of animals caught in the act of running. Their colors of dark reds, browns, and blacks—still visible after so many thousands of years—raise questions about what the artists used for paints-mixed

SOURCE: From ART IN CONTEXT by Jack A. Hobbs, © 1975 by Harcourt Brace Jovanovich, Inc. Reprinted by permission of publisher.

pigments of red ocher and manganese with animal fat, and then used reeds or animal tails for transferring this mixture to the walls. There is also reason to believe that some of the artists developed a prototype of the air-brush, a painting tool of the twentieth century. The images in the caves of Font-de-Gaume and Altamira are even more lifelike than those in Lascaux. They are extremely convincing because of their shapes and details, but mostly because of their sense of volume, a chiaroscuro effect that may have been accomplished by spraying paint with a blowpipe.

There is a sharp contrast in levels of sophistication between the images of animals and the images of other subjects. Representations of people are like stick figures; the rare references to landscape features such as rocks, plants, and streams are more like schematic symbols than images. Likewise, the arrangements of the animals (with or without other images) reveal none of the sophisticated methods—overlapping, vertical placement, variations in size, and linear perspective—for showing spatial depth in a landscape picture. Indeed, few of the arrangements seem determined by any identifiable logic; one animal overlaps another for no apparent reason other than being painted on the same space at a later time. Occasionally two or more animals are purposely juxtaposed to illustrate an event such as a chase or combat, but beyond this they are not related to what we would consider a pictorial setting. The intense realism of Paleolithic art is restricted almost entirely to the portrayal of the individual animal.

But if we speculate on the kind of lighting (or lack of it) that was available, we can guess that prehistoric people probably could not have viewed more than one painting at a time anyway. Imagine what it must have been like to see one of these beasts leap into view as a torch was waved in front of it. This intriguing mental image leads us to wonder about what an animal picture meant to these hunters. It requires quite a lot of imagination to piece together the few bits of evidence and guess the purpose and meaning of prehistoric art. The awkward location of many of the murals and the poor ventilation of the various chambers disprove theories that these caves were used as art galleries or dwellings. This, plus the fact that many of the images of beasts show the marks—real or painted—of weapons, suggests that they did not serve purely aesthetic purposes.

The best guess is that the awkward locations served as privileged sanctuaries for religious rites and that the murals of beasts contained within served magical purposes. Religion and myth mirror the needs of a society. And animals, which to the Paleolithic hunters meant nothing less than survival, must inevitably have been at the center of their religion.

There is a parallel both in art and crafts between Paleolithic culture and the recently extinct society of African Bushmen. Totemism, a belief that animals are ancestrally or spiritually related to humans, thrived among the Bushmen, and their myths are laced with stories of people turning into animals and vice versa. Their sacred rites, accordingly, focused on animals. Sexual initiations were woven in with ritual killings of animals or symbolic killings performed by hunter-dancers dressed in animal costumes. The existence of illustrations of men-beasts on Paleolithic walls further strengthens the parallel, suggesting that those prehistoric hunters, like the African Bushmen, performed animal rites and believed in a form of totemism.

In such societies distinctions were not made between the supernatural and the natural. Since Paleolithic man's world was totally bound to animals, the art of the animal in this world must have assumed awesome significance. Its magic would not only have been sought to ensure success in the hunt but would have been part of the very structure of belief and social continuity. In a sense, these paintings were not images but real spirits occupying the same magical stage as the hunter-dancers.

Ending Time:

_____

WPM: _____

Comprehension Check: Images of Nature

Directions: Complete each statement by circling the correct answer.

1. The first subject matter of art was
   a. animals.
   b. landscapes.
   c. people.

2. In Paleolithic painting, the people are portrayed
   a. with sophisticated overlapping and linear perspective.
   b. as stick figures.
   c. with clay.

3. The awkward locations of the paintings served as sanctuaries for religious rites.

   True   False

4. Totemism is a belief that animals are ancestrally or spiritually related to humans.

   True   False

5. Paleolithic paintings were merely expressions of art to the people.

   True   False

Comprehension Accuracy:

_____

Record your ending time. Check your answers to the comprehension questions for "Images in Nature" in the Answer Key at the end of Unit 1. Compute both your rate of reading and comprehension accuracy scores. Then plot your scores for Selection 3 on the Sample Reading Progress Chart on p. 6.

Are you a flexible reader? Examine the Sample Reading Progress Chart. Were your rates approximately the same while reading the three different types of materials? If they were, you are using the same reading speed for three very different types of reading materials. To be a flexible reader, you must learn to adjust your reading rate according to the level of difficulty of the selections and the purposes for which you read them. For instance, you should have read Selection 1 on "Car Rentals," an example of pleasure reading, much more quickly than you read Selection 3 on "Images in Nature," an example of a study assignment. Interesting, informative materials will be read with normal or fast speeds depending on how much you want to remember of the articles. But study materials should be read much more carefully and slowly because of the importance of the information. You may be asked, for example, to answer questions, take an exam, or write a paper on those topics presented in the study material. The ability to vary your rate of reading for such materials can be developed and improved through practice. This flexibility can be acquired only after you master the many speed reading techniques presented in *Speed Reading*.

What Do You Know About Your Speeds of Reading?

At this point you have determined how quickly you normally read and, in general, the accuracy of your comprehension. Future growth will be measured by the amount of gain you show over your scores for Selections 1, 2, and 3.

You have also demonstrated to yourself whether you flexibly switch from one speed to another to read as quickly and efficiently as possible. If you read everything at the same rate, you will need to develop flexibility; all techniques and practice exercises presented in *Speed Reading* are designed to help you acquire this important skill. Further, you will learn to use high-powered speed reading for easier materials and to develop efficient study reading rates.

Which Speeds Are Appropriate?

When you consider which speed you should apply to a particular selection, you can draw from a "collection" of many. You may choose to *skim* or *scan*—two of the high-powered speed techniques. Or you may apply an actual reading rate— slow for study or fast for pleasure—appropriate to your purpose. Table 1.2 gives approximate speeds suitable for reading certain types of materials.

As you examine Table 1.2, you see that the high-powered technique of skimming is inadequate for careful study reading and perhaps much too fast even for pleasure reading. If you want only to determine whether or not you wish to read a particular book, then skimming would be most appropriate. Selection of appro- priate speed depends on what you want to gain from the reading—your purpose.

Table 1.2   *Different Speed for Different Purposes*

Type of Speed	Rate	Usability for Type of Reading Material
Scanning	Approximately 1,500 or more	Locating a date, name, etc. on a page or in a column
Skimming	Approximately 800–1000	To get the "gist" of an article or passage, locating the overall idea
Actual Reading		
Very fast	400+	Entertaining materials
Fast	350	Light, fairly easy materials, looking only for main idea
Average	250	Novels, some texts or magazines such as *Scientific American*, etc.
Slow or study	Below 250 to 50 or less	Study materials or scholarly works

SOURCE: From Ellen Lamar Thomas and H. Alan Robinson, IMPROVING READING IN EVERY CLASS, Second Edition. Copyright © 1977 by Allyn and Bacon, Inc., Boston, pp. 157–60. Reprinted with permission.

When selecting the appropriate speed at which you will read, you must recognize that another factor, "internal rate adjustment,"[3] will affect your reading rate. This simply means that an author may begin writing with an easy explanation that can be read quickly. The main body of the report or essay probably contains solid facts and explanations that require more careful reading. The summary or closing becomes simpler as the writer "winds down" her explanations. Major points discussed in the body of the paper are reiterated in closings. Thus, the reader is already familiar with the ideas and can again increase his reading rate.

Obviously then, you as a reader may practice flexibility in choice of rate even *within* a single article. For example, you might choose to read at approximately 150 words per minute overall. You may find as you begin reading that you are very familiar with the material and may speed up to 250 or 300 words per minute only to slow down again if you reach more difficult passages.

Other factors such as temperament and intelligence also affect the reading speeds you use. Obviously, each reader selects his or her own speeds; one speed for everyone is not attainable.[4]

Practice Sheet—What Approach Will You Take? **Table 1.3**

Remember: Your purpose
Difficulty of the material for you
Your familiarity with material

Deliberate Choice of Approach

1. Scanning
2. Skimming
3. Actual reading

   a. very rapid reading
   b. rapid reading
   c. average reading
   d. slow and careful reading

Suppose you are to read the following materials for the purposes as stated.

Think over the considerations listed above, then select your approach. Of course, practice in setting your approach by examining the actual material you're to read is essential, and your training will provide such practice soon. This practice exercise is just to alert you to the considerations which should control your reading rates.

Type and Difficulty of Reading Material	Your Purpose in Reading It	Estimate the Approach for You
1. The chapter on Reconstruction after the Civil War in a social studies textbook.	Your instructor has announced that thorough understanding and retention are expected. There is to be a test on the details.	
2. A light, fast-moving Perry Mason story, *The Case of the Borrowed Brunette*.	You are reading only to pass time pleasantly.	

Type and Difficulty of Reading Material	Your Purpose in Reading It	Estimate the Approach for You
3. A chapter on "The Chemical Basis of Life" in a science textbook.	You want to retain the main ideas and all the important details in this chapter.	
4. Your science teacher has assigned the problem "What are the factors that influence the climate of any area of the earth's surface?"	You want to look through various books to locate the parts that offer material you will read carefully later.	
5. A *Reader's Digest* article.	You would like to find out the general content before deciding whether you want to read the article.	
6. An encyclopedia article on the life of President Franklin D. Roosevelt.	You want to learn what college President Roosevelt attended.	
7. The various essays on friendship by Emerson, Aristotle, and Bacon. The rhetorical patterns are complex. Some of the concepts are abstract and difficult to comprehend.	You are reading for ideas that will guide your own thoughts and actions in your relationships with your own friends.	
8. The chapter on American colonial life in a social studies textbook.	Your teacher has explained that you are to get an overall picture of what it was like to live in colonial times. You are expected to gain from your reading just a general impression, not specific facts.	
9. News stories of local interest in your daily paper.	You wish to keep informed about what is happening in your city.	
10. One of Shakespeare's sonnets that "defines" enduring love.	You want to grasp Shakespeare's ideas about the experiences of a love that lasts. As you read, you will be comparing Shakespeare's experiences with your own.	

SETTING YOUR GOALS FOR SPEED READING GROWTH

At the outset, you the reader must establish your speed reading goals and work consistently toward achieving them. However, you must set realistic limits for yourself. Follow these steps as you identify your goals for speed reading growth.

First, look back at your present rates of pleasure and study reading, your speeds for Selections 1 and 3. Then, consulting Table 1.2, determine your desired reading levels for each kind of reading; set your goals. For future reference, record these numbers on your Sample Reading Progress Chart on p. 6.

Observe one caution when determining desired reading rates: it is more realistic to set a series of short-range goals than it is to try to achieve a major goal all at once. Short-term goals will help you reach your ultimate goal in time but without the frustration that often occurs when you try to learn too much all at once. Approaching reading in this way will also permit an increase in speed without the drastic loss in comprehension that can sometimes occur. Such a procedure assures continuous advancement toward your goals.

NOTES TO UNIT 1

1. Ellen Lamar Thomas and H. Alan Robinson, IMPROVING READING IN EVERY CLASS (Boston: Allyn & Bacon, Inc., 1977), pp. 153–55.

2. Nila Banton Smith, *Read Faster and Get More From Your Reading* (Englewood Cliffs, N.J.: Prentice-Hall, Inc., 1958), p. xi.

3. Thomas and Robinson, IMPROVING READING, pp. 160–61.

4. Thomas and Robinson, IMPROVING READING, pp. 160–61.

Answer Key:
Unit 1

Selection 1: Car Rentals, p. 1

1. b   **2.** a   **3.** a   **4.** Give size of car desired, dates, and points of departure and return. In addition, have alternative rent and travel plans in mind.   **5.** False

Selection 2: Look Out, Your Punctuation is Showing, p. 7

1. c   **2.** c   **3.** c   **4.** True   **5.** apostrophe

Selection 3: Images of Nature, p. 9

1. a   **2.** b   **3.** True   **4.** True   **5.** False

UNIT 2

Crucial Techniques for Both Efficient Study Reading and High-Powered Speed

As you begin to pursue faster reading rates, your major objective will be to rid yourself of the habits of slowness and inefficiency. Two effective techniques that will help you develop new habits to improve both your reading rate and comprehension accuracy are previewing and phrase reading.

Previewing, or examining a selection quickly before reading, is often used by a good reader to help him determine his purpose. A quick preview of the material allows the reader to decide how much he wants to know about the topic and how closely he will read to get the amount of information necessary for his purposes.

Once he does begin to read, he does not read every word; he focuses only on key words related to his purpose. Thus, a good reader does not linger on each word in a line of print. He pauses after each thought unit instead. This technique is *phrase reading*.

In Unit 2, you will first learn the steps for following the procedures of previewing and phrase reading and then apply these techniques to several reading selections. Supplementary readings are provided for additional practice.

PREVIEW: ESTABLISH YOUR PURPOSE FOR READING

When university students approach a reading task, they are often interested in completing it in the least amount of time possible because of other study and social obligations. This is a justifiable position. Why dawdle or struggle ploddingly through a reading assignment? Doing the job well in the least amount of time is excellent conservation of time and energy. Major corporations spend billions of dollars on task analysis—helping the worker produce at a maximum level within the time limits. Why shouldn't students aim for a similar productivity?

The first step toward improving your reading productivity is to realize that many university-level reading assignments contain little or nothing to motivate you to want to read them. Forcing yourself to concentrate as you read takes major effort. At their best, such efforts are usually inefficient. A better procedure would be to ''psyche'' yourself into full concentration when you do read. Whether you like the material or not does not matter; getting the job done does. Most readers pause in the middle of a reading to think of other things like finances, dates, or clothes—a habit that leads to gross inefficiency. Because of this habit, most students will have to reread to be certain they understand the material. As a result, the reading time required becomes even longer and comprehension is usually spotty.

The *preview*, a view of the information before you read it, is a technique that will help you cut your reading time to a fraction of what it was formerly. This process alerts you to the specific topic being discussed and clues you in on the major points made about that topic. Then as you read, you concentrate only on explanations of those points and how they relate to the major topic. You do not dawdle or think of other things; you are too busy concentrating on the topic as it unfolds. *You have a purpose for your reading.* Purpose is critical to both pleasure reading and efficient study reading.

Another valuable by-product of previewing is that it helps you decide how you will read the selection. How long will this reading task take? Which rate will you apply? You set your own time goal to prevent dawdling and apply your full concentration.

Table 2.1 lists the steps Nila Banton Smith suggests you should use when previewing a reading selection. Read through and study these steps before beginning the section on "Applying the Preview."

Table 2.1   *Steps to Follow When Previewing*

1. Study the title.
    (What do you think the author will discuss?)
2. Are subheadings or subtitles used in this selection?
    (What are they and how many?)
3. Locate and examine any audiovisual aids that are provided.
    (For example, what do the pictures, charts, tables, graphs, or maps tell you?)
4. Examine the lengths of the paragraphs.
    (Long, short, average?)
5. Estimate how long it will take you to read the selection.

SOURCE: Nila Banton Smith, *Read Faster and Get More From Your Reading* (Englewood Cliffs, N.J.: Prentice-Hall, Inc., 1958), p. 67. Used by permission.

Applying the Preview to a Reading Selection

The best way to master the preview is to do one. The first reading selection in this Unit, "A Science of Man," clearly demonstrates the efficiency of the preview. Let's begin.

Step 1

Read the title of Selection 1 on p. 19. What does this mean to you? What do you think this selection will discuss? Jot down your ideas in the space provided.

Major Points:

1. _____

2. _____

3. _____

    _____

Main Idea:

To be filled in at a later step. (Do not complete now.)

Step 2

Examine each subheading. Underline the actual points discussed about the topic. Place a check before each point you identified earlier that will actually be discussed in the selection. In the extra space, jot down any points that you did not identify earlier. The total number should equal the number of subtopics in the selection.

Step 3

Now find any visual materials that are provided. Is there a photograph? If so, read the caption. Does it illustrate the title or major idea? Or does it illustrate the meaning of one of the points being made about the major topic? Be sure to determine exactly to what each photograph relates. Did you find a chart, graph or table? If so, these usually depict facts about the title or main idea. One table or chart usually demonstrates how each of the subpoints relates; therefore, the most important information for a whole chapter is identified here. However, if the selection contains no visual aids, you will have to identify the main idea and its supporting details from the title and subtopics alone. Once you have identified the main idea and the subtopics, you know exactly what you should be aware of as you read. Other information provides only explanatory detail. You need to remember it only if it is absolutely necessary to your understanding of the major point. Therefore, to cut down on reading time, preview to identify the main idea and major points made about it. Explanations that clearly illustrate these points should be read carefully. Others that only expand or give further details are less important and can be read quickly. You actually read only the key words in such explanations— not every word. Since your selection contains no visual aids to clarify the main idea and its supporting details, you will have to rely solely on the information given in the title and subtopics to determine what the main idea is.

Go back to Step 1. What is the main idea? Write your answer in the line below "Main Idea."

Step 4

You are almost ready to read the selection, but before you do, take a second to "size up" the paragraphs in the selection. Are they long? Short? Medium-sized? How will you read them?

Step 5

Estimate how long you will give yourself to read this selection. *Don't* give yourself time to dawdle or coast. Read only for explanations of the main idea or title. Force yourself to meet this time limit. Do *not* think of other things. Now begin.

Selection 1: A Science of Man

Beginning Time:

_____

Total Words: 1667

The archives are old; some of the strange letters carved into the rock tablets have been worn almost smooth in the vast sea of time. Yet they remain the only link between Then and Now—and for a race that has clung so romantically to its past, they are a precious link indeed.

It was a young shepherd who first found the tablets, scattered about in the remote corners of a cave to which he often went for shelter when the rain came down too hard and too cold. At first he was amused by the strange lines on the faces of the flat stones, but in time he lost interest and put them back in the shadows that they had occupied for countless years.

But one day he brought one of the stones to his home to place in front of his hearth, for it was wide and flat, and on it he could set the soup pot without spilling it and without burning another hole in the ancient floor—and baby was not so likely to trip over such a flat stone and fall into the fireplace.

The stone was there when it was discovered by a hot and thirsty archeologist who stopped for a drink fifty years later. He was led by the now aged shepherd to the cave in the hills, and in time all the tablets were collected in a far away museum, and stored there in the dark shadows where they remained through several wars and many years. From time to time an enthusiastic graduate student came eagerly to look for a doctoral dissertation in the script on the worn rock faces, eventually lost his enthusiasm, and returned again to the more legible writings of his contemporaries. But some stayed and marveled at the stories on the rocks and translated them for others to read and marvel at.

Among the many tales told on these stones, there is one that must be told here again. It is the story of Oog, a man who professed to be among the first of the thinkers of the People. It is a story told by Oog, and it is about him. Oog writes that it occurred to him that a great many children of the People did not know very much. They did not know that they should walk on the top of the hills where their scent would be carried away into the skies, rather than at the bottom where the scent would find its way to the beasts that lie on the hillsides. They did not know that the huge Bela snake hides among the branches of the Kula berry bushes, not because the snake likes the berries, but because he likes the children. Of this they were ignorant, even as they were ignorant of the skills required to fashion the houses of the People so that the rain would not come in, and of a thousand other things that the People must know. And so the children of the People died like the small rabbits that their mothers cooked; and like the small rabbits, the People continued to make children, but barely managed to keep pace with the heavy losses that they suffered.

It is written on the tables that for these reasons Oog took it upon himself to gather the wisdom of the People in his mind, and to gather the children of the People at his feet—and he became their teacher. And it is written that the People soon flourished, grew greatly in number, and chose others who would also be teachers, for there were too many to sit at the feet of Oog. When this happened, Oog withdrew from the tiring business of transmitting the wisdom of the people to its children, and thought instead of how this could be done in a better way. Accordingly, he thought of education, and in time he came to think of psychology. And because he was clever as well as industrious, he eventually thought of educational psychology.

The story of Oog is therefore the beginning of the story told in this book. It is the story of man, of children, and of the attempts that man makes to impart enough of his wisdom to his children to enable them to obtain more of it by themselves, and to survive. The story of man and his children is the story of psychology; the story of the imparting of wisdom is the story of education, and the story of this book, since it deals with both of these, is the story of educational psychology. Man is therefore the central theme of this book.

And who and what is man?

MAN, THE ANIMAL. Man is the species Homo sapiens. He is an unattractive, smelly, pugnacious creature that walks upright, grunting and bellowing. He is the only one of many species that live on this planet, and he appears to be among the worst adapted. His young are helpless for longer than the young of any other species. He has lost most of his hair and what he has left is of little protection against the cold. His eyesight is weaker than that of most species, and his sense of smell responds only to the strongest odors. If pursued he can run only a very short distance, and that very slowly. He is remarkably unskilled at climbing trees or digging holes; he cannot live under water, and he swims with less grace than almost any other animal, if he swims at all. He is heavy and awkward and cannot fly—he can't even jump very high. He is singularly unequipped with weapons either for defense or for killing food. It is absolutely remarkable and utterly fascinating that this species has survived at all.

And yet it has. Why?

MAN, THE THINKER. If one animal is being pursued by another which is faster and stronger, and which has more highly developed senses, the pursued animal will probably be captured. Yet it may escape by climbing a tree where the predator cannot follow; it may jump into a hole too small for the pursuer, or it may hide somewhere where predators seldom venture. Some of these animals will survive—but most of their energy will be devoted to finding food and avoiding enemies.

If, on the other hand, this animal could amplify its *motor capacities*—make itself stronger, faster, less vulnerable—it might avoid its enemies, and perhaps even find food, more easily. In short, such an animal as man was could best survive by changing its motor capabilities.

This might be accomplished genetically. Through an incredibly slow evolution where only the fittest would survive, man might eventually come to run faster and perhaps swim naturally with some grace. However, if such a change were left to evolution alone, the fittest of man's enemies would also survive and, through their offspring, keep pace with changing man. One can image Thros, a Neanderthal caveman, turning to his wife one morning and saying, "Nghaaa! Gor quinted cor cora corraturi potu. Lesj tunc chica ngha quis." ("Nghaaa! We have to amplify our motor capacities. They got the kid last night.")

But man took the course of evolution into his own hands, to become the first, and perhaps the only, animal to exercise significant control over his world and its future. How does one become stronger? By inventing simple machines—levers, pulleys, wheels, screws, and inclined planes—and by using them to make uncomplicated weapons—bows and arrows, spears, slings, and hatchets. How does one become less vulnerable? By using machines to make both weapons and shelters. Bruner (1964, 1966) sees man's inventions as beginning with the amplification of motor capabilities (the invention of simple machines), followed by amplification of human *sensory capacities* (the invention of telescopes, radio, television, etc.) and culminating in amplification of *ratiocinative* (intellectual) *capacities* (the invention of theory). At present, man appears to be trying to understand and develop his intellectual capacities—and this is one of the functions of psychology.

This physically inferior specimen has survived because of a tremendous advantage that it acquired probably very early in its evolution—the capacity to think. Man's capacity to think allowed him to foresee the consequences of his actions, leading him to devote the time and energy required to escape from the dangers that beset him at the dawn of civilization. In the same way, it is the child's ability to think which allows him to adapt to the world well enough to ensure his survival. Survival simply means learning to cope with the world, however structured and socialized it may be. True, the price of nonsurvival in this sense, is no longer swift and painful death (but it may be incarceration in a mental hospital). Nor has man's increasing ability to amplify his capabilities made survival in the world he has created any simpler. Probably it has become even more difficult. Man has amplified his capabilities to the point where his mushrooming technology is consuming the resources of his planet and replacing them with garbage. Individals can, in their wisdom, speak of Utopia and environmental control; but the human race often appears to be a blundering idiot.

But now we can do much more than simply think—we can think about our thinking. At that, in large part, is psychology.

MAN, THE RACE. Psychological literature, particularly when it deals with individual differences, with measuring intelligence, or with personality, tends to stress the differences among people and to account for variations in behavior on the basis of these differences. For *learning, developmental*, and *motivation theory*, it is probably more useful to deal with similarities. How much more significant it is that all men walk upright than that some men walk faster than others! In the same way, the fact that man can communicate is more important than the fact that he uses many different languages. It is those broad characteristics of human functioning which are relatively common to all men that permit the development of a science of man—a science which, among other things, attempts to answer the questions: "Why does man behave?" and "How does he learn?"

Ending Time:

_____

WPM: _____

Comprehension Check: A Science of Man

Directions: Complete each of the following questions by writing in or circling the correct answer.

1. This selection implies that early man's knowledge was very carefully recorded and preserved for future generations.

    True   False

2. The science of mankind's accomplishments and behavior is known as

    a.   education.
    b.   psychology.
    c.   epidemiology.

3. What role does the author of this selection assign to man's ability to think?

    _____

    _____

4. Humans' success in developing survival strategies has provided time for them to explore more fully

   a. the world of sensations.
   b. the limits of the human physical capacity.
   c. the workings of their intellect.

5. Because all humans share certain _____, it became possible for them to develop the study of their own behavior into a full science.

Comprehension Accuracy:

_____

Did you come close to staying within your time limit? Do you feel that most of the ideas presented were already familiar to you as a result of previewing. Great! Familiarity with the material helps you read much faster.

A second selection is provided for your application of previewing to an actual reading. Remember to follow carefully Smith's steps (on p. 18) for the preview. Now preview Selection 2.

Selection 2: How I Learned to Sleep

Beginning Time:

_____

Total Words: 3592

My bedside clock has a luminous dial, and night after night I was accustomed to watching its ghostly glow at hours off limits to the blessed. Pillows were my punching bags, the mattress my fighting ring. Sheets and blankets served as the ropes against which my body plunged, as I lost, once more, my contest with the night. I was one of the millions of people plagued by chronic insomnia.

One sunny morning last spring, when I got out of bed especially exhausted, I knew I was tired of being tired. I had heard of clinics that help people suffering from troubled sleep. In a burst of faith, I decided to give one a try.

In late May I became a patient at the Sleep-Wake Disorders Unit at Montefiore Hospital in the Bronx, New York. The secretary to whom I'd spoken by phone had inspiringly attested to a high rate of cure. Yet, despite the promise of relief in the offing, I was uncomfortable about the venture. Casually, I studied the literature introducing me to my treatment. Not so casually, I surveyed the sleep-wake log I had been asked to keep—a kind of diary in graph form, on which I would indicate the hour I went to bed, the hour I awoke, an estimate of when I had gone to sleep, when I had awakened in the night, and so forth.

Never a big one for rules (which I would later discover was half my problem), I felt a stir of rebellion at having to pencil in the hours and minutes of my "sleep-wake cycle." Moreover, there was a space on the log where, by circling a number from one to seven, I was to note my state upon arising. Number one (clearly the best) was "Feeling active, vital, alert;" seven (the worst) was, "Almost in reverie. Cannot stay awake. . . ." None matched the way I felt every morning; "rotten" wasn't listed. Still, I had been told to change nothing yet. For the time being, compliance amounted merely to keeping track.

On the day of my first appointment, two weeks after receiving the log, I took the subway to the Bronx. The log had been no bother, but now many tests lay ahead of me, and lengthy interviews to boot. I was nervous.

Upon reaching the clinic, I was quickly closeted in a room and seated at a desk, on which was a stack of papers and one enormous form. It amounted to 24 pages, with 550 questions, going by the ominous title of Minnesota Multiphasic Personality Inventory, the famous MMPI. I tried not to laugh at some of the true-false choices. "I like tall women" was one. "I used to like 'drop-the-handkerchief' " was another. Well, I'd been told that it all adds up to a composite picture of who you are.

Several hours later, my hand aching from holding the pencil so long, I was ushered into see the psychologist. He was a kindly man, and I was encouraged. So I laid it on thick, telling him that, yes, I had several personal crises in recent months, but that I had always been a poor sleeper. Maybe it was my upbringing. I ventured, my family's almost Puritanical view that sleeping long was self-indulgent. For years I've waked at around six or seven A.M. The psychologist listened patiently.

After a break for lunch, I was shuttled along to another interview, this time with a neurologist, Dr. Charles P. Pollak, co-director of the clinic. In response to his warm questioning, I went over my travails once more. Yes, I fell asleep quickly enough; no, I could not stay there. My wee hours were spent in endless worry.

"About what?" he asked.

"You name it," I answered.

Then he asked to see my sleep log. I handed it over and warily watched him frown as he scanned it. I had been bad, I knew—my log was hopelessly erratic. I am a free-lance writer, with no boss or live-in family to dictate when I get up or go to bed. I do my work and get it in on time—but I do it, have always done it, at whatever hour of day or night suits me.

Besides my cock-eyed nocturnal habits, my log also revealed that every day I'd had a nap. "This isn't Mexico, you know, where we have to have a siesta," Dr. Pollak said. Why did I always need a nap? Not for sleepiness, I recognized; it was merely something to do—a brief escape from whatever work I was involved in or from momentary boredom. Cut out the naps, I was admonished. Instead, I was to set up a schedule: to go to bed nightly at a strict and regular time, and similarly to set my alarm for a strict and regular arousal. The idea was so foreign to me that I had difficulty picking a time at which I'd agree to go to bed. But keeping "The Late Show" in mind, I decided to retire at one A.M. and to get up at 7:30. I was instructed to keep another sleep log to record this expected change in pattern.

And there was more, which I liked even less. I was not to read in bed. As for "The Late Show," if I wanted to watch it, I'd have to do it elsewhere than from the comfort of my mattress. I was to adhere as carefully as I could to this schedule until I returned to the clinic for my next appointment.

I wanted the insomnia to go away. I didn't want to work at it. With reluctance and indignation, I accepted the rules nonetheless, really as some sort of challenge. Four weeks commenced during which I struggled to maintain my new rigid schedule and I managed in the face of overwhelming frustration. No decent "Late Show" had hit the screen for ages. Listing like a sinking ship from weariness, I cheated—but not severely—going to bed several evenings at midnight and arising when I chose. Though I awakened throughout the night, I was surprised to find that I was returning to sleep more quickly than I was previously wont to do. Perhaps having a schedule did improve my sleep. I was beginning to wonder just how serious my insomnia actually was.

The question evolved naturally enough. I was besieged by something Dr. Pollak describes as akin to a headache; it exists primarily as a symptom or a complaint, rather than an illness in itself. My curiosity was piqued. Entering the clinic had aroused my writer's instinct, too, and staying up until one A.M. gave me plenty of time to delve into the labyrinthine facts at the core of sleep and sleeplessness.

The most basic facts are these: In its beginning stages, sleep progresses in an orderly fashion. The drowsiness preceding sleep is marked by the alpha waves coming from the brain; gradually the brain waves slow down; thoughts start to splinter; images whirl: Stage I of sleep has begun. State II begins when the character of the brain waves changes again. The normal sleeper reaches that point in less than 15 minutes, and soon proceeds down deeper to that luxurious slumber known as delta sleep which, depending on the sleeper's age, may last from 20 minutes to about an hour. In these three stages, the eyes are motionless. But then, some 90 minutes following the onslaught of sleep, a change occurs: The eyes begin to dart rapidly about. This is REM (Rapid Eye Movement) sleep: We are dreaming.

After the first REM sleep, which may last no longer than five minutes, the normal sleeper moves back and forth from State II to REM again, perhaps returning to delta, and almost always returning to an intense REM sleep just before waking.

Sleep researchers think of life as governed by three separate systems of the brain: one for wakefulness, one for sleep, one distinct system for REM. All are contained within the circadian rhythm ("circa" for "about;" "dian" for "day") that roughly corresponds to 24 hours in keeping with the spinning of the earth.

Occasional instances of startling departure from this 24 hour cycle have been noted. Peter Hauri, director of the Dartmouth-Hitchcock Sleep Clinic, in a pamphlet on sleep disorders, cites an astonishing example. A young woman has been fired from her job for habitually arriving late, her morning lethargy provoked by persistent insomnia. When she came to the sleep center, she was out of work and free to retire and get up when she chose. Advised to do exactly that, she kept a sleep log, which took an amazing turn: Her insomnia disappeared. Unrestricted by the requirements of an office job, she was able to sleep normally, living at her pace. Which amounted to work on a book for 20 to 22 consecutive hours, a couple of hours spent at leisure and solid sleep for ten to twelve. Clearly, she was marching to the beat of a different drummer, with a circadian rhythm that ran in the vicinity of 36 to 38 hours!

Disturbed sleep is frequently seen in those whose lives—like mine—demand no more than a sketchy adherence to time cues. Along those lines, Dr. Pollak had indicated that he strongly suspected my living habits to be the major root of my sleep deprivation. It was not impossible, however, that recording the processes of my sleep—by a procedure known as polysomnography—would disclose some organic cause. At any rate, when I returned to the clinic in July, it was to take the first of two polysomnograms.

I arrived at the clinic around ten P.M. Feeling both foolish and apprehensive, I changed into my nightclothes and began to chat with the technician who was preparing to hook me up to what looked like enough wires to garrote a roomful of people. I tried to concentrate on his words, though my mind was naturally dwelling upon the prospect of attempting to sleep while smothering in wires and electrodes. Some of his stories made me feel ordinary. A woman from England, he told me, came and slept in her mink coat—not from cold or fear of theft, but because it was her habit. A man showed up in bandages, having walked right out a second-story window in the middle of a night-terror siege only two nights before he was due for his polysomnogram. "Some people bring their own pillow," the technician said. "We've seen everything here."

As he began to plaster electrodes and other recording gadgets to my head, my brow, my nostrils, my chin, my chest, my legs, another patient arrived. He was voluble; people with sleep problems are prone to rattle on. "I haven't slept well for twenty years," he moaned. "I wake up constantly; I feel lousy all day. I don't believe this place can help me. I've tried every pill there is."

The following evening I was back at the clinic for my second polysomnogram. To my amazement, I had slept the night before, despite the electrodes and wires. I was told that I was not unusual: A number of people claim to sleep better at the clinic than they do at home. Well, the room I was in was black as coal because there were no windows, though the walls were covered with draperies to convey a homey feeling. And the insulation had to be stupendous; I had not heard a single noise. But most of all, I realized, my worries had been deposited, if only temporarily, in some back pocket of my mind. I had only one responsibility that night, which was to go to sleep.

Once again I was buried in equipment. On some forms I was given, I answered questions as to how well I expected to sleep. My estimates would later be measured against the recording. (Some people, called pseudoinsomniacs, sleep well enough but think they don't; as it turned out, I was not one of them.)

With less nervousness than the previous night, I fell asleep rather quickly. But then, at heaven knows what hour, I awoke, from a need to go to the bathroom. The preceding night the technician had assured me that all I had to do in such a circumstance was tap on the wall—he would be there pronto to unleash me; and he had been true to his word. So I tapped on the wall, but what I got this time was absolutely no response. I tapped again. Silence. Peering through the circle in the wall, through which the wires were connected to the pens of the polysomnogram, I saw the top of a head above a chair back, and the head was immobile. Oh, no, I realized—the sleep technician had fallen asleep! Frantically, I scrambled for the light switch. Staring at the jumble of wires, I carefully assessed the odds. What can get plugged in can get plugged out, I managed a release from my harness. Stumbling into the other room, I shouted the technician's name. Jolting awake in shock, he whirled around to look at me, a wraithlike apparition trailing streamers everywhere. "Must have had a good old delta attack," I said, laughing. Apologizing profusely, he shortly afterward escorted me back to bed.

Sleeping pills are big business. How ironic that chemical compounds specifically developed to destroy insomnia so often end up destroying sleep! What happens is that the patient, desperate for sleep, may gain relief for several nights. But the effectiveness of drugs is rapidly lost and the user increases the intake. The person previously suffering from a period of troubled sleep now can barely sleep at all, and what sleep there may be is severely distorted. Barbiturates (Seconal is one brand name) and others of the so-called hypnotic drugs tend to suppress REM sleep as well. And once withdrawn from the drugs, the patient can be subjected to rebound dreaming of a particularly frightening nature.

Some clinicians, nonetheless, find the careful administration of hypnotics permissible in specialized cases. Flurazepam (Dalmane) is one drug that maintains its effectiveness for a month or perhaps longer, and occasions arise when a knowledgeable doctor will resort to prescribing it. At Montefiore, however, few patients are found to require hypnotics; almost always they are only used in a diagnostic framework. "If a drug would work indefinitely, or would not alter sleep except to improve it, and had no serious side effects," says Dr. Pollak, "that would be fine. But even if such an ideal substance existed, I am not sure how often we would need it."

As for alcohol, a cocktail or two before dinner is harmless; but if you're drinking throughout the evening, expect trouble. Belting down a number of drinks before bedtime will guarantee a quick, stuporous knockout, and then a jack-in-the-box pop-up soon down the line, with a near-interminable thrashing about in an effort to recover peace. One more relevant matter: alcohol and drugs depress the central nervous system. Taken together, they may produce a synergistic reaction—as if two and two suddenly added up to six. In the files of medical examiners all over the country are testimonies to the outcome of such combinations.

So pills and alcohol, as well as erratic scheduling and emotional problems, are among insomnia's most frequent causes. Another is conditioning. During times of stress, sleep is often disrupted; but when the stress lifts, an association often remains. The very act of getting into bed brings on an attack of worry that a troubled night is ahead—and the worry ensures that such a night occurs. There are many reasons for insomnia, yet this generality holds: Either the victim has too much activity in the wake system, which may be associated with tension and anxiety, or there is some malfunction in the networks of the brain that aid the progress of sleep. Insomnias that are clearly traceable to a weakness in the sleep system have turned out, so far, to be rare—but specialists have not ruled out biochemical factors that could be present in a small part of the population. What a research bonanza that discovery would be!

How much sleep do we really need and what, in the long run, is sleep's purpose? The need for sleep is remarkably variable in respect both to age and personal requirements. Babies sleep approximately 16 hours. The magical "figure eight" is drawn from the patterns of adolescence, which we perhaps would all like to maintain. Between the ages of 25 and 45, an average sleep plateau remains at about seven hours. In old age, six and a half hours is customary. Yet there is no absolute number of hours that can be cited as "normal" for any age group. Some people are satisfied to get a mere three hours. In rare instances, people have managed to do quite well sleeping just one hour a day. Once they get over the fixation that a specific number of sleeping hours is essential to good health, many supposed insomniacs will find themselves victims only of misinformation. In short, if you feel fine after four hours, stop worrying. Get out of bed and live!

When it comes to the purpose of sleep, experts are of two minds. A minority believes that the requirement for sleep is a matter of conditioning, a hand-me-down business dating back to the days of primitive man, when retiring into the recesses of the cave served as protection from dangerous surroundings. Today more evidence points to sleep as containing genuine restorative properties. Hormone secretions intensify while we sleep; drying cells are replaced by new ones with greater rapidity than when we are awake; dreams are known to be psychologically important, reflecting our unconscious fears and wishes. Sleep renews us—that we know.

Nobody yet has all the answers. But for the vast majority of poor sleepers there are sufficient solutions at hand:

• Measure, on the basis of past experience, just how much sleep you really need to feel fresh and healthy throughout the day. Try setting up a routine such as I've described. My schedule has certainly proved of benefit to me. And consider this: Sleeping a little *less* than you think you must can turn out to be a surprising boon, improving the quality of your rest. Learn to regard your alarm clock as a friend and not as your archenemy.

• Develop an exercise routine. Take up dancing; join the joggers. Sporadic exercise won't be of help—a daily workout is necessary. But steer clear of exercise right before bedtime. For promoting sleep, it works best in the afternoon or in the early evening.

• Food intake seems to have an effect on the quality of sleep. Going to bed hungry brings on discomfort. But so does going to bed after a heavy meal. There is the possibility, according to some researchers, that an amino acid known as L-tryptophan, found in many foods, such as milk, cheese, meat and tunafish, helps bring on sleep. They believe that L-tryptophan contributes to the production of serotonin, a substance found in the centers of the brain that are involved in sleep regulation. Lately, the exact role of serotonin has been questioned, but there is something to L-tryptophan. If your sleeplessness is not too serious, then, a light snack just may improve your slumber. But of course stay away from caffeine, contained in coffee, tea, cola drinks and chocolate.

• If a stressful event has affected your sleep, try setting up new rituals to crack the frustration you've come to associate with bed. Don't force yourself to retire unless you are very sleepy. Get accustomed to the bed for sleep, not watching television or reading. If you can't sleep, get up until you feel intolerably tired and then you can try again. None of these methods will work right away. Gradually, however, the bedroom should no longer be associated in your mind with anger and defeat.

• If your sleep is very bad, the daytime use of mild tranquilizers, in relatively small doses, is medically acceptable—provided your own doctor approves.

• Finally—and this may be the hardest for the insomniac to face—a long delay in being able to fall asleep is often the result of anxiety; difficulty in *staying* asleep and waking excessively early in the morning are more commonly related to depression. Admitting that something is emotionally askew is often the first step toward cure. Examine your sleep patterns closely, and discuss them with your doctor. Some form of psychotherapy might well be of aid.

As for my own specific problem, I was told at my follow-up appointment that the insomnia troubling me so much was of the mild-to-moderate variety. My polysomnograms revealed nothing remarkable—though I was stunned when Dr. Pollak let me know that I got no delta sleep.

"But I thought I slept especially well," I protested.

"No delta sleep," he repeated.

He assured me, however, that I could get along without it. Apparently, I get plenty of REM, and my delta sleep could easily return when my general sleeping pattern improves. Relieved by his words, I began to relax and ponder the techniques he had suggested.

I've followed those guidelines for improving sleep and have done so fairly faithfully. No miracles have occurred. I am convinced that the cure will take a long-range effort. I thought I loathed exercise; I'm learning to like it, and I'm considering a try at Yoga or even meditation. And these behavioral realignments—because that's what they really are—have started to pay off. My daytime weariness has somewhat abated; my night-time tumult is easing. Miracles, no—but I didn't expect them. I'm making peace with the darkness and, bit by bit, I'm on my way.

Ending Time:

_____

WPM: _____

What did you learn from your preview?

Main Idea: _____

Major Points: 1._____

2._____

3._____

_____

_____

_____

Now pretest yourself on Selection 2. Answer as many questions as you can about the story. Check your answers in the Answer Key on p. 65.

Preview Test: How I Learned to Sleep

Directions: Complete the following statements by filling in the missing words.

1. This story is a factual account about _____.

2. There are _____ phases of actual sleep.

3. The author is attending a _____.

4. Sleep and wakefulness cycles seem to revolve around _____

_____.

5. The test that determines if the person experiences all phases of sleep is

the _____.

6. Many Americans must have trouble sleeping because _____

_____.

7. How much sleep a person needs is determined by _____

_____.

8. There are _____ schools of thought about the purpose for sleep.

9. The author's insomnia could be described as _____

_____.

Now read Selection 2 carefully as you had planned. Time yourself. Answer the comprehension questions that follow. Check your accuracy and compute your rate of reading.

Comprehension Check: How I Learned to Sleep

Directions: Complete each of the following statements by writing in or circling the correct answer.

1. Sleep, as the author learned, progresses through stages.
   True   False

2. Time cues play which role in the life of an insomniac? _____
   _____.

3. Drugs such as sleeping aids are very highly effective in at least 90 percent of cases of sleeplessness.
   True   False

4. The biggest fallacy or piece of misinformation about sleep is _____
   _____.

Comprehension Accuracy:

_____

5. Pills, alcohol, erratic scheduling, and emotional problems are among the most frequent causes of insomnia.
   True   False

Making the Preview

Now you are ready to preview a reading selection. This should last only a few seconds; so time yourself, beginning and end. Be certain to read and carry out all of the following instructions.

1. Examine the title to identify the main topic.
2. Examine each subheading to gather as much information as you can about the topic.
3. Note your finishing time.
4. Take the Preview Test that follows the reading selection.

Beginning Time:

_____

Total Words: 1244

Selection 3: The Jogging-Shoe Race Heats Up _____

Jogging is no longer the simple sport it used to be when all that was needed was a T-shirt, some shorts, and a pair of battered sneakers. It is a crusade that involves 25 million Americans. And it is also a $500 million industry that has become as competitive as the New York and Boston marathons.

For years, the running-shoe business was dominated by such foreign manufacturers as Adidas and Puma from Germany and Tiger from Japan. But in the past few years, U.S. brands—Nike from Oregon, and Brooks, New Balance, and Etonic from New England—have become major contenders in the running-shoe race. And conventional athletic-shoe producers Converse and Uniroyal, and even Sears, J. C. Penney, and K Mart, have taken up the cause.

As with sports cars, design and state-of-the-art technology have become major considerations. In fact, the titles of such top-rated running shoes as Nike LDV, Brooks Vantage, Saucony Hornet, and New Balance 320 resemble the names of the hottest racing cars. So do their shapes, which are a streamlined heel-to-toe "wedge," and color schemes that contrast two or more bright tones with a dazzling array of stripes, swirls, and letters. Then there are the science and the technological breakthroughs in air and cantilevered soles, lace-around and flaired heels, and other foot-comforting developments.

Rapid growth. These not only keep runners on their toes and heels but jogging back to their neighborhood stores for the latest models. Increasingly, these shops are part of national chains such as Athlete's Foot, Athletic Attic, and Kinney Shoe's Foot Locker. Fast-footwear franchises also are expanding rapidly. Athletic Attic Inc., based in Jacksonville, Fla., has 138 outlets, and President Marty Liquori, who is also an Olympic middle-distance runner and TV sportscaster, says his operation recently has been opening one new franchise a week.

If any sport should present hurdles to sportswear suppliers, it is probably running, which is more solitary than social, and there is scant need for equipment. Nevertheless, one Berkeley (Calif.) born-again runner, who has a closet full of jogging shoes to fit most seasons and moods, muses, "Manufacturers have overcome all obstacles and made running big business." Indeed, products range in price from $15 to $50, and the advertising manager of Boston's New Balance Athletic Shoe Inc. notes that many suppliers have taken "a Procter & Gamble approach to brand segmentation." In its fourth annual shoe-rating issue last October, *Runner's World* magazine ranked no less than 103 different training and racing flats. And the one to five stars allocated each contender signified as much to the magazine's half-million readers as the Michelin guide ratings mean to French restaurant buffs.

There are other periodicals, too, like *The Runner* and *Running Times*, and these publications explore marathons and medical issues in exhaustive detail as well as advertise chronographs, bumper stickers, thirst quenchers, herbal potions, jogger lights, jewelry, and, of course, shoes. One crepe-soled, cross-country model is promoted as "dirt-kicking, grass-grabbing, and mud-slinging."

More than occasionally, these terms describe the manufacturers as much as the products they make. Adi and Rudolph Dassler, who put tiny Herzogenaurach, Germany, on the map with their respective Adidas and Puma topselling brands, reputedly were not on speaking terms. Although the brothers are dead (Adi died last year), there remains intense rivalry between Adi's technically oriented Adidas, which sold 40 million pairs of shoes last year, and Rudolph's marketing-oriented Puma, with sales of 10 million pairs. Puma customers reportedly cannot even stay in the hometown hotel owned by Adidas.

The Competition. For years Adidas was undisputed front-runner in the U.S. jogging-shoe market, but it now has far more than Puma to contend with. Adidas' share of the market has dipped to 20% from 25% last year and trails that of Nike, which now has 33% of the market and New Balance with 10%. With its line of "action clothes," Adidas has about $1 billion sales and is still No. 1 in world market, but because the number of U.S. joggers has doubled in the past two years to 25 million, while another 10 million Americans wear running shoes around home and town, U.S. manufacturers have been growing faster. Nike's sales have grown from $28 million in 1977 to $71 million in 1978, and the company expects to top $125 million for the year ending May 31.

Companies such as New Balance also have seen sales more than double each year since 1975 when the running-shoe business began to take off. Some traditional sports-shoe manufacturers like Eltra Corp.'s Converse, which makes two-thirds of U.S. basketball shoes, stayed on the sidelines. "We thought jogging would be more of a fad," says Frederic J. Huser, Converse's running-shoe group marketing manager. But when sales continued to soar, the country's largest athletic-shoe producer jumped in. With a lineup of nine training models, Converse was able to double volume in running shoes last year and with a 5% share of the U.S. market is in a dead heat with Puma, which in the early '70s had 15% of the U.S. market.

Part of Puma's problem has been its distribution, but the declining market share also indicates that U.S. companies are awakening, not only from a marketing point of view but with technology.

Developing the tailwind. The most innovative competitor of all has been the Nike brand, made by BRS Inc., of Beaverton, Ore. Its latest offering, introduced in January, is the Tailwind, which rides on a cushion of polyurethane-encapsulated air chambers. Touted as "the next generation of footwear" and advertised as "air travel" and backdrop picture of the Wright Bros. at Kitty Hawk, the Tailwind was developed by an aerospace engineer from Rockwell International Corp. BRS President Philip Knight claims the Tailwind is just the latest in a chain of pioneering developments by BRS.

M. Frank Rudy, a former aerospace engineer, took three years and more than 1,000 designs to come up with a Tailwind model that neither went flat nor had a pronounced pogo-stick effect. Before the Tailwind hit the market, it underwent extensive testing by everyone from podiatrists to policemen and was followed by an intensive promotion. Shoe dealers, Knight says, are waiting in line for the $50 shoe because the company has been forced to allocate them.

Nike, however, is not likely to hold a marketing edge long. Converse will introduce soon the $35 Arizona, which uses a proprietary cushioning compound (similar to that in football helmets) developed by former employees of the National Aeronautics & Space Administration. According to the Company, it will allow "more stability in landing and liftoff."

Inflatable air shoe. Some running-shoe executives, such as Jerome A. Turner, vice-president of Brooks Shoe Mfg. Co., suspect that Converse models and Uniroyal Inc.'s new Pro-Keds T/Racer may be unable to overcome the research and development edge built up by running-shoe companies that got in earlier. His Hanover (Pa.) company's latest product is a $49 air shoe introduced at the February National Sporting Goods Show in Chicago. It has a replaceable air liner, similar to a mini air mattress, that fits in the bottom of the shoe and can be inflated to fit each runner.

Although some runners swear by these new shoes. others swear at them. For its part, Adidas suggests that BRS and other manufacturers are turning to gimmicks to expand market share.

Maintaining the recent growth of the running-shoe industry is unlikely. But there is still plenty of room for expansion. BRS, with just 10% of its sales abroad, is looking to Europe where runners still prefer cross-country jaunts to road-racing. And then there is the vast leisure market. Specs International Inc., of Avon, Mass., is doing a $25 million annual business selling to independent shoe stores what one official calls "casual athletic shoes with the jogger look." And Liquori of Athletic Attic talks about "the whole geriatric market" and contends more people are finding that "a $20 nylon jogging shoe might beat out a $100 Gucci as the most comfortable shoe in their closet."

Ending Time:

_____

WPM: _____

Preview Test: The Jogging-Shoe Race

Directions: Complete each of the following statements by writing in or circling the correct answer.

1. The "jogging-shoe race" refers to _____

   _____.

2. Fast footwear franchises now include jogging-shoes as parts of their selections.

   True   False

3. Adidas and Puma are _____-made shoes.

4. _____-owned companies entered the jogging-shoe market to challenge foreign manufacturers.

5. The _____ brand outchallenged all other brands in the U.S. market as the jobbing-shoe race went into full swing.

6. The new technicians who are responsible for developing these newer and

   better jogging-shoes are _____

   _____

   _____.

7. The jogging-shoe industry will continue to grow at this highly rapid pace for years to come.

   True   False

8. The next market to be reached by the jogging-shoe industry is _____

   _____.

   _____.

Check your answers by referring to the article.

Read the Article

Reading just as quickly as possible, find out about the jogging-shoe race. Time yourself. Then check your comprehension with the following questions.

Comprehension Check: The Jogging-Shoe Race

Directions: Complete each of the following statements by writing in or circling the correct answer.

1. The two factors that jogging-shoe manufacturers must consider when developing such shoes are _____

    _____.

2. 1975 was the year the jogging-shoe business began to expand rapidly.
    True   False

3. The two best known brands of jogging-shoes originated in _____

    _____.

4. An American-made brand, the _____, now rivals the best of the foreign-made jogging shoes.

Comprehension Accuracy:

_____

5. The jogging-shoe business will continue to expand for many more years allowing many smaller companies to enter the market.
    True   False

Check your answers by the Answer Key provided at the end of this unit.

Beginning on p. 67 you will find several supplementary reading selections that may be used for further practice in applying the preview technique. If you feel unsure of your previewing abilities or desire further practice, turn to the supplementary selections now.

PHRASE READING FOR BETTER COMPREHENSION

It has been said that the "eye is the mirror of man's mind." If this is true, then when your eyes focus on single words, you mentally consider each word separately, not as part of a meaningful thought unit. If you read in this word-by-word fashion you must reconstruct all the separate impressions into a meaningful whole. If you are this kind of reader, you will probably be able to quote the facts given in an essay but may fail to understand its overall idea. You may not be able to grasp the relationship of all the small parts to the central theme. Learning to read in groups of words—in phrases—can help deepen your understanding of all that you read. But before we begin to explore phrase reading, first read Table 2.2, which presents an informal check to help you determine how often your eyes pause as you read.

Table 2.2   *What Type Reader Are You?*

Directions: There are three sentences below. Each has been marked with slanting lines. Let your eyes pick up the words between the slants, pausing at each slant to take in what is said. Circle the category you felt most comfortable using. This is a good representation of the kind of reader you are now.

SOURCE: Nila Banton Smith, *Read Faster and Get More From Your Reading* (Englewood Cliffs, N.J.: Prentice-Hall, Inc., 1958), p. 17. Used by permission.

Poor

Many / adults / are / now / suffering / from / habits / that / became / fixed / during / the / early / stages / in / which / they / were / learning / to / read. /

Average

Many / adults are / now suffering / from habits / that became / fixed during / the early stages / in which / they were / learning / to read. /

Good

Many adults / are now suffering from habits / that became fixed during the early stages / in which they were / learning to read. /

Reading in phrases or by thought units is a crucial skill in both high-powered speed and efficient study reading. Even if you find yourself reading much more easily with the last pattern, you can improve your skill even more by learning to read in thought units. Readers who are using the Poor or Average patterns will show much growth from training.

Grasping Phrases Quickly

Most readers already phrase-read to a certain extent. A sentence may be read in differing ways; words can be grouped into various ways and still produce meaning. If you are to build speed and efficiency in reading, you must train your eyes to take in larger groups of words at a glance, without losing any of the message. A simple procedure may be used to acclimate yourself to phrase reading in larger and larger units.

Your first reading selection, "Women Become Farm Managers," is written in phrases in column form. This is designed to help you take advantage of a special visual ability that you possess—peripheral vision. Your peripheral vision enables you to focus on one object but at the same time be able to identify what is to the right or left of that object or above or below it. In reading, this ability enables you to focus on a key word yet perceive the other words immediately surrounding it. Scanning involves the ability to perceive what is above or below the focal point. Those who read very fast using phrase reading skills can perceive and understand words to the left and right of the focal point. Therefore, focusing on each word in the line is unnecessary and wasteful of both time and energy.

At first when you begin to read phrases in columnar form, you will be tempted to read every word. To keep yourself from doing so, try this procedure.

Place the tip of your index finger or eraser end of your pencil at the top of an imaginary line running down through the center of each column. As it passes down through the line of print, focus on the word immediately above your finger or eraser. Do not permit your eyes to move toward either side. Keep your pointer moving continuously downward. Don't worry about comprehension at first, but be sure to check your percentage of accuracy anyway. Your comprehension will grow stronger as your phrase reading skills improve.

Now put this procedure to use as you read "Women Become Farm Managers." Force you eyes to move down the center of each column. *Do not time yourself*. But *do* answer the comprehension questions at the end of the selection and compute your accuracy score.

Selection 4: Women Become Farm Managers ────────

More women
are taking
an active interest
in managing farms,
but the male-dominated
farm organizations
are not yet
willing to treat
women as equals
according to
Jim Thomson,
editor of
Prairie Farmer,
a national
farm magazine.
 "Are
farm organizations
ready to treat
women as equals?

Not so you
would notice it,
but some changes
may be
in the wind,"
he said
in an editorial.
"With farming
becoming more
of a business
that involves
someone handy
with a pencil
and a calculator
more women
are taking on
this chore."

SOURCE: Reprinted by permission of The Associated Press.

Comprehension Check: Women Become Farm Managers

Directions: Select the best ending for each of the statements below. Circle your
answer.

1. Jim Thomson is

    a. a farmer himself.
    b. a women's lib advocate.
    c. editor of a national farm magazine.

2. Women are now taking

    a. a less active role in farming.
    b. a more active role in agriculture.
    c. a more active role in forcing the liberation movement.

3. Farm organizations have traditionally been
    a. male dominated.
    b. female dominated.
    c. operated on a co-equal basis.

4. Farm organizations are

    a. less ready to treat women as equals.
    b. treating women on the same basis as they always have.
    c. more ready to treat women as equals.

5. More women are assuming responsibility for
    a. operating the heavy machinery.
    b. serving on the board of directors of farm organizations.
    c. managing the books or business accounts.

Comprehension Score:

_____

Check your answers by the Answer Key at the end of this unit. Allow yourself a score of 20 for each correct answer.

Selection 5: Chinese Greet Year of Horse _____

Directions: Read as you did for Selection 4.

Chinatown greeted
the Year
of the horse
today with
the hope
that the
bleak specter
of a bloody massacre
has slipped away
with the Year
of the Snake.
It has been
five months
since three masked
gunman invaded

the Golden Dragon
restaurant and sprayed
a crowd
of 75 diners
with bullets,
killing five
and wounding 11.
No one
has been arrested
in connection
with the shootings.
The Sept. 4 outburst—
blamed
on warring
between rival

Chinese youth gangs—
cast a pall
over the
ricky-ticky
neighborhood,
the largest enclave
of Chinese
outside Asia.
Sidewalk traffic
thinned and
once-bustling
restaurants began
to close early,
spurring rumors
that several would
go out of business.

_____

SOURCE: Reprinted by permission of The Associated Press.

Comprehension Check: Chinese Greet Year of Horse

Directions: Select the best ending for each of the following statements. Circle your answer.

1. Chinese calendar years are identified by
    a. the names of famous Chinese poets.
    b. the names of animals.
    c. the most important events of the year.

2. The events in this article took place in
    a. the Republic of China.
    b. the United States of America.
    c. Chinatown in a country outside Asia.

3. Several tourists were killed and others wounded when

   a. holiday celebrants became too rowdy in Chinatown's streets.
   b. fire broke out in the motels where they were staying.
   c. rival youth gangs battled in a restaurant where they were eating.

4. Chinese officials were concerned about

   a. the effect the incident would have on business.
   b. the dampening of religious fervor in the community.
   c. the increase in the number of such happenings in the community.

5. The bloody massacre took place in the Chinese

   a. Year of the Horse.
   b. Year of the Snake.
   c. Year of the Cow.

Comprehension Score:

_____

Check your answers by the Answer Key at the end of Unit 2. Allow yourself a score of 20 for each correct answer.

Rapid Phrase Perception Practice

If, at this point, you feel slightly frustrated, don't. Frustration is a natural feeling until you develop your phrase reading skills. Exercises 2.1 through 2.10 are designed to train you to perceive phrases very rapidly. Do them as directed. You will need a watch with a second hand.

Directions: For Exercise 2.1 through 2.5, move your pencil point down the center of each column looking for the key phrase. Remember to focus in the center of the phrase just above your pencil point. When the key phrase appears, place a dot over it. Do not use just one word in the phrase as a clue to identification.[1] Use your peripheral vision. Force your eyes to focus on one word in the center while taking in what is to the left or right without moving your eyes. Work quickly. Try to finish each exercise in less than 25 seconds.

☐ Exercise 2.1 ☐

Key Phrase: time-honored tradition

time line	tap water faucet	time-honored tradition
tardy for school	tall and gangly	thumpity-thump-thump
time-honored tradition	tested and tried	tremble and sway
thimble and thread	tumblers and goblets	two tall trees
tremble in fear	time-honored tradition	tamper with it
tumbling down hill	tub of lard	throw the ball
thoughtless and rude	tune in a bucket	time-honored tradition
time-honored tradition	table and chairs	traditions time honored
traditions time honored	time-honored tradition	tacks and nails
to and fro	turn over and over	tea and toast
time for tea	thicker than water	time-honored tradition

Time: _____ seconds

The Key Phrase appears seven times. Check your answers.

Number of key phrases you marked: _____ out of 7.

Key Phrase: unsung hero

up and down	under the weather	undue stress
uttermost ends	unsung hero	heroes gone unsung
utter dejection	unchanging ways	unassuming individual
unsung hero	heroes gone unsung	unbending will
under the sun	uncle and aunt	unsung hero
heroes gone unsung	unearth the bone	uncivil tongue
unusual display	unsung heroes	heroes gone unsung
uncle and aunt	unusual display	undeniable error
unsung hero	utter dejection	underground hideout
unsung hero	heroes gone unsung	underneath the porch
		unsung hero

Time: _____ seconds.

The key phrase appears seven times. Check your answers.

Number of key phrases you marked: _____ out of 7.

Key Phrase: beauteous young lady

barber shop quartet	bated breath	barrier reef
bargain store suit	beachhead patrol	beauteous young lady
beauteous young lady	beauteous young lady	beauty salon
barefaced lie	bearer of tales	barricade the door
beautiful young lady	beauty salon	bipartisan relationship
barricade the door	behind the door	beauteous young lady
basketball player	bevelled edged mirror	beautiful young lady
beauteous young lady	beautiful young lady	bizarre incident
baste the meat	beauteous young lady	black and blue
beautiful young lady	between the walls	beauteous young lady
barrier reef	bipartisan relationship	between the walls

Time: _____ seconds.

The key phrase appears seven times. Check your answers.

Number of key phrases you marked: _____ out of 7.

☐ Exercise 2.4 ☐

Key Phrase: unscrupulous merchant

ultraviolet light	unscrupulous merchant	urgent message
unsharpened sword	useful service	unscrupulous merchant
unappetizing dinner	ultimate decision	unscrubbed merchant
unscrupulous merchant	usurp another's power	ultraviolet light
ugly duckling	urban dwellers	ultimate decision
ultimate decision	unscrupulous merchant	uttermost end
unscrubbed merchant	umbrella effect	usurp another's power
unscrupulous merchant	unscrubbed merchant	unscrupulous merchant
umbrella effect	ultraviolet light	utilitarian object
urban dwellers	unscrupulous merchant	ultimate decision
urinary tract	useful service	unscrupulous merchant

Time: _____ seconds.

The key phrase appears eight times. Check your answers.

Number of key phrases you marked: _____ out of 8.

☐ Exercise 2.5 ☐

Key Phrase: mock battle

masterful execution	matted hair	material witness
mock battle	mockery in battle	maternal grandmother
mastermind the plan	mock battle	meaningful glance
materialize from air	material witness	mockery in battle
maternal grandmother	meadow lark	mock battle
matted hair	mockery in battle	medicine man
material witness	mastermind the plan	membership drive
maturity level	mock battle	mock battle
mock battle	maturity level	maturity level
mockery in battle	meaningful glance	mock battle
meaningful glance	mockery in battle	mockery in battle

Time: _____ seconds.

The key phrase appears seven times. Check your answers.

Number of key phrases you marked: _____ out of 7.

Directions: For Exercises 2.6 through 2.10 *do not* pull your pencil down the center of each column. This time find the center of the column with your eyes. Force your eyes down the center of each phrase. If the phrase is the Key Phrase, place a dot over it with your pencil.

□ **Exercise 2.6** □

Key Phrase: squander your savings

squander your inheritance	square dance routine	steamroller effect
squeal and squall	stabilizer effect	squander your savings
squander your savings	squirrel your savings	steak and eggs
sacrificial lamb	squander your savings	squirrel your savings
saffron yellow	stampeding herd	squeal and squall
sharp-witted reply	starry eyes	staying power
spontaneous reaction	squander your savings	squander your savings
splutter and sputter	staunch advocate	splutter and sputter
squander your savings	startling discovery	sterling silver
spend your savings	squander your savings	squirrel your savings
spurious report	spontaneous reaction	squander your savings

Time: _____ seconds.

The key phrase appears eight times. Check your answers.

Number of key phrases you marked: _____ out of 8.

□ **Exercise 2.7** □

Key Phrase: curdle the blood

clamoring crowd	cold-blooded animal	classic example
blood curdling yell	curdle the blood	curdle the blood
classic example	colloquial expression	blood curdling yell
curdle the blood	combination lock	commonplace remark
clean-cut fellow	blood curdling yell	coast guard cutter
clandestine affair	colorful setting	curdle the blood
clamor and climb	coast guard cutter	curdle the blood
coast guard cutter	commendable progress	commendable progress
curdle the blood	curdle the blood	comic strip character
cocaine and heroin	commonplace remark	curdle the blood
blood curdling yell	curdle the blood	curdle the blood

Time: _____ seconds.

The key phrase appears eight times. Check your answers.

Number of key phrases you marked: _____ out of 8.

☐ Exercise 2.8 ☐

Key Phrase: fervent prayer

frequent pain	favorable results	fervent prayer
fervent prayer	fervent prayer	frequent pain
faithful few	faithful few	fervent prayer
pray faithfully	fully guaranteed	fairly strong
faithful to prayer	pray fervently	faithful to prayer
falsely accused	frequent pain	frosty panes
fairly strong	falsely accused	flooded walkways
fully guaranteed	fervent prayer	favorable results
fervent prayer	frosty panes	fervent prayer
falsely accused	flooded walkway	pray faithfully
fervent prayer	pray fervently	frequent pain

Time: _____ seconds

The key phrase appears eight times. Check your answers.

Number of key phrases you marked: _____ out of 8.

☐ Exercise 2.9 ☐

Key Phrase: replenish the larder

replace the leader	refueling the plane	replay the record
replay the record	recreational vehicle	replenish the larder
replenish the larder	rotating wheel	recreational vehicle
recreational vehicle	replenish the larder	replace the leader
relieve the pain	refunding the money	replenish the larder
replenish the larder	relocate the refugees	relevant application
replace the leader	replace the leader	rippling effect
release the prisoner	replenish the larder	relieve the pain
relevant application	rippling effect	replay the record
rotating wheel	rogue in rags	replenish the larder
replenish the larder	release the prisoner	release the prisoner

Time: _____ seconds.

The key phrase appears eight times. Check your answers.

Number of key phrases you marked: _____ out of 8.

Key Phrase: natural habitat

nationalistic trends	neighborly deed	neutral party
neutral party	nightly foray	noiseless flight
natural habitat	nameless individual	nameless individual
naughty habit	natural habitat	natural habitat
nightly foray	nobody knows	neighborly deed
neighborly deed	naughty habit	naughty habit
naughty habit	natural habitat	nationalistic trends
nameless individual	neutral party	neutral party
natural habitat	nationalistic trends	natural habitat
nationalistic trends	noiseless flight	nightly foray
nightly foray	neighborly deed	natural habitat

Time: _____ seconds.

The key phrase appears seven times. Check your answers.

Number of key phrases you marked: _____ out of 7.

APPLYING PHRASE READING SKILLS

It is now time for you to apply this skill in reading a selection. The thought units in Selection 6 are longer than those in Selections 1 and 2 read earlier. Force your eyes down the center of each column. *Do not* time yourself, but check your comprehension.

Selection 6: Pop-Eyed in Moscow

The Soviet Union's
first public showing
of American pop art
and photo-realism
has met with
guarded approval
from Soviet critics.
One said the show
"awakens a sincere liking
for the American people."
Breaking with
traditional Soviet condemnation
of such controversial styles,
the critic used
such words as
"attractive" and "talented"
and said the spirit
of the paintings
"touches our hearts."

Since mid-December
long lines of Russians
have waited in the snow
outside the Pushkin Museum
to see the exhibit
from New York's
Metropolitan Museum of Art.
It was sent
in exchange for an exhibit
of Soviet realism
that New York critics
hosted last year.
The exhibit also contains
representational art
from the late 19th century
through the present,
including classics
by Thomas Eakins,
Winslow Homer, Grant Wood,
and Edward Hopper, who are
known and respected in the
Soviet Union.

SOURCE: Reprinted by permission of The Associated Press.

Comprehension Check: Pop-Eyed in Moscow

Directions: Mark a T or an F in the blanks preceding these statements to indicate which ones are true or false.

_____ 1. The Russians are a pop-eyed people.
_____ 2. The Soviet Union and the United States exchange art exhibits.
_____ 3. American artists such as Winslow Homer are popular even in the Soviet Union.
_____ 4. American realism as an art form for Russian viewing was not acceptable in earlier times.
_____ 5. The American art exhibit shown in the Soviet Union was sponsored by the Metropolitan Museum of Art in New York City.

Check your answers by the Answer Key at the end of Unit 2.

Selection 7: Business, Labor Join to Battle Alcoholism ▬▬▬▬

A telephone lineman in Michigan
with a penchant for blended whiskey
has curtailed his drinking—
and his absenteeism—
and is back on the job
after a brief stint
at a detoxification and counseling center.
Bell Telephone Co. sent him there
and paid the bill.
Standard Oil Co. of California
is treating one of its executives
for a bad case
of too many martini lunches—
before the martinis became
more important to him
than the job.

At the State Department,
an administrator's secretary
has been referred
to a special alcoholism program
within the agency
to find out if her drinking habit
has anything to do
with her tardiness habit.
The treatment is
confidential and free—
courtesy of the federal government.
Throughout the country,
business, government, and labor
are joining forces to fight
alcoholism where it can
usually be identified first,
on the job.
And both management and labor
are finding that a company program
designed to treat employers
with drinking problems
is mutually beneficial.

SOURCE: Reprinted with permission of *The Washington Post*. Copyright © 1978.

Comprehension Check: Business, Labor Join to Battle Alcoholism

Directions: Mark a T or an F in the blanks preceding these statements to indicate which ones are true or false.

_____ 1.   The home is where an alcoholic's problem is first identified.

_____ 2.   Only the alcoholic benefits from the treatments.

_____ 3.   Persons with an alcoholic problem are sent to a detoxification and counseling center.

_____ 4.   Persons with potential alcoholic problems also receive treatment in order to prevent "on the job" problems.

_____ 5.   Costs for employees' receiving help at the detoxification and counseling centers is borne by their employer.

Making the Transition to Regular Materials

Most reading materials are not written in columns. A line of print from top to bottom is more usual. Exercises 2.11 through 2.20 will help you make the transition from rapid phrase reading in columns to rapid phrase reading in rows of print.

Directions: This time you will find the Key Phrase every time it appears in a row of print. Force your eyes to take in a whole phrase at a time. Do not read every word separately in each phrase. Place a dot over each Key Phrase as you come to it. *Time yourself.*

☐ Exercise 2.11 ☐

Key Phrase: alien being

almost alone	in the garden	under the weather
alien being	mostly unkempt	force of habit
completely wet	alien body	out of alignment
over the seas	mark of dignity	alien being
steering the ship	faster than rain	out of sight
endless chain	alien being	light in the dark
alien being	star-studded course	from the deep
over your head	mark my word	bubbling over
cause of concern	alien body	faster and faster
a host of ills	ahead of time	alien being
wearing a watch	alien being	marvelous sight
alien being	a broad back	pull in the reins

Time: _____ seconds.

The key phrase appears seven times. Check your answers.

Number of key phrases you marked: _____ out of 7.

☐ Exercise 2.12 ☐

Key Phrase: from exotic ports

fountain of youth	from exotic ports	of foreign lands
port of call	knives and scissors	bow at the knee
twist and turn	about to fall off	from exotic ports
bishop and queen	jack of all trades	beautiful bride
from exotic ports	raid and plunder	call the dog
hook and ladder	fall around his ears	move away
do him in	from exotic ports	rain cats and dogs
hardly a word	rock me to sleep	from exotic ports
with bated breath	black and blue	harbor a fugitive
from exotic ports	many a day	horrible nightmare
heavenly hash	a collapsible frame	completely ignored
from exotic ports	old wives tales	from exotic ports

Time: _____ seconds.

The key phrase appears eight times. Check your answers.
Number of key phrases you marked: _____ out of 8.

☐ Exercise 2.13 ☐

Key Phrase: his primeval desires

humble the proud	dare to be brave	down and out
fly the coop	his personal desires	never lose hope
his primeval desires	duly obey	more dead than alive
forget his past	the primeval forest	fang and claw
fat and sassy	thrown for a loop	his primeval desires
practical yet attractive	prime the pump	so rudely interrupted
his primeval desires	in rare form	totally ignored
harmless old man	from sheer delight	hardly a sound
his perennial desires	burst the bubble	from down under
his holy personage	his primeval desires	rustle the leaves
bright and gleaming	stitch the seam	douse the fire
his primeval desires	nevertheless he is	his primeval desires

Time: _____ seconds.

The key phrase appears six times. Check your answers.

Number of key phrases you marked: _____ out of 6.

☐ Exercise 2.14 ☐

Key Phrase: eccentric old man

ode to spring	eccentric old man	automatically excluded
electrifying feeling	please the crowd	simply fabulous
fabulous wealth	rumble like thunder	eccentric old man
eccentric old man	place of rest	electrifying feeling
very much a lady	fold like an umbrella	an abiding fear
gone with the wind	break like glass	registration in advance
holier than thou	eccentric old man	eccentric old man
eccentric old man	unpleasant experience	where are you
usable no more	greener than grass	hang the man
dimwitted soul	satiny glow	his feeble attempts
braver than most	eccentric old man	up and down
coming unglued	for no conceivable reason	eccentric old man
roared with anger	at feverish pitch	

Time: _____ seconds.

The key phrase appears eight times. Check your answers.

Number of key phrases you marked: _____ out of 8.

☐ Exercise 2.15 ☐

Key Phrase: standing ovation

floating on water	a maze of roads	flat like a pancake
wearing a smile	roaming the hills	standing ovation
smart and sassy	hardly a day	gun the motor
standing ovation	standing ovation	glorious array
hold the line	abject proverty	standing room only
grossly misrepresented	standing room only	fledgling pilot
standing in line	among the rubble	forbidden fruit
labor of love	almost persuaded	standing ovation
lonely and blue	flight of the arrow	evade his captor
stubbornly refuse	falling like rain	distribute the mail
medley of tunes	completely unbending	standing ovation
profound statement	some of these	
standing ovation	winter's last breath	

Time: _____ seconds.

The key phrase appears six times. Check your answers.

Number of key phrases you marked: _____ out of 6.

☐ Exercise 2.16 ☐

Key Phrase: most harrowing experience

most horrible experience	probably not true	most harrowing experience
marketing analyst	over my head	noble experiment
maybe tomorrow	bright and beautiful	wonder of wonders
flying by night	fire-eating dragon	trail of tears
very frequent guest	golden sands of Wai Kee Kee	beautiful blue sky
intolerable situation	most harrowing experience	most harrowing experience
most harrowing experience	honorable mention	beads and baubles
fallen from grace	make the most of it	free as the wind
battle the elements	most horrible experience	mow the grass
from morning to night	live life to its fullest	most harrowing experience
most harrowing experience	fallen from grace	never on Sunday
rejuvenating experience	uphold the tradition	

Time: _____ seconds.

The key phrase appears six times. Check your answers.

Number of key phrases you marked: _____ out of 6.

□ Exercise 2.17 □

Key Phrase: unsavory individuals

unusually lovely	unlucky chap	favored individuals
ultimate decision	homing device	chocolate and vanilla
unsavory individuals	arbitrarily chosen	go for broke
unwanted and unloved	favored individuals	this is the day
useless and old	forgotten son	unsavory individuals
ukeleles and guitars	pitiless tyrant	father knows best
unsavory individuals	unsavory individuals	the worst is yet to come
leap and gallop	sun and surf	favored individuals
roses are red	head-hunting aborigine	solid or veneer
unsavory idiosyncrasies	only a day	maimed and crippled
tall as a pine	daddy is here	unsavory individuals
unsavory individuals	antiques and junk	costlier than most
a jumble of things	unsavory individuals	blatant opportunists
		unsavory individuals

Time: _____ seconds.

The key phrase appears eight times. Check your answers.

Number of key phrases you marked: _____ out of 8.

□ Exercise 2.18 □

Key Phrase: ornate facade

ornery and mean	ornate facade	suave and articulate
featured attraction	an ominous warning	ornate facade
fountain of youth	orchids and lace	mourning a friend
ornate facade	tie one on	bitter reprieve
facial expression	frosty and cold	an equestrian's delight
oblique triangle	ornate facade	dole expression
hesitant and fearful	hamming it up	ornate facade
kick up your heels	symbol of courage	avenue of time
horrendous affair	lonely solitude	audit the books
ornate facade	ship of fools	thoughtful individual
musical score	ornate facade	fractional number
fanciful tale	sickening sight	force of habit
the mounted police	free flowing design	ornate facade
		removal of sand

Time: _____ seconds.

The key phrase appears eight times. Check your answers.

Number of key phrases you marked: _____ out of 8.

☐ Exercise 2.19 ☐

Key Phrase: opinionated dowager

orphaned child   unduly alarmed   it's true nevertheless
toe-tapping rhythm   orphaned child   somewhere in space
opinionated dowager   dank and cold   opinionated dowager
doe-faced girl   opinionated dowager   numbers of clues
lonely and blue   fractious youth   spicy with sauce
downright ornery   ominous storm cloud   peppered with gray
opinionated dowager   beloved yet feared   fun and games
orphaned child   opinionated dowager   too frequent visitor
remarkable resemblance   smothered with love   frothy milkshake
soft and soothing   romp through the snow   opinionated dowager
infamous individual   orphaned child   rant and rave
opinionated dowager   opinionated dowager   under his wing
favorable first impression   far and near

Time: _____ seconds.

The key phrase appears eight times. Check your answers.

Number of key phrases you marked: _____ out of 8.

☐ Exercise 2.20 ☐

Key Phrase: quizzical expression

quotable quotes   quizzical expression   proud and lofty
reeks with onion   have no qualms   quietly in control
fast and furious   bustling with business   fume and fuss
quizzical expression   quaint customs   quizzical expression
bus terminal   in an equivocable position   known for that
the majestic spire   quizzical expression   quotable quotes
favorable moment   well-guarded secret   stop squirming
quizzical expression   its monetary value   quaintly beautiful
politely cold   quaint customs   comical relief
the quizzed witness   monetary discomfort   quizzical expression
ran a furlong   quizzical expression   related causes
his raucous call   lunge forward   quizzical expression
rather ridiculous   a brush with the enemy   foregone conclusion
well-guarded secret

Time: _____ seconds.

The key phrase appears eight times. Check your answers.

Number of key phrases you marked: _____ out of 8.

Applying Phrase Reading Skills to Regular Materials

You are now ready to learn how to apply your phrase reading skills to reading materials that follow the usual format. Read Selection 8 to yourself, just for meaning.

Selection 8: East Asia—Japan

Beginning Time:

_____

Total Words: 243

Simplicity has become a cult to the Japanese, best expressed in their dwellings, particularly since the Tokugawa period. A great and abiding love of natural wood takes full advantage of its ingrained beauty, achieving pleasing contrasts of wood against wood or white plaster. To withstand frequent earthquakes, each beam is fitted without relying on nails, and supports a heavy roof of gray tiles or thatch. The size of rooms is determined by the number of rice-straw mats, or tatami, it accommodates. 2-inches thick and measuring about 3 × 6 feet, they are placed on the polished floor and used for sleeping. The house is divided into rooms by sliding screens; light is admitted by a paper-covered lattice mounted as a sliding window. These screens are removable so as to throw all rooms into one. At night the house is shuttered by wooden panels running in grooves along the outside. Bare of major furniture, at one end of the room is the "tokonoma," a raised alcove, framed by a pillar of some exceptional wood, and featuring a hanging scroll and perhaps a single azalea bonsai, or a style arrangement of flowers, intended to direct the attention of all eyes to the beauty of nature, and its inner meanings. An all-absorbing love of nature makes a garden an integral part of the Japanese home. When opening wide the "shohi" or sliding screens, there is revealed, as on a stage, and changing with the seasons, a make-believe landscape in miniature. Deceivingly, great mountains are expressed by hills or rocks, distant forests by a few bamboo, the sea with its rolling waves by neatly combed sand, a lake by a pool, grassy meadows by varying types of moss, individual trees by dwarfed bonsai, and a distant road by stepping stones. The half-moon bridge reflects a full moon, and each treasured tree has its symbolic meaning. In meditation, and by capturing its feeling, the restless mind finds harmony with nature, and with it a deep serenity.

Ending Time:

_____

WPM: _____

Comprehension Check: East Asia—Japan

Directions: Complete each question by writing in or circling the correct answer.

1. The scene described is that of a typical _____

_____.

2. The force that receives primary consideration in the decoration of a Japanese home is

   a. the type furniture to be used.
   b. nature.
   c. the central living area.

3. From its architectural designs it may safely be assumed that the Japanese have many earthquakes.

   True   False

4. The one term that describes Japanese tastes in home furnishings is _____.

5. Identify the symbolic purpose that each of the following decorative elements serves in the Japanese home:

   a. Hanging scroll and flowering arrangement for bonsai _____

   b. Green mountains _____

   c. Forests _____

Comprehension Accuracy: d. Sea _____

_____   e. Individual trees _____

    What is Selection 8 about? If you chose "Japanese homes reflect their feelings about nature and simplicity," you are correct.

    Suppose you had to show a friend who was having difficulty understanding Selection 8 how to read it in such a way that the meaning would become clear. How would you group the words for meaning? Using the slash (/), mark the words of Selection 8 into groups as you would recommend that your friend read them.

    You have just marked Selection 8 into phrases. Now read Selection 8 aloud phrasing or grouping the words as you intend them to be read. Do the groupings or phrases sound correct according to the meaning the author wishes them to have? If they sound correct, then they are. If one phrase is awkward or sounds odd, then regroup at that spot until you find a logical way to group them for clear understanding. Meaningful phrases are usually four to five words long.[2]

    You are now ready to mark the phrases for selections that you yourself will read, Selections 9 through 11.

    The first step is to read quickly through the selection to get the gist of the message. When you are first learning to mark the phrases you will read, you must be aware of the author's message and how the selection should be read. That is why the preview is so important in longer selections. It alerts you to the author's meaning and clues how you must phrase to fathom that meaning quickly.

    The second step is to mark how you will read each sentence. Remember, you want to force your eyes to take in longer phrases of four to five words. Very short sentences should be read as one unit or phrase. Longer ones must be divided into meaningful units.

Directions:

1. Quickly preview Selections 9 through 11 for general meaning.
2. Decide one sentence at a time how you will read the selection. Use slashes to separate the phrases.
3. When you have marked the phrasing for the entire selection, begin to read. Force your eyes to take in all words between slashes. Focus in the center of the phrase letting your peripheral vision take care of the other words in the same phrase. Read as quickly as possible. Time yourself. Check your comprehension.
4. Record your scores on the Reading Progress Chart on p. 117.

Selection 9: Pyramid Yields Priceless Art ━━━━━━━━━━━━

Beginning Time:

Total Words: 489

The full moon rose directly behind the Temple of the Masonry Altars, outlining the squat truncated pyramid against the tropic night. A damp sea wind rattled the cohune palm fronds overhead, and a pair of nightjars called to each other in whippoorwill voices. Atop the ancient Maya monument two priests watched in motionless silence as the moon goddess Ix Chel began her stately stroll among the stars.

Climbing the vaulted sky, Ix Chel shed a ghostly light over the brooding scene, etching sharp shadows on the silvered grass. Presently, one of the priests bent low. I shivered, feeling like a forbidden witness to arcane rites of a thousand years ago. The figure straightened. I could see a small, dark object in his hand—an incense burner, perhaps, or a jade idol to be shattered on one of the circular altars as a propitiatory offering.

A fearful din suddenly shook me from my reverie: It was the frantic beat of a rock group. The mysterious object at once became a transistor radio turned to Radio Belize. The "priests" were watchmen guarding a precious archeological dig at Altun Ha.

Two days before, Dr. David M. Pendergast of the Royal Ontario Museum in Toronto had extracted from a tomb inside the 58-foot-high pyramid a magnificently carved jade head. A representation of Kinich Ahua, the sungod, it was the largest carved jade object ever found in the Maya area—a region where, in pre-Columbian times, jade was one of the most valuable materials.

Since 1964, Dr. Pendergast, his wife Esther, and a small team of local Maya and Creole workers had been excavating jungle-covered mounds that contained houses, priests' palaces, tombs, and temples in this small coastal city-state. From the Temple of the Masonry Altars they painstakingly peeled away six layers of limestone construction that had covered, onion-fashion, an impressive structure of the Classic Period, probably built around A.D. 600.

"The Maya apparently believed that buildings, like people, had a definite life-span," Dr. Pendergast told me. "In some cases they would erect a new palace or temple right over the existing one every 50 years or so."

I asked Dr. Pendergast about the significance of the jade head.

"It underscores something we have suspected for some time—that this was a major trade and ceremonial center," he replied. "The people have supplied marine materials to inland Maya settlement— pearls, shells, coral, possibly also fish bones and stingray spines—some things that were ritually valuable. In exchange they received such things as jade and obsidian, which are not found locally."

In his thatch house next to the ruin, he brought out the jade head and let me hold it. It was green and polished, in a way grotesque, with crossed eyes and bulbous nose. But its beauty was magical, mysterious.

How many more such treasures lie buried in Belize, no one can guess. But to retrieve some ancient Maya artifacts an archeologist doesn't even need a spade.

Limestone caves formed by underground streams underlie large areas of the country, especially in the west. The Maya used many of them.

SOURCE: Reprinted by permission of *National Geographic Magazine.*

Ending Time:

WPM: ━━━━━━━

Comprehension Check: Pyramid Yields Priceless Art

Directions: Complete each question by writing in or circling the correct answer.

1. The author allowed his imagination to run wild as he viewed the ancient Maya ruins during the tropical night.

   True   False

2. The author's area of study was _____

   _____.

3. Jade was an important clue to the diggers since _____

   _____.

4. Many Mayan artifacts do not have to be dug from the ground since _____

   _____.

Comprehension Accuracy:

_____

5. The Maya looked upon a building as having a specific life span and built other structures upon existing ones every 50 years or so.

   True   False

Beginning Time:

_____

Selection 10: The Miraculous Swiss Landscape _____

Total Words: 945

On a map of Europe, Switzerland is the size of a postage stamp; on a map of the world, little more than a pinhead. A population of approximately six million and a half—half that of Greater London—is densely distributed in the fertile regions of the country: in Alpine and Jura foothills, along the broad Central Plateau, in remote valleys. A confederation of twenty-two sovereign states covering a total area of sixteen thousand square miles, 22.6 percent of which is composed of the High Alps, forest lands and barren rocks: a country that has no seaboard, virtually no natural resources except hydraulic power, and which, despite all this, is prosperous.

Approaching Switzerland by a land route from the south or northwest, one is eager to escape the flat monotony of the Plain of Lombardy, of central France, or even the green and orderly undulations of Burgundy and the Cote d'Or. Traveling north from the Riviera, however, one finds the steep escarpment of the Maritime Alps, which merge into the Mont Blanc range, south of Lake Geneva, rising over 250 miles to the Alpine heart of Europe.

Western Switzerland shares its Jura and Lake Geneva frontiers with France and incorporates the three French-speaking cantons—Vaud, Neuchatel, and Geneva—and the two bilingual cantons, Fribourg and Valais, which are also Catholic states. Even in Fribourg and Valais, French is predominant and the Swiss call this region ''Suisse Romande,'' recognizing the Latin ascendancy of the populations here. Here lies the great basin of Lake Geneva, fed by the Rhone, which enters the lake after crossing the large alluvial plain between St. Maurice and Villeneuve.

The Swiss shore of Lake Geneva faces south and has a rich, agricultural hinterland rising in the east to the lovely Pays D'Enhaut, in the foothills of the

SOURCE: Reprinted with permission from FODOR'S SWITZERLAND © copyright 1977. Published by Fodor's Modern Guides.

Fribourg Alps, and in the west to the Jorat, the wooded foothills of the bleak rolling Jura Mountains, with their long, narrow valleys. South of Lake Geneva, along the French coast, lie the impressive Savoy Alps, which incorporate Mont Blanc (Europe's highest peak, 15,777 feet, standing guard at the Franco-Italian frontier) and stretch from south of Geneva into the upper Rhone Valley. This towering mass forms the frontier between France, Switzerland, and Italy: The Valley of Chamonix, at the foot of Mont Blanc, leads northeast into the Rhone Valley, from which radiate the Great St. Bernard and the Simplon Passes.

The Rhone Valley is bounded on the south by the Valais (or Pennine) Alps, which include the great triangular peak of the Matterhorn (14,690 ft.), and Mont Rosa (15,210 ft.), the second-highest mountain in Europe.

From the Swiss shore of Lake Geneva, with the town of Lausanne as its central point, the Jorat provides the main access into the Central Plateau, a rich agricultural region of orchards and pasturelands running northeast and broadening in the north to include the Lakes of Constance and Zurich. In the Central Plateau, which is bounded on the west by the Jura Mountains, also lie the Lakes of Neuchatel, Bienne, and Morat, and the cities of Fribourg and Bern, to the east of which, again, rise the Fribourg Alps and the Bernese Oberland. Central, eastern, and northern Switzerland have German-speaking populations.

Central Switzerland incorporates the classic Alpine scenery of Lucerne and its lake, known as the Vierwaldstattersee (Lake of the Four Forest Cantons), Lake Zug, and the more southerly lakes of Thun and Brienz.

The most easterly of the Swiss cantons is the Grisons (in German, Graubunden), which, like the canton of St. Gallen, shares a frontier with Austria. The Grisons and its beautiful Engadine district lie across two chains of the Alps, known as the Lepontine and Rhaetian Alps; it is also the home of Switzerland's fourth national language, Romansch. Leading south into Italy are the less well-known, dramatically beautiful, Alpine passes, the Splugue, San Bernardino, Maloja, and Bernina.

The Engadine (the valley of the Inn River) is accessible either from the north (from Zurich along Lakes Zurich and Walen; from the Lake Constance region up the Rhine); via Coire (Chur), Lenzerheide and the Julier Pass, or from the Central Alps via Andermatt on the St. Gotthard route (only during the summer season), over the Oberlap Pass through Disentis and Thusis and over the Julier Pass.

The lower Swiss Rhine is a very long region, extending from Lake Constance through Schaffhausen and Aargau to the canton and city of Basel, the great river port. Here there are lovely orchards, peaceful homesteads and small, medieval towns, whose architecture reveals German influence.

One canton only is Italian-speaking, the Ticino, somewhat isolated on the south of the St. Gotthard. As one crosses this great international pass and descends into the Valley of Bellinzona, scenery and atmosphere change miraculously. Here already is the vegetation and climate of the Italian lake district. Behind, to the north, lie the immense barriers of the Alps; southwards there are palm trees, flowering camellias, and sweet chestnut groves.

Travel in Switzerland offers an immense variety of natural scenery and atmosphere, ranging from the bleakness of polar landscapes to the sunny warmth of the Mediterranean. The Alps, romantic and beautiful as they are, are not the only high spots of a Swiss tour. Off the beaten track lie the rural charm of easterly Appenzell, the orchard lands of Lake Constance, the lovely rolling Jura. There are picturesque small cities such as Solothurn, with its indefinable elegance, legacy of

Ending Time:

_____

WPM: _____

the Swiss confederation of the French ambassadors who, for 150 years, had their official residence here. There are rich pastoral valleys, such as the Emmental, with its flaxen-haired, sturdy population and geranium-decked farmsteads. There are utterly rustic villages of clustering brown-roofed chalets in the rugged lateral valleys branching out from the upper Rhone Valley. Evolene or Herens, for example: unbelievable nooks, such as the hamlet of Iserables, perched on a rocky crag and accessible only by a mule track or by an aerial cable cabin which swings perilously over a deep grove. Plain and mountain alternate with foothills and pastureland, Mediterranean warmth with glaciers at 14,000 feet above sea level.

Comprehension Check: Miraculous Swiss Landscape

Directions: Complete each question by writing in or circling the correct answer.

1. The geographical features of Switzerland are described in a manner that

_____

_____.

2. The landscape of Switzerland ranges from the bleakness of polar scenes to the sunny warmth of the Mediterranean.

   True   False

3. The traditional Alpine scenery that comes to mind as one thinks of Switzerland is centered mainly

   a. in Central Switzerland—Lucerne.
   b. in Southern Switzerland—Ticino.
   c. in Western Switzerland—Geneva.

4. The dense population regions of Switzerland are to be found _____

_____.

5. The ethnic origins of the Swiss include primarily

   a. English, German, French.
   b. Asiatic, German, French.
   c. Italian/Roman, German, French.

Comprehension Accuracy:

_____

Beginning Time:

_____

Total Words: 3796

Selection 11: Nineteenth-Century Niagara

When Wild Bill Hickok, the legendary western scout and gunfighter, arrived in Niagara Falls, Ontario, as the star of the world's first wild-west show, he looked like almost any other prosperous visitor in a neat business suit—without his colorful frontier trappings or his fabled pearl-handled .44's. But Wild Bill walked with both hands in his pockets where he carried two small but deadly derringers.

His caution was well taken. Hickok was the continent's most notorious

SOURCE: Reprinted by permission of Hawthorn Properties (Elsevier-Dutton Publishing Co., Inc.) from MACLEANS CANADA, ed. Leslie F. Hannon. Copyright © 1960 by McClelland and Stewart Ltd.

target—he had killed eighty men—and the Front facing the Canadian Falls was, in 1872, the playground and workshop of some of the continent's worst scoundrels. It became so infamous that many tourists were afraid to go there. Visitors were so systematically humbugged, swindled, blackmailed and bullied that newspapers in both Canada and the United States tarred the resort with their blackest prose, vaudeville comics made wry jokes about it, poets wrote rhymes about the mulcting of the innocents, guidebooks warned of the dangers awaiting the gullible, and angry voices were raised against it in the New York state legislature.

From 1825 to 1888 the mile-long Front, stretching from what is now Oakes Gardens to Table Rock at the brink of the Falls, was one of the most ruthless and ingenious clip joints in history. Originally it was a military reserve of Upper Canada, but piecemeal—except for a government road—it was taken over by a group of businessmen and showmen. To attract customers to their taverns, hotels, museums, bazaars, and curio shops they sailed wild animals in schooners over the Falls, staged an elaborate Indian burial ceremony and a farcical buffalo hunt—with Wild Bill Hickok in charge—and they encouraged or hired daredevils to jump into the raging river or walk across the Gorge on tightropes. They also perpetrated some of their country's most blatant hoaxes.

Derby-hatted sharpers imported white pebbles from England and sold them to visitors as congealed Niagara spray. At Burning Spring, where natural gas bubbled through the water and could be set afire, tourists bought bottled water, and found out later of course that it didn't burn. One forgotten curio dealer launched the legend of Niagara Falls as a honeymoon resort by telling his customers the story of a beautiful Indian princess thrown into the Falls to become the bride of a god who dwelt in the mist and spray. He also sold them paintings and medallions of a bare-bosomed princess.

The Front itself, squeezed between the Niagara escarpment and the Gorge, was only three hundred yards wide, but in character it was almost as unbridled as its strange inhabitants. From the spidery suspension bridge spanning the Gorge to Table Rock, there were six large and, for those days, magnificent hotels—the Clifton House, Robinson House, Brunswick House, Museum House, Prospect House and Table Rock House. Scattered between them were souvenir stands, taverns, refreshment booths and a forest of Indian tepees. In the middle of the Front stood Colonel Thomas Barnett's Museum, a costly ($150,000) ornamental stone building filled with everything from Egyptian mummies to Mohawk arrowheads. In a park surrounding the museum were buffalo, rare flowers, rattlesnakes and raccoons, among other attractions.

At tollhouses guarding the roads to the Front along the escarpment, sightseers were charged a fee just to enter this curious Casbah, and inside they were boldly robbed and cheated on almost every side. Barkers dressed like Mississippi gamblers in checkered waistcoats, tight pants and carrying yellow Malacca canes marched along the Front in raucous hordes, shouting the merits of this or that hotel or tavern, trying to lead visitors to tepees where Irish "Indians" in feather headdress and beaded leggings sold cheap and often spurious handicraft for whatever they could extract from their customer.

There were barkers for the rattlesnakes, the Egyptian mummies, Indian antiquities and Niagara spray, barkers for the firewater in the bars, for the false firewater sold at Burning Spring and for the battlegrounds of the War of 1812, just a few hundred yards from the Front. Other barkers lured the curious or the witless to see the Whirlpool and the Lower Niagara Rapids from Termination Rock at the base of the Falls, where guides charged you nothing to go down but made you pay a "ransom" to get up again. And through the dust and din of the whole Front, hackies drove visitors to the hotels and taverns or other stopping places, where they later collected a percentage of any money solicited or stolen from their passengers.

After a visit to the Front in 1871 Henry James, the American author, wrote in disgust: "The spectacle you have come so far to see is choked with horribly vulgar shops, booths and catch-penny artifices which have pushed and elbowed to the very spray of the Falls. The inopportunities one suffers here amid the central din of the cataract from hackmen, photographers and vendors of gimcracks is simply hideous and infamous. Their cries at times drown out the thunder of the cataracts."

Often the cries of the victims were even louder. Some were beaten when they refused to pay a ransom to get out of the Front's more infamous establishments. The Table Rock House, a curio shop and hotel operated by "Old Sol" Davis and his several sons and daughters, was openly described as "the den of forty thieves" by the Hamilton *Evening Times*. Davis sued the *Times* for libel, and at the trial several visitors to the Front, including women, testified that they had been threatened or beaten or forced to pay ransoms in Davis's place.

The Front, with its cupidity and crookedness, could not have survived in a more sophisticated era, but in the Canada of 1825 it would have been surprising if it had not flourished. For the hayseed with straw in his hair was not only a literal reality but, with the rube and the hick, he represented the average Canadian. It was an age of which P. T. Barnum later said, "There's a sucker born every minute, and two to take him." Upper Canada had only 130,000 people; Kingston was the biggest town (2,336); London had not yet been founded and Ottawa was still called Bytown. The United States frontier had just reached the Mississippi and the midwest still belonged to the Indians.

In such a backwoods most of the social pleasures were improvised. A barn-raising, a wedding, an auction or a revival meeting was the occasion for a celebration. These affairs were usually accompanied by roisterous square dancing as fiddles scraped out such tunes as "Monkey Musk," "Old Dan Tucker," and "Pop Goes the Weasel." Whiskey was twenty-five cents a gallon, and fighting, gambling and drunkenness went with almost every public gathering.

Any excuse for a holiday from farm work or land clearing was seized eagerly, so when the enterprising tavern keepers and merchants at the Front began to stage their stunts thousands came by oxcart over muddy roads through the bush, by Lake Ontario schooners and by flatboats up the Erie Canal to join the fun.

The first man to appreciate the commercial possibilities of the Front was a farmer named William Forsyth. He owned land above the escarpment, and in 1817 built a hotel on it and ran a fence down to Table Rock, overlooking the Horseshoe Falls. Only guests at the hotel were permitted inside the fence to view the Falls from this superior vantage point. When Sir Peregrine Maitland, the lieutenant governor of Upper Canada, ordered him to remove the fence from military property, he refused. Maitland sent a squad of soldiers and they tore it down. Forsyth promptly sued for damages.

The suit dragged on and Forsyth, running short of money, sold his hotel and the property above the escarpment to Samuel Street, a wealthy and politically influential neighbor. From a later lieutenant-governor, Sir John Colborne, Street got a license to occupy the military reserve. The government kept only a sixty-six-foot-wide strip along the bank of the Gorge for a public road, but Street was told he could not place any obstruction along the Front.

Street's answer was to call together a group of businessmen and propose a City of the Falls. They built a railway to bring Americans down the Canadian side of the Niagara River from Buffalo, and they began putting up baths, hotels, souvenir stands, taverns and a museum. When Colborne heard about it he ordered the army to halt the work. The officer in charge, remembering the Forsyth suit, had his men remove only one stone from a fence. Street sued the government for trespassing, was awarded five hundred pounds, got a deed to the whole Front and the government was left with only its road.

That was the start of a wild tawdry seventy years on the Front. In addition to the cataract itself, the first big attractions at Niagara were the battlefields of the War of 1812. Nine hundred men had been killed at Lundy's Lane, about a mile from the Falls, and Street and his friends provided guides for visitors. Street also built a pagoda, a towerlike affair from which his patrons could view the country-side without walking or riding in a carriage. When the lure of the battlefields wore thin, the promotors groped for a new attraction. In the summer of 1827, in towns and villages on both sides of the border, handbills appeared with a startling notice: "The pirate ship 'Michigan' on the eighth day of September will sail down the deep and furious rapids of the Niagara and over the precipice and into the abyss below with a cargo of furious animals."

When the day came the Canadian bank of the Gorge and the rapids was black with sightseers. The excitement mounted as word swept down their ranks that the "Michigan" had been cast loose. On board were stuffed effigies of several notables, a buffalo, three bears, two foxes, a raccoon, a dog, a cat and four geese. All except the buffalo were loose on deck.

On the ship's bowsprit was the American ensign; at her stern, the British Jack. People with field glasses could see the foxes running around the deck in terror; the two bears climbed a mast, didn't like it there and jumped overboard. The crowds cheered as they struggled to reach shore and shouted in glee as they finally climbed up the bank and vanished into the forest.

Then the "Michigan," her sails billowing, struck the rapids. She pitched and shook—and broke into pieces. A cry of disappointment went up from the bank. All that could be seen going over the Falls were bits of wreckage. These were later salvaged and sold as souvenirs.

Among those who witnessed the Michigan's last trip was Sam Patch, of Rochester, N.Y., who had made a local reputation by jumping off bridges and other high places into rivers. Patch announced he would jump off a hundred-foot ladder into the river below the Falls. The merchants on the Front quickly rushed out handbills and thousands gathered on the Front. Then the merchants announced that Sam had broken his leg. By that time it was too late for many to go home and they had to stay overnight in the expensive hotels and inns. The next day Sam appeared, sound of limb, and made his leap. But the Front had wrung two days' lodging and food out of thousands, and many angry visitors cried "Hoax!"

It was one of the first, but far from the last, swindles worked on tourists at the Front. One guide showing a visitor around the base of the Falls picked up a white stone one day.

"What's that?" asked the tourist.

"Why," said the guide, suddenly surprised, "it's congealed mist. Very rare."

The tourist bought the stone for three dollars, and the Niagara Spray racket soon became one of the most popular and profitable at the Falls. When the guides could no longer find this variety of white stone, souvenir dealers found there were mountains of it in Derbyshire, England, and began importing it.

One souvenir dealer with a slow-moving supply of medallions and paintings of Indian maidens hatched the idea of building a myth around them. The maiden, he told customers, was a princess sent over the Falls as a bride for a god who lived there. Although North American Indians never have sacrificed human beings to their gods, the gullible public liked the story and romantic women took it to their hearts.

Soon the honeymooners began coming to the Falls. The astute merchants encouraged the legend and named the spume of mist in the cataract The Bridal Veil. In 1846, when the first little boat sailed around the bottom of the Falls, it was named the "Maid of the Mist," and so were all its successors. Oscar Wilde visited the Falls in 1883, observed the honeymooners and then the cataract, and wrote pointedly: "This must be the second major disappointment of American married life."

Many of these smaller hoaxes were in good fun, and it's almost certain the public helped them along to some extent, as people do today at carnivals. But organized robbery, extortion and swindling—often helped by hoodlums and strongarm boys—was a different thing. It became the rule on the front, brought the whole resort into ill repute and finally helped to kill it.

The key man in this skin game was the hack driver, usually an obsequious creature who picked up visitors on their arrival by train and offered to show them the sights for a small fee. He drove them to the Whirlpool and the Lower Gorge and finally landed them at Table Rock House, the headquarters of "Old Sol" Davis and his clan. From there, stairs led to Termination Rock; nearby were Burning Spring and Colonel Barnett's Museum.

Barnett, enterprising and honest, charged a straight fifty-cents admission, but at all the other places sightseers were told there was no fee. Inside, however, tawdry saleswomen sold worthless knickknacks at fancy prices, and visitors had to pay pug-ugly doormen anything from fifty cents to two dollars to get out again. From the owners of these places the hackies collected fifty percent of the money extorted from customers, and when the ride was over they charged their passengers whatever the traffic would bear.

As the systematic swindle continued through the Fifties, tourists became more and more wary of the Front, and the merchants began to look for new lures. In 1859 they found a prize one in Jean Francois Gravelet, known as Blondin, a tightrope artist who did incredible things on his rope above the Gorge. He ran, turned somersaults, lay down, put baskets on his feet, while a hundred thousand people gasped and hundreds of gentlewomen fainted.

Blondin started a new golden era for the Front. Other tightrope experts and daredevils followed, though none were as expert as Blondin. Railway excursions came to the Falls from the American midwest and from New York. The merchants prospered and the crooks got even richer.

In 1867 the Front's reputation was blacker than ever. In the New York legislature a resolution was passed protesting to Canadian authorities "the outrages on American citizens at Niagara Falls." The Toronto *Telegram* countered that the worst outrages were perpetuated by a "Yankee and a scoundrel, Sol Davis."

Then the Hamilton *Evening Times* referred to "the robbers at Niagara—the cave of the forty thieves, otherwise known as the Table Rock House and kept by the notorious Sol Davis and his progeny." It was a dangerous locality for strangers, said the *Times*.

Old Sol promptly sued, and now, for the first time, the ruthlessness and crudity of the swindles and extortions on the Front began to come to light. At the trial witnesses came forward and told how they had been robbed and threatened, and how sometimes beaten, if they refused to pay a ransom to get out of the Davis establishment.

"Enter . . . all is free," they had been told by an oily individual when they went in. Then. . . .

Dr. E.P. Miller, New York City, said he refused to pay four dollars for going to Termination Rock, and he was caught by the whiskers by one man, the throat by another, pushed out of the door and thrown to the ground. He was in bed for six weeks.

S.L. Kilbourne, a lawyer from Lansing, Michigan, had to pay $4.50 for a photograph worth fifty cents. He thought it was a joke, but when Sol Davis gave a whistle and two "large Ethiopians and two equally large Irishmen" charged into the room, he changed his mind and paid.

John Crist, from Lockport, N.Y., when told he had to pay five dollars, made a dash for the door, but was caught and flung back. "Here is one dollar in my purse," he wailed. "It's all I have except a quarter. I'll give you all I have."

"You're a damned pretty fellow to come all the way to the Falls with only a dollar in your pocket," cried Davis. "You'll stay here until you pay."

"Is there no law in Canada that will give me redress?" cried Crist.

One of the Davis's sons shook his fist in Crist's face and cried: "That's the law in Canada, and we're the officers to carry it out."

John Weir, a farmer near Peterborough, refused to pay four dollars and was threatened by Davis who said: "Damn you, I have something here that will put a window through you." Weir paid.

Even the American consul at Niagara Falls was a victim. W. Martin Jones told how he had gone to the Falls with his wife and a secretary of the Department of State in Washington. A man named Jess Burkin opened their carriage door at the Table Rock House and said: "Ladies and gentlemen, please step out. All is free."

Jones told him to close the door as he knew the character of the house. Burkin then "commenced to use language I would not like to repeat and threatened to throw me over the bank into the Gorge. He went away and returned with Edward Davis, son of the proprietor, who also threatened to throw me over the bank."

The jury took only three minutes to decide that the *Times* was not guilty of maligning Davis's reputation.

As a result of the trial the Canadian government, which owned the entrance from the road, canceled Davis's license to guide tourists to Termination Rock. Davis then made plans to blow off part of the rock so he could build a staircase outside the government's property. He had the dynamite ready when Colonel Barnett tipped off the authorities. Enraged, Davis sued Barnett for perjury, but lost again in the courts.

Now, like a disgraced and jaded rake, the Front became the butt of wits and rhymers—the last stop before oblivion. By 1870 many tourists were afraid to go there. Tightrope walkers had lost their appeal. Colonel Barnett thought he saw the solution in an Indian burial ceremony to attract sightseers to his museum. He imported Indians togged out in ceremonial dress and painted to the eyebrows and he displayed a coffin reported to contain the ashes of twenty Indians unearthed from a mound near Queenston where they had lain for a thousand years. It was pretty tame fare for tourists accustomed to boatloads of "furious animals" and death-defying stuntmen, and what was supposed to have been a serious ritual was greeted with whimsical good humor by a small crowd. Barnett admitted the venture was a flop and looked around for something more exciting.

The great buffalo hunts of the western plains had excited public imagination in the United States. Barnett got the idea of staging a buffalo hunt at Niagara Falls and sent his son Sydney west to hunt buffalo and hire some performers. In Kansas City he met Wild Bill Hickok and engaged him to manage the show. He also hired some Sac and Fox Indians and Mexican cowboys.

When Wild Bill arrived at the Front, Blondin was forgotten. The frontiersman, with his long blond hair, broad shoulders, handsome features and his amazing record of gun victories, was quickly made a hero. He was not a show-off, but when one day he walked into a bar and saw a friend asleep in a chair, he fired between his feet with a derringer. When his friend didn't bat an eye Wild Bill roared with laughter and the incident became the talk of the town.

On August 28 about three thousand people gathered to see the Great Buffalo Hunt. The arena was an enclosure of about eighty acres above the Horseshoe Falls, fenced with ten-foot-high boards. In the centre two buffalo bulls grazed peacefully. In a far corner of the enclosure were four Texas steers. Cheers went up as Wild Bill, dressed in buckskin-fringed frontier costume, rode into the arena followed by four Mexican vaqueros and three Indians. After saluting the crowd, the little band rode out to do battle. The buffalo turned docilely and watched the cowboys riding about hallooing. Finally one stepped defiantly toward his adversaries. With his huge head and beard he seemed of enormous proportions in contrast to the prairie ponies. For a while he charged the cowboys, as the crowd gasped. Then a vaquero lassoed one of his feet. At that moment a second Mexican and his pony were knocked over by the enraged animal and it seemed to the horrified spectators as if the buffalo was only stopped from killing both rider and pony by the lasso, held by several straining cowboys. Another lasso was thrown over his horns and the struggle ended.

The other buffalo was lassoed in the same way but broke the rope. Indians approached him on foot and on horseback, shooting blunt arrows. For a time the buffalo pursued one of the vaqueros, but the sport degenerated into a farce when it became evident that he was driven by a motley crowd of Indians, white men and boys. At last he was left in his ignominy on the grounds.

The Great Buffalo Hunt received a bad press. One correspondent wrote that it was a mere sham. "Many of the Indian chiefs had to take a buffalo by the horns to make him run. Wild Bill managed by the aid of his satellites to secure a cow, which had to be goaded into desperation before it would run. The chase after the

Texan cattle was also a farce, since the Indians were evidently chasing a cow that had been roaming about for the last two years in the pasture of some peaceful agriculturist.''

A second hunt was held two days later, but the effect was no better. Four buffalo were turned loose, but they had to be goaded to gallop. Three, it turned out, were from Colonel Barnett's museum park. Artistically and financially, the whole venture was a flop, Barnett was forced into bankruptcy and his museum sold to his old enemy, Sol Davis.

For the whole Front, the Great Buffalo Hunt was also the end. The public felt it had been cheated once too often and refused to go back. In 1888 the Ontario government expropriated the Front and created a public park. Souvenir stands, hotels, taverns, tepees—all were torn down and flowers and grass planted in their place.

In 1901 Mrs. Anna Edson Taylor went over the Falls in a barrel, and lived, and there was a slight, renewed flurry of excitement, but it didn't last. For years she sat on a street in Niagara signing autographs for pennies, and eventually she died in a poorhouse. Four others—Bobby Leach in 1911, Charles Stephens in 1920, Jean Lussier in 1928 and William (Red) Hill, Jr. in 1951—went over the Falls and Stephens and Hill died in the attempt. In each case the old memories of Blondin and Wild Bill were revived, but only for a day.

Today the raucous roistering Front is scarcely recognizable in quiet Queen Victoria Park with its green lawns and colorful flowers where even an Eagle Scout isn't permitted to sell an apple on Boy Scout Day. But in a nearby souvenir shop you can buy a little white stone for a dollar. It's really imported from England, but ask the salesgirl what it is and she'll tell you: "It's congealed mist from the Falls.''

Ending Time:

_____

WPM: _____

Comprehension Check: Nineteenth-Century Niagara

Directions: Complete each question by writing in or circling the correct answer.

1. The Niagara area was a historically significant site since _____

   _____.

2. Nature had endowed the Niagara region
   a. with numerous species of animal and plant life.
   b. with precipitous mountains.
   c. with majestic falls.

3. Niagara gained infamy because _____

   _____.

4. The legend of Niagara as a honeymoon resort

   a. stemmed from an Indian legend from the area.
   b. was a hoax as were most attractions that the tourists frequented.
   c. was a prefabrication spread by a group of silly romantic women.

5. From this selection, list ten words that describe how the author and writers of the nineteenth century felt about the happenings at Niagara.

Comprehension Accuracy:

_____

The Supplementary Selections at the end of this unit on pp. 99–114 are provided for further practice of phrase reading skills on regular materials. Turn to these now if you need more work.

NOTES TO UNIT 2

1. Royce W. Adams, *Developing Reading Versatility* (New York: Holt Rinehart and Winston, Inc., 1973). p. 51.

2. Nila Banton Smith, *Read Faster and Get More From Your Reading* (Englewood Cliffs, N.J.: Prentice-Hall, Inc., 1958), p. 28.

Answer Key: Unit 2

Selection 1: A Science of Man, p. 19

1. True **2.** True **3.** True **4.** True **5.** True

Selection 2: How I Learned to Sleep, p. 23

Preview Test, p. 29

1. sleeplessness or insomnia. **2.** three **3.** sleep clinic **4.** the 24-hour spin-ning cycle of the earth **5.** polysomnogram **6.** so many sleeping pills are sold **7.** how much it takes for the person to function well **8.** two **9.** mild to moderate

Comprehension Check, p. 30

1. True **2.** they are usually of little significance; is a free spirit **3.** False **4.** every one needs at least eight hours **5.** True

Selection 3: The Jogging-Shoe Race Heats Up, p. 30

Preview Test, p. 33

1. competition among manufacturers or makers of such shoes **2.** True **3.** German **4.** American **5.** Nike **6.** scientists from NASA and the aerospace industries **7.** False **8.** the leisure market

Comprehension Check. p. 34

1. Design and technology **2.** True **3.** Germany **4.** Nike **5.** True

Selection 4: Women Become Farm Managers, p. 36

1. c **2.** b **3.** a **4.** b **5.** c

Selection 5: Chinese Greet Year of Horse, p. 37

1. b **2.** c **3.** c **4.** a **5.** b

Selection 6: Pop-Eyed in Moscow, p. 44

1. F **2.** T **3.** T **4.** T **5.** T

Selection 7: Business, Labor Join to Battle Alcoholism, p. 45.

1. F **2.** F **3.** T **4.** T **5.** T

Selection 8: East Asia—Japan, p. 51

1. Japanese home **2.** b **3.** True **4.** simplicity **5. a.** beauty of nature **b.** hills or rocks **c.** bamboo **d.** sand **e.** bonsai

Selection 9: Pyramid Yields Priceless Art, p. 53

1. True   **2.** archeology   **3.** it provided a valuable clue to the importance of the site, (commercial, religious, etc.) because jade was not found there naturally   **4.** the Maya used open caves that are easy to locate and enter   **5.** True

Selection 10: Miraculous Swiss Landscape, p. 54

1. causes a person to want to visit there; shows its great beauty   **2.** True   **3.** a
4. in the foothills, Central Plateau and valleys   **5.** c

Selection 11: Nineteenth-Century Niagara, p. 56

1. Several battlefields of the War of 1812 were located there.   **2.** c   **3.** because of the dishonesty and brutality shown to tourists by its businessmen   **4.** b   **5.** Choose any ten: infamous, humbugged, blackmailed, ruthless, ingenious, raucous, extortion, wild, elaborate, hordes roi, roistering, farcical, sharpers, magnificent, ornamental, boldly, hackmen, gimcracks, vulgar, hideous, cupidity, crookedness, tawdry, racket

Supplementary
Selections for Unit 2

You must practice the previewing technique many times before you become a proficient user. The supplementary selections provided here will help you develop and strengthen your skills.

Efficient previewing follows a systematic procedure which you should apply to *everything* you read. Now review the suggested sequence for the preview:

1. *Study the title.*
2. *What are the subheadings or subtitles? How many are there?*
3. *Inspect any visual aids.*
4. *Examine the lengths of the paragraphs.*
5. *Estimate how long it will take you to read the selection.*

Remember, the preview does not slow you down. The preview actually increases your reading rate because it familiarizes you with the topic before you read it thoroughly.

Once you do begin to read through these selections, read as rapidly as possible. Time yourself. Check your comprehension. Plot your scores on the Reading Progress chart on page 117. Your comprehension should be at seventy-five percent accuracy or better.

If your comprehension is lower than seventy-five percent, you will need to study other techniques to increase your accuracy. These include phrase reading (Unit 2); identifying organizational patterns (Unit 5); and paragraph reading and diagramming for effective recall (Unit 5). As you work on these skills, continue to preview all materials before reading. Your comprehension levels will steadily increase if you consistently apply your previewing skills and other speed reading techniques to everything you read.

Selection 1: Accounting as a Tool of Management ⎯⎯⎯⎯⎯

Beginning Time:

_____

Accounting is sometimes said to be the language of business. As language is a means of expressing and communicating ideas in general, so accounting in

Total Words: 1843

67

business is a means of expressing managerial plans and a tool for communicating managerial results.

Language uses words as a means of expression; accounting uses both words and figures. To express and communicate ideas effectively, some familiarity with the meaning and syntax of words is needed. Similarly, to present managerial plans clearly and to communicate and interpret managerial results effectively, some understanding of the significance and limitations of accounting data is necessary. . . .

ACCOUNTING AS A TOOL FOR THE STEWARDSHIP FUNCTION OF MANAGEMENT

Historically, accounting development has been made in response to business needs. As commerce has expanded, so has the use of accounting data.

To an owner-manager of a business in the Middle Ages, the need for organized accounting information was not apparent. He supplied all the necessary capital to the business; he was responsible to no one but himself. He managed his own business affairs and was fully aware of day-to-day activities. Further, since each business transaction was concluded with an exchange of goods for currency or other valuables, committing such activities to writing was not a necessity. In short, the factors responsible for accounting's development were not present at this time.

As an Aid in Completing Credit Transactions

The need for accounting information was first felt during the Renaissance period in Italy. With an expansion of trade and a consequent broadening of competition, it became necessary for the merchants in large Italian trading ports, such as Florence and Genoa, to sell their goods to customers on the latter's good name: that is, on credit.

These credit transactions, the completion of which might take months or even years, prompted the Florentine and Genoese merchants to keep written records. Such records served as a reminder for collections to be made in the future. In addition, the courts were known to have used this information, if it was systematically recorded, as one of the proofs of sales made in cases concerning the merchants' claims against their customers for nonpayment of debt.

The need to record credit transactions was directly responsible for the creation of the two most frequently heard bookkeeping terms, *debit* and *credit*. As they were originally used, *debit* referred to a person from whom we shall receive payment (a debtor), and *credit* referred to a person to whom we shall give payment (a creditor). With later expansion of accounting functions, the original meaning of these two words became inappropriate and obsolete, though their use as two technical terms is still retained.

As a Report to Credit Grantors

Commerce expanded as the use of credit increased and large amounts of circulating capital were often required. Many owners of business could not provide this, so short-term, "self-liquidating" loans were frequently used.

In application for such loans, some owners-borrowers thought it desirable to submit a list of financial resources and obligations related to their business enterprises. This listing, which has become known as a statement of financial position, was intended to convey the owners-borrowers' financial integrity; it generally facilitated the credit grantors in reaching a decision. It became so popular with bankers that they soon required submission of such statements with nearly all applications for loans: many even designed proper forms for supplying the necessary information. In the United States, a standard form, designed and endorsed by the American Bankers' Association, was put into use in 1899.

Submitting statements of financial position with loan applications to credit grantors was the first time that accounting data were released to non-owner groups. Since this information was compiled by one group, the owners-borrowers, and interpreted by another group, credit grantors—each with their own interests in mind—conflicts sometimes arose. Suggested forms of presentation, like those prepared by the bankers' group and later by the professional accountants' group, were attempts directed toward a reconciliation of these conflicting interests.

As a Report to Absentee Owners

Industrialization further widened the scale of business operation and increased the need for more capital for acquiring machines and plant facilities. Relying upon a few persons to supply this amount of capital became exceedingly difficult. Using short-term bank loans to finance plant acquisitions seemed to be too hazardous and impracticable. This series of events made the corporation, with its ability to secure sizable amounts of capital from a large group of people, the dominant form of business organization. In addition, a corporation offered distinct legal advantages, considering the attendant risks and slow maturity of industrial enterprises. It protected its stockholders with limited liability in the event of financial failure, and it assured continued existence regardless of ownership changes.

The diversity of ownership interests coupled with the growing complexity of the process of decision-making for large enterprises prevented the stockholders as a group from exercising direct, day-to-day operating control over their business interests. By necessity, this responsibility and authority had to be delegated to a select group of people versed in the conduct of business affairs, the professional management group. The delegation of authority increased the necessity for reporting accountability. Accounting information came to be the principal means of reporting the results achieved by management to the absentee stockholders.

Though stockholders are interested in the financial solidity of a corporation, their primary interest seems to be with its long-continued economic success. As a result, two reports are generally submitted by management to stockholders: a statement of financial position and an income statement. A statement of financial position indicates the status of assets and liabilities as of a given date. An income statement reports the consumption of existing resources and the generation of new resources in connection with the rendering of services over a period of time.

Since stockholders place emphasis on the income statement, their interests are in conflict with those of short-term credit grantors. The latter evaluate the statement of financial position for clues about a corporation's loan-repaying ability. The interaction of these two statements is responsible for the development of many areas of accounting theory. . . .

As a Report to Governmental Agencies

Modern tax levies by governmental agencies based on the extent of corporations' net income have further broadened the use of accounting data. Since what constituted income was subject to various interpretations, detailed regulations concerning the methods to be followed in computing net income for tax purposes have been prescribed. In the fields of public utilities and transportation, many governmental agencies have turned to the prescription of uniform accounting systems as a means of control and to the use of the accounting data derived as an aid in rate-making.

As a Report to the Employees and to the Public

Big industrial enterprises, with investments in millions and employment in thousands, are commonly considered to be quasi-public institutions. Their success or failure affects directly the welfare of those employed, and indirectly that of the communities in which plants are located. The two accounting reports, statement of financial position and income statement, are sometimes used by management as a means of discharging some of the public aspects of corporate responsibilities.

ACCOUNTING AS A TOOL FOR THE PLANNING AND CONTROL FUNCTIONS OF MANAGEMENT

As a tool for reporting the results of management's stewardship to various interested parties, the statement of financial position and the income statement are generally considered adequate. They indicate the results of managerial decisions already made and the efficiency of managerial performances already completed. They relate, however, only to the past: only to the period covered by the two statements.

For managerial use such statements are inadequate unless supplemented. Forward planning and decision-making affecting the future require data relevant to the future. Accounting, as a tool for the planning and control functions of management, is designed to provide supplementary data in a systematic and timely manner to facilitate the evaluation, selection, and subsequent analysis of plans.

As an Aid in Evaluating Overall Plans

One of the functions of top management is to plan ahead, to set policies for implementation and execution. The main objective of this type of planning and policy-making is to attain and maintain a high level of economic competence consistent with public policies and business statesmanship.

An overall plan in its final version, one which is to be used as the basis for implementation and action, is generally a coordination of various divisional plans. To evaluate these plans in terms of profit potential, a projected income statement may be prepared; in terms of financial commitments, a budgeted statement of financial position may be needed. These projected or budgeted statements differ from regular statements only in that the former use projected data and the latter use historical data.

As a means of evaluating plans in terms of operating risks, cost-volume-profit analysis is a convenient tool. As a means of evaluating plans in terms of financial flexibility, cash forecasting tends to provide the necessary clues.

As an Aid in Establishing Responsibilities and Providing Guides for Effective Control

To implement top management plans and policies, management in general is charged with the function of delegating the authority and responsibility of execution to subordinates and of supervising and evaluating the subordinates' performances.

A divisional budget, if all members within the division are encouraged to participate in its preparation, permits in an informal but effective way the establishment of each member's responsibility. This, together with performance standards, can serve also as a guide for subsequent evaluation.

The use of management control reports tends to facilitate the supervision and evaluation of subordinates' performances. Through such reports, management is informed of the actual level of effort and accomplishment as well as the extent and probable cause of deviation from the expected. If such reports are timely, management's attention may be directed promptly to areas requiring remedial action and factors pertinent to the solving of such problems are elusive. The objective of such decision-making is the most effective use of business capital and facilities.

Accounting data compiled for regular use are generally irrelevant and sometimes misleading for solving such problems. Instead, a special study, known as project planning, must be made for each problem. This study considers only factors and data relevant to the problem.

SUMMARY

Accounting is a tool of management. To be useful, it must adapt itself to the needs of management.

Management first conceived of accounting as a written reminder in aiding the completion of credit transactions. With the expansion of commerce and the extended use of credit, accounting function was broadened to include supplying financial data of business enterprises to credit grantors at the time of loan applications. With industrialization and the corporate form of business organization, the accounting function was further broadened to a means of reporting the results of management stewardship to absentee owners. The inception of income taxes and the growth of corporations that became, in effect, quasi-public institutions paved the way for using accounting information as a means of discharging the public aspects of corporate responsibilities.

The complexity of business decision-making resulted in a systematic use of accounting for managerial planning and control purposes. Projected statement of income, budgeted statement of financial position, cash forecast, and cost-volume-profit analysis were designed to permit the selection of the most suitable plan for implementation and action. Performance standards and management control reports were instituted to facilitate the establishment of operating responsibilities and the supervision and evaluation of subordinates' performances. Special project planning was aimed at providing clues for decisions related to making effective use of business capital and facilities.

Ending Time:

_____

WPM: _____

Comprehension Check: Accounting as a Tool. . . .

Directions: Complete each of the following statements by writing in or circling the correct answer.

1. As with many other important developments in our world, the growth of accounting was an evolutionary one.

    True   False

2. The stewardship function of accounting refers to _____
_____

3. Managerial functions are more precisely described when the language of _____ is applied.

4. The event of _____ prompted the first felt need for a system of accounting.

5. In top level management obtaining the most efficient use of business capital and facilities is made possible with specialized data made available by accounting.

   True   False

Comprehension Accuracy:

_____

Beginning Time:

_____

Total Words: 4468

Selection 2: Secretaries: Are Bosses Getting Their Message? _____

In the beginning was the secret. Secretary was the title devised for an employee who, among other things, could be entrusted with the most private of confidences. Also in the beginning, of course, was the male secretary: Almost all such workers were men, until the advent of the typewriter and the large corporation freed them for higher managerial positions.

Today 99.1 percent of all secretaries are female. The original concept of the confidential secretary is still alive and well, as Rose Mary Woods showed the world during the saga of Watergate. Yet every day more and more secretaries are becoming increasingly vocal about certain aspects of the job itself. The "secret," they are saying, must no longer remain in the dark.

Consider the revelations of Ann Butler. She was a Phi Beta Kappa with a master's degree in English and a dream of teaching literature. She entered the labor market at a time when teaching positions were as scarce as English majors were plentiful, and so she took a secretarial job instead. After handling everything from keeping track of her employer's dental appointments to planning his business calendar to rinsing out coffee mugs to dusting shelves to taking care of the most urgent business questions when he was away, not to mention the usual load of typing and dictation, she realized: "I was completely unprepared for the rigors of a job I had heretofore considered a cinch . . . I will never sneer at secretaries again. They are superhuman, fonts of practical and useful knowledge . . . I am convinced that if one can survive being a secretary, one can survive anything."

Her words, which appeared in the January, 1978, issue of *McCall's* clearly touched a nerve. Or, rather, two nerves. Secretaries throughout the country wrote back both to praise and to protest. On the one hand were those like the woman who wrote: "Thank God, someone said something good about being a secretary . . . Now I know that there are other women who work in offices who get blamed when things go wrong, and when they go right the boss gets all the praise. I am giving this article to my boss, so that he can see why I need a raise." And another wrote: "I'm sure you'll get countless letters like this from other . . . secretaries who have been reduced to acting as coffee makers and maids along with other tasks performed beyond the call of duty. Maybe we should form a Secretaries' Union. The bosses will never admit it, but secretaries run the world."

There were, however, an equal number of equally passionate letters from

SOURCE: Reprinted by permission of *McCall's* Magazine.

women who felt they sniffed a strain of snobbism in Ann Butler's story. From one of the most eloquent: "Secretaries have come a long way and we have a long way to go, but we're proud of our chosen field. We are a vital part of every business, industry and public office—they would collapse without our support. Don't make us feel as though we should hang our heads low and say, "I'm just a secretary!"

Just a Secretary.

It immediately brings to mind that other self-derogatory phrase that is imposed on women (and that women too often impose on themselves): *just a housewife*. Since homemaking and secretarial work are still by far the two most prevalent occupations of American females, what is really being said is: "just a woman's job." For some reason, those engaged in the traditional pursuits never feel they have to say, "just an insurance salesman" or "just a policeman." Only women are asked to downplay the work they do. In any case, despite their decidedly different reactions to Ann Butler's article, both groups of secretaries were making the same point:

Our work is extremely important. It can also be fulfilling, absorbing, challenging, and provide opportunities to participate closely in a vast array of interesting projects. The job of secretary should not be undervalued.

It should not be, but it often is, and that is what growing numbers of secretaries are now trying to change. In Boston, Cleveland, Chicago, San Francisco, New York, Dayton, Minneapolis and a dozen other cities, secretaries have joined with other office workers to fight for better conditions. Called by different names in different cities (Nine to Five in Boston, Women Employed in Chicago, Cleveland Women Working, Sixty Words per Minute in Washington, D.C., Women Office Workers in New York) the groups are using a wide variety of techniques to get their point across. They stage "pettiest office procedures contests" to publicly expose the unreasonable chores demanded of workers. Among the winners have been an employer who insisted on having freshly peeled carrots every day, another who wanted his picture taken before and after he shaved off his moustache, and a third who required his secretary to sew up his pants while he still had them on. They pass out leaflets and balloons on National Secretaries Day, calling for "raises, not roses."

Most strenuously, they pressure corporations to comply with affirmative action regulations, filing complaints and initiating lawsuits against those who do not. In a variety of cases they have helped office workers win large back-pay and salary-increase awards, including settlements of over a million dollars from several corporations in Chicago.

Meantime, while secretaries have begun fighting for change, employers are increasingly worrying about secretaries, too. But their concern is quite different: Will there be enough qualified secretaries to go around in the future? Already an immense shortage exists in many cities, and according to the business publication, *Dun's Review*, if the current rate continues, there could be as many as 600,000 unfilled openings by 1985. "The women's movement has been a primary cause of changing attitudes toward secretarial jobs," the Review warns employers. "Many are deserting . . . If you have a good secretary, you better do everything you can to keep her."

This, then, should be the perfect time to help employers understand exactly what secretaries want. Obviously differences exist. Obviously much depends on the individual worker and the individual job. At latest count there are over three and a half million secretaries in the nation, and there is no job with a greater diversity of openings listed day after day in the help-wanted ads: Medical secretary, legal secretary, executive secretary, secretary to famous writer, sec'y real estate, sec'y airline—special benefits, sec'y insurance, sec'y small one-person office; sec'y large multinational corp., part-time sec'y, temporary sec'y, sec'y to bank president, to publisher, to producer, to professor, to proctologist, to priest . . . the list and variety go on and on.

As does the range of women in such jobs. Secretaries straight out of high school, secretaries returning to the labor force after years at home with the kids, secretaries who always wanted to be secretaries (''our chosen field''), secretaries like Ann Butler who never conceived of being secretaries but could find no other work, secretaries who are using the position as a way of gaining entry into the fields of their choice, secretaries who are only working temporarily, until they finish school or find an opening in an entirely different career—plus a slowly growing smattering of men. Before presuming to say ''what secretaries want,'' one would first have to reconcile a myriad of different impressions and goals and expectations.

But certain fundamentals apply for all secretaries. A ''Bill of Rights for Women Office Workers,'' prepared by several of the office workers' groups, lists a number of them. They include the right to comprehensive medical coverage, having pregnancy treated as a temporary medical disability, compensation for overtime written and systematic grievance procedures. Again, each item on the bill of rights is fundamental, but the following are perhaps the most pressing, both to the wide variety of secretaries I've been talking with lately and to those who wrote letters responding to Ann Butler's article.

The Right to Respect

One might assume that respect from her employer was something a secretary could take for granted.

''It's the main reason why I took this job,'' Arline, a legal secretary, told me. ''He really respects my intelligence and he gives me a chance to use it.'' A secretary before getting married, Arline stopped working while her two daughters were growing up. ''When I decided to go back, like a lot of other women, I wasn't sure at first what I was going to do. You know you hear about all these fantastic opportunities, most of which probably don't exist, and I was thinking of maybe getting into wholesale sales or possibly doing something related to art. I decided to work as an office temp while I was thinking things over, and that's when I walked into this particular job. It was amazing. An hour after I got there he offered me a permanent position. I thought, What's going on? He seemed so ecstatic about the way I was talking to his clients on the phone, so thrilled that I was able to take his dictation accurately. I had to wonder who had been working for him before. I didn't realize how rare good secretarial skills are today.

''Anyway, I told him I'd think it over, but after a while I could see this was probably going to be as fine a job as I would find. The money was good, and so were the benefits; and that of course was a big influence. But the main reason was the way I was being treated and the fact that I was working in a relaxed atmosphere with pleasant, considerate people, not cold and rude; the way I'd seen at some other places.

"Also, the one thing I would never do is work in a place where there's no room for self-expression, and here there's plenty. The work is interesting, I'm learning new things all the time, and the days fly by. As any secretary can tell you, interpersonal skills—you know, the ability to deal intelligently with a whole bunch of different people with different problems—can be as important as your typing and shorthand skills. Much more important a lot of the time. In my own case, my typing and shorthand are okay, although I'm sure there are secretaries who are faster. But I think my intelligence is really my strongest point. I can't count the times when I've had to calm down a panicky client on the phone and even offer some practical advice when my boss is away. And that really does give me a sense of accomplishment.

"We've gotten to the point, the two of us, where we really work as a team. Oh, of course, he's still the employer, but if he screws up, I tell him, and vice versa. For example, time and time again I'll catch a gaffe in his dictation and I'll say, 'Did you really mean to write that?' And he'll say, 'Arline, thank God you caught that.' Or at the end of a letter or contract, he'll sometimes ask, 'Is there something you think I left out?' And naturally there are times when I make mistakes—I'm human, too—and he'll tell me about them in the nicest possible way. All in all, he appreciates me beyond belief. Which of course he should, since no matter how successful he is, if I don't come through, he's in trouble."

But contrast Arline's situation with this secretary's:

"My boss wrote 'damn you' on manuscripts if I made mistakes. He expected me to vacuum the office even if I was busy—I could go on and on. Even though I had very little money at the time, I quit because of his condescending and poor treatment of me. Now I am faced with a situation where, when I go to apply for a new job, I cannot put him down as a former employer. Otherwise, he would give me a poor reference."

So wrote a woman to Karen Nussbaum of the Working Women Organizing Project, which is helping office workers in different cities launch groups of their own. This particular story is just one of thousands the various groups have heard from secretaries decrying the disrespectful treatment they have received, including the most pernicious: sexual harassment. "And I'm convinced," Ms. Nussbaum says, "that we've still only seen the tip of the iceberg."

The Right to Choose Whether to Do the Personal Work of Employers

In her book *Men and Women of the Corporation*, Rosabeth Moss Kanter discusses the old analogy of the secretary and the wife. Just as a wife's status in society has been traditionally dependent on her husband's, a secretary's status within an organization has been directly tied to that of her boss. Like a wife, she is expected to be loyal and devoted; she is expected to care. Otherwise there's always the possibility of "divorce."

And also like wives, secretaries are typically the ones to bring a humanizing touch (what used to be called the feminine touch) into cold, impersonal settings. Collections for workers who are getting married, parties for those who are leaving, freshly baked cookies—these are often the contributions of secretaries. To her own boss, again like a wife, a secretary is frequently the source of emotional support. "He'll call me at the end of the day just to talk and unwind," one said. And when there is a crisis, a business setback, it's the secretary, many times, who will tell the executive not to worry. "Sometimes an unfavorable report will come in, and I won't show it to him right away. I don't want to ruin his whole day." Just like a wife. Or maybe a good friend.

And when the relationship is a close one, it can be a two-way street. Arline's employer is truly concerned about her welfare. And one year the employer of a recently divorced secretary I know paid for her children's camp expenses as a bonus. Another sent his secretary to his own physician when she was stricken with cancer, kept her on the payroll until the day she died two years later and grieved bitterly with members of her family at the funeral. From strictly impersonal to highly personal, grossly insensitive to acutely sensitive, thoughtless to caring, the employer-secretary relationship is lived daily in an infinite variety of ways. As is the one between husbands and wives.

However, also like wives, secretaries are living in an era of profound social change. If the greatest distinction between wives today is between those with traditional and those with egalitarian views of male-female roles, the same, Dr. Kanter believes, can be said of secretaries. In analyzing the different attitudes at one large corporation, she found:

"The traditional secretary, usually an older woman, knew her place, served with a smile, was willing to be scapegoated and take the blame for the boss's mistakes and did not presume. . . . She never called him by his first name. . . . At the other end of the continuum were the new "liberated' office marriages, generally involving younger women. Some secretaries refused to do 'housework' and insisted on participating in a process of contracting that defined the relationship as they wanted it defined. . . . However, even this liberated secretary was still merely 'the wife' without a clear career territory of her own but in a new kind of marriage in which she could demand privileges."

What proportion of women working as secretaries today fall into which category? My feeling, after talking with many, is that for the majority such clear-cut distinctions are impossible, since so much depends on other factors. (And needless to say, the marriage metaphor is a very limited one. In their most crucial aspects, the roles of secretaries and wives bear no resemblance at all.)

"I've had three different bosses in the last eight years," one secretary told me, "and each one expected different things. My last boss never asked for anything personal. My current boss expects his coffee served and I'm doing it, but it's not because I'm traditional or untraditional. It's because I have two kids to support and I want to keep getting paid." Said another: "I figure, if he wants to be called by his last name, that's his hangup, not mine."

Although their reactions differ, depending upon which particular chore was required of them, most of the women I talked with had deeply mixed feelings about performing personal tasks in general. "In a way," one said, "it can be fun to do his Christmas shopping or pick up his theatre tickets; it breaks up the routine." Then she paused: "But, you know, sometimes when I'm doing it, it's the middle of winter and I'm freezing and I really resent it terribly." True, there were some who seemed to have no objection at all to such tasks and who also took pride in keeping their employer's office immaculate, the plants watered and healthy. But others believed that one of the reasons secretaries have been undervalued is that they have allowed themselves to be treated as "gofers." "We have to show our employers that this not the job applied for."

Of course, the biggest symbol in the controversy about personal chores has been the issue of serving coffee. In Chicago, 50 members of Women Employed demonstrated in the office of a secretary who was fired because she refused to make another cup. The woman was rehired. In Cleveland, another secretary almost lost her job when she refused to serve lunch to a group of executives. Eventually the lunch chores were taken away—only to be given to another woman. As for Arline, the legal secretary I mentioned earlier, her attitude is this: "I guess I'm secure enough not to mind getting his coffee now and then. Or calling downstairs for a jelly doughnut. Big deal. But, in my opinion, he should also return the favor. In any case, when I do it, I let him know it's not because I have to. I let him know I have the right to say no." Which is exactly what the Bill of Rights for Women Office Workers asks for—"the right to choose"—and that is why the next item is so important.

The Right to Comprehensive, Written Job Descriptions Specifying the Nature of All Duties Expected of the Employee

Job descriptions are important, not only because executives often take advantage of secretaries by asking them to perform the most petty of chores, but also because they add on to the job the most complex tasks as well. Ann Butler wrote about having to take care of urgent business questions when her employer was away. Arline is learning to prepare contracts. A secretary who works at a small art studio told me she sometimes writes advertising copy. An editorial secretary screens manuscripts.

In almost all cases, the women were delighted to be performing these additional tasks. (There were exceptions, but a far more frequent complaint was that the employer refused to delegate the more interesting work.) These secretaries were constantly learning. "He's giving me a chance to stretch my brain," said Arline. They were experimenting. "If I'm any good, maybe I'll get a job writing copy full time," said the woman at the art studio. However, they were not receiving any additional pay or benefits for assuming the extra work; nor was there any talk about their being groomed for another job.

In most large corporations, according to management consultant Marcy Murninghan, the average secretary uses far more skills than she gets credit for. And her employer is often blind to the scope of her activities. "You'll ask him what she does, and he'll say 'typing and taking dictation,' that's all. In fact, she's taking care of much of his job. That's why we feel it's so important to have both secretaries and their bosses prepare detailed job descriptions. We ask the secretaries to keep a record of all their different activities for about a week, and then try to list all the various skills they've used. Most of the time, they and their employers are shocked to realize how much they've been doing. When it's time for salary review, they now have an excellent case to make. Also, the job descriptions can help the secretary and her employer decide which skills she particularly wishes to develop further, either as a way of making the work more interesting or as a step leading toward promotion."

The use of comprehensive job descriptions has also been of utmost importance in connection with the federal Equal Pay Act. Under the Act, suit can be filed with the Labor Department's Wage and Hour Division by any woman who believes she is doing the same work as a man but is receiving less pay or benefits simply because she is a woman. She need not be performing the identical job, but must prove she is doing substantially equal work that requires equal skill, effort and responsibility. Through the use of job descriptions, women labeled "secretaries" have been able to show that they were performing the tasks of male "executive assistants" who had much higher salaries.

The Right to Equal Access to Promotion and Training Opportunities

For most secretaries, despite the laws against discrimination, the opportunities for promotion are still extremely slim. Again, there are exceptions. Numerous editorial secretaries have become editors. Many secretaries to managers, particularly those in companies under the gun of affirmative-action regulations, have become supervisors and assistant managers. But in the vast majority of corporations career-development ladders for secretaries still do not exist. And now, with the increasing shortage of qualified secretaries, employers are likely to be even more reluctant to let the best ones move up and away. "I know," one woman who typed nearly 100 words a minute told me, "that I can do the work of three secretaries. After all, I've been at it almost twenty years. I've asked for a transfer at least three times, and each time he tells me, 'Are you kidding? How would I survive without you?' I'm finally beginning to realize that if I want to advance I'll have to leave."

Can this office marriage be saved? Should it be saved? In the short run, the employer's position is pragmatic: He doesn't want to lose her. But in the long run, if employers want to attract the secretaries they desperately need, they are going to have to come up with jobs that offer opportunities for mobility and growth. "I think it must be spelled out at the beginning," one secretary said. "When you apply for the job, there should be a discussion of where you hope to go and what you can reasonably expect. Of course, you can change your mind—it might not work out—but there should be some sense at the beginning of what is truly possible. As it is, so much is left to luck."

Another problem for the secretary in the large corporation is that she is so often isolated in a particular department without links to others in the firm. To increase her awareness of opportunities that might exist in other departments, corporations have been asked to provide "job posting" in central spots where all can come to see and possibly apply. But it is also necessary, Marcy Murninghan believes, to begin restructuring the secretarial job itself so that there are more chances to move around within the corporation.

In addition to pressuring companies to change their promotion policies, secretaries should also be encouraged to think about their goals. So believes Alice Quill Sweeney, marketing and advertising director of the nation's most famous secretarial school, Katherine Gibbs, which now offers a half-dozen separate programs for women (and men) who want to stay permanently in the secretarial or administrative-assistant job and those who eventually want to move on. "You know," Ms. Sweeney said at her office, "men are used to thinking about where they want to be in five years and then planning how to get there. We find that women are still unaccustomed to thinking that way, but that's what we urge them to do.'' Then she looked wistfully at her own secretary who was standing near the office door. ''Still, I do hope she'll remain with me for at least three years.''

The Right to Regular Salary Reviews

Even in the best of all possible worlds, not every secretary will be promoted; and not every secretary will want to be promoted. For many it will continue to be ''our chosen field.'' ''I really find it extraordinarily satisfying, and I wish I didn't have to retire,'' one secretary at a junior college said to me. And another: ''I'm not the slightest bit interested in becoming a tense workaholic like the woman I work for. I don't believe in putting your whole life into your work.'' A college graduate in the ''Entree'' program at Katharine Gibbs said, ''I think I eventually want to get into TV production, but it's hard to say how I'm going to feel later. I think so much depends on the particular secretarial job. The particular person you work for. I mean, suppose I was secretary to someone like Bill Moyers. That could be fascinating, more exciting than most other jobs, and you probably couldn't drag me away.''

But even if not every secretary is in search of a promotion, I've yet to meet one who doesn't want a decent salary. Once again, your earning status generally depends on the status of the person you work for. If you are Rosalynn Carter's social secretary, you are currently topping $40,000 a year. If you are working for the supervisor of a small suburban office in the Middle West, you may be earning considerably less than a fourth of that. According to the Labor Department, a secretarial salary usually rises with the size of the firm as well as the rank of the particular corporate executive she works for. Salaries also are somewhat higher in the West and Northeast than they are in the North Central states, and they are lowest of all in the South.

''When you look at the way prices have risen and then try to live on the salaries they pay most of us, it's simply horrifying,'' said Helen Williams, director of Cleveland Women Working. In fact, in recent years the average wages of secretaries and other clerical workers have grown less rapidly than those of most other workers. And since one out of every three women in the labor force is a clerical worker, that is a prime reason why, despite the women's movement, the gap in earnings between men and women has actually widened in the past decade.

''How do we get these salaries up?'' Helen Williams continued. ''Of all the issues facing secretaries, that has to be number one.'' And so, if employers are truly concerned about growing shortages of secretaries, if they agree with *Dun's Review* that they should ''do everything'' to keep the ones they have, if they want to know how to recruit more in the future, they would do well to bear in mind the main slogans of the office worker's group, the three R's: Raises, Rights, and Respect.

Ending Time:

_____

WPM: _____

Comprehension Check: Secretaries

Directions: Complete each question by writing in or circling the correct answer.

1. A move toward ''collective bargaining'' is now invading the secretarial field as secretaries are banding together to improve conditions on the job.

    True   False

2. A direct comparison was made between secretaries and _____, both occupations which are much undervalued by society.

3. Serving the boss his coffee has become a symbol for which basic principle so important to secretaries? _____

_____

4. Changing attitudes toward secretaries stem directly from _____

_____.

Comprehension Accuracy:

_____

5. Raising the salary level is a low priority item for secretaries.

True   False

Beginning Time:

_____

Total Words: 2817

Section 3: Racial and Ethnic Discrimination _____

1. STATE-SPONSORED SEGREGATION

The Equal Protection Clause covers only "state action" and, therefore, prohibits only state-fostered discrimination. Racial or ethnic segregation that is derived from the influence of law is called *de jure* segregation and is unconstitutional; but segregation or imbalance created by social forces, independently of government sponsorship, is called *de facto* segregation and is not unconstitutional.

Three elements must exist for de jure segregation:
1. It must have been initiated or supported by government action.
2. The action must have been taken with the intent or motive to discriminate.
3. The action must actually create or increase segregation.

Despite powerful criticism, the Supreme Court has repeatedly approved the de jure-de facto distinction in ruling that public school authorities have no constitutional obligation to eliminate de facto segregation. Given the difficulty of proving unconstitutional purpose as well as segregative effect, the distinction has proven critical in recent Supreme Court cases. "Our cases have not embraced the proposition that a law or other official act . . . is unconstitutional *solely* because it has racially disproportionate impact." The difficulty of determining what kind and degree of proofs are required to establish unconstitutional purpose has been recognized, but not resolved by, the Supreme Court. Some lower courts accept statistical evidence of racial concentrations as sufficient proof of segregative intent or purpose. The Supreme Court has stated that "discriminatory purpose may often be inferred from the totality of the relevant facts" including a law's disproportionate impact on one race only. It has, nevertheless, rejected the position that disproportionately adverse impact of official actions alone (viz. from employment screening tests) is inherently unconstitutional.

Unconstitutional (de jure) segregation is not subject to a fixed definition:

"What is or is not a segregated school will necessarily depend on the facts of each particular case. In addition to the . . . composition of a school's student body, other factors, such as the racial and ethnic composition of faculty and staff and the community and administration attitudes toward the school must be taken into consideration." *Keyes v. Sch. District No. 1*, Denver, 413 U.S. 189, 196 (1973).

Although states are constitutionally free to tolerate de facto segregation, they are not constitutionally prohibited from attacking it as a matter of educational policy (such voluntary actions are considered in a later section).

In 1954 the Supreme Court struck down state laws that *required* public schools to be racially segregated. This ruling was later extended to cover ethnic minorities (Hispanos, Indians), northern states, and federal enclaves that practiced de jure segregation.

Official segregation of school faculty and staff and official discrimination in the hiring and treatment of minority teachers and administrators equally violate the equal protection rights of teachers.

The constitutional *remedy* for de jure segregation was first pronounced in the second Brown case (*Brown II*) where the Court ordered public school authorities to take immediate action toward desegregating their schools under the continuing supervision of the lower federal courts. *Brown II* failed to set any time deadline for completing the desegregation process and merely instructed the lower courts *to proceed with all deliberate speed*. The dragging pace of desegregation through the ensuing decade prompted the Court in 1964 to declare that: "The time for mere 'deliberate speed' has run out, and that phrase can no longer justify denying . . . school children their constitutional rights. . . ." *Griffin v. School Board*, 377 U.S. 218, 234 (1964).

Court-ordered desegregation was stalled by numerous evasionary devices, which required further decrees. When state authorities closed public schools in Little Rock, Arkansas, and in Prince Edward County, Virginia, the courts held such action unconstitutional in that it frustrated and defeated court ordered desegregation. State encouragement of private school segregation by providing funding or leasing public school buildings to segregated private schools was held equally unconstitutional. In the latter cases, the Supreme Court stressed that state aid to private education was not per se unconstitutional, but was unlawful when used to avoid and defeat outstanding desegregation orders.

Other unlawful actions to defeat desegregation included school district reorganization that resegregated schools.

School authorities must also avoid discrimination in the methods used to desegregate schools. Casting the entire burden of travel and relocation only on black students where less burdensome alternatives were available was held impermissible, as was the closing of a black school in the belief that white students would not go to that school. Where, however, the closing of a black school, without cross transfers was made to provide students with better resources in a newer school, the court found no discrimination by reason of the incidental burdens on black students.

2. INTRADISTRICT SEGREGATION

a. School sites and attendance zones. School boards may not create racially identifiable schools in the guise of fixing school locations or of drawing attendance boundaries. Where board action produced unlawful segregation in only part of the city, however, the Supreme Court ruled that the constitutional remedy was limited to that part of the city in which the board fostered de jure segregation. While the Court recognized that segregation in one part of the city could in certain cases have citywide impact as to justify citywide desegregation, it insisted that the constitutional remedy must be confined to territory actually affected by unconstitutional action. In addition to ordering reassignments of teachers and students, courts may remedy the adverse *effects* of past segregation by ordering offending states and districts to initiate and fund special education programs (remedial speech and reading, in-service teacher training) for the injured minority group.

The cases have been divided on whether changes in student assignment plans of predecessor boards that were intended to eliminate de facto segregation could amount to intentional de jure segregation.

b. Open transfers.   School districts cannot avoid desegregation orders by allowing students to elect any school they wish to attend. A "minority-to-majority" transfer plan permitted a student to transfer from a school where he was in the racial minority to a school where he would be in the racial majority. The plan, which resegregated the schools, was unanimously struck down. "Freedom of choice" plans met the same fate when they operated to block a desegregation decree:

> "The burden on a school board today is to come forward with a plan that promises realistically to work, . . . *now*. We do not hold that 'freedom-of-choice' plan might of itself be unconstitutional. . . . Rather, all we decide today is that a plan utilizing 'freedom of choice' is not an end in itself. . . . 'If the means prove effective, it is acceptable, but if it fails to undo segregation, other means must be used. . . .' " *Green v. County School Board*, 391 U.S. 430, 439–40 (1968).

> "The only school desegregation plan that meets constitutional standards is one that works." *United States v. Jefferson County Bd. of Education*, 372 F.2d 836, 847 (5th Cir. 1966).

c. Racial disproportion in testing and placement.   The validity of tests that result in lower evaluation and lower-level student or teacher placement of blacks or other minorities depends in part upon the school district's record of de jure segregation. For districts undergoing desegregation with a duty to eliminate the effects of past segregation, courts nullified tests that produced racially imbalanced classes for underachievers or learning disabled since the tests themselves tended to perpetuate unlawful segregation. For nonsegregated districts, however, there is no foursquare Supreme Court decision to resolve the conflict in lower court cases.

Disproportionate racial impact of teacher employment tests does not automatically establish unconstitutional discrimination. In a 1976 decision, the Supreme Court overturned many lower court cases by holding that statistical evidence of disproportionate exclusion of black job applicants under police department examinations was not sufficient to prove intentional discrimination or to render the test practice unconstitutional. In so ruling, the Court noted that the burden of proving purposive discrimination under the Constitution is heavier than that required to show a violation of employment discrimination statutes. While recognizing that statistical evidence may be relevant for both purposes, the Court noted that the weight of such evidence is very much a matter of case-by-case analysis: "Statistics . . . come in an infinite variety . . . [T]heir usefulness depends on all of the surrounding facts and circumstances."

In public schools the legal effect of disparate impact of employment tests has been complicated by the lack of dominant, objective standards to validate testing procedures: "It appears beyond doubt by now that there is no single method of appropriately validating employment tests for their relationship to job performance." *Washington v. Davis* 426 U.S. 229, 247 (1976).

In 1978 the Supreme Court again considered a challenge, under both the constitution and Title VII (employment discrimination) of the 1964 Civil Rights Act, to the National Teachers Examination, which was used to determine teacher certification and rate of pay in South Carolina. The plaintiffs charged the test was discriminatory because it resulted in excluding 83 percent of the black applicants against 17.5 percent of the white applicants and produced a white/black ratio of 96/1 in the newly certified teachers. Since the plaintiff did not prove discriminatory *intent* in selecting the test and the state established that the test was objectively valid, the trial court found no illegality. The United States Supreme Court summarily affirmed this decision.

The importance of statistical impacts was also limited by safety factors. In a Title VII case, the Supreme Court found no employment discrimination where an employer, in order to assure safety in a hazardous project, passed over three qualified black firebrick artisans to employ more experienced white artisans. Since other, experienced blacks were not systematically excluded, the Supreme Court sustained the defense, notwithstanding possible disproportionate racial impact. How these rulings will apply to the school context in a district found not to have violated the constitution remains to be seen.

The *American Bar Association Journal* summarized the changes and rapid development in the law of employment discrimination as of March, 1978:

> "Cases deal with a variety of issues, ranging from housing to the classroom, and those that have gained review have sometimes been hard to distinguish from those that have not. Comparing lower court decisions that the Justices have not taken on petitions or appeals may be even more bewildering. Decisions that have been allowed to stand often have supported conflicting approaches to discrimination law. . . . School-desegregation problems have prompted the largest number of requests for review, but so far the Court has not granted any. Its failure to step into the area leave standing such decisions as the imposition of a plan welding the Wilmington (Delaware) School District and several suburban ones . . . without specific findings of discriminatory intent (77–131, *Delaware State Board of Education v. Evans*), but the Court allowed to stand the use of 'natural and foreseeable consequences' as a test for intent in a school desegregation case from the Sixth Circuit, . . . (77–600, *Lansing Board of Education v. NAACP*) . . . In a teacher employment case, denied review, there was a conclusion by the Fifth Circuit that the discriminatory intent could be presumed from the firing of seventeen black teachers after different criteria were employed to evaluate black and white teachers (77–392, *Sweeney Independent School District v. Harkness*). On the other hand, the Justices summarily affirmed a ruling . . . that found intentional bias was lacking in school certification and evaluation procedures. . . . (77–422, *National Education Association v. South Carolina*). In the employment sphere in general, the significance of statistics appears to be the greatest area of uncertainty. . . . Although the Court appears to be moving cautiously in the discrimination area, it is moving, developing what may be new lines in social philosophies. And if there is anything that can be said with certainty about the balance of interests of racial groups or other classes of citizens, it is that the questions will never be settled for all time."

Title VI of the 1964 Act generally prohibits racial (but not sex) discrimination in any federally aided program or activity (see appendix 7-A). Conflicting interpretations of that title by the courts leave its impact uncertain.

3. INTERDISTRICT SEGREGATION

Federal courts have no authority to order one school district to cross-assign or cross-bus its students or teachers into another district *unless* both districts or their parent state fostered segregation between districts. The lack of jurisdiction to remedy de facto interdistrict racial imbalance has been confirmed by the Supreme Court in later cases. However, where adjoining school districts or the parent state fostered interdistrict segregation, the Supreme Court sustained interdistrict desegregation orders because they matched the scope of de jure segregation found to exist in those districts. It is possible to find intentional de jure segregation where officials act to *freeze* existing de facto segregation by prohibiting natural changes that would undo such segregation.

4. AFFIRMATIVE ACTION AND REVERSE DISCRIMINATION

The use of racial standards, goals, or quotas, benignly described as affirmative action and perjoratively condemned as reverse discrimination, has different implications in different fact settings. Where an official finding of past unconstitutional discrimination exists the law is clear:

> "Just as the race of students and teachers must be considered in determining whether a constitutional violation has occurred, so also must race be considered in formulating a remedy. To forbid this . . . would deprive school authorities of the one tool absolutely essential to fulfillment of their constitutional obligation to eliminate existing dual school systems." *North Carolina State Bd. of Education v. Swann*, 402 U.S. 43 (1971).

State and federal lawmakers may not prohibit race-conscious court remedies through antibussing statutes that would frustrate court-ordered desegregation, nor can state statutes be enforced where such action would undercut the constitutional power of federal courts to use bussing as a tool to undo unconstitutional segregation.

Where there is no *official determination* of past unconstitutional discrimination, the legal limits of minority preference are not clear. The ambiguous phrase *affirmative action* can mean very different things. If a program seeks to improve the lot of a minority by special efforts that do not subject other groups to adverse discrimination, such as by special training programs, little difficulty is encountered. If, however, the means used to help a minority involve removal of other groups from like opportunities, major difficulties are presented. Unfortunately, the courts have not developed clear guidelines to distinguish between permissible affirmative action and illegal reverse discrimination.

Any racial preference in teacher promotion that is not tied to remediation of past injury may thus violate equal protection as well as Title VI and Title VII of the 1964 Act, which proscribe antiwhite as well as anti-black discrimination. But a school board's preference of black candidates who were best able to identify with a predominantly black student body was held nondiscriminatory since whites were not excluded from consideration. A similar preference standard (ability to identify with a predominantly white student body) was found discriminatory in a different setting. Minority preference as a matter of administrative discretion was upheld as compensatory in one case, but condemned as reverse discrimination in another. These case variations may rest more on differences in fact interpretation than on constitutional principle.

Prior to the milestone case of *Regents, U. of California v. Bakke*, the lower courts did not agree on whether public administrators could on their own initiative, and without judicial, statutory, or executive authority, adopt minority preference programs. In *Bakke*, the Supreme Court Justices split 4–1–4 on the legality of minority quotas for admission to a state medical school. Five justices held the practice unlawful, and four voted to sustain it. Four of the five-man majority held that fixed minority preference amounted to unlawful discrimination under Title VI of the 1964 Act. . . . The fifth concluded that Title VI was no stricter than the federal constitution, and voted that the use of race as an *exclusive* test of admission was unconstitutional. This crucial "swing" opinion of Mr. Justice Powell significantly made no reference to the slogan terms: "affirmative action" and "reverse discrimination." He stressed that race may be a relevant, but not exclusive, consideration in admitting students to a professional school because "diversity" of student bodies enhances the educational process.

The *Bakke* limitation on racial quotas was confined to its facts, if not undone, with respect to "affirmative action" in private employment by the later Supreme Court decision in *Kaiser Aluminum & Chemical Corp. v. Weber*. The Court there sustained a training program set up by company-union agreement that assigned a fixed ratio of openings to minority races as lawful under Title VII. The *Bakke* and *Weber* opinions are guarded in tone to avoid suggesting that all racial preferences for beneficent purposes will be upheld. How *Weber* will operate upon *public* employment in public schools remains, therefore, to be clarified in pending cases. It makes clear, however, that some form of voluntary affirmative action in employment will survive legal challenge.

a. Termination of constitutional oversight. The Supreme Court has limited the power of federal courts in several ways. As previously stated, their jurisdiction is limited to de jure violations. They may not act arbitrarily: "Remedial judicial authority does not put judges automatically in the shoes of school authorities . . . judicial authority enters only when local authority defaults. . . . No fixed, or even substantially fixed, guidelines can be established as to how far a court can go, but it must be recognized there are limits." *Swann v. Charlotte-Mecklenberg Bd. of Education*, 402 U.S. II (1971) at p. 16, 28.

Considerations, such as child welfare, educational efficiency, financial resources, demography, and the geography of involved districts must be weighed in deciding the propriety of particular desegregation plans. The Supreme Court stated that even one-race schools could be justified in special circumstances.

Once de jure segregation is eliminated, the court's jurisdiction terminates, and it cannot be revived unless a new suit is brought to establish new de jure violations. Thus a court order to compel a previously desegregated school district to eliminate de facto racial imbalances arising from later population shifts was reversed by the United States Supreme Court.

5. ANTIDISCRIMINATION STATUTES

a. Federal laws. The federal statutes have hastened school desegregation by providing federal aid for desegregation expenses; by authorizing federal agency regulations and supervision of desegregation plans; and by authorizing court action by the Attorney General to complete desegregation. The combination of fiscal incentives and enforcement advanced desegregation without displacing the power of federal courts to act directly under the Fourteenth Amendment. The federal statutes allow the courts broad discretion in fashioning relief. For example, courts may deny advanced seniority status to a victim of discrimination where other remedies will make that victim "whole" without injuring the interests of other employees.

b. State laws. The "floor" requirements of federal laws do not disable individual states from adopting more stringent antidiscrimination rules under their own constitutions and statutes. . . . For example the California court ruled that the California constitution required school districts to make reasonable efforts to undo de facto as well as de jure segregation. Several courts held that their state constitutional provisions were violated by tax laws that produced materially disproportionate per pupil expenditures in the school districts, notwithstanding the Supreme Court's decision that such tax schemes did not violate the federal constitution.

Under their general welfare powers, states may outlaw discrimination in private as well as public schools, establish compensatory education programs for disadvantaged minorities even though no de jure segregation exists; and fix racial balance ratios for public school students and staff, regardless of the causes of such imbalance. The rule against arbitrary action will still operate, however, to stay a racial balance scheme that unfairly burdens a particular racial group.

Reasonable measures to achieve racial balance by out-of-neighborhood bussing are within the state's police power, but a state is not bound to elect such an approach. For example, under the Illinois Fair Employment statute, a state court deprived school authorities of the power to transfer teachers merely to improve racial balance among teachers.

Ending Time:

_____

WPM: _____

Comprehension Check: Racial and Ethnic Discrimination

Directions: Complete each of the following statements by writing in or circling the correct answer.

1. Desegregation occurs most frequently as a result of the actions of various levels of government.

    True   False

2. De facto segregation occurs when _____

    _____

    _____.

3. Segregation when knowingly committed for discriminatory purposes becomes

    _____.

4. The courts' power for dealing with antidiscrimination situations ends when de jure segregation has been disproved.

   True   False

5. This selection discusses racial and ethnic discrimination as they affect school policies and students of school age.

   True   False

Comprehension Accuracy:

_____

Selection 4: The Shot Heard Round The World ━━━━━━━━━

Beginning Time:

_____

Total Words: 2441

Just 200 years ago, Americans took up arms against the British in two villages outside Boston-Lexington and Concord, and this "shot heard round the world" ignited the Revolution in the Colonies. Following is a vivid account of the battle, condensed from "200 Years," a Bicentennial history of the United States published by U.S. News & World Report Book. The day-long battle, which took place on April 19, 1775, marked the culmination of months of disorder in rebellious Massachusetts following the Boston Tea Party, where fiery patriots vented their anger at what they considered to be growing British suppression of colonial rights. This was the moment when the Crown—its patience already frayed—acted decisively.

On April 14, 1775, new orders arrived from London. Massachusetts had been declared in a state of rebellion—as indeed it was—and Gage (Lt. Gen. Thomas Gage, the British governor and military commander in Boston) was ordered to take immediate action.

The provincials had assembled their military stores in Worcester and Concord. Worcester was too distant to reach through a hostile countryside, but Concord was near enough for a surprise foray. Gage went quietly to work, but his plans were soon discovered.

With hundreds of unemployed men loitering on street corners and along the waterfront, little went unnoticed. Paul Revere had his organization of spies, and there were similar groups throughout the city. They patrolled the streets and met secretly to exchange information. Among other things, they noticed that the boats belonging to the troop transports, which had been pulled up on shore for repairs, were no longer there.

This news they immediately reported to Dr. Joseph Warren (physician, major general and Whig leader), who concluded that Gage was planning to raid Concord. Moreover, as the preparation of the ships boats showed, Gage was not going to march his troops out across Boston Neck; he was going to ferry them across the Charles River, a shorter route and one that avoided most villages, thereby making it possible to take Concord by surprise—or so Gage thought.

Having reached this conclusion, Warren sent Paul Revere on April 16 to warn John Hancock and Samuel Adams, who were staying in Lexington, and to tell the people of Concord to hide the weapons and supplies.

On his way home that evening, Revere stopped in Charlestown to talk to Col. William Conant "& some other Gentlemen." He arranged "that if the British went out by water, we would show two lanthorns in the North Church Steeple,

_____

SOURCE: Copyright 1975 U.S. News & World Report, Inc. Reprinted from the 14 Apr. 1975 issue of *U.S. News and World Report*, pp. 57–59.

and if by land, one, as a signal.'' Longfellow's poem notwithstanding, the lamps were not a signal to Revere; they were a signal from Revere to alert other couriers, especially in case he did not himself get across with the message.

Long after dark on the night of April 18, sergeants moved among the sleeping redcoats, waking their men, cautioning them to be quiet as they sleepily dressed, forming them up outside their barracks, marching them toward the waterfront. There were six to eight hundred men—10 companies of light infantry, 10 of grenadiers, 1 of marines—and no matter how silently their sergeants tried to move them, they were observed by many eyes.

Word was brought to Dr. Warren that the regulars were abroad and heading for the waterfront. Warren sent one of his dispatch riders, William Dawes, off to Lexington and Concord by way of the road that led across Boston Neck.

Paul Revere waited only long enough to see that the two signal lanterns in North Church were lit; then two friends rowed him across to Charlestown. On the opposite shore Colonel Conant and others waited. Revere mounted a horse and galloped off. His fellow patriots disappeared down other dark roads to alert minutemen and militia in many quarters.

Revere raced toward Lexington, rousing farmers along the road, awakening the villages of Medford and Menotomy (now Arlington), and galloping on again. Once he ran into two officers of Gage's patrol but wheeled about in time to dash down another road and escape in the dark. He reached Lexington about midnight, roused Hancock and Adams and, while they prepared to flee, waited about half an hour until Dawes arrived by his longer route. Then the two, along with Dr. Samuel Prescott, who had lingered long courting a young lady in Lexington, continued on toward Concord.

About halfway there, two of Gage's redcoats suddenly appeared and stopped them at pistol point. The three broke and ran. Dawes turned and headed back toward Lexington. Prescott jumped his horse over a stone wall, escaped and went on to give the alarm in Concord. Revere headed for a wood, but was hopelessly surrounded when half a dozen more British guards appeared.

When questioned, Revere boldly informed his captors that 500 American militia were even then assembling on Lexington Green. At the sound of shots—a rallying signal used by the Americans—the British became alarmed and set Revere free after putting him afoot. He walked back to Lexington, arriving there in time to help Hancock and Adams load a last chest of papers in their carriage. He then climbed in and rode away with them. Thus ended Paul Revere's ride.

In the meantime, the British force, commanded by Lt. Col. Francis Smith and Major John Pitcairn, had set out for Lexington. As the redcoats trudged silently through the dark countryside, they soon realized that they were not the only men stirring in the night. They heard the eerie tolling of church bells in the darkness, now near, now far; they heard musket shots and knew that no hunters were in the field at that hour.

Now and then they caught a glimpse of shadowy figures stealing by on mysterious errands, and a general unease grew in the ranks. By the time they reached Menotomy, even their slow-witted leader, Colonel Smith, was aware that a great many Americans were abroad in the night, and he sent an express rider back to Boston to ask Gage for reinforcements.

The sun rises about 5 o'clock on April 19, and it was above the horizon when the British column came over a gentle hill and saw the Lexington village green.

The green was—and still is—triangular in shape, with one side of the triangle formed by the road to Concord. Drawn up on the green were some 75 men, about two thirds of the Lexington Minute Company, under the direction of Captain John Parker.

Upon seeing the minutemen, Major Pitcairn, who was at the head of the British column, led his men off the road and onto the green, at the same time changing then from column into line; then, as the redcoats swept toward the forlorn band of minutemen, he called on the Americans to disperse.

At first, Parker ordered his men to stand their ground; then, realizing the hopelessness of their situation, he commanded them to disband.

Pitcairn had orders to disarm any rebels he came upon; now, as the minutemen were leaving the field in response to his command, he bawled out to his men the somewhat contradictory order to surround the Americans. Don't fire, he shouted, but disarm them.

At this uneasy moment, as the redcoats line bore down on the minutemen and extended its flanks to surround them, there was a shot, followed by two or three more. No one knows who fired that first shot. It may have been discharged by a minuteman, probably panicked by the line of regulars bearing down on him. One redcoat was very slightly wounded, and Pitcairn's horse was grazed.

The British troops, ignoring Pitcairn's orders not to fire, began a general and enthusiastic blasting at the retreating minutemen. Some shouted that the village should be set afire; a number headed for a tavern whence, it was claimed, shots had come.

Eventually their officers got them under control again, and as they formed up in ranks on the green where eight minutemen lay dead—another nine were wounded—they gave three cheers. They resumed the march to Concord with fifes and drums playing since there was no longer any need to keep up the pretense of secrecy.

The Concord militia, now reinforced by men from nearby Lincoln, deliberated and decided to reconnoiter in force. Some 150 strong, they marched toward Lexington until they saw the British column approaching and heard its fifes and drums.

It took no second look at the long redcoat ranks to tell the Americans that they were outnumbered. Whereupon they very sensibly countermarched; their fifes and drums picked up the British cadence, and the provincial militia preceded the regulars almost like an escort of honor.

The Americans retreated through Concord village, across North Bridge over the Concord River, and up a hill on the other side. The British stationed three light-infantry companies to guard North Bridge and sent four more to search for arms and supplies at the farm of Col. James Barrett, the commander of the Concord militia. The remaining three were dispatched to guard South Bridge.

The grenadier companies began searching the village for military stores, and Colonel Smith established a command post on a vantage point in the village burying ground. It was then about 8 o'clock in the morning.

A number of wooden gun carriages were found in the meetinghouse, dragged outside and set afire, but when the meetinghouse ashes began smoldering, grenadiers yielded to the entreaties of an old woman and doused the flames with water.

Across the river the Americans had moved down the hill to a position nearer North Bridge and the British. They had been joined by men from Acton, Bedford and other nearby towns; their numbers had grown to several hundred, far outnumbering the British at the bridge. While they were discussing their course of action, they saw the pillar of smoke from the burning gun carriages and drew the obvious but wrong conclusion: The British were putting the torch to Concord. They decided they could no longer stand indecisive, but must "march into the middle of the town for its defence or die in the attempt."

Captain (Walter) Laurie, commanding the British at the bridge, withdrew his men to the Concord side of the river when he saw the Americans coming, leaving only a small detail to take up the bridge planking. This gross mistreatment of town property outraged the Americans, and an officer shouted to the British to leave the bridge alone, whereupon the men meekly stopped what they were doing and joined the rest of the redcoats across the bridge.

Smith and his rescue force were still on the way when the American column reached the bridge. The British opened fire, first a few harmless shots, then a volley that killed Capt. Isaac Davis and drummer boy Abner Hosmer of the leading Acton company and injured several provincials. The American muskets fired in return, and 3 redcoat soldiers fell dead or dying; 4 officers and 5 men were wounded. Then, incredibly, these disciplined British troops broke and fled in utter panic, leaving their dead and wounded.

Smith, back at his vantage point in the cemetery, could see that the number of provincials across North Bridge was growing steadily larger; he also saw that American units were drifting down and spreading out on all sides of the village. His force was not only outnumbered, it was being surrounded. He called in the three companies that had been uneventfully watching South Bridge, got his troops in marching order, and at noon led his forces out of Concord, carrying his wounded in commandeered carriages.

About a mile out of Concord the Bedford road from the north joins the Lexington road at a point called Meriam's Corners. Now striding down the Bedford road came minutemen from more-distant towns: Billerica, Reading, Chelmsford, Wilmington, Woburn. These men, some of whom had come as far as 15 miles on foot, were informed of the situation by messengers from Concord. They took up positions along the Lexington road, where they were joined by many Concord men who had circled ahead of the British.

There is disagreement over what happened when the redcoats came down the road. The British claim that the Americans fired first. The American story is that the rear ranks of the redcoat force, exasperated by the way the provincials dogged their steps, turned and fired a harmless volley.

The American reply killed two redcoats and wounded others, and the shooting that began there did not stop for hours—not until, as one American was later to recall, "A grait many Lay dead and the Road was bloddy."

The Americans did not come off untouched. British fire from the road got some; others were so absorbed in getting close for a good shot that they did not see British flankers behind them, and more than one was thus shot in the back. But by and large the (British) regulars could only plod their nightmare way along, leaving their dead and badly wounded where they fell, not even daring to think of all the miles that still lay between them and safety. By the time the column neared Lexington most of the men were no longer making an attempt to return the rebel's fire.

The American farmers and townspeople were on the verge of victory.

On the edge of Lexington village the British officers still on their feet resorted to a desperate measure to bring the column back to some semblance of order and discipline: They put themselves at the head of it and threatened to shoot their own men if they did not stop and straighten up their ranks. Even as they made this hopeless gesture, the officers were astounded to hear their men break into cheers; turning around they saw the leading company of a powerful force of redcoats about to enter Lexington from the other direction. At the same time they heard the report of a cannon.

The rescue force was the one Smith had sent for early that morning.

Percy (Lord Percy, commander of the British relief force) allowed the exhausted men to rest for an hour; then at 3:30 he started for Boston. Once more the Rebel muskets began firing. Hundreds of fresh men were arriving from eastern towns now, all eager for their chance at the redcoats. By this time, the British troops were not only searching every roadside home; they were looting as well.

The fighting was especially bitter in Menotomy, where the British had to march between rows of houses and other buildings held by rebel snipers. There was house-to-house and often hand-to-hand fighting. The British lost 40 men killed and about 80 wounded at Menotomy, just about half their casualties for that entire bloody day.

Ahead of Menotomy lay Cambridge village, and beyond that Brookline and Roxbury—and evening was approaching. Percy did not fancy any more house-to-house fighting, especially in the dark.

In a surprise move he took the fork leading to Charlestown, a much shorter route than the road to Boston. A force of Rebels held the hill beside the Charlestown road, but Percy's cannon and men forced them off.

Now the way was clear. Soon the grimy, dazed redcoats had crossed the narrow neck of land that connected the Charlestown peninsula with the mainland. In the river between Boston and Charlestown lay British warships, their guns ready. The redcoats were safe at last.

That day 73 regulars had been killed, 174 wounded and 26 missing, not a rousing tribute to the shooting of the Americans. Still, it must be remembered that the musket was not a sharpshooter's weapon and that the Americans were farmers, not marksmen.

Ending Time:

The Americans lost 49 killed, 41 wounded and 5 missing.

WPM: _____

Comprehension Check: The Shot Heard. . . .

Directions: Complete each of the following statements by writing in or circling the correct answer.

1. ''The Shot Heard Round the World'' refers to _____

_____

_____.

2. Paul Revere's famed ride was made in two phases, the first by boat and the second by horse.

   True   False

3. The lanterns in the North Church steeple were placed there by Revere to signal others of the British troop movements—not placed there to signal to Revere himself.

True   False

4. The purpose of the British raids on Lexington and Concord was to _____

_____

_____.

Comprehension Accuracy:

_____

5. The American militiamen were highly organized throughout the battles of Lexington and Concord.

True   False

Selection 5: Modern Bioengineers Reinvent Human Anatomy with Spare Parts

Beginning Time:

_____

Total Words: 3737

A 19th-century English humorist, Jerome K. Jerome (*Three Men in a Boat*), once opened a medical tome and discovered, he said, that he had every ailment in the book except for housemaid's knee. By the 21st century, a man in Jerome's shoes may be able to order a replacement for almost every ailing part of his body, including the knee. That is the promise of a revolution which had its beginnings 40 years ago.

When Dr. Willem Kolff began practicing medicine in the 1930s, his first patient died of kidney failure. There was nothing the young Dutch physician could do to save the boy. His helplessness, and the family's grief, set him off on a quest that revolutionized medical practice. If he had only been able to remove some of the wastes that had accumulated in his patient's blood, he reasoned, this young man might have survived and led a normal life.

So Kolff began a stubborn search for a material that would contain blood, yet let impurities seep through. He hit on an unlikely one: sausage casings made of thin cellophane, which was then a new material. When these casings were submerged in salt solution, they became porous to many chemicals, but not to blood. Eventually Kolff built a Rube Goldberglike device of cellophane tubes wrapped around a drum which he partially immersed in saline solution, and ran a patient's blood through the tubes to purify it, a technique known as dialysis. Only the weakest and most desperately ill patients were entrusted to this device at first, and 14 patients died. But Kolff continued to modify the technique and patients began to respond. The 17th patient, a woman, lived for many years with the help of Kolff's machine—the first artificial kidney.

Its success marked the birth of modern bioengineering, an extraordinary field applying engineering principles to biology and medicine. Since 1943, when Kolff's artificial kidney made its debut in Holland, kidney dialysis has saved the lives of hundreds of thousands of people around the world. Some 40,000 Americans are alive today because of it. The artificial kidney was followed by the heart-lung machine (in which Kolff also had a hand). Soon afterward, bioengineering began to produce a cornucopia of spare parts: cardiac pacemakers, patches, valves and bypass units, intra-aortic balloon pumps, artificial arteries, artificial joints and sophisticated artificial limbs. It has also produced experimental models of artificial lungs, eyes, ears, pancreases and hearts.

So splendid are these achievements that bioengineering has become the victim of its own success. Rapid progress in space technology, the advent of miniaturized electronic devices, and a heady supply of research funds, have inspired unrealistic expectations about artificial organs and limbs—as seen in TV shows about a "six-million-dollar man" and a "bionic woman" whose man-made parts give them superhuman powers.

Yet, just as some critics are focusing on the limitations of existing medical technology—and its cost—the pioneers of bioengineering see their field on the verge of a new flowering. The future they envision includes a whole new family of instruments to monitor body chemistry, computer systems to provide instant medical diagnosis and perhaps even treatment, synthetic materials tailor-made for use inside the body, and new tools for research into the mysteries of such diseases as atherosclerosis, cancer and schizophrenia.

There is promising work all over the country, in countless laboratories. At the University of Southern California, for example, a medical research team has developed tiny glucose sensors that can be implanted into the body tissues of diabetic dogs to watch for excessive concentration of sugar; whenever the level of sugar approaches a danger point, the sensor switches on a miniature pump (implanted in the dog's peritoneal cavity) which "secretes" insulin in appropriate quantities. Taking a different tack, researchers in New England are relying on living cultured cells rather than on hardware to deal with the same problem. After removing some insulin-producing cells from pancreases of normal newborn rats, they culture the cells on the outside of synthetic capillaries. Dozens of these cell-coated capillaries, in cigar-sized units, are then connected to the blood vessels of diabetic laboratory animals. As the animal's blood circulates through the capillaries, the cultured cells release insulin as needed. In time, both methods may be tried on human beings for the treatment of diabetes.

Patients who suffer from emphysema or other chronic lung diseases may someday benefit from implantable "booster lungs" which will do part of their breathing for them, if experiments now underway at Brown University prove successful. Prototypes of such booster lungs, made of spongy Teflon will soon be implanted in sheep, says Dr. Pierre Galletti, a professor of medical science at Brown, and past president of the American Society for Artificial Internal Organs.

Elsewhere various laboratories are developing "noninvasive" imaging techniques, based on X-ray scans or ultrasound probes and computers, that will allow doctors to diagnose a variety of ills without resorting to painful tests or exploratory surgery. Other labs are working on ways to receive and monitor information from electrodes which are placed over the brain, eyes, muscles or hearts of ambulatory patients who may be miles away.

Dr. Kolff himself has attracted an energetic and talented group of researchers to the University of Utah, which he joined in 1967. As a result, some of the most exciting work in bioengineering is now taking place in Salt Lake City, where surgeons, mathematicians, physiologists, mechanical engineers, metallurgists, electrical engineers, anesthesiologists, chemists, computer scientists, veterinarians and hematologists form a sort of critical mass in which the solution of one problem helps to deal with another, and a variety of projects are about to pay off.

There is, for example, the Wearable Artificial Kidney, or WAK—a device that could make the lives of thousands of kidney patients more bearable because it would allow patients to treat themselves comfortably and more cheaply at home, rather than in hospitals or other institutions. At present, people who undergo dialysis must generally lie down and stay connected to a bulky machine for five hours three times a week—a thoroughly demoralizing and fatiguing experience. However, with the help of WAK, which packs in a suitcase and weighs only eight pounds, one patient was able to travel to California recently and work at his desk even during the treatments. He was also free to disconnect himself from the 20-liter tank that contained the blood-cleansing fluid for as much as 15 minutes at a time during the treatment, to open the door or do anything else he'd like.

The WAK was designed by Dr. Stephen Jacobsen, an associate professor of mechanical engineering who also runs the university's large Projects and Design Laboratory, where all the parts and supplies for the WAK were made. The lab is also developing a small, implantable access device which could make peritoneal lavage—dialysis within the abdomen—convenient and practical for a large percentage of patients.

Like many of the Utah bioengineers, Dr. Jacobsen is a dynamic man who tackles several different problems at once. Besides working on kidney devices, he has been designing a revolutionary artificial arm which amputees will be able to move just by thinking about it. In an office lined with medical antiques—such as an 1866 artificial hand made of leather and metal, with a hook attached fork and spoon—Jacobsen described the plight of thousands of persons who have lost an arm above the elbow: in many cases they wear artificial limbs which serve little more than a cosmetic purpose (and which are often discarded by people who have use of the other arm), since anything more functional is disturbingly noisy, heavy, awkward, and difficult to operate. So Jacobsen tried something new. Instead of relying on gear trains, screws, and pulleys, he designed an artificial muscle made of flexible plastic fibers that works much like the real thing. This, he believes, can provide graceful motion. Then he studied the exact role of 30 separate muscles which are involved in arm motion, to identify those which could be used to control an artificial arm. He made a map of the electrical signals from the muscles in the amputee's shoulder and remnant limb, which can be picked up by electrodes embedded in the artificial arm's socket. Finally Jacobsen and his colleagues designed an "anthropomorphic hook," with forefinger and thumb, to serve as an artificial hand. The arm can grasp objects delicately, lift four pounds actively and withstand static loads of up to 50 pounds. For cosmetic reasons, the team added a lifelike plastic glove, complete with finger creases and nails, which slipped over the hook to look like a real hand.

An amputee who receives a Utah arm will not have to learn complex rules of operation, as he would with other kinds of full-arm prostheses. He will simply think of moving his elbow or hand, and a microcomputer which processes signals from his shoulder muscle will deliver the right amount of energy to appropriate motors in appropriate parts of the arm. So far the arm has been used only in Jacobsen's lab, but preliminary models (limited to elbow flexion) will soon be tried out by amputees under normal conditions, to be followed by models that allow full and graceful motion of the entire arm, the elbow, the wrist and the hand.

Meanwhile, in another part of the University, many of the functions of a hospital chemistry lab are being designed into a tiny, implantable chip. This is the "superprobe" only one millimeter wide, a powerful sensor relying on microscopic integrated circuits, which could be inserted into a patient's arm to give continuous reading on the vital chemicals in his blood without withdrawing a drop. The superprobe has proven remarkably sensitive to concentrations of hydrogen, potassium and calcium ions. It is hoped that in the future it will be able to monitor other vital chemicals in the blood, as well as antibodies an enzyme substrates—and it is bound to produce some radical changes in medical care.

For example, patients who are in intensive care today must have blood drawn repeatedly for tests; the blood is then carried to the hospital's lab for analysis—possibly by undergoing subtle changes in transit—and a few hours late, the relevant information is given to the doctor. Meanwhile the patient's condition may have changed.

Stanley Moss, an electronics engineer who has done pioneering work on the superprobe, foresees a time when it will be used together with computers to control the injection of various types of ions into patients' blood, in order to maintain a constant balance of vital chemicals without having to call in the doctor for each one. This would create a feedback system much like the body's own.

A Marriage Made in the Laboratory

"We have married the technology of minaturized integrated circuits to new discoveries in membrane chemistry," Moss declares. The superprobe consists of almost invisible membranes which are designed to react to specific ions and are linked to miniature transistors. Traditionally, chemists analyze body fluids by taking a sample of fluid and separating it into various components, points out Jiri Janata, an electrochemist who is also working on the superprobe. With the ionsensitive field-effect transistors (known as ISFET) which are used in the superprobe, each membrane reacts to one component selectively, making it unnecessary to do any preliminary separation. And because of their microscopic size, ten different kinds of membranes could easily fit on a tiny chip.

Eventually the most selective system in nature, the immune system, will be tapped in this way, Janata predicts, and he looks forward to the monitoring of many kinds of antibodies and antigens. "That would be invaluable" he says, "as an early warning system to alert doctors about various infections, and as a measure of how well the organism is fighting back." Such a system would be particularly useful in watching for signs of rejection in organ transplants and in monitoring the effects of chemotherapy.

The limiting factor in nearly all the products of bioengineering has been the lack of materials which are truly compatible with living tissues. Before the superprobe is tested on human beings, for instance, many more studies will have to be done on animals to determine whether the materials on its surface will cause blood to clot, and to find out how long the membranes can continue functioning before various substances in the blood adhere to them, blocking their accessibility to other chemicals.

The University of Utah has just received a $1.4 million grant from the National Institute of General Medical Sciences to study such problems in a polymer implant center directed by Dr. Donald J. Lyman, a polymer chemist. Lyman is greatly excited by the possibilities this will open up. "How many times in life does a person have a chance for so many successes?" he asks delightedly.

His projects include an artificial ureter which is proving successful in dogs and may one day help many cancer patients. "At present, if a tumor compresses the ureter, surgeons simply cut it out and let the urine collect in a bag at the patient's side," Lyman explains. "Though this is easy for the surgeon, it's traumatic for the patient."

He is also working on a macaroni-sized artificial blood vessel which can flex and pulsate as if it were made of living cells. The material for it was tailormade in Lyman's lab so that it would not clot blood and would be able to form a good junction with natural blood vessels.

Dacron and Teflon Didn't Really Work

"In the past, people used whatever materials were commercially available," says Lyman. In the mid-1950s, the first vascular grafts were made of Dacron, "which had been designed for wash-and-wear clothes," as he puts it. Then Teflon and nylon were tried out for various implants. But none of these materials was really adequate for use in the body, mostly because they stimulated the formation of blood clots which could break loose and do serious damage to the brain or heart. Lyman noticed that the blood clots seemed to form wherever certain proteins stuck to a surface. So he decided to study and manipulate the atoms in a polymer chain in order to achieve exactly the kind of surface he wanted: one to which specific proteins would not adhere.

This kind of research, he notes, has implications for the control of atherosclerosis, a disease characterized primarily by the adhesion of fatty substances in the inner lining of the artery wall—and the underlying cause of most heart attacks and strokes. It may also lead to new ways of diagnosing cancer, for normal cells will stick to certain surfaces and cancer cells will not. In fact, with a basic understanding of surface structures, almost anything becomes possible. His lab has already developed smaller and more compactible artificial blood vessels, including tiny, three-millimeter tubes which could be used by neurosurgeons to bypass obstructed blood vessels leading to the brain. But now the lab is also learning how to control the growth of different kinds of human cells by synthesizing special surfaces on which only certain types of cells will stick. This means that someday doctors may be able to grow natural tissues for implanted organs, or regenerate the skin of burn victims.

Lyman envisions implants made of materials that need not last forever—they would just serve as scaffolding for the natural growth of various kinds of cells and when the man-made materials disintegrate, there would remain a natural surface made of living cells. This would make it possible to put implants into babies, for the regenerated tissues would continue growing after the implant disintegrates. He also hopes that his group will soon reach the long-hoped-for goal of reconnecting severed nerves so they work again. He plans to use polymer cuffs over the cuts to serve as bridges. The inside of the cuff would be designed to make neurons (nerve cells) grow, while the outside would stimulate the growth of glial cells that insulate and support the nerve cells. "Then, if you could get nerve signals through these cuffs, as we are attempting to do in the lab across gaps of one centimeter, you could repair different types of nerve loss and paralysis," he says.

Meanwhile, a daring attempt to develop artificial sight and hearing through the electrical stimulation of nerve cells in the brain or ear is under way both at the University of Utah and at Columbia University in New York City. This work seems more startling than other forms of bioengineering because some of it involves penetrating the human skull. But it also holds a strange fascination because if the research ever does produce useful results—which is still in doubt—these will be modern miracles.

The strategy of the artificial sight program is to bypass the eye itself, ignore the optic nerve which normally relays impulses from the retina to the back of the brain, and rely on direct stimulation of a small area in the brain—the visual cortex—through implanted electrodes. Ten years ago a British physiologist, Dr. Giles Brindley, showed that when he inserted electrodes into the visual cortex of a blind nurse, who had volunteered for the experiment, and then ran a mild electric current through them, she saw isolated points of light, called phosphenes. Shortly afterward Dr. William Dobelle, who was then director of the University of Utah's neuroprostheses program (and now runs the Division of Artificial Organs at Columbia University's College of Physicians and Surgeons), started a series of experiments to find out whether such stimulation could be carried out without damage to the brain, and whether the resulting phosphenes would form meaning-ful patterns. A computer graphics program was developed by Dr. Michael Mladejovsky at Utah to "map" whatever phosphenes might be produced by the brain electrodes.

Artificial Sight: "It's a triangle"

In 1973 the researchers used this program to map the phosphenes produced by electrodes which they temporarily implanted in the brain of a blind volunteer. Once they had a map, they selected only a few electrodes to activate and asked the volunteer what he saw. "Why, it's a triangle, of course—and it's pointing up," he replied. He also identified letters, geometric shapes and other patterns. Encour-aged, in 1975 the team proceeded to implant 64 electrodes more permanently into the visual cortex of two other volunteers. Although in one case they produced almost no usable phosphenes (the electrodes had been placed too far forward in his brain), the other man—a 33-year-old who had been blinded by gunshot—saw 60 separate points of light in response to the stimulation. These were still not enough points to form all the letters of the alphabet, however, so the researchers decided to program braille characters instead. When these were flashed into his brain, the volunteer read them five times faster than when he used his fingertips. Further-more, when a TV camera was connected to the system, he was able to detect white lines on a dark background—much like the flashing lights of a football scoreboard. He still has the electrodes in place now, three years later, and has suffered no ill effects. However, they do not benefit him in any way, and they don't produce any phosphenes unless he comes to the lab to be stimulated by the research team.

For a system of this sort to be effective, a blind person would have to have a miniature TV camera set in his eyeglasses (or enclosed in a glass eye) and powered by a battery. He would have to have a computer translate the information from the TV camera into stimuli that would fit his internal phosphene map. The computer would have to be connected to a wire coming out of his skull through an opening the size of a dime, and leading to an array of at least 256 electrodes for each brain hemisphere, or a total of 512 separate electrodes. And he would need assurance that the electrodes could function over a long period of time without damaging his brain cells, or without themselves being damaged by the corrosive environment of body fluids. None of this can be provided in the near future.

The artificial hearing program, run by Dr. Mladejovsky and also in its infancy, involves electrodes inserted in the cochlea, part of the inner ear, within the skull. Instead of phosphenes, they produce sensations of sound, "audenes." But it has proved to be extremely difficult for a totally deaf person to describe such audenes—to estimate their pitch, for example—so no computer program has yet been developed to map them. Besides, only a minority of deaf people have the kind of impairment which lends itself to stimulation of the nerves in the cochlea. Others would need to have the electrodes placed directly into their brains—a particularly tricky problem, since unlike the visual area the auditory cortex is deep in the gray matter. Altogether "it will be many years before something is developed that is of real use to a patient," according to Dr. Mladejovsky.

While all these diverse efforts are going on at Utah, an ambitious project which was dreamed up by Dr. Kolff 21 years ago is finally nearing fruition: an implantable artificial heart, made of polyurethane parts and powered either by compressed air or by electric batteries. Kolff put a crude model of such a heart in a dog in 1957 when he was at the Cleveland Clinic, but it soon became clear that developing an artificial heart for human beings—or even for calves, the currently favored experimental animal—would strain every aspect of bioengineering beyond its limits. There were problems of design, materials, power, operating procedures, and even controversies about the quality of life with such a device. A lesser man would have given up long ago. Instead, in 1970 Kolff recruited an imaginative medical student, Robert Jarvik, and let him loose on the project. Dr. Jarvik, now a seasoned researcher, believes that a battery-powered artificial heart of his own design could be developed for human use within five years. He also feels that this could save the lives of some 50,000 persons a year—people who might otherwise die from heart attacks, heart disease or during open-heart surgery.

The most successful model so far has been an airdriven heart, with all its bulky machinery remaining outside the body. One calf survived six months with such a heart recently, and another was thriving five months after its operation, gaining weight and exercising on a treadmill. However, all these animals have long, thick hoses sticking out of their chests to bring in the compressed air that drives their hearts. They are permanently attached to a compressed-air machine—a fate which Jarvik would not want to inflict on human beings. He is betting, instead, on a new electrohydraulic pump he has just developed, which should make battery-powered hearts much more practical.

Kolff, on the other hand, emphasizes that even paraplegics who are confined to a wheel chair can lead rewarding lives—and that a person with an air-driven artificial heart could have a relatively happy existence. "When you see those calves stand up the day after the operation, eat and exercise," he says, "and then compare them with cardiac patients who are in bed, too weak even to shave, you realize what an artificial heart could mean. There must be thousands of people who would prefer to be tethered to a drive system, especially one that has wheels, than to be dead."

Incorrigibly optimistic and impatient, Kolff does not want to wait for the perfect model before starting to save lives. Improvements can come later, he says, and anyway most doctors are too cautious.

Kolff's optimism is based not only on the great advances he has witnessed and helped to engineer since his first patient died some 40 years ago, but also on the array of medical problems where bioengineering has not even been applied yet. "If you want to understand the future of bioengineering," he says, "don't talk to doctors, talk to high school students, whose minds have not been ruined."

Ending Time:

WPM: _____

Comprehension Check: Modern Bioengineers. . . .

Directions: Complete each question by writing in or circling the correct answer.

1. The father of modern bioengineering
   a. is the Dutchman, Dr. Wellem Kolff.
   b. is the Englishman, Jerome K. Jerome.
   c. is the University of Utah professor, Dr. Stephen Jacobsen.

2. The major deterrent to former and present advances in bioengineering is

   _____

   _____

   _____.

3. The significance of such television programs as "The Six-Million Dollar Man" and "Bionic Woman" is that the public expects more progress in bioengineering than can now be delivered.

   True   False

4. The first major breakthrough in bioengineering
   a. was the cardiac pacemaker.
   b. was kidney dialysis.
   c. was artificial joints and limbs.

5. Through help from _____, tasks such as developing artificial limbs that respond to brainwaves have become feasible.

Comprehension Accuracy:

_____

PHRASE READING PRACTICE

These Supplementary Selections are provided to enhance your phrase reading skills. They are to be used for rapid reading practice in which you gather ideas by clustering groups of related words. Since phrase reading increases your speed in both pleasure reading and effective study reading, you should strive to perfect your use of this skill.

For each of the readings in this supplementary section, follow these directions:

1. *Preview*. Identify words that are unfamiliar to you and learn about the general idea being presented.
2. *Read the selection*. Remember that not every word must be read separately. Cluster the words in groups and phrases as you read. Focusing on the center of the cluster forces you to use your peripheral vision, eliminating the need to see each word separately.
3. *Time yourself as you read*. Record beginning and ending times. Compute your reading rate (WPM).

4. *Check your comprehension accuracy* with the Answer Key provided on p. 115.

5. *Plot both your rate and comprehension scores on the Reading Progress Chart on p. 117.* Your scores should now show a consistent increase in level of comprehension. If your scores have not increased, find an interesting paperback novel to practice on. Unit 4's "Home Practice" section offers some excellent suggestions on how to proceed as you read the novel.

Beginning Time:

_____

Total Words: 551

Selection 1: ABC's of Veneering in Easy Photo Steps ——————

Egyptian woodworkers had a problem 3,500 years ago. Pretty hardwoods were scarce. So, being clever Egyptians. they devised a way to slice off thin layers from hardwood logs and glue them over common wood constructions. They were the first to develop what we call wood veneering.

Wood veneering is a finishing technique you can do, too, with beautiful results. We show how you can make a start with the easy photo steps illustrated here. And you don't have to slice your own veneering from a log, either. Just buy it in sheets and rolls from a display rack.

To help illustrate the veneering process, we've chosen a simple end table as our common wood construction. You can build it according to our specs or enlarge it. The basic veneering steps, however, remain the same.

The parts for our table are cut from a piece of ¾-in. fir plywood measuring only 26 x 66 in. The interlocked leg-and-apron sections are ripped on a table saw by making a series of internal cuts. You can do this by positioning the panel over the recessed saw blade.

With the rip fence set, you turn on the power, then slowly elevate the arbor until the blade cuts through the top of the sheet to within approximately ½ in. of an inside corner. Finish the inside corners later with a hand or saver saw.

In order to know exactly where the blade surfaces, make a test cut on a scrap piece. As the blade comes through, cut power and mark the rear and forward limits of the kerf on the rip fence. Use these marks as a guide for positioning the actual panel.

Additional tips: Work with a sharp blade, cutting the panel into three sections first, for easier handling. Then start the internal cuts. Use 2-in. finishing nails and glue to assemble the parts. Perfectly flush butt joints are essential. Be sure, too, to countersink the nails and wipe off all glue squeezings.

The veneering we chose for our table is zebrawood stripe, available from Constantine's (2050 Eastchester Rd., Bronx, NY.) They have a large variety to choose from. There also are other sources, such as lumberyard showrooms and craft supply stores, as well as mailorder wood suppliers. In all, there are about 100 varieties on the market.

You'll need 18 sq. ft. for the table project. That allows for some waste. A pint of veneer glue should be enough if you're careful. The only equipment you need is a veneer saw and a roller. The photos show you how to apply the veneer.

With a veneering project like this under your belt, you might be turned on to trying a more advanced technique, such as inlaying. For example, the Romans improved on the Egyptian veneering discovery by using it in a purely decorative way. Inlaying is a process of insetting a variety of thin

SOURCE: Reprinted from *Mechanix Illustrated Magazine.* Copyright © 1977 by CBS Publications Inc.

veneers into a recessed solid surface.

Then, perhaps, you'd like to get into marquetry, which was developed in the 16th century. In the process, cut-out parts of veneer are assembled into a one-piece veneer face (or picture) and the face is glued to a mounting board.

A knowledge of basic veneering techniques also can be applied to old pieces of furniture with simple lines. Just strip them first, then lay them on an all-new finish. It's just that easy.

Ending Time:

_____

WPM: _____

Comprehension Check: ABC's of Veneering

Directions: Complete each of the following statements by writing in or circling the correct answer.

1. The woodworking technique called veneering was developed
   a. as an ornamentation process during the surge of creativity of the arts in ancient Egypt.
   b. as a means of making scarce hardwoods go farther in the building trade.
   c. by ancient Rome to help cover unsightly buildings.

2. Veneering is a technique for _____ wood.

3. Inlaying is a simpler process than veneering.
   True   False

4. The technique of gluing thin cut-out wood parts into a picture is known as

_____.

5. The author's purpose for writing this selection is to
   a. give a history of woodworking techniques.
   b. make the reader aware of the complexities involved in the process of using woodworking techniques.
   c. help the reader acquire skill in veneering wooden objects.

Comprehension Accuracy:

_____

Selection 2: Biases, Prejudices, Tolerance

Beginning Time:

_____

Total Words: 697

The quantity and quality of sports participation is directly related to the attitude of the participant. His biases, prejudices, and value orientation condition his choices and direct his behavior. This is true in all aspects of life; sports participation is no exception.

It is generally accepted by most sociologists and social psychologists that games play a significant role in the socialization process of man. They are vital to the internalizing of normative behavior. As Mead writes, when one plays baseball, he not only assumes the role of throwing the ball but must anticipate the role of the batter and all other members of the team. He learns to cooperate and function through the play process. He becomes a member of a corporate body and takes on the attitudes of his team—his group. The quality of experience he enjoys as a child, the degree of skill he develops, depends to a large degree on the views of his group.

SOURCE: Reprinted with permission of Macmillan Publishing Co., Inc. from ENCYCLOPEDIA OF THE SPORT SCIENCES AND MEDICINE by Leonard A. Larson. Copyright © 1971 by Macmillan Publishing Co., Inc.

We are very conscious of what others do and the way our behavior is interpreted by those we respect. This has been demonstrated most effectively in studies of aging and juvenile delinquents.

In explaining why over 3 percent of the aging do not participate in organized recreation activities, Miller cited that the aged do not consider "recreation activities" meaningful. They do not see them in the same context as they view work. No longer able to work because of retirement or infirmity, they are encouraged to participate in recreation activities as a means of "occupying their time." This results in boredom and increased frustration. Their value orientation and their biases will not allow them to enjoy those activities that they have held in the past to be childish or frivolous. Yablonsky describes the same phenomenon among members of violent gangs. These youths reject participation in organized sports, holding these activities to be sissy or what the middle-class kids do. To establish their own identity, they reject the values and activities of the larger society. Basketball becomes a sissy's game and few gang members are going to play that which their peers reject.

Through the socialization process, society imposes its values, biases, and prejudices—its culture—on its young. Although the dominant values and attitudes of the larger society tend to condition the behavior of the people, each social class, minority group, regional faction, and gang creates patterns peculiar to itself. Packard and Warren speak of social-class attitudes, citing that the leisure patterns, including the participation of the group in sports activities, vary among social classes. The tolerance of the class for an activity such as golf becomes a measuring rod for the individual's willingness to participate in the activity. If his group sees golf as a weekend sport or one to be played while conducting business transactions, the participant, regardless of his interest in the activity, will tend to restrict his participation to the weekends. If, on the other hand, his class tolerates playing golf during the week for the sheer pleasure of playing golf, he can enter fully into the game without feelings of guilt. There are definite attitudes and expectations for each game; the participant has been socialized by his culture (his subgroup) and expects to derive certain benefits or have certain experiences each time he plays. Some recent research at the University of North Carolina in activity perception supports this observation.

Lest we conclude that participation in sports is totally dependent on one's cultural orientation, it should be remembered that individual biases and beliefs are shaped by personal experience. Both Keogh and McCloy report that participation in sports is directly related to the degree of skill one has developed in the activity. If one perceives himself as being good at an activity and that sport is accepted by his group or if he receives recognition from people he respects by participating in the activity, he will continue to play the sport. In fact, the sport may become a vehicle for moving from one social class to another. The prejudices, biases, and beliefs of the culture shape the attitudes of the individuals, but individual experiences are the means for altering these attitudes and values.

Ending Time:

WPM: ——————

Comprehension Check: Biases, Prejudices

Directions: Complete each of the following statements by writing in or circling the correct answer.

1. In this selection, the author equates sports with _____.

2. The biases, prejudices, and tolerance shown by a group are those factors that combine to produce the culture of that group.

    True   False

3. Experts of human behavior feel that the socialization process of mankind depends heavily on _____.

4. The most commonly accepted recreational activities are rejected by both youth gangs and work-oriented retirees because _____

    _____.

5. The experiences of an individual have little bearing on culturalization.

    True   False

Comprehension Accuracy:

_____

Selection 3: Will Pollution Controls Boost Electric Bills? _____

Beginning Time:

_____

Total Words: 729

The switch to coal as a primary energy source has already begun, dictated because domestic reserves of coal are enormous compared to those for oil and gas. But power companies that burn more coal will also be increasingly obligated to install expensive pollution control equipment. How will these added environmental costs affect the power industry? And even closer to home, how will they affect your monthly electric bill?

A study entitled Economic and Financial Impacts of Federal Air and Water Pollution Controls on the Electric Utility Industry attempts to project answers to these questions. The report was prepared for EPA's Office of Planning and Evaluation.

According to James Speyer, Acting Division Director of Policy Planning, the study indicates that "the cost of electricity in the future will still remain affordable, despite increased capital investment in pollution controls.

"It is projected that in 1985, the average consumer will be paying about $5.80 per month more than in 1975 for all goods and services because of such pollution abatement. This includes an increase of $2.80 in the average electric

bill of $42.40 per month," Speyer said.

The study estimates capital expenditures for a plant in service during the 1975–1985 period will increase by 10.5 percent over normal as a result of added environmental controls. In hard figures, this translates to $25 billion more than regular expenditures of $237.1 billion. It is projected that 60 percent of this increased capital investment in pollution abatement technology will be required through 1980, and the remaining 40 percent through 1985.

Water pollution control regulations will account for only a small percent of this increase, six percent by 1980, and the remaining 20 percent by 1985. The rest will go into air pollution prevention equipment.

Most expensive per kilowatt of the devices to protect air quality are scrubbers, which remove sulfur oxides from gases released during combustion. These will account for 39 percent of future capital outlays for environmental protection. Precipitators and wet scrubbers, used to capture particulate fly ash, will account for 36 percent, and cooling towers will make up 16 percent of the capital expenditures.

Meeting this increased level of capital investment will mean increased external financing (floating of bond issues, etc.). The report predicts that during the 1975–1985 period, external financing will increase for investor-owned power-producing utilities by 12.5 percent, or $19.3 billion over the $155 billion required before consideration of pollution control equipment.

The report states that "assuming the power industry is able to pass on the costs of pollution control equipment to its customers and to offer investors a competitive return on equity, the industry generally will be able to obtain the financing required both for regular needs and for pollution control equipment . . . The financing outlook for pollution control is guardedly optimistic due to favorable trends in earnings and in recent regulatory decisions."

Speyer explained that "what is meant by 'favorable trends in regulatory decisions' is that the states which regulate power companies have been willing to allow them larger returns of revenue. The plants usually accomplish this by increasing utility bills. The study indicates that larger power companies should encounter little difficulty with external financing of pollution control equipment. In the case of smaller companies, states may have to allow them higher returns on their service."

With regard to what kind of utility bills we can expect to be receiving in the future, the report states, "To view these costs in perspective, it is useful to relate them to the average bill paid by customers. The average bill is projected to increase even in the absence of pollution control impacts at a real growth of approximately five percent per year, or from $25.60 per month in 1975 to $42.40 per month in 1985.

"The direct increase in an average residential electric bill as a result of federal pollution control regulations will be approximately $1.80 per month in 1980 and $2.80 per month in 1985. In relative terms, those impacts represent 5.3 and 6.6 percent increases."

When price increases other than the $2.80 added to the electric bill are included—such as increased cost of products produced by electricity-intensive industries—the entire monthly increase attributable to costs for environmental controls is $5.80 per month, as Speyer previously noted.

"Generally the impacts of expenditures on pollution controls will be very small both on major users of electricity and on other areas such as the sulfur industry," the report indicates.

"Product price increases in the most electricity-intensive industry, primary aluminum, would be only 1.1 percent by 1985 if all increased electricity costs due to pollution control were passed directly on in the form of increased product prices."

The report states that when broken down by geographical region, percentage increases in average customer charges are expected to be as follows: Mountain, 11.1 percent; East South Central, 10.2 percent; West North Central, 10.1 percent; West South Central, 9.0 percent; East North Central, 8.3 percent; South Atlantic, 5.2 percent; Middle Atlantic, 4.1 percent; New England, 1.8 percent; and Pacific, 1.3 percent.

Ending Time:

_____

WPM: _____

Comprehension Check: Will Pollution Controls. . . .

Directions: Complete each of the following statements by writing in or circling the correct answer.

1. Pollution control has become of intense interest to residents of the United States since

   a. shortages of natural gas and oil have again made coal one of our primary sources of energy.

   b. major industrial companies have been cited for repeated violations of the clean air laws.

   c. utility bills will reflect the costs of power companies incurred from the use of coal as a major fuel.

2. Water pollution is less expensive to control than air pollution is.

   True   False

3. The _____ section of the United States will experience the least increase because of pollution controls.

4. Utility companies have been able to absorb the costs of pollution controls

   because _____

   _____.

5. The expected percentage of increase found in customer utility bills is between

   a. 10–20 percent.

   b. 5–6 percent.

   c. 50–75 percent.

Comprehension Accuracy:

_____

Selection 4: Run the Gamut to Jogging Comfort _____

Beginning Time:

_____

Total Words: 333

If, overcome by your first few days of warm weather, you've probably discovered that plain old shorts, sometimes called short-shorts, hardly exist.

They've almost been replaced by a new fashion look—jogging shorts, and never mind the fact that you rarely take a walk, let alone work up a sweat hoofing around the neighborhood. Jogger or no, they're the shorts to have.

People in the clothing industry say the current boom in physical fitness has given leisurewear definite sports overtones. And the growing number of people participating has brought about a change in real sports togs.

Alongside plain gray sweatshirts and sweatpants are brightly colored velour, terrycloth, fleece, cotton and even satin-finished polyester togs. Fashion trims include racing stripes up the leg and colorful contrast piping on all the gear; shirts, shorts, warm-up jackets and tank tops.

The worst of this new, sports-oriented gear is so ill-suited for athletics that it will only see duty in places like supermarket checkout lanes.

The best will deliver both good performance and good fashion. That winning combination is a result of several things. Tight is out; fit should allow for movement. Shorts, for instance, should be cut full enough in the leg to make running comfortable.

Webbed belts on warmup jackets and pants provide better fit than simple drawstrings. Waistbands on running shorts should be elasticized.

Fabrics should breathe. And, of course, everything should be washable and should never, ever need the services of an iron.

Perhaps one of the nicest things about these action clothes is the price. Charlotte stores are full of jogging shorts, some as low as $2, and t-shirts that are only $1 or so more. Thus, while a pair of jeans may set you back $15–$20, with judicious shopping you can get a comfortable, color-coordinated outfit for $10 or less.

The sports influence isn't limited to adult clothing. Kid's clothes are action-oriented, too.

While it may not be true in fact, Americans this summer at least will look like a nation of athletes.

Ending Time:

_____

WPM: _____

Comprehension Check: Run the Gamut

Directions: Complete each of the following statements by writing in or circling the correct answer.

1. Leisurewear has been unaffected by trends in athletics.

   True   False

2. That America will look like a nation of athletes this summer refers to

   _____

   _____.

3. Utility is the best term for describing _____

   _____

4. Shorts shorts are used by this author to represent _____

   _____.

Comprehension Accuracy:

_____

5. Children's and adults' clothes are not affected by the same trends of fashion.

   True   False

Beginning Time:

_____

Total Words: 858

Selection 5: Nativist Theory _____

Language is a biological endowment unique to a human species, Lenneberg . . . has argued. He is joined in this belief by McNeill . . . and others. The nativist, or biological, theory of language acquisition is based on the belief that the human nervous system is innately predisposed, through the evolutionary process, to the development of language. Maturation in language development parallels related growth in thinking and motor ability. Assuming the absence of some massive abnormality or injury, every child will naturally and rapidly learn to speak whatever language he or she is exposed to. Learning to talk is as natural and inevitable as learning to walk. The nativist theory emphasizes what occurs inside the child whereas the behaviorist theory emphasizes the role of events in the child's exterior environment.

Lenneberg has presented a number of arguments supporting the notion that the human ability to acquire language is due to biologically inherited capabilities. His evidence is based on normal and abnormal language development in children, as well as evidence which suggests the possibility of an innate biological capacity for language, unique to the human species. Lenneberg . . . has cited the following evidence to support his theory:

1. *Language is unique to the human species.* While it is apparent that animals can communicate in some interesting and even complex ways, there is no evidence to show that any nonhuman species has learned to communicate using the complex syntactic properties of human language. The learned behavior of parrots, pets, and chimpanzees shows only a superficial resemblance to human language.

2. *Every human language is based on similar universal principles of semantics, syntax, and phonology.* This is sometimes referred to as the principles of linguistic universals, an argument that maintains that certain features of language and language learning are universally similar in key respects.

3. *The developmental schedule for language learning is uniform in all cultures.* In all cultures, for example, children have mastered the essential elements of their native language between the ages of four and six.

4. *Language is learned with such ease and is so deeply rooted in humans that children learn it even in the face of enormous handicaps.* Even blind, retarded, and criminally neglected children learn to speak and often with only a minimal delay.

5. *There is evidence that language learning is related to certain anatomical and physiological correlates.* There is reason to believe, for example, that certain parts of the human brain contain specialized structures for the production of speech, and these structures are apparently species specific.

The theory of biological endowment for language ability has gained a considerable following in recent years. Perhaps this trend is at least partially attributable to the failure of psychologists and linguists to adequately account for recent linguistic observations, particularly the existence of language universals, in any other satisfying way.

The nativist theory of biological determination of language acquisition must be taken seriously. However, like other theories, it leaves some basic matters unexplained. For example, the theory does not adequately account for the actual mechanisms of language acquisition except in a general way. How the child moves from biological endowment to actual linguistic performance is not adequately explained.

The fact that environmental factors are relatively unimportant in nativist theory (since children are presumed to possess certain general language abilities before specific elements are ever produced) tends to make the theory considerably less interesting to educators because it seems to negate the importance of applications of language learning processes to reading and writing.

Cognitive Theory

The cognitive theory of language acquisition is similar to the nativist theory in that it postulates innate structures which make language learning possible. However, the cognitive theorist claims that universal thought structures, rather than linguistic universals, account for the capacity to learn language.

Slobin . . . for example, seems to suggest that the child may be preprogrammed, in effect, with such cognitive abilities as short-term and long-term memory facility, information processing capacities, and cognition of the categories and processes of human experience. These factors, along with other developing cognitive abilities, determine and control the pace of language acquisition.

Similarly, Cromer's . . . research indicates that as the children increase their cognitive ability they free themselves to learn and express new language abilities. Having developed the necessary cognitive structures, children immediately extend their linguistic performance in concert with their newly developed cognitive ability.

Cognitive theorists, such as Piaget, Vygotsky, and Bruner, have not been primarily concerned with describing a language acquisition theory. Rather, they have concerned themselves with the development of a theory which accounts for cognitive development. Consequently, they have discussed the mechanisms of language acquisition mainly in terms of how it is acquired. Athey . . . has responded to this tendency with the following critique:

> Perhaps the greatest criticism of cognitive models is that they fail to account specifically for the facts of language development. It is not so much that linguistic facts are incompatible with the models as that they seem irrelevant to them. Yet the cognitive and language functions are so interdependent, and their developmental paths are intertwined. It is difficult to see how a theory in either area can be considered adequate if it fails to take account of existing theories and facts in the other. . . .

Ending Time:

WPM: ───────

Comprehension Check: Nativist Theory

Directions: Complete each of the following statements by writing in or circling the correct answer.

1. Contrast the nativist theory of language development with that of the behaviorist theory. ──────────────────────────

──────────────────────────

──────────────────────────

──────────────────────────

2. The nativist theory of language development stresses what occurs outside the child rather than inside.

   True   False

3. The major proponent of the nativist theory of language development is

   a. Piaget.
   b. Lennenberg.
   c. McNeill.

4. The scientists who study language development are the ───────────

   ─────────────── and ───────────────.

5. Because a reasonable explanation for the human's development of language cannot be given by present day scientists, most people accept the theory that

_____

_____   Comprehension Accuracy:

_____.   _____

Selection 6: How To Choose a Dog ━━━━━━━━━━━━

Beginning Time:

_____

Total Words: 2756

It's easy to be charmed by the look of a little dog and take it home as a pet for your children—only to discover as it grows up that the animal has a strong sense of privacy and prefers to be left alone. Or you can buy a pup for a watchdog—and find it turning into a timid soul that needs protecting itself. An apartment dweller can acquire a dog that works out fine for the first year but eventually becomes so large and lively that it's exhausting to manage.

The problems that result from this sort of incompatibility can be distressing at best and heartbreaking at worst—and that's why it is necessary to know as much as possible about the various breeds of dogs before your purchase one.

Selecting a breed is not like deciding on a make of automobile or style of dining-room furniture. The dog you choose will become an integral part of your life, and will grow and develop just like the other members of your family. There is an incredible variety of purebred dogs to choose from. My first piece of advice is *not* to go to a commercial pet store and pick a pup from their limited selection. For one thing, do you really want a purebred? You may well be better off with a good mongrel pup, and your local humane society or animal shelter has any number of them waiting to be adopted. In terms of all-around temperament, physical vigor and genetic soundness, mongrels generally have it over the purebreds.

Where purebreds "outclass" the mongrels is in their predictability. You know what kind of temperament, specific traits and eventual body size and coat type you are going to get. But beware the pet suffering from the "pure-bred-dog syndrome"—a serious problem among the more popular breeds. This overbreeding to meet the demand has resulted in some animals that have no character at all, or are emotionally unstable, high-strung, hyperactive, timid or aggressive. It may be hard to tell this in the brief time you spend in the pet store, and so you are better off locating a small breeder who takes an obvious pride in his dogs. You can find such breeders at dog shows, in national dog magazines, or simply listed in your local newspaper. Familiarize yourself with the various breeds by reading as much as you can about them—and then by visiting dog shows and talking to the owners or handlers of the breed that you're interested in.

First of all, purebred dogs are divided into six categories: terriers, toys, working breeds, hounds, sporting breeds and nonsporting breeds.

The terriers are mainly medium-to-small-size dogs that are notoriously bold, alert and active. Their name comes from the Latin terra, meaning earth, and they were originally used in hunting such prey as rabbits, foxes and badgers. They were the allies of the huntsman, gamekeeper and farmer, and became such popular pets that they were often allowed to live in the house with the family. Terriers in general can be spitfires, especially when another dog approaches their territory. This strong territorial instinct makes them excellent house protectors.

Terriers are generally very good with children and always ready for fun and games. They don't adapt particularly well to a sedentary life, so if you want a quiet, sedate dog, forget a terrier.

With few exceptions, their coats need only occasional grooming. Wire-coated types include the wirehaired fox terrier as well as the Irish, Scottish, West Highland, Welsh and Sealyham Terriers. These medium-size dogs weigh around 20 pounds, but the largest, the Airdales, can weigh as much as 50. The smallest are the Norwich and Border Terriers and the cairns, which run about 14 pounds.

The types with smooth, short coats include the fox terrier, the bull terrier (it's quite pugnacious and difficult to handle if you have other dogs) and the Manchester terrier, which is the leanest and looks like a greyhound (there is a toy variety of this breed that weights a mere six pounds).

Curly-coated types—which are cuddly though still fiesty—are the Skye and Dandie Dinmont terriers. Both are short-legged characters weighing in at about 25 pounds. If you want a larger dog, a 35-to-40 pound Kerry Blue may be your breed. At first glance, The Bedlington terrier looks more like a lamb than a dog, but it is a tough breed, once used in England as a ratter.

One of the most popular curly-coated terriers is the miniature Schnauzer (15 pounds), which was used on German farms as a rat catcher. Like other terriers of this coat class, Schnauzers require frequent grooming and trimming. Some people like to have a vet crop their ears to make them stand up, but you should know that the American Veterinary Medical Association does not condone this practice. It can be extremely painful and does the animal no real good.

The toy breeds weigh about six to eight pounds, and include the diminuitive Chihuahua—the smallest of all breeds at four pounds! "Tea cup" Chihuahuas may weigh less than one pound, but they are extremely rare and don't survive well.

Don't let the size of toy dogs deceive you: They are not delicate and timorous, but very active, curious and outgoing, often getting into fights with much bigger dogs. I often wonder, when I see toys challenging dogs five or ten times their size, if they have any concept of how small they really are. In domesticating them, humans have shrunk their bodies but not their egos!

The toy breeds were created principally to be pets. They were first owned by aristocrats, who could afford to keep animals for pleasure rather than work. Some were, and still are, miniature replicas of larger breeds. They are responsive to training, make good apartment pets, and are excellent companions for elderly or sedentary people because they can get adequate exercise indoors.

All toys from a good lineage are loyal and intelligent, make good companions and will let you know when there is someone else around. Some strains are yappier and snappier than others, so be considerate of neighbors when making your selection. Buying a pair of dogs is a good idea if you plan to leave them alone for any length of time.

Wiry-coated toys don't need much grooming, but long or silky-coated animals need owners who have the time to pet and primp them. Low on the ground as they are, some of these breeds are not outdoor dogs, since their silken tresses would soon be muddied. Those who do get outdoors need a good trim first. In this category are the ancient Maltese terrier, a six-pound ball of dynamite and affection, purportedly a pet of Roman ladies; and the Shih Tzu, or Chinese lion dog, which is very popular today. The "Yorkie," or Yorkshire terrier, is the smallest of the long-haired toys—a mere five to seven pounds—but full of energy and fight.

Other breeds in this category include the Pomeranian, a miniaturized version of a Baltic sled dog. There are also three miniature spaniels—the Tibetan, Japanese, and English or King Charles. A popular pet from China is the Peking-ese, one of the most ancient of all toys.

The most popular toy breed today is the toy poodle—an exact replica of the two larger kinds of poodles. Because of its popularity, though, be alert for overbreeding; this kind of pet may have a finicky temperament and genetic defects, so here again it is very important to check the background and breeder.

The working breeds were originally developed to protect livestock, to drive cattle to market, to serve as guards on estates and game preserves and to pull carts and sleds. Some make good watchdogs and guides for the blind and are used for police and military work. But be warned: Working dogs from good stock *need* to work; they don't thrive when cooped up. Some of these breeds are highly trainable but, if given no obedience training, they can become difficult to handle and be a potential danger to your family and to society in general.

Pets that once pulled sleds include the Siberian Husky (weighing about forty-five pounds) and Alaskan Malamute (75 pounds). Although these animals are increasing in popularity, the problems they create are increasing as well; these breeds do not adapt well to a sedentary life. Also, if you live in a hot climate, they are apt to show great discomfort as the temperature rises. The Samoyed, another sled dog (35 to 45 pounds), is more adaptable to hot weather, having been kept as a pet for a longer time over the centuries. All three enjoy sleeping outdoors in the coldest weather. and, in fact, when given a good kennel and run, do best when kept outside.

Another category of working breeds might be called the rescuers. The Newfoundland, famed for saving lives in shipwrecks, and the Saint Bernard, the Swiss mountain rescue dogs, are giant breeds (weight 145 to 165 pounds and up, respectively). Overbreeding has given the Saint Bernard a bad reputation, and people should think carefully about owning one of these giants. They can be gentle—but unpredictable, too.

There are also the guards: The English mastiff (185 pounds) and the bull mastiff (110 pounds) have impressive physiques that will intimidate any would-be intruder. Also in this category are the German Rottweiler, the Doberman pinscher, and the German shepherd. Although naturally protective, it is very important that these dogs be obedience trained; otherwise, their potential will go to waste. Worse, they may not know *when* to defend you—which could mean real trouble. But *never* have one of these breeds attack trained, since the animal will never again be a reliable house dog.

Finally, there are the herders—farm dogs from all over the world that have become established as specific breeds. Some of them, like the collie and Shetland Sheepdog, have been bred for so long as pets that they are no longer working dogs. As such, they adapt better to a more sedentary life.

Herders include the beautiful Belgian sheepdog and the Tervuren (good alternatives if you want a dog that looks like a German shepherd but is highly trainable). Another popular pet in this category is the old English sheepdog, that shaggy-haired drover's dog of old. Its cuddly coat and bouncy, playful nature have contributed to its popularity, but again beware of the pitfalls of overbreeding.

Also, its coat requires constant attention, and while it makes a good family pet, it does need space and freedom.

I have the same reservation about the Great Dane from Germany—a boarhound and America's most popular giant breed, measuring 32 inches and more at the shoulder. But like many Saint Bernards, collies, Afghans and Irish setters, some Great Danes are just big quiet "boneheads"—sweet nothings, lacking both character and vitality. They may be handsome to look at, but if you want a spirited and intelligent one, you will have to find a reliable, noncommercial breeder.

The hound breeds: There are two basic types—the long-limbed gazehounds built for speed, possessing stamina and keen vision, and the somewhat smaller tracking hounds that hunt by scent. No longer used for hunting, many of these hounds have been altered through selective breeding to adapt to a passive life as a household pet. But this is not always the case, and a large gazehound, cooped up all day and never allowed to race, may develop serious behavior problems. The smaller scent hounds can be a problem, too, since once they pick up a scent, they may rush off, leaving you miles behind!

The largest of all breeds is the Irish deerhound (33 inches or taller at the shoulder), and a leaner version is the Scottish deerhound. The aristocratic Borzoi is Russia's wolfhound, and is certainly one of the most distinctive of the hounds. The greyhound and the silky shag-coated Afghans come from the Mideast and are of a very ancient lineage.

Larger hounds include the bloodhound, foxhound, coonhound, and Rhodesian Ridgeback; they are generally easy-going and are usually quiet and gentle with children.

Smaller breeds include the huskylike Norwegian Elkhound, a robust, outgoing and very ancient breed, and the beagle, a hunter's rabbit dog that often makes a good family pet. Remember, however, that hounds in general are harder to train than other breeds, because they were originally bred to work alone, with the hunter following behind. A case in point is the easygoing Basset hound, the comic of the dog world with his chubby legs and forlorn, droopy face. Very nice with children, the Basset may frustrate some owners who discover it is hard to train—not because it is stupid but because it is an affectionate, nonaggressive groupie with a heritage of following its nose rather than somebody's instructions.

The dachshund—there are long and silky, short and smooth, and wire-haired varieties—are the badger hunters of Germany. Although classified in the hound category, their temperaments are closer to the terriers. They make wonderful pets, but aren't always good around children. There are the miniature varieties of the dachshund, too, which in temperament are not unlike the toy breeds described earlier.

The sporting breeds: There are three types in this category: the tall, keennosed pointing breeds (65 pounds or so), the retrievers, who are of a similar size and are excellent swimmers, and the smaller spaniels (35 to 45 pounds) who are quick in finding and fetching game birds. Unlike the more independent hound breeds, these sporting breeds were bred to work in very close association with the hunter. For that reason, they tend to be easier to train, and many of them make the transition to a non-hunting pet relatively easily. In fact, there are some breeds, like the Irish Setter and the cocker spaniel that have been bred for many generations exclusively for show as pets. Like the hounds these sporting breeds are usually good with children. But before you decide to bring one into your home, be sure, unless you intend to hunt with it, that it is not from an active hunting lineage. A good bird dog will not adapt well to a sedentary life.

The silky-coated setters—so named because they "set" their sights on their prey—include the Irish, English, and Gordon Setters. The first two breeds have been excessively overbred as "show-pets" in this country to the point that here again they may be striking in appearance but less than energetic and bright in your interaction with them. On the other hand, though, a sweet, dopey dog may fit into your home far better than an active and quick-witted animal.

Then there are the pointers, who actually do point the way to an animal in its lair (the German short- and wire-haired pointers and the Weimaraner are some of these).

Other sporting breeds are retrievers (in this country we find the Chesapeake Bay, golden and Labrador). The golden retriever is my first choice of the larger purebreds as a family dog—it is sweet, gentle and very understanding and patient with children.

More active—and, in a way, half-terrier and half-hound in temperament—are the smaller spaniels such as the Welsh Springer and the English cocker spaniel. The smallest is the American cocker, whose popularity a few years ago was followed by a sudden decline in its numbers; overbreeding had resulted in unstable, hysterical temperaments, as well as genetic defects.

Nonsporting breeds: In this category is a whole smorgasbord of breeds that have endured as pets long after they ceased to be used for the specific purposes for which they were originally bred. Some of these include the English and French bulldogs; the Boston terrier; the small, shaggy Tibetan Lhasa Apso; the Dalmatian or coach or fire dog; and the Chow Chow from China (originally bred to hunt and to be eaten!).

Also in this category are the standard and miniature Poodles, whose ancestry is derived from European hunting and circus trick dogs. The Poodles are the most popular today, but a little Lhasa Apso or Schipperke is an interesting pet for someone who wants something relatively small and different. Dalmatians and Chows, however, can be difficult to handle and are not the kind of dog an inexperienced person should acquire. Other than that, the members of this breed are generally even-tempered and adaptable—and more specific information about the characteristics of each can come from a breeder or owner.

Getting a dog can be akin to adding a whole new member to your family, one with whom you hope to be living for a number of years. For your sake and your dog's, don't buy on impulse. Know your breed—and select carefully and wisely.

Ending Time:

_____

WPM: _____

Comprehension Check: How to Choose a Dog

Directions: Complete each quesion by writing in or circling the correct answer.

1. Shopping for a dog should be like shopping for any other large, important item

   because_____

   _____

2. A purebred dog may not be the best buy in these modern times since
_____ is about the only characteristic he has above that of the lowly
mongrel.

3. A basic flaw that one must guard against when buying purebred dogs is
   a. the costs, which are highly inflated.
   b. illegal issuance of pedigrees even though the dogs are of impure bloodlines.
   c. the "syndrome" caused by overbreeding.

4. Selecting a dog who by size and temperament will be appropriate for a family
   or individual's life style is of the utmost importance if one is to be happy with
   his pet.
   True   False

5. Name the breeds of purebred dogs that are available._____

Comprehension Accuracy: _____

_____   _____

                            _____.

Answer Key: Supplementary Selections

Selection 1: Accounting as a Tool. . . ., p. 71

1. True **2.** the businessman's responsibility to provide information used for making decisions or knowing the true circumstances of a business or corporation **3.** accounting **4.** credit **5.** True

Selection 2: Secretaries: Are Bosses Getting Their Messages?, p. 79

1. True **2.** housewives **3.** the right to choose whether to do the personal work of employers **4.** the women's liberation movement **5.** False

Selection 3: Racial and Ethnic Discrimination, p. 86

1. False **2.** imbalances in social forces create segregation in a population **3.** unlawful, illegal **4.** True **5.** True

Selection 4: The Shot Heard, p. 91

1. The Battle of Lexington and Concord which was the beginning of the American Revolution against the alleged tyranny of England, a major colonial power **2.** True **3.** True **4.** to destroy ammunition storage sites **5.** False

Selection 5: Modern Bioengineers Reinvent, p. 99

1. a **2.** the lack of materials that are compatible with body tissues **3.** True **4.** b **5.** microcomputers

Selection 1: ABC's of Veneering, p. 101

1. b **2.** finishing **3.** False **4.** marquetry **5.** c

Selection 2: Biases, Prejudices, p. 103

1. games **2.** True **3.** Game participation **4.** both groups feel they are childish, frivolous, or unacceptable **5.** False

Selection 3: Will Pollution Controls Boost. . . ., p. 105

1. c **2.** True **3.** Northeast or New England area **4.** increased earnings and favorable regulatory decisions that allowed them to pass the costs to the customer have provided the necessary financing **5.** b

Selection 4: Run the Gamut, p. 106

1. False   **2.** sportswear's becoming fashionable for the leisurewear dress of numbers of Americans   **3.** trends in present day leisure- and sportswear   **4.** the status of the leisurewear industry before the sports influence became so strong   **5.** False

Selection 5: Nativist Theory, p. 108

1. The Nativist Theory says that the human's ability to develop language is physical but the behaviorists say it comes from the outside, from outside forces found in his environment, his experiences, education, etc.   **2.** False   **3.** b   **4.** psychologists, linguists   **5.** Language is a product of biological development or native to humans

Selection 6: How to Choose a Dog, p. 113

1. the shopper should know as much as possible about the different breeds and their habits, sizes, needs, etc. in order to make the best choice   **2.** predictability of size, habits, etc.   **3.** c   **4.** True   **5.** terriers, toys, working breeds, hounds, sporting breeds, nonsporting breeds

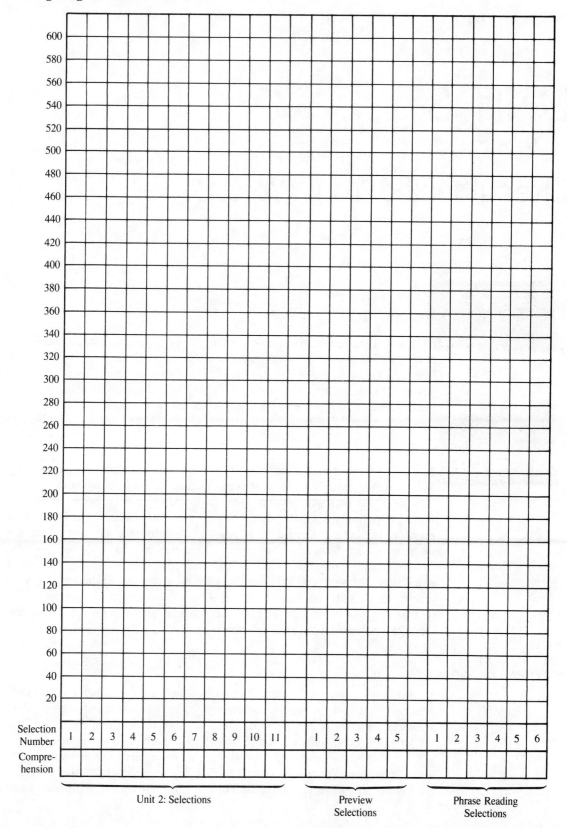

Selection Number	1	2	3	4	5	6	7	8	9	10	11		1	2	3	4	5		1	2	3	4	5	6
Compre-hension																								

| Unit 2: Selections | Preview Selections | Phrase Reading Selections |

UNIT 3

Strengthening Your Word Power

TIPS FOR INCREASING COMPREHENSION

Having a strong vocabulary is essential for increasing your comprehension. Rapid recognition of numerous words and the ability to associate them with specific ideas and topics are skills that can be developed with practice. Three techniques that you can learn are particularly helpful in strengthening and extending your word power: using previewing, structural or syntactic clues, and semantic or significant meaning clues.

Previewing for Unfamiliar Words

In Unit 2 you learned that previewing to gain quick information about the topic and subheadings should be the first step in reading for both pleasure and study. As you make this preliminary check, you should also preview for any unfamiliar words. Simply place a dot over each word you don't understand. Then take a minute or two before you read the selection to check the pronunciation and general meaning of each word in a dictionary or glossary. As you work, ask yourself, "How does this term relate to this topic?" Studying the words in this way reveals much about the topic and helps you identify the technical vocabulary associated with it. As a result, you won't be stumped by unfamiliar words as you read. You will thus be able to read the selection more quickly and with greater comprehension. Remember, high speed is effective only if you are familiar with the material being read.

Structural or Syntactic Clues

Because a word can often be identified through the context in which it appears in a selection, you may be able to define a word by studying the structure of the sentence. Structure or syntactic clues refer to word order within sentences. Syntax, or word order, signals to the reader what has been acted on in each sentence and by what or by whom. By identifying the actor, action, and object of the action, you select the most important facts in any sentence. Being able to do this quickly not only helps you understand better, but it also speeds up the reading.

Practice with this sentence:

The archives are very old; some of the letters are worn too smooth to be recognized.

Let your eyes travel to the ending punctuation, the period. Did you notice the semicolon as your glance swept over the text? It signals that there will be two thoughts in this sentence—two different actors, two sets of actions and things acted upon. The first step is to identify the first thought. What is told before the semicolon? Ask yourself:

Who or What?	archives
Action?	are
What?	old

Now find the actor, action, and object of the second thought given after the semicolon.

Who or What?	some of the letters
Action?	are worn
What?	too smooth to be recognized

Simply program yourself to identify who, what, when, where, and why as your eyes scan the sentence.

Semantic Clues

Semantic clues, or clues that can be picked up from the meaning of other words in the sentence, the **context** of the sentence, can also help you increase your comprehension. Whenever you recognize a word, phrase, or sentence, each reminds you of something you have seen, heard, or read. If you recall nothing, you then must set out to construct or build meaning of what you are reading. For example, take a look at the following sentence from a selection you read in Unit 2, "Secretaries: Are Bosses Getting Their Message?"

Time and time again I'll catch a gaffe in his dictation and I'll say, "Did you really mean to write that?"

Suppose that you do not know what the word "gaffe" means. You can get the general idea that a "gaffe" is a mistake of some sort from the rest of the sentence, "Did you really mean to write that?" Looking for semantic clues such as this one can help you understand unfamiliar words even when you don't have access to a dictionary. But it is always good practice to look up the meanings of unfamiliar words in a dictionary or glossary. A check in the dictionary will provide you with a *specific* definition of the word in question. For example, you would find that the word "gaffe" mean a "social blunder." Only by repeatedly analyzing the words you don't recognize and checking their dictionary meanings can you extend and strengthen your vocabulary.

In using each of these tips for increasing comprehension, remember to read only as fast as you can comprehend. The following exercises will help build your word power. Each demonstrates an efficient strategy you can use when you run across unfamiliar vocabulary while reading. Complete each exercise as indicated.

USE OF COMBINING FORMS OR DERIVATIVES

☐ **Exercise 3.1** ☐

Review the meaning of the following prefixes.

Prefix Review

Prefix	Meaning	Example
ad	toward, to, at	admit
re	again	regroup
in	into, in, upon	intake
en	into, in, on	encompass
be	all around, thoroughly	beware
pro	forward, for, ahead	productive

Using this knowledge of prefixes, change each of the following phrases to one word. Use the dictionary if needed.

Example: soiled, made dirty all over   <u>besmirch</u>

1. to put information into code _____
2. to moan about, lament _____
3. throw back light _____
4. to return as to the starting point or source, reacted _____
5. to break in on _____
6. a person who supports or speaks for a cause _____
7. to send back _____
8. to warn of a fault _____
9. to cloud over, obscure _____
10. lying next to, near _____
11. to shut in all around _____
12. something that is closed in all around _____
13. a natural tendency or inclination toward _____
14. to admit _____
15. a number of persons or things moving forward _____
16. to cover as with a flood _____
17. to besiege by surrounding _____
18. the result of being cut into _____
19. to lengthen in time _____
20. to stick to _____

Directions: Fill in the blanks below with the appropriate words that you identified in Excercise 3.1.

1. The intern _____ in horror at the sight of blood.

2. The new suggestion will only _____ the issue.

3. The _____ of the new law worked diligently for its passage.

4. The spring floods will _____ the land and bring new soil.

5. The elderly gentleman will strictly _____ to the dictates of his
    religious faith.

6. The _____ made from the exploding bomb bled profusely.

7. The ranch is _____ to the newly planned interstate highway system.

8. Continuing the hearing will only _____ the suffering of the victim's
    family.

9. The _____ mayor finally gave in to the striking workers' demands.

10. The reader will _____ the message given by the words of the text.

11. The minister will _____ his congregation of the dangers inherent
    in being complacent about the suffering of minority groups.

12. An object that is white is known to _____ light rather than absorb
    it.

13. The _____ was not large enough to house a car.

14. Large companies diversify and therefore _____ many smaller ones
    into the conglomerate.

15. The _____ wound slowly through the streets.

16. The plans are for the apartment building to _____ the quaint older
    home rather than have it demolished.

17. The aging model will _____ the day when she was tops in her
    field.

18. The rules of conduct seemed to _____ upon the individual's
    personal liberties.

19. His _____ for rich, creamy foods resulted in obesity in the man's
    middle years.

20. The court will _____ custody of the children to their grandparents.

□ Exercise 3.3 □

Directions: Review the meaning of these prefixes. Then complete the following
exercises.

Prefix Review

Prefix	*Meaning*	*Example*
com	together, also	complete
sub	under	substandard
ab	from, away from	abduct
un	not	unfavorable
dis	not	disabled
in	not	inconvenient

Prefix + *Word*	=	*New Word*	*Meaning*
Example: dis + abled	=	disabled	not able
1. com + passionate	=	_____	_____
2. sub + terraneous	=	_____	_____
3. un + savory	=	_____	_____
4. ab + solution	=	_____	_____
5. dis + continued	=	_____	_____
6. com + press	=	_____	_____
7. dis + comfort	=	_____	_____
8. sub + merge	=	_____	_____
9. in + disposed	=	_____	_____
10. un + fortunately	=	_____	_____
11. dis + interested	=	_____	_____
12. com + pose	=	_____	_____
13. sub + soil	=	_____	_____
14. in + continent	=	_____	_____
15. un + believable	=	_____	_____
16. sub + marginal	=	_____	_____
17. dis + avow	=	_____	_____
18. in + active	=	_____	_____

□ **Exercise 3.4** □

Directions: Change each word in the following Vocabulary List to a noun. Use the dictionary if necessary. Then complete the sentences that follow with the appropriate word from the list.

Example: disabled   disability

Vocabulary List

Word	Noun	Word	Noun
1. insubordinate	_____	6. submerge	_____
2. compassionate	_____	7. indisposed	_____
3. discontinue	_____	8. disinterested	_____
4. unbelievable	_____	9. disavow	_____
5. compress	_____	10. inactivate	_____

1. The _____ provided the energy source for air-conditioning the travel trailer.

2. The physician showed no _____ for the trauma experienced by the wreck victim.

3. The students' _____ became apparent with the advent of the football season.

4. The magazine's _____ was protested vigorously.

5. The _____ will not be rewarded.

6. The _____ of the bus in the river rendered it useless to the transit authorities.

7. The man's _____ to his superior officer caused great difficulties for him at a later time.

8. The accused's _____ of any connection with the crime confused authorities.

9. The _____ of the nuclear power plant caused "brownouts" in several metropolitan areas.

10. The _____ caused by the illness made Mr. Jones feel depressed.

□ **Exercise 3.5** □

Directions: Match the word in the first column with its definition in the second column. Complete Exercise 3.6 before checking your answers in the Answer Key on p. 139.

_____   1. disband   a. to put into position again

_____   2. insatiable   b. not suitable for surgery

_____   3. reinstall   c. to deprive an attorney of privileges and status

_____ 4. inoperable   d. to break up the organization of
_____ 5. disbarred   e. not capable of being satisfied
_____ 6. invigorate   f. not likely to be true or occur
_____ 7. disappearance   g. to give life or energy to
_____ 8. improbable   h. a vanishing or going away
_____ 9. reimposed   i. to subject to a change or penalty again
_____ 10. reinterred   j. to place in the earth or tomb again

☐ Exercise 3.6 ☐

Directions: On the line below each sentence rewrite the sentence in your own
words.

1. His appetite seemed to be *insatiable* as he ate and ate and ate.

   _____

2. It is *improbable* that another earthquake will occur along the Mississippi
   River again.

   _____

3. Most rock and roll groups *disband* when their members grow older and no
   longer appeal to the younger set.

   _____

4. A good slow rain will help *invigorate* the dying grass.

   _____

5. Will the repairperson *reinstall* the vandalized telephone booth?

   _____

6. The tumor was determined to be *inoperable* and the man was sent home.

   _____

7. The banker's *disappearance* aroused immediate suspicion.

   _____

8. Will military rule be *reimposed* on the rebellious natives?

   _____

9. The body will be *reinterred* the day after the autopsy.

   _____

10. The dishonest lawyer will be *disbarred* because of his illegal business deals.

    _____

☐ Exercise 3.7 ☐

Match the meanings in the second column with the root or base in the first column.

————— 1. scribe   a. to carry
————— 2. par   b. to talk
————— 3. port   c. to write
————— 4. dic   d. to hear
————— 5. aud   e. to make ready
————— 6. corp (cors)   f. the body
————— 7. ject   g. to break, burst
————— 8. tract   h. to throw
————— 9. rupt   i. to break
————— 10. fract (frag)   j. to draw, drag

☐ Exercise 3.8 ☐

Directions: For each base word, make four new ones, using the definition as your guide.

1. SCRIBE

    a. to write ahead,   c. to take,
       ————— SCRIBE   —————SCRIBE

    b. to copy onto,   d. to give to,
       ————— SCRIBE   —————SCRIBE

2. PAR

    a. to make ready   c. to regard as similar,
       beforehand, —————PARE   —————PARE
    b. thing done beforehand,   d. noting similarities,
       —————PAR—————   —————PAR—————

3. PORT

    a. able to be carried,   c. to carry boats and supplies overland
       PORT—————   from river to river, PORT—————
    b. carry across distance,   d. bring in from outside,
       —————PORT—————   —————PORT

4. DICT

    a. book of words,   c. words taken down,
       DICT—————   DICT—————
    b. official saying,   d. one who tells others what to do,
       DICT—————   DICT—————

5. AUD

   a. having a hearing,
      AUD_____

   b. of hearing, AUD_____

   c. not capable of being heard,
      _____AUD_____

   d. place where one goes to hear,
      AUD_____

6. CORP

   a. dead body, CORP_____
   b. so as to form one body,
      _____CORP_____

   c. fat, obese CORP_____
   d. collection of writings and laws,
      CORP_____

7. JECT

   a. turn or throw down, refuse,
      _____JECT

   b. throw out, _____JECT

   c. something thrown or jutting out,
      _____JECT_____

   d. deserving contempt, thrown down
      in a low position, _____JECT

8. TRACT

   a. draw away from,
      _____TRACT

   b. capable of being pulled or
      controlled, TRACT_____

   c. drivable machine for pulling,
      TRACT_____

   d. draw together, _____TRACT

9. RUPT

   a. break off suddenly,
      _____RUPT

   b. break apart, _____RUPT

   c. break into or between,
      _____RUPT

   d. a break, RUPT_____

10. FRACT

   a. break back or bend,
      _____FRACT

   b. break or crack,
      FRACT_____

   c. one or more parts,
      FRACT_____

   d. likely to break out into a passion,
      FRACT_____

☐ Exercise 3.9 ☐

Directions: For each word on the left, form a new word by adding the given ending. Watch your spelling.

1. prepare	_____ed	_____ing	_____ation	_____atory
2. scorn	_____ed	_____ing	_____ful	_____fully
3. predict	_____ing	_____ed	_____tion	_____able
4. comfort	_____able	_____ing	_____ed	_____er
5. prosecute	_____ing	_____ed	_____or	_____tion

6. project	_____ed	_____ing	_____tion	_____ile
7. abstain	_____ed	_____ing	_____tion	_____ance
8. emit	_____ed	_____s	_____sion	_____ing
9. form	_____ation	_____al	_____ality	_____ulation
10. grant	_____ed	_____ing	_____or	_____ee
11. transgress	_____ed	_____ing	_____sion	
12. revert	_____ed	_____ing	_____sion	
13. sedate	_____ed	_____ing	_____tion	
14. recur	_____ed	_____ing	_____ence	
15. hurry	_____ed	_____ing	_____edly	

☐ **Exercise 3.10** ☐

Directions: From the noun given, write an adjective and an adverb.

Example: storm   stormy   stormily

Noun	*Adjective*	*Adverb*
1. beauty	_____	_____
2. peace	_____	_____
3. athlete	_____	_____
4. unbelief	_____	_____
5. substance	_____	_____
6. prefer	_____	_____
7. intermission	_____	_____
8. ignominy	_____	_____
9. finance	_____	_____
10. compulsion	_____	_____
11. prediction	_____	_____
12. expression	_____	_____
13. definition	_____	_____
14. dejection	_____	_____
15. formality	_____	_____

USE OF SYNONYMS AND ANTONYMS

☐ **Exercise 3.11** ☐

Directions: Examine the word in the left column. In the blanks provided, label each of the four words to the right of it. If they are the opposite of the word in meaning, label them with an *O*. If they are similar in meaning, label them with an *S*.

1. analogy   ____ a. comparison   ____ c. difference

        ____ b. identical   ____ d. similarity

2. bigoted   ____ a. humble   ____ c. narrow-minded

                ____ b. meek   ____ d. intolerant

3. axiomatic   ____ a. reasoned   ____ c. questionable

                ____ b. self-evident   ____ d. conjecture

4. indubitable   ____ a. certain   ____ c. questionable

                ____ b. doubtful   ____ d. indisputable

5. fallacious   ____ a. misleading   ____ c. deceptive

                ____ b. truthful   ____ d. honest

6. illusion   ____ a. real   ____ c. false impression

                ____ b. misconception   ____ d. misleading appearance

7. preposterous   ____ a. absurd   ____ c. irrational

                ____ b. senseless   ____ d. reasonable

8. rational   ____ a. reasonable   ____ c. unreasonable

                ____ b. intelligent   ____ d. sensible

9. speculate   ____ a. reflect   ____ c. meditate

                ____ b. assured   ____ d. conjecture

10. plausible   ____ a. reasonable   ____ c. absolutely true

                ____ b. trustworthy   ____ d. genuine

□ Exercise 3.12 □

Directions: Fill in the blanks with the appropriate word.

1. Comparing life to a candle is a very common _____.
   a. axiom   b. analogy   c. speculation   d. bigot

2. The town drunk has an _____ reputation.
   a. analogous   b. bigoted   c. illusionary   d. indubitable

3. It is not _____ to say that any dormant volcano may erupt again.
   a. preposterous   b. rational   c. plausible   d. speculative

4. The administrative assistant was _____ and arrogant toward his fellow workers.
   a. rational   b. indubitable   c. bigoted   d. axiomatic

5. Scientists _____ about what happens but then seek to prove or disprove their ideas.
   a. axiom   b. speculate   c. illusion   d. falsify

6. To say that wild animals will become dangerous when threatened is _____.
   a. preposterous   b. speculation   c. analogous   d. axiomatic

7. Expensive entertainment outside the home was a (an) _____
   explanation for the young married couple's financial difficulties.

   a. axiomatic   b. illusionary   c. plausible   d. indubitable

8. The dishonest executive gave a _____ account of the
   firm's assets in order to secure his position with the board of directors.

   a. fallacious   b. rational   c. speculative   d. axiomatic

9. The suggestions offered by the elderly gentleman were both _____
   _____ and ingenious.

   a. bigoted   b. rational   c. illusionary   d. speculative

10. The color and weave of the fabric gave the _____ of
    nudity.

    a. analogy   b. axiom   c. illusion   d. fallacy

□ **Exercise 3.13** □

Directions: Add words similar in meaning to the two words already given. Use a
thesaurus or dictionary if needed.

1. affinity	likeness	_____	_____
2. blithe	cheerful	_____	_____
3. clamorous	noisy	_____	_____
4. compunction	regret	_____	_____
5. deceptive	misleading	_____	_____
6. dour	gloomy	_____	_____
7. elite	superior	_____	_____
8. fallacy	error	_____	_____
9. gruesome	horrifying	_____	_____
10. ignominy	shame	_____	_____
11. inflexibility	rigidity	_____	_____
12. juvenile	immature	_____	_____
13. lithe	agile	_____	_____
14. malleable	adaptable	_____	_____
15. obligatory	required	_____	_____
16. oust	expel	_____	_____
17. precipice	cliff	_____	_____
18. reprehensible	blamable	_____	_____
19. sanguine	confident	_____	_____
20. sobriquet	nickname	_____	_____

□ Exercise 3.14 □

Directions: Study the vocabulary list given below. In the sentences that follow, replace each italicized word with an antonym, or word meaning the opposite, from the list.

Vocabulary List

incontrovertible	flawless	exaltation
repulsion	sedate	inflexible
dour	optional	rejoice
scintillating	indubitable	peon
pessimistic	surname	inept

1. He shows a great *affinity* for lovely young ladies.

   _____

2. The *clamorous* crowd waited impatiently for the game to begin.

   _____

3. The manager's *dour* expression cast doubt on whether the staff would leave

   _____

   early that afternoon.

4. The teenager could not face the *ignominy* of telling his parents of his arrest.

   _____

5. The *lithe* movements of the dancer entranced the audience.

   _____

6. The opinions of youth are more *malleable* than those of their elders.

   _____

7. Their *obligatory* activities consumed all of the staff's working hours.

   _____

8. The senator's behavior was *reprehensible* since his district had placed com-

   _____

   plete trust in his judgment.

9. The *sanguine* executive strode boldly into the boardroom.

   _____

10. Her *sobriquet* mislead everyone, for all thought she was a man.

    _____

11. The beginner's *blithe* attitude irritated many of her co-workers.

    _____

12. The sailor who demonstrated no *compunction* angered his commanding officer.

    _____

13. The salesman's *deceptive* statements were meant for the unwary buyer.

_____

14. The sharpshooters were from an *elite* force.

_____

15. The *fallacy* of the scientist's projections was quite evident.

_____

ASSOCIATING WORDS WITH AN IDEA

□ **Exercise 3.15** □

Directions: Circle the word that does *not* mean the same as the underlined word.

1. isolate:	insulate	separate	expose	disassociate
2. cravat:	sombrero	tuxedo	cummerbund	shirt
3. contour:	concave	dogmatic	rotund	symmetrical
4. doldrum:	apathy	sluggishness	passivity	vehemence
5. diffident:	modest	reluctant	brazen	hesitant
6. elation:	ecstasy	despair	rapture	gratification
7. wane:	reduce	devitalize	energize	exhaust
8. fallible:	axiom	evasive	erroneous	illusionary
9. versatile:	tractable	constrained	pliable	ductile
10. specious:	dubious	apparent	probable	ostentatious
11. arrogant:	submissive	affected	pompous	disdainful
12. primeval:	primitive	olden	future	patriarchal
13. nepotism:	usefulness	beneficial	convenient	unfavorable
14. ostentatious:	demureness	vaunting	magnificence	pompousness
15. gradual:	progressive	perpetual	continuous	intermittent
16. jocund:	bacchic	sober	jovial	humorous

□ **Exercise 3.16** □

Directions: The following terms identify a quality of human behavior. Pretest yourself to determine how many you already know. Match every word in the first column with its identifying characteristic in the second column.

——————— 1. prudence   a. head in name only
——————— 2. benevolence   b. robot
——————— 3. figurehead   c. good judgment
——————— 4. automaton   d. doubter
——————— 5. skeptic   e. good will
——————— 6. belligerent   f. receiver
——————— 7. despondent   g. opponent
——————— 8. pacifist   h. warlike
——————— 9. antagonist   i. discouraged
——————— 10. recipient   j. believer in peace
——————— 11. lassitude   k. inclination
——————— 12. penchant   l. buoyant
——————— 13. resilient   m. weariness
——————— 14. subterfuge   n. strategem

☐ Exercise 3.17 ☐

Directions: Using the words you identified in Exercise 3.16, complete the following sentence with the appropriate term.

1. He was so stunned that one would think he was an ——————— from the way he moved.

2. The ——————— of the scholarship was so happy with his good fortune.

3. The man seemed to have a ——————— for embarrassing himself.

4. The young man refused to go to war since he was a ———————.

5. The proud woman used all types of ——————— to conceal the fact that she needed glasses for better sight.

6. The crotchety old man did not believe anything told him, for he was a born

   ———————.

7. His ——————— could not be matched, as he seemed to know the needs of his people and was always ready to help.

8. The rebellious youth was quite ——————— whenever anyone spoke to him.

9. The elderly woman's ——————— was evident in every step that she took.

10. The beautiful young mother was quite ——————— over the death of her only child.

11. His personality was quite ———————; he bounced back quickly from the loss of his job.

12. The lion-maned elderly judge served as a ——————— only in the law firm of Rhodes, Ryan, and Rodgers.

☐ Exercise 3.18 ☐

Directions: Write two synonyms, or words having the same meaning, for each of the following words. Use your thesaurus if needed.

1. prudence   ———————   ———————

2. benevolence   _____   _____

3. figurehead   _____   _____

4. automaton   _____   _____

5. skeptic   _____   _____

6. belligerent   _____   _____

7. despondent   _____   _____

8. pacifist   _____   _____

9. antagonist   _____   _____

10. recipient   _____   _____

11. lassitude   _____   _____

12. penchant   _____   _____

13. resilient   _____   _____

14. subterfuge   _____   _____

☐ **Exercise 3.19** ☐

Directions: Each of the sentences below uses a word referring to height. On the line below each sentence write two or three words that identify the idea associated with height as used in the italicized word.

Example: For many American children, becoming President is the *acme* of their ambitions.

<u>top or highest point</u>

1. Albert Einstein's ideas on relativity remain *preeminent* in the field of

_____

mathematics.

2. Astronomy deals with *ethereal* bodies such as the sun and the Milky Way.

_____

3. Beethoven's *Fifth Symphony* contains many *climactic* movements.

_____

4. The woodcarver wielded his knife with *consummate* skill.

_____

5. His *eminence* brought great respect at home for the new ambassador.

_____

6. The weary pilgrim stopped at the foot of the mountain and gazed at the *precipitous* climb ahead of him.

_____

7. Women who have been elevated to managerial levels *exult* over their accep-

_____

tance into a once male-dominated territory.

8. Being able to sing with the Metropolitan Opera is the *zenith* of a small town

_____

opera singer's career.

9. The *vertex* of the triangle was eight inches from its base.

_____

10. Riders who experience motion sickness dread the *acclivity* of mountainous roads.

_____

☐ Exercise 3.20 ☐

Directions: Write an antonym, or word with a meaning opposite, to the words
listed in the first column.

1. preeminent   _____
2. ethereal   _____
3. climactic   _____
4. consummate   _____
5. eminence   _____
6. precipitous   _____
7. exult   _____
8. zenith   _____
9. vertex   _____
10. acclivity   _____

☐ Exercise 3.21 ☐

Directions: In the space provided, design a sentence in which the idiom in
quotation marks substitutes for the phrase that explains its meaning.

1. "of his own accord"—of his own choice

_____

2. "act one's age"—behavior that is expected

_____

3. "up in arms"—angry

_____

4. "availed himself"—took advantage of

_____

5. "have one's back to the wall"—be in a difficult situation

_____

6. "on the beam"—doing well, correct

   _____

7. "in the clear"—free from suspicion, guilt

   _____

8. "throw dust in someone's eyes"—do something for the purpose of misleading

   _____

9. "in the face of"—when confronted with

   _____

10. "in harness"—working energetically

    _____

11. "on thin ice"—in a risky situation

    _____

12. "go ill with"—to work against

    _____

13. "irons in the fire"—business undertakings in which one has an interest

    _____

14. "the jig is up"—it's all over

    _____

15. "mad as a hatter"—completely demented, foolish

    _____

USE OF THE DICTIONARY

After examining the entries from *Webster's New Collegiate Dictionary* on p. 136, answer each of the questions in Exercise 3.22.

☐ **Exercise 3.22** ☐

1. *Use of Guide Words.* Circle the words from the following list that will not be found on dictionary page 585. Use only the guide words at the top of the dictionary page to complete this exercise. *Do not look down the columns of words.*

inequitable	infarct	infer	inflect
innocence	infamy	infanta	infectious

in·ex·is·tent \-tənt\ *adj* [LL *inexsistent-, inexsistens,* fr. L *in-* + *exsistent-, exsistens,* prp. of *exsistere* to exist] : not having existence : NONEXISTENT

in·ex·o·ra·ble \(ˈ)in-ˈeks-(ə-)rə-bəl, -ˈegz-ə-rə-\ *adj* [L *inexorabilis,* fr. *in-* + *exorabilis* pliant, fr. *exorare* to prevail upon, fr. *ex-* + *orare* to speak — more at ORATION] : not to be persuaded or moved by entreaty : RELENTLESS ***syn*** see INFLEXIBLE — **in·ex·o·ra·bil·i·ty** \(ˌ)in-ˌeks-(ə-)rə-ˈbil-ət-ē, -ˌegz-ə-rə-\ *n* — **in·ex·o·ra·ble·ness** \(ˈ)in-ˈeks-(ə-)rə-bəl-nəs, -ˈegz-ə-rə-\ *n* — **in·ex·o·ra·bly** \-blē\ *adv*

in·ex·pe·di·ence \ˌin-ik-ˈspēd-ē-ən(t)s\ *n* : INEXPEDIENCY

in·ex·pe·di·en·cy \-ən-sē\ *n* : the quality or fact of being inexpedient

in·ex·pe·di·ent \-ənt\ *adj* : not expedient : INADVISABLE — **in·ex·pe·di·ent·ly** *adv*

in·ex·pen·sive \ˌin-ik-ˈspen(t)-siv\ *adj* : reasonable in price : CHEAP — **in·ex·pen·sive·ly** *adv* — **in·ex·pen·sive·ness** *n*

in·ex·pe·ri·ence \ˌin-ik-ˈspir-ē-ən(t)s\ *n* [MF, fr. LL *inexperientia,* fr. L *in-* + *experientia* experience] **1** : lack of practical experience **2** : lack of knowledge of the ways of the world — **in·ex·pe·ri·enced** \-ən(t)st\ *adj*

in·ex·pert \(ˈ)in-ˈek-ˌspərt, ˌin-ik-ˈ\ *adj* [ME, fr. MF, fr. L *inexpertus,* fr. *in-* + *expertus* expert] : not expert : UNSKILLED — **in·ex·pert** \(ˈ)in-ˈek-ˌspərt\ *n* — **in·ex·pert·ly** \(ˈ)in-ˈek-ˌspərt-lē, ˌin-ik-ˈ\ *adv* — **in·ex·pert·ness** *n*

in·ex·pi·a·ble \(ˈ)in-ˈek-spē-ə-bəl\ *adj* [L *inexpiabilis,* fr. *in-* + *expiare* to expiate] **1** : not capable of being atoned for **2** *obs* : IMPLACABLE, UNAPPEASABLE — **in·ex·pi·a·bly** \-blē\ *adv*

in·ex·plain·able \ˌin-ik-ˈsplā-nə-bəl\ *adj* : INEXPLICABLE

in·ex·pli·ca·ble \ˌin-ik-ˈsplik-ə-bəl, (ˈ)in-ˈek-(ˌ)splik-\ *adj* [MF, fr. L *inexplicabilis,* fr. *in-* + *explicabilis* explicable] : incapable of being explained, interpreted, or accounted for — **in·ex·pli·ca·bil·i·ty** \ˌin-ik-ˌsplik-ə-ˈbil-ət-ē, (ˌ)in-ˌek-(ˌ)splik-\ *n* — **in·ex·pli·ca·ble·ness** \ˌin-ik-ˈsplik-ə-bəl-nəs, (ˈ)in-ˈek-(ˌ)splik-\ *n* — **in·ex·pli·ca·bly** \-blē\ *adv*

in·ex·plic·it \ˌin-ik-ˈsplis-ət\ *adj* : not explicit

in·ex·press·ible \-ˈspres-ə-bəl\ *adj* : not capable of being expressed : INDESCRIBABLE — **in·ex·press·ibil·i·ty** \-ˌspres-ə-ˈbil-ət-ē\ *n* — **in·ex·press·ible·ness** \-ˈspres-ə-bəl-nəs\ *n* — **in·ex·press·ibly** \-blē\ *adv*

in·ex·pres·sive \-ˈspres-iv\ *adj* **1** *archaic* : INEXPRESSIBLE **2** : lacking expression or meaning ⟨an ~ face⟩ — **in·ex·pres·sive·ly** *adv* — **in·ex·pres·sive·ness** *n*

in·ex·pug·na·ble \ˌin-ik-ˈspəg-nə-bəl, -ˈspyü-nə-\ *adj* [MF, fr. L *inexpugnabilis,* fr. *in-* + *expugnare* to take by storm, fr. *ex-* + *pugnare* to fight — more at PUNGENT] **1** : incapable of being subdued or overthrown : IMPREGNABLE ⟨an ~ position⟩ **2** : STABLE, FIXED ⟨~ hatred⟩ — **in·ex·pug·na·ble·ness** *n* — **in·ex·pug·na·bly** \-blē\ *adv*

in·ex·pung·ible \ˌin-ik-ˈspən-jə-bəl\ *adj* [*in-* + *expunge*] : incapable of being obliterated ⟨~ scent of a bottle of perfume he had . . . broken —Louis Auchincloss⟩

in ex·ten·so \ˌin-ik-ˈsten(t)-(ˌ)sō\ *adv* [ML] : at full length

in·ex·tin·guish·able \ˌin-ik-ˈstiŋ-(g)wish-ə-bəl\ *adj* : not extinguishable : UNQUENCHABLE ⟨an ~ flame⟩ ⟨an ~ longing⟩ — **in·ex·tin·guish·ably** \-blē\ *adv*

in ex·tre·mis \ˌin-ik-ˈstrā-məs, -ˈstrē-\ *adv* [L] : in extreme circumstances; *esp* : at the point of death

in·ex·tri·ca·ble \ˌin-ik-ˈstrik-ə-bəl, (ˈ)in-ˈek-(ˌ)strik-\ *adj* [MF or L; MF, fr. L *inextricabilis,* fr. *in-* + *extricabilis* extricable] **1** : forming a maze or tangle from which it is impossible to get free **2 a** : incapable of being disentangled or untied ⟨an ~ knot⟩ **b** : not capable of being solved — **in·ex·tri·ca·bil·i·ty** \ˌin-ik-ˌstrik-ə-ˈbil-ət-ē, (ˈ)in-ˌek-(ˌ)strik-\ *n* — **in·ex·tri·ca·bly** \ˌin-ik-ˈstrik-ə-blē, (ˈ)in-ˈek-(ˌ)strik-\ *adv*

inf *abbr* **1** infantry **2** infinitive

in·fal·li·ble \(ˈ)in-ˈfal-ə-bəl\ *adj* [ML *infallibilis,* fr. L *in-* + LL *fallibilis* fallible] **1** : incapable of error : UNERRING ⟨an ~ memory⟩ **2** : not liable to mislead, deceive, or disappoint : CERTAIN ⟨an ~ remedy⟩ **3** : incapable of error in defining doctrines touching faith or morals — **in·fal·li·bil·i·ty** \(ˌ)in-ˌfal-ə-ˈbil-ət-ē\ *n* — **in·fal·li·bly** \(ˈ)in-ˈfal-ə-blē\ *adv*

in·fa·mous \ˈin-fə-məs\ *adj* [ME, fr. L *infamis,* fr. *in-* + *fama* fame] **1** : having a reputation of the worst kind **2** : causing or bringing infamy : DISGRACEFUL **3** : convicted of an offense bringing infamy ***syn*** see VICIOUS ***ant*** illustrious — **in·fa·mous·ly** *adv*

in·fa·my \-mē\ *n, pl* **-mies** **1** : evil reputation brought about by something grossly criminal, shocking, or brutal **2 a** : an extreme and publicly known criminal or evil act **b** : the state of being infamous ***syn*** see DISGRACE

in·fan·cy \ˈin-fən-sē\ *n, pl* **-cies** **1** : early childhood **2** : a beginning or early period of existence **3** : the legal status of an infant

¹in·fant \ˈin-fənt\ *n* [ME *enfaunt,* fr. MF *enfant,* fr. L *infant-, infans,* fr. *infant-, infans,* incapable of speech, young, fr. *in-* + *fant-, fans,* prp. of *fari* to speak — more at BAN] **1** : a child in the first period of life **2** : a person who is not of full age : MINOR

²infant *adj* **1** : of, relating to, or being in infancy **2** : being in an early stage of development **3** : intended for young children

in·fan·ta \in-ˈfant-ə, -ˈfänt-\ *n* [Sp & Pg, fem. of *infante*] : a daughter of a Spanish or Portuguese monarch

in·fan·te \in-ˈfant-ē, -ˈfän-(ˌ)tā\ *n* [Sp & Pg, lit., infant, fr. L *infant-, infans*] : a younger son of a Spanish or Portuguese monarch

in·fan·ti·cide \in-ˈfant-ə-ˌsīd\ *n* [LL *infanticidium,* fr. L *infant-, infans* + *-i-* + *-cidium* -cide] **1** : the killing of an infant **2** : one who kills an infant

in·fan·tile \ˈin-fən-ˌtīl, -tᵊl, -ˌtēl, -(ˌ)til\ *adj* **1** : of or relating to infants or infancy **2** : suitable to or characteristic of an infant; *esp* : very immature ⟨the immature parents . . . who have so many ~ traits themselves —H. B. Peck⟩ **3** *of topography* : being in a very early stage of development following an uplift or equivalent change — **in·fan·til·i·ty** \ˌin-fən-ˈtil-ət-ē\ *n*

infantile paralysis *n* : POLIOMYELITIS

in·fan·til·ism \ˈin-fən-ˌtīl-ˌiz-əm, -tə-ˌliz-; in-ˈfan-tᵊl-ˌiz-\ *n* **1** : retention of childish physical, mental, or emotional qualities in adult life; *esp* : failure to attain sexual maturity **2** : an act or expression that indicates lack of maturity

in·fan·tine \ˈin-fən-ˌtīn, -ˌtēn\ *adj* : INFANTILE, CHILDISH

in·fan·try \ˈin-fən-trē\ *n, pl* **-tries** [MF & OIt; MF *infanterie,* fr. OIt *infanteria,* fr. *infante* boy, foot soldier, fr. L *infant-, infans*] **1 a** : soldiers trained, armed, and equipped to fight on foot **b** : a branch of an army composed of these soldiers **2** : an infantry regiment

in·fan·try·man \-trē-mən\ *n* : an infantry soldier

infant school *n, Brit* : KINDERGARTEN

in·farct \ˈin-ˌfärkt, in-ˈ\ *n* [L *infarctus,* pp. of *infarcire* to stuff, fr. *in-* + *farcire* to stuff — more at FARCE] : an area of necrosis in a tissue or organ resulting from obstruction of the local circulation by a thrombus or embolus — **in·farct·ed** \in-ˈfärk-təd\ *adj* — **in·farc·tion** \in-ˈfärk-shən\ *n*

in·fare \ˈin-ˌfa(ə)r, -ˌfe(ə)r\ *n* [ME *infer,* fr. OE *infær* entrance, fr. *in* + *fær* way, fr. *faran* to go — more at FARE] *chiefly dial* : a reception for a newly married couple

¹in·fat·u·ate \in-ˈfach-ə-wət\ *adj* : being in an infatuated state or condition

²in·fat·u·ate \-ˌwāt\ *vt* **-at·ed; -at·ing** [L *infatuatus,* pp. of *infatuare,* fr. *in-* + *fatuus* fatuous] **1** : to affect with folly **2** : to inspire with a foolish or extravagant love or admiration — **in·fat·u·at·ed** *adj* — **in·fat·u·a·tion** \-ˌfach-ə-ˈwā-shən\ *n*

in·fau·na \ˈin-ˌfón-ə, -ˌfän-\ *n* [NL, fr. ²*in-* + *fauna*] : benthic fauna living on the substrate and esp. in a soft sea bottom — compare EPIFAUNA — **in·fau·nal** \-ˌfón-ᵊl, -ˌfän-\ *adj*

in·fea·si·ble \(ˈ)in-ˈfē-zə-bəl\ *adj* : not feasible : IMPRACTICABLE

in·fect \in-ˈfekt\ *vt* [ME *infecten,* fr. L *infectus,* pp. of *inficere,* fr. *in-* + *facere* to make, do — more at DO] **1** : to contaminate with a disease-producing substance or agent (as bacteria) **2 a** : to communicate a pathogen or a disease to **b** *of a pathogenic organism* : to invade (an individual or organ) usu. by penetration **3 a** : CONTAMINATE, CORRUPT ⟨manages to ~ her with a sense of guilt⟩ **b** : to work upon or seize upon so as to induce sympathy, belief, or support ⟨the teacher *~ed* his pupils with his enthusiasm⟩ — **in·fec·tor** \-ˈfek-tər\ *n*

in·fec·tion \in-ˈfek-shən\ *n* **1** : the act or result of affecting injuriously **2** : an act or process of infecting; *also* : the establishment of a pathogen in its host after invasion **3** : the state produced by the establishment of an infective agent in or on a suitable host; *also* : a contagious or infectious disease **4** : an infective agent or material contaminated with an infective agent **5** : the communication of emotions or qualities through example or contact

in·fec·tious \-shəs\ *adj* **1 a** : capable of causing infection **b** : communicable by infection — compare CONTAGIOUS **2** : that corrupts or contaminates **3** : capable of being easily diffused or spread : readily communicated ⟨~ excitement⟩ — **in·fec·tious·ly** *adv* — **in·fec·tious·ness** *n*

infectious hepatitis *n* : an acute virus inflammation of the liver characterized by jaundice, fever, nausea, vomiting, and abdominal discomfort

infectious mononucleosis *n* : an acute infectious disease characterized by fever, swelling of lymph glands, and lymphocytosis

in·fec·tive \in-ˈfek-tiv\ *adj* **1** : producing or capable of producing infection **2** : affecting others : INFECTIOUS — **in·fec·tiv·i·ty** \(ˌ)in-ˌfek-ˈtiv-ət-ē\ *n*

in·fe·lic·i·tous \ˌin-fi-ˈlis-ət-əs\ *adj* : not appropriate in application or expression ⟨essays written in an ~ style⟩ — **in·fe·lic·i·tous·ly** *adv*

in·fe·lic·i·ty \-ət-ē\ *n, pl* **-ties** [ME *infelicite,* fr. L *infelicitas,* fr. *infelic-, infelix* unhappy, fr. *in-* + *felic-, felix* fruitful — more at FEMININE] **1** : the quality or state of being infelicitous **2** : something that is infelicitous

in·fer \in-ˈfər\ *vb* **in·ferred; in·fer·ring** [MF or L; MF *inferer,* fr. L *inferre,* lit., to carry or bring into, fr. *in-* + *ferre* to carry — more at BEAR] *vt* **1** : to derive as a conclusion from facts or premises ⟨we see smoke and ~ fire —L. A. White⟩ — compare IMPLY **2** : GUESS, SURMISE ⟨your letter . . . allows me to ~ that you are as well as ever —O. W. Holmes †1935⟩ **3 a** : to involve as a normal outcome of thought **b** : to point out : INDICATE ⟨this doth ~ the zeal I had to see him —Shak.⟩ **4** : SUGGEST, HINT ⟨another survey . . . *~s* that two-thirds of all present computer installations are not paying for themselves —H. R. Chellman⟩ ~ *vi* : to draw inferences ⟨men . . . have observed, *inferred,* and reasoned . . . to all kinds of results —John Dewey⟩ — **in·fer·able** *or* **in·fer·ri·ble** \in-ˈfər-ə-bəl\ *adj* — **in·fer·rer** \-ˈfər-ər\ *n*

syn INFER, DEDUCE, CONCLUDE, JUDGE, GATHER *shared meaning element* : to arrive at a mental conclusion

in·fer·ence \ˈin-f(ə-)rən(t)s, -fərn(t)s\ *n* **1** : the act or process of inferring: as **a** : the act of passing from one proposition, statement, or judgment considered as true to another whose truth is believed to follow from that of the former **b** : the act of passing from statistical sample data to generalizations (as of the value of population parameters) usu. with calculated degrees of certainty **2** : something that is inferred; *esp* : a proposition arrived at by inference **3** : the premises and conclusion of a process of inferring

in·fer·en·tial \ˌin-fə-ˈren-chəl\ *adj* [ML *inferentia,* fr. L *inferent-, inferens,* prp. of *inferre*] **1** : relating to, involving, or resembling inference **2** : deduced or deducible by inference — **in·fer·en·tial·ly** \-ˈrench-(ə-)lē\ *adv*

in·fe·ri·or \in-ˈfir-ē-ər\ *adj* [ME, fr. L, compar. of *inferus* — more at UNDER] **1** : situated lower down : LOWER **2** : of low or lower degree or rank **3** : of little or less importance, value, or merit ⟨always felt ~ to his older brother⟩ **4 a** : situated below another and esp. another similar superior part of an upright body **b** : situ-

ə abut	ᵊ kitten	ər further	a back	ā bake	ä cot, cart
aü out	ch chin	e less	ē easy	g gift	i trip	ī life
j joke	ŋ sing	ō flow	ȯ flaw	ȯi coin	th thin	t͟h this
ü loot	u̇ foot	y yet	yü few	yu̇ furious	zh vision

SOURCE: From *Webster's New Collegiate Dictionary* © 1981 by G. & C. Merriam Co., Publishers of the Merriam-Webster Dictionaries.

2. *Codes*. Which codes are used to indicate the parts of speech of the words found on dictionary page 585. Give the codes, their meaning, and a sample word for each.

Code	Meaning	Sample Word
_____	_____	_____
_____	_____	_____
_____	_____	_____

3. *Etymology*. Identify the etymology, or origins, of the following words.

Word	Country of Origin	Original Word
infantry	_____	_____
infer	_____	_____
infamy	_____	_____
infante	_____	_____

4. *Pronunciation Key*. Give three words that contain the sound demonstrated by the following Key words found at the bottom of dictionary page 585. Circle the portion of the word which is like the Key sound.

Key Word	Sample	Sample	Sample
abut	_____	_____	_____
easy	_____	_____	_____
life	_____	_____	_____

5. *Word Meanings*. After studying the meaning of the italicized words in the following sentences, look at the words' meanings on dictionary page 585. Which meaning of the italicized word has been used? Place the number of the meaning in the blank before each of the following sentences.

_____ a. The young lady was *infatuated* with the musclebound youth.

_____ b. The *infamy* of Benedict Arnold will never be forgotten by Americans interested in the history of their country.

_____ c. The *infantry* was crucial to the winning of the battle.

_____ d. The working girl felt *inferior* to the socialite who walked into the room.

_____ e. Her jubilance will soon *infect* those who are celebrating with her.

6. *Derivatives*.

a. What is the most frequently used prefix on dictionary page 585?_____

b. List five derivatives for the word *infer*._____

Answer Key:
Unit 3

Exercise 3.1, p. 120

1. encode **2.** bemoan **3.** reflect **4.** recoil **5.** infringe
6. proponent **7.** remand **8.** admonish **9.** becloud **10.** adjacent
11. encompass **12.** enclosure **13.** propensity **14.** incorporate
15. procession **16.** inundate **17.** beleagured **18.** incision
19. prolongate **20.** adhere

Exercise 3.2, p. 121

1. recoiled **2.** becloud **3.** proponent **4.** inundate **5.** adhere
6. incision **7.** adjacent **8.** prolongate **9.** beleagured **10.** encode
11. admonish **12.** reflect **13.** enclosure **14.** incorporate
15. procession **16.** encompass **17.** bemoan **18.** infringe
19. propensity **20.** remand.

Exercise 3.3, p. 122

1. compassionate feeling or showing sorrow for the troubles of another
2. subterraneous underneath the earth
3. unsavory not pleasing to the taste or smell
4. absolution freeing from question or guilt
5. discontinued to stop doing
6. compress to bring together
7. discomfort uneasiness
8. submerge to place under
9. indisposed not willing or inclined
10. unfortunately not lucky, unfavorable
11. disinterested not interested, impartial
12. compose to put together
13. subsoil layer of earth below the surface soil
14. incontinent without self-restraint
15. unbelievable not credible
16. submarginal below standards
17. disavow not claim
18. inactivate not active

Exercise 3.4, p. 123

1. insubordination **2.** compassion **3.** discontinuance **4.** unbeliever
5. compressor **6.** submergence **7.** indisposition **8.** disinterest
9. disavowal **10.** inactivation

1. compressor   **2.** compassion   **3.** disinterest   **4.** discontinuance
5. unbeliever   **6.** submergence   **7.** insubordination   **8.** disavowal
9. inactivation   **10.** indisposition

Exercise 3.5, p.123

1. d   **2.** e   **3.** a   **4.** b   **5.** c   **6.** g   **7.** h   **8.** f
9. i   **10.** j

Exercise 3.6, p. 124

Answers will vary.

Exercise 3.7, p. 125

1. c   **2.** e   **3.** a   **4.** b   **5.** d   **6.** f   **7.** h   **8.** j   **9.** g
10. i

Exercise 3.8, p. 125

1. SCRIBE PRESCRIBE TRANSCRIBE SUBSCRIBE ASCRIBE   **2.** PAR PREPARE PREPARATION COMPARE COMPARISON   **3.** PORT PORTABLE TRANSPOR-TATION PORTAGE IMPORT   **4.** DICT DICTIONARY DICTUM DICTATION DICTATOR   **5.** AUD AUDITION AUDITORY INAUDIBLE AUDITORIUM **6.** CORP CORPSE INCORPORATE CORPULENT CORPUS   **7.** JECT REJECT EJECT PROJECTILE ABJECT   **8.** TRACT DETRACT TRACTABLE TRACTOR CONTRACT   **9.** RUPT ABRUPT DISRUPT INTERRUPT RUPTURE **10.** FRACT REFRACT FRACTURE FRACTION FRACTIOUS

Exercise 3.9, p. 126

1. prepared	preparing	preparation	preparatory
2. scorned	scorning	scornful	scornfully
3. predicting	predicted	prediction	predictable
4. comfortable	comforting	comforted	comforter
5. prosecuting	prosecuted	prosecutor	prosecution
6. projected	projecting	projection	projectile
7. abstained	abstaining	abstention	abstinence
8. emitted	emits	emission	emitting
9. formation	formal	formality	formulation
10. granted	granting	grantor	grantee
11. transgressed	transgressing	transgression	
12. reverted	reverting	reversion	
13. sedated	sedating	sedation	
14. recurred	recurring	recurrence	
15. hurried	hurrying	hurriedly	

Exercise 3.10, p. 127

1. beautiful	beautifully
2. peaceful	peacefully
3. athletic	athletically
4. unbelievable	unbelievably
5. substantial	substantially
6. preferable	preferably
7. intermittent	intermittently
8. ignominious	ignominiously

9. financial   financially
10. compulsive   compulsively
11. predictable   predictably
12. expressive   expressively
13. definitive   definitively
14. dejected   dejectedly
15. formal   formally

Exercise 3.11, p. 127

1. a. S   **b.** S   **c.** O   **d.** S
2. a. O   **b.** O   **c.** S   **d.** S
3. a. S   **b.** S   **c.** O   **d.** O
4. a. S   **b.** O   **c.** O   **d.** S
5. a. S   **b.** O   **c.** S   **d.** O
6. a. O   **b.** S   **c.** S   **d.** S
7. a. S   **b.** S   **c.** S   **d.** O
8. a. S   **b.** S   **c.** O   **d.** S
9. a. S   **b.** O   **c.** S   **d.** S
10. a. S   **b.** S   **c.** O   **d.** O

Exercise 3.12, p. 128

1. b   **2.** d   **3.** a   **4.** c   **5.** b   **6.** d   **7.** c   **8.** a
9. b   **10.** c

Exercise 3.13, p. 129

1. attraction   relationship
2. joyful   vivacious, animated
3. tumultuous   uproar
4. repentance   lamentation
5. deceitful   fraudulent
6. morose   moody, sullen
7. unsurpassed   distinguished
8. delusion   misconception
9. hideous, ugly   ghastly, fearful
10. disgrace   dishonor
11. stiffness   tenaciousness
12. undeveloped   infantile
13. graceful   flexible, supple
14. accommodating   conforming
15. compelled   coerced, forced
16. evict   remove
17. peak   cliff, drop, bluff
18. contemptible   reproval
19. optimistic   enthusiastic
20. pen name   appellation, diminutive

Exercise 3.14, p. 130

1. repulsion   **2.** sedate   **3.** scintillating   **4.** exaltation   **5.** inept
6. inflexible   **7.** optional   **8.** flawless   **9.** pessimistic   **10.** surname
11. dour   **12.** rejoice   **13.** indubitable   **14.** peon   **15.** incontrovertible

Exercise 3.15, p. 131

1. expose   **2.** sombrero   **3.** dogmatic   **4.** vehemence   **5.** brazen

6. despair   **7.** energize   **8.** axiomatic   **9.** constrained   **10.** dubious
11. submissive   **12.** future   **13.** unfavorable   **14.** demureness
15. intermittent   **16.** sober

Exercise 3.16, p. 131

1. c   **2.** e   **3.** a   **4.** b   **5.** d   **6.** h   **7.** i   **8.** j   **9.** g
10. f   **11.** m   **12.** k   **13.** l   **14.** n

Exercise 3.17, p. 132

1. automaton   **2.** recipient   **3.** penchant   **4.** pacifist   **5.** subterfuge
6. skeptic   **7.** benevolence   **8.** belligerent   **9.** lassitude   **10.** despondent
11. resilient   **12.** figurehead

Exercise 3.18, p. 132

1. discretion, caution	carefulness
2. kindness, tenderness	love
3. symbolic	ornamentation
4. robot	slave
5. doubter	unbeliever
6. warlike	quarrelsome
7. downcast, discouraged	depressed
8. peacemaker	conciliator
9. enemy	opponent
10. receiver	heir, beneficiary
11. lethargy	weariness
12. inclination	flair
13. elastic	resistant
14. ruse	pretext

Exercise 3.19, p. 133

1. most outstanding in worth   **2.** heavenly   **3.** highest points   **4.** perfect, complete   **5.** superiority, greatness   **6.** almost vertical   **7.** leap for joy, elated   **8.** highest point, peak   **9.** highest point, zenith, peak   **10.** upward slope of ground

Exercise 3.20, p. 134

1. undistinguished, lowly   **2.** earthy, mundane   **3.** anticlimactic, less important, last of a series   **4.** imperfect, flawed   **5.** low status, lack of rank, disrepute   **6.** deliberate, cautious, studied   **7.** humiliate, embarrass   **8.** nadir, lowest point   **9.** base, foundation, bottom   **10.** declivity, descent, downward slope

Exercise 3.21, p. 134

Possible answers are:

1. He went of his own accord.   **2.** The elderly man was told to act his age.   **3.** The pacifists were up in arms about the latest sale of nuclear weapons.   **4.** The obese gentleman availed himself of the bounteous table set by his hostess.   **5.** The increase in property taxes has the farmer's back to the wall.   **6.** The executive who was on the beam received a generous increase in salary.   **7.** The thief thought he was in the clear and returned to the scene of his crime.   **8.** The outlandish tale was spread just to throw dust in the eyes of those who had formerly trusted the politician.   **9.** The coward always ran in the face of danger.   **10.** The gardener was in harness at daybreak.   **11.** The desperate young man was walking on thin ice when he turned to a loan-shark for money. **12.** Her indecisiveness will go ill with her chances to become an administrator. **13.** The woman has more irons in the fire than she knows what to do with. **14.** The FBI agent told the counterfeiter that the jig was up. **15.** The abandoned woman was as mad as a hatter.

Exercise 3.22, p. 135

1. inequitable   innocence   inflect

2.

code	*meaning*	*Sample Word*
adj.	adjective	inexhaustible, inexorable or other words so labeled
n	noun	inexperience, infamy or other words so labeled
vt	verb	infatuate, infect or other words so labeled

3.

Word	*Country of Origin*	*Original Word*
infantry	France	*infante*—boy, foot soldier
infer	France	*inferre*—to carry, bear
infamy	England	*in + fama*—fame
infante	Spain	*infant, infans*—infant

4.

Key Word	*Sample*	*Sample*	*Sample*
abut	infanticide	infantile	inexplicable or other word in which the sound is heard
easy	infamy	infelicity	inferior
life	infanticide	Inez	infantile

5. a. 2   **6. a.** in
   b. 3   **b.** inferred, inferring, inferable, inferably, inferer
   c. 1
   d. 2
   e. 4

UNIT 4

Pleasure Reading: Building High-Powered Speed

As you have already learned in Units 1 and 3, the speeds you use for pleasure and study reading differ greatly. Now that you have been introduced to the techniques of previewing and phrase reading and have learned some useful tips for strengthening your vocabulary, you have probably improved your reading rate for both pleasure and studying. However, because the complexities of these two different kinds of reading require varying degrees of concentration, you should practice developing high-powered speed on one kind of reading at a time.

Pleasure reading is, of course, less complex than study reading and demands less concentration. The material is easy. Understanding what you read is still very important, but you do not want to remember every word—only those that develop the topic.

In this unit eight selections are provided for practicing high-powered speed. As you read through them, use the techniques of previewing and phrase reading. (You will learn about other ways to increase your speed—skimming and scanning—in Unit 6.) Force your eyes to gather in as many words as possible in a glance. Concentrate on attaining faster and faster speeds without sacrificing your understanding of the material. Comprehension will improve as your eyes become adjusted to the new demands on them.

Go through the brief directions that follow. Do not try to read all the selections in one sitting. Space your practice. Build your speed. But remember, read only as fast as you can comprehend.

Directions: For each of the selections in this unit, follow these steps:

1. Preview to determine what you want to learn from the reading.
2. Record beginning time.
3. Read the selection. Force your eyes to take in longer phrases.
4. Record ending time.
5. Check your comprehension by answering the questions at the end.
6. Using the Answer Key on p. 180, determine your percentage of accuracy.
    Refer to p. 5 in Unit 1 if you have forgotten how to compute this.

7. Compute your speed of reading in words per minute (WPM). Refer to page 4 in Unit 1 if needed.
8. Plot your speed and comprehension accuracy scores on the Reading Progress Chart for Unit 4 on p. 181.

Beginning Time:

_____

Total Words: 1681

Selection 1: Only One Came Back _____

It was a glowering evening—March 21, 1973—when the 20,787-ton Norwegian freighter Norse Variant eased out of the harbor at Norfolk, Va., bound for Glasgow, Scotland, with a cargo of coal. From the bridge, Capt. Hens-Otto Harsem could barely tell where the wind-streaked sea ended and the sullen sky began. Yet captain and crew had a good feeling about their ship, despite the weather. Storms had been routine that winter, but the freighter had always shrugged off the North Atlantic's worst moods.

Below decks, as the Norse Variant plowed ahead, 23-year-old ship's mechanic Stein Gabrielsen began stowing the food and drink that he had purchased for a birthday celebration. A shipmate would be 25 the next day, and Stein planned to surprise him.

Thursday, March 22, dawned cold and raw. The wind shrieked out of the north, and huge seas bore down on the freighter, exploding heavily against her bows. Inside, the 29-man crew had to brace against bulkheads to keep from being tossed about like dice in a cup. Stein realized the celebration must wait; the going was simply too rough.

Around 10 a.m., Norse Variant ran headlong into an enormous wave that thundered down on her bow and smashed the forward hatch. No. 1 Hold began to take on water as waves kept sweeping across the deck. Although pumps were handling the problem, Captain Harsem decided to return to Norfolk for repairs.

Another great wave struck about an hour later with such devastating force that the welds holding the forward crane to the deck zippered open, and the seas poured into Hold No. 2. Now, under almost continuous battering of wind and water, Norse Variant started to come apart. With leaks erupting, the ship grew increasingly nose-heavy. The radio officer began signaling the U.S. Coast Guard for assistance, giving Norse Variant's course and position.

The lifeboat alarm sounded at 1:45 p.m. Grabbing his life jacket, Stein rushed to the afterdeck where the crew was gathering. Norse Variant was now wallowing like a harpooned whale. Captain Harsem ordered: ''The life rafts! Throw them overboard and jump after them! The Coast Guard will pick you up.'' Almost as he spoke, two monstrous breakers crashed amidships, plunging the freighter under huge masses of water. In a matter of seconds, Norse Variant was gone.

Stein found himself fighting the suction of the sinking vessel as it dragged him downward toward the Atlantic floor. After what seemed like an eternity, the pull weakened. Lungs near bursting, Stein struggled to the surface, boosted by the buoyancy of his life jacket. Keep calm, he told himself, amazed at being alive. Save your strength. The men on the rafts will pick you up.

He hung limply in his life jacket, trying to catch his breath in the almost unbearably cold water as waves lifted, then dropped him. Each time he was swept

_____

SOURCE: Reprinted by permission of *Reader's Digest* (March, 1976), pp. 64–68.

up to a 50-foot crest, he scanned the sea around him for his shipmates. There must be others, he thought. Then he spotted a raft. There they are! He struggled toward it and heaved himself aboard. It was empty.

As Stein tried to pull his thoughts together, waves showered sickeningly over the pitching, tossing raft, threatening to wash him back into the sea. Hurricane-force winds were driving needles of sleet and spray into his face. Stein determined to cling to hope. The Coast Guard is out looking. It will be only a few hours.

The Coast Guard was looking. Norse Variant's distress signals had been picked up at 12:28 p.m., and the search was under way even before she sank. All through the rest of March 22, rescue planes criss-crossed the storm-swept sky, while Coast Guard cutters plowed the heavy seas. But no clue to Norse Variant's fate could be spotted. The Atlantic, it seemed, had swallowed the ship whole.

Meanwhile, clinging to the ropes inside the reeling raft, Stein was grateful that he had put on his windbreaker under the life jacket. Like a diver's wet suit, it gave some protection from the cold. He had just learned to parry the tossing effect of each wave by shifting his weight when, suddenly, a churning breaker drove him deep beneath the surface, chewed up the raft and spat it out in little pieces. Again Stein fought to the surface, and there bobbed helplessly in the mountains and valleys of the seething sea.

Once more now, he began scanning the horizon at each opportunity. Incredible! Over there, a few hundred yards away, a second empty raft was bucking! He fought his way into its path, hauled himself aboard, tied its lifeline securely to his left arm and settled back to wait. Hang on, he kept telling himself. It won't be long now.

Shortly before nightfall, Stein heard a welcome sound above the roaring of the wind. A plane! He grabbed a rocket flare from the raft's emergency compartment, and—with numbed fingers working in maddeningly slow motion—managed to release the safety and fire. As the drone of the plane grew steadily weaker, in desperation Stein fired another rocket—his last one. But the plane was gone. The young seaman was alone once more with the pitching raft and the roar of wind and sea.

Several hours later, a ship's searchlights appeared, sweeping wide arcs through the murk. Stein waved his arms, shouting vainly into the howling wind, "I'm over here! Can't you see me?" But the searchlights blinked off, and the ship churned past only a quarter-mile away.

At least they're looking, he consoled himself. There will be another chance. He settled down to parrying the seas and keeping himself awake.

Next morning—Friday, March 23—Stein was exhausted. His feet were blue and numb, and he knew he had to get the circulation going in his legs. Sliding into the water and holding tight to the side of the raft, he began slowly kicking until he felt a measure of warmth returning. Still worried about the condition of his legs, however, he tried to wrap them with the tattered remains of a canvas shelter. It was a mistake. A mighty wave capsized his craft again and hurled Stein beneath it, his feet imprisoned in the canvas.

Kicking and clawing frantically, he managed to free himself, only to find his life jacket so buoyant that it trapped him against the raft's floor like a bubble caught under ice. His air almost gone, he pushed up with all his strength and barely managed to squeeze out from beneath.

Late that afternoon, the storm dealt its cruelest blow. An immense breaker—a great, gray monster the size of a five-story building— thundered down on Stein. The turmoil of raging water tore away his life jacket, snapped the lifeline and sent the raft swirling out of reach. Once more he made a desperate swim—and barely got back aboard.

By dawn Saturday, Stein was almost ready to give in. It had been nearly two full days since he had last closed his eyes. How pleasant it would be to stretch out in the raft and drift off to sleep, he thought. No, Stein. If you doze, you are finished. Hang on just one more day.

Saturday, the storm at last began to taper off. But, as the hours dragged on, the ocean remained empty. Stein began to wonder: Could the search have been called off? His muscles ached; his eyes were swollen and nearly blinded by the driving spray. And now his throat was too raw to swallow any of the raft's emergency rations. He felt giddy from lack of sleep. His strength was ebbing fast.

That morning, the search was continuing full-scale. At Coast Guard headquarters in New York, a computer had calculated wind and current and mapped out the area most likely to contain survivors. Coast Guard and Air Force planes were to search a grid of 12,600 square miles that day, but engine trouble forced one plane back early. When the last aircraft returned to base, 2200 square miles had been left uncovered— precisely where Stein Gabrielsen was fighting his battle against the sea.

As daylight faded that Saturday, the temptation to sleep was overwhelming Stein: Even if you freeze to death, there are worse ways to die. The word brought him to his senses. Don't be a fool, he kept repeating. You are not going to die. Somehow, he managed to stay awake another night.

On Sunday morning, the seas were calmer. The exhausted seaman decided that it was finally safe to allow himself the luxury he had not dared yield to for almost three days. He closed his eyes and dozed off.

Minutes later, at 9 a.m., the roar of a jet plane jolted him awake. It streaked by, several thousand feet above, and disappeared. How could they miss again? he asked as he gazed with frustration at the empty horizon.

The men aboard Air Force HC-130 had been out for nearly three hours when—at 9:06 a.m., Sunday, March 25—co-pilot Lt. Ronald Balleu spotted something off to starboard. It passed out of sight behind them before he could tell what it was. On the return pass, it was clearer: an orange bubble shining like a tiny beacon on the empty sea. It was unmistakably a life raft.

"My God, there's someone in there!" screamed Balleu. The entire crew jammed into the cockpit as the pilot, Lt. Cmdr. Edward L. Weilbacher, brought the plane down for a closer look. They could not believe their eyes. Not only was there someone there, but he was very much alive, jumping up and down. Balleu dropped flares to assure the war-dancing figure that he had been seen, then radioed his base. Within minutes, the nearest vessel, an oil tanker half an hour away, had set course for the little raft.

Meanwhile, a plane from the 54th Aerospace Rescue and Recovery Squadron at Pease Air Force Base in New Hampshire arrived overhead. Two frogmen bailed out, carrying plastic-wrapped medical equipment, blankets and a radio transmitter. They splashed down a few dozen yards from the raft. Then, as they clambered aboard it, Stein, who a minute before had been dancing for joy, went limp as a rag. "He's okay," they radioed to the plane circling overhead. "It's unbelievable."

There was something Stein had to know. "Have you found any others?" His voice was so hoarse it was barely audible. "I'm sorry," one of the frogmen answered gently. Stein lay back and closed his eyes.

For nearly 70 hours Stein Gabrielsen—alone in a stormy sea without sleep, food or drink—had survived conditions that no man should have been able to survive. In an incredible feat of human endurance, he had struggled against screaming 75-mile-an-hour winds and 50-foot killer waves. He had endured freezing temperatures, snow, sleet and hail. Amazingly, there was no frostbite. He was dehydrated, and bruised, but that was all. After a few days' rest, he would be on his way home to his native Norway. For Stein Gabrielsen, the long ordeal was over.

Ending Time:

_____

WPM: _____

Comprehension Check: Only One Came Back

Directions: Circle the correct answer for each of the following statements.

1. The freighter Norse Variant

    a. had seen many a North Atlantic storm.
    b. was an icebreaker used in sailing Arctic waters.
    c. was a U.S. Coast Guard cutter.

2. Stein Gabrielsen

    a. was a cook aboard the Norse Variant.
    b. was a U.S. citizen.
    c. was one of the Norse Variant's mechanics.

3. When the Norse Variant broke during the North Atlantic storm,

    a. she sustained damage at successive periods then broke apart.
    b. she only became too water-logged to stay afloat.
    c. she splintered into thousands of bits in one instant.

4. Stein was able to withstand the weather and seas due to

    a. his luck in salvaging a portion of the broken ship.
    b. his care in dressing wisely in life-saving equipment.
    c. his early rescue by a Coast Guard cutter.

5. Stein's will to live during the first days of his ordeal

    a. developed from his intense desire to return home to his native land.
    b. was sustained by the hope of being picked up by some of his fellow crewmen.
    c. was the result of his intense desire to cheat the sea of yet another victim.

Comprehension Accuracy:

_____

Selection 2: Teaching Your Body to Work Better _____

Beginning Time:

_____

A few years ago there was a lot of talk about a technique called biofeedback. Companies sold "brain-wave" machines for electronic meditation, promising they would foster deep relaxation and creativity in their users, while many doctors

Total Words: 870

SOURCE: © 1978 by the McCall Publishing Company. Reprinted by permission, from the December, 1978, *McCall's*.

dismissed the treatment as a fad—and most people simply wondered what "bio-feedback" meant.

Now medical professionals agree that, although in many cases the method is still experimental—especially for controlling states of mind—it is a legitimate tool in the treatment of certain disorders. Biofeedback can help people suffering from such conditions as headaches, muscle pain, anxiety or hypertension who have found little relief from other therapies.

Biofeedback is a way of learning to control normally involuntary functions such as pulse rate, muscle tension and skin temperature. Patients who master the technique can stop pain, relax muscles and even reactivate impaired ones. This is done with the help of special machines attached to the patients that pick up internal information and feed it back to them via flashing lights, beeps or meter movements on a video screen. As patients try to relax muscles to ease lower back pain, for example, flashing lights immediately signal the results of their efforts.

Despite the sophisticated machinery, the key to biofeedback is not the device itself. "The machine is only one part of the training process; it's a springboard to helping patients learn self-regulation by showing them how well they are doing," explains psychologist Elmer Green, director of a biofeedback research program at the Menninger Foundation in Topeka, Kansas, and a pioneer in biofeedback training. The major part of the training is a series of deep-relaxation exercises, similar to those used in yoga or meditation. Patients practice these until eventually they don't need the machine.

One of the most effective uses of biofeedback is in the treatment of stress and its related symptoms, such as chronic tension and migraine headaches. Because people respond to stress differently, many don't even realize how tense they are until they see evidence on the machine. Once they recognize their stressful response, they can learn to relax the area of the body that is affected.

To control migraines, sufferers are taught to raise the temperature in their hands. Although the hand seems an unlikely connection to head pain, researchers think that the method may work because as blood flows to the hand to warm it, the blood vessels in the head shrink and pressure is reduced. To make their hands warm, patients do relaxation and breathing exercises, repeating such phrases as "my hands are getting warm, they feel heavy." Many also concentrate on an image—of themselves lying on a beach, for instance. Meanwhile, very sensitive thermometers taped around a finger monitor their efforts. (This approach is also used to relieve Raynaud's disease, a circulation condition that, until biofeedback, was difficult to treat, even with surgery.)

Biofeedback as an adjunct to regular physical therapy, has also helped the victims of such neural disorders as strokes, brain or spinal cord injury and cerebral palsy to rehabilitate muscles formerly considered lost. In these cases, patients watch a screen as they move unimpaired muscles. Then, still watching the screen, they try to duplicate the effort in the impaired muscles. Gradually, the brain learns to use a new message to carry out an old command.

Most patients can learn some degree of self-regulation after several hours with a biofeedback machine, but it usually takes months to achieve long-lasting results. Besides sessions with the machines several times a week, most therapists prescribe daily exercises to do at home, which may be accompanied by tape cassettes of recorded instructions or even small portable biofeedback machines.

"The most important part of biofeedback therapy is home exercise. Like tennis, the more one practices, the better he or she gets—until the motions become automatic," says Lorraine Rose, a biofeedback therapist at the Professional Associates of the Psychiatric Institute, a clinic in Washington, D.C. When that happens, regular exercises are no longer needed, the patients simply get periodic checkups.

Biofeedback practitioners say that the method's greatest potential lies in preventive medicine. Migraine sufferers, for example, learn to ward off headaches with relaxation exercises at the first sign of an impending attack, such as dizziness or nausea. In stress management programs, executives across the country are learning biofeedback to prevent tension. And at the University of Michigan, biofeedback is one of the techniques used in a special program to teach students to control anxiety over exams.

But practicing biofeedback methods to the point of self-regulation requires willpower, and that is why the technique does not work for everyone. "With proper training people have approximately an eighty-percent success rate in reducing or eliminating their ailments," says Dr. Green of the Menninger program. "But some patients are so used to thinking that there must be drugs or other cures for them that they can't believe they could control the disorder themselves." Too much motivation isn't good either: Practitioners warn patients not to try too hard, since the therapy requires complete calm and relaxation.

Although biofeedback becomes a do-it-yourself therapy, professionals emphasize that it must first be learned under a doctor's supervision. For one reason, it is generally used in conjunction with other treatment. . . . People who think they might be helped with biofeedback training are advised to find it through their own doctor, a nearby major medical hospital, since unreliable practitioners do exist. . . .

Ending Time:

_____

WPM: _____

Comprehension Check: Teaching Your Body. . . .

Directions: Complete each statement by writing in or circling the correct answer.

1. Although it is still experimental, the biofeedback technique has proven itself to be useful in certain cases where other therapies give no relief.

   True   False

2. The biofeedback technique has established its value as

   a. a preventive medicine.
   b. a cure for all illnesses.
   c. a psychological device.

3. The major use of the biofeedback machinery is _____

   _____

   _____

4. As biofeedback is primarily a "do-it-yourself" therapy, the services of a doctor are not needed.

   True   False

5. Biofeedback has revealed that migraine headaches can be controlled by raising the temperature of the hands.

Comprehension Accuracy:

_____

Beginning Time:

_____

Total Words: 2395

True   False

Selection 3: Fire Building ─────────────────────

Fire building is an essential skill in outdoor cooking. Prepare to master fire building before learning to cook. A basic need for a camp is a good fire not only for cooking but for warmth and for protection from animals at night. Improperly made or tended fires can become destructive. Take precautions in preparing fires and putting them out by following a few simple rules.

RULES TO FOLLOW

Be sure to follow the fire rules of the particular area you are visiting.

For building the fire, select a spot fifteen feet from trees, bushes, and fallen trees. Fires built over roots are dangerous because the fire can follow the roots back to the trees or bushes and cause larger fires. Never build the fire directly under branches or near dry grass or weeds. When possible, either use rocks to enclose the area where you plan to build the fire or dig a fire pit or trench and clear away flammable fuel within a ten-foot area around the fire.

Build the fire only large enough to satisfy your needs. Big fires are not required in cooking; too much heat makes it difficult to control the cooking temperature. Most cooking can be done best on hot coals rather than on direct flames.

Never leave a fire unattended, and always have a bucket of water and a shovel near the fire to extinguish it in case of emergency. Report any wild fire to the nearest forest or fire officer as soon as possible. Put out your fire and your matches—dead out.

Before leaving campsite, make sure the fuel is cool, the fire is completely out, the ashes are buried (if you are in a primitive area), and the fireplace area is back to its natural state.

WOODPILE

Upon your arrival at the campsite, your first and perhaps most important activity is building a goodsized woodpile. After you are in the process of cooking, it is inconvenient to stop and look for wood. Outdoor meals are more successful if an ample supply of wood is available during the cooking time.

PILING THE WOOD

Care in piling wood can protect it from moisture. Begin at least ten or fifteen feet from the fire circle. Place side by side horizontally two large poles, on which to place the wood so that it will be protected from ground dampness. Stack the wood into separate stacks: tinder, kindling, and fuel, placing the stack of fuel closest to the fire, since it is used most often. Large sticks can be driven into the ground to

SOURCE: From ROUGHING IT EASY, by Dian Thomas. Copyright 1974, by Brigham Young University Press, Provo, Utah. Reprinted by permission.

divide the stacks. Use a large piece of plastic or a poncho to cover the woodpile when it rains.

TYPES OF WOOD

The three basic types of wood to gather are tinder, kindling, and fuel.

TINDER. For material to start the fire, use anything that will burn which is smaller than your little finger. Some examples of tinder are dry grass, dry leaves, small twigs, dry pine needles from evergreen trees, fine shavings, and bark. A fuzz stick, carved from a small twig, will catch fire more rapidly than another twig. After a rain the best place to find dry wood is on the lower inside branches of little evergreen trees.

Good tinder can be prepared at home in egg cartons. Fill each egg cup with dry, red pine needles, pieces of paper, and any other dry materials that will burn quickly. Pour paraffin over the material. Then place a looped string in the wax to be used later as a wick. When it becomes difficult to start a fire because of wet wood or other reasons, cut one of the egg cups off and place the other tinder around it. After the carton is lighted, it will create a large flame which should burn for about ten minutes.

Cotton balls soaked in paraffin or bottle caps filled with paraffin and topped off with a string wick are also good fire-starting materials.

KINDLING. Kindling is wood which ranges in diameter from the size of the little finger to the size of the wrist. It is used to feed the fire until larger pieces of wood will burn.

FUEL. Pieces of wood the size of the wrist and larger are classed as fuel. This type of wood is used to sustain the fire.

BUILDING AN A-FRAME

Make a basic A-frame, or triangle, in the center of the fire-circle with three sticks approximately one inch in diameter and one-half foot long. One end of each stick should overlap another stick, and the other end should rest on the ground.

In the center of the A-frame make a teepee with tinder, starting with very fine materials and graduating to more coarse materials. Place some kindling around the teepee.

Over the A-frame lay the type of fire structure you desire. Light the tinder while it is still accessible, even if the fire structure is not entirely laid.

Lay the fire structure so that air can circulate between the materials. Without enough air the fire will not continue to burn. If necessary, fan the smoldering fire with a paper plate to aid the circulation of air.

TYPES OF FIRES

Fires are generally named from the manner in which the wood is stacked.

TEEPEE. A basic fire used to begin other fires is the teepee fire. Lay the A-frame and the tinder. Then set the kindling and fuel on end in the form of a teepee. The high flames of this fire are good for one-pot cooking and for the reflector oven.

LOG CABIN FIRE. To get a good bed of coals, build the log cabin fire by forming a basic A-frame and a teepee of tinder, then placing logs in the center as if you were building a miniature log cabin. Gradually lay the logs toward the center as you build the cabin. It will have the appearance of a pyramid, and coals will form quickly.

CRISSCROSS FIRE. For a large, deep bed of coals for Dutch oven cooking or roasting, prepare a crisscross fire. After forming a basic A-frame and a teepee of tinder and kindling, place the logs on the fire in layers, one layer crossing the other. Leave a little space between each log for air to circulate.

INDIAN OR STAR FIRE. This fire is sometimes called the lazy man's fire because, as the logs burn down, they are simply pushed farther into the flames. It is a useful fire for preparing one-pot meals. Use the basic A-frame and the teepee of tinder and kindling to begin the fire, then feed the long logs into the center as needed.

METHODS OF STARTING A FIRE

There are many ways to achieve actual combustion. Some of the more primitive methods need be used only in emergency.

MATCHES. The most common method of starting a fire is to use matches. They can be protected against moisture by dipping them into either paraffin wax or fingernail polish. After dipping them in wax, place them in the holes of a corrugated cardboard, then roll the cardboard. It should be transported in a water proof container.

FLASHLIGHT BATTERIES AND STEEL WOOL. A rather dramatic method of starting a fire is to conduct the electricity from two flashlight batteries through steel wool: Use 00 or a finer grade steelwool roll, cut or tear it into a ½-inch strip (which will lengthen out to a strip seven or eight inches long), and use two good flashlight batteries. . . . place one battery on top of the other making sure both are in an upright position. Take one end of the strip of steel wool and hold it against the bottom of the lower battery. Then take the other end of the wool and rub it across the top of the top battery. After the steel wool sparks, place it next to the tinder and blow on it to start the fire.

FLINT AND STEEL. A meat-cutter's steel, a steel knife blade, or a file struck against stone will cause sparks. The sparks will create a thin wisp of smoke if they come in contact with very dry tinder. When smoke appears, blow gently with short puffs of air until the tinder bursts into flame. Very fine tinder or charred cloth will facilitate ignition.

MAGNIFYING GLASS. A strong magnifying glass placed in the direct sunlight so that a fine point of light is focused into dry tinder will cause the tinder to smoke and eventually break into flame.

BOW DRILL. If constructed properly, a bow drill, consisting of a fireboard, a drill, a socket, and a bow, will create heat that can light tinder. A notch must be cut in the side of a fireboard through which a drill will pass and rest on a flat grooved surface below. A socket (lubricated with grease) to fit the hand will allow the drill, operated with the string of a bow, to rotate first one way and then another, until a fine, hot dust results. The dust will smoke when it becomes heated. Then it should be placed into the tinder and blown into flame.

EXTINGUISHING A FIRE

Knowing how to extinguish a fire properly is as important as, if not more important than, knowing how to start one. First, break up the fire with a stick and spread out the coals. Sprinkle water over the coals. Keep stirring the fire with the stick and drenching it with water until the coals are cool enough to touch. Take precautions not to pour large quantities of water on a hot fire because a sudden issue of steam might burn bystanders. A fire is not out until the coals are cool enough to touch.

If large logs have been burning, make sure all sparks are put out.

If no water is available, dig a hole or a trench and bury all hot materials, or stir dirt thoroughly through the hot material and cover it with dirt at least two inches deep.

HEAT WHEN OPEN FIRES ARE NOT PERMITTED

In many camping areas open fires are illegal because of fire hazard. Increasingly, picnickers are forced to use other methods of heat for cooking food out of doors.

TABLETS. Commercial tablets, available at camping goods stores, can be placed in a small stove and lighted. These tablets are about one inch in diameter and about ½-inch thick. They are very good for warming canned food and for cooking things that don't take long periods of time. They may be used either with the tin-can stove or with a small commercial stove made expressly for their use. If a stove is not available, place stones in close proximity around tablets to serve as a stand to hold small cooking pots and cans.

CANNED HEAT. Canned heat can be commercially purchased and used for cooking or warming food in cans. Special stoves made to use with canned heat may be purchased.

PARAFFIN. Make your own can of heat by rolling narrow strips of corrugated cardboard into a tuna-fish can with paraffin. . . .

NEWSPAPERS. Newspapers can be used in the tall-can stove for cooking meat. . . .

CHARCOAL BRIQUETS. Charcoal is one of the best kinds of fuel to use when open fires are not permitted or when it is against the law for wood to be gathered. Charcoal briquets are good for grilling meat, for cooking foil meals, for spit or stick cooking, and for the Dutch oven. Charcoal briquets should never be burned in a closed area. They give off carbon monoxide which can be deadly. Two rules to remember when you are using charcoal briquets are these: (1) never light the briquets with homemade lighting fluid or gasoline; it could explode. Also, the briquets tend to give food an offensive flavor. (2) Always allow forty to fifty minutes for the briquets to become hot.

A good way to shorten the preparation time of charcoal briquets and to insure an even heat is to use the chimney starter method. Using two or three sheets of newspaper, matches, and a number-ten tin can, follow these steps:

—Punch holes every two inches around the lower edge of the can with a punch-type can opener.
—Cut both ends out of the can.
—Set the can down so that the holes are next to the crumpled newspaper.
—Crumple two or three sheets of newspaper and place them in the bottom of the can.

—Place charcoal briquets on top of the crumpled newspaper.

—Lift the can and light the newspaper. Prop a bottom edge of the can on a rock to create a good draft. The briquets will be ready to use in thirty to forty minutes.

—If a greater draft is necessary, prop the can on small rocks and fan the flames with a paper plate.

—When the briquets are hot, lift the chimney off the coals and spread the coals out. They are ready to use.

The chimney starter is also useful for more rapid heating of briquets when lighter fluid is used. The can will insure an even heat for all the fuel.

Egg carton briquets: Another way of lighting the briquets is to use wax in a cardboard egg carton. Separate the lid from an egg carton and set the bottom of the carton inside the lid. A little wax is poured inside the lid first will make the cupped half adhere to it. Then pour approximately ¼ inch of melted paraffin into each egg cup and let the wax cool. When it is cool, set a charcoal briquet in each cup, then continue to stack briquets over the carton. Light the carton and wait for the briquets to heat.

Starting briquets over a campfire: Briquets can also be added to wood fires to provide a better and larger bed of coals. Pour the briquets into the hot fire and allow them to heat for twenty to thirty minutes. An effective way to start charcoal briquets over an open fire is to shape a screen into a bucket or bowl-shaped basket. Make a wire bale for lifting or carrying. Place the desired amount of charcoal briquets into the basket and set it over an open fire. If the fire is hot, particularly if there are good flames, the charcoal will start quickly, and it will heat evenly.

Commercial starters: Commercially prepared charcoal starters and jellies can be purchased. It is important that you put the right amount of the mixture on the briquets, close the container of the starter, and place out of the way of sparks or flames before lighting the briquets.

Electric starters: If electricity is available, it can be used to start the briquets. Place an electric coil in the fire bed and place the briquets over these.

Extinguishing briquets: Use your briquets over and over again until they are burned out. Put them out by using one of the following methods: (1) Place them in a can which can be covered with a lid or with foil. The cover cuts off the oxygen supply, and the briquets will cease to burn. (2) Place them in a can of water. The briquets must be allowed to dry before using them again.

Ending Time:

WPM: _____

Comprehension Check: Fire Building

Directions: Complete each question by writing in or circling the correct answer.

1. Since different areas observe varying fire rules, the camper should become aware of those where he plans to camp.

   True   False

2. The first thing the author recommends that the camper do, is _____

   _____

   _____.

3. Three types of wood that should be collected before cooking begins are:

   a. teepee, log cabin, and crisscross.
   b. canned heat, paraffin, and newspapers.
   c. tinder, kindling, and fuel.

4. Knowing how to extinguish a fire properly is as important as knowing how to start one.

   True   False

5. Name three alternative sources of heat when open fires are not permitted in a camping area.

   a. _____

   b. _____   Comprehension Accuracy:

   c. _____   _____

Selection 4: Nixon's Embarrassing Road Show _____

Beginning Time:

_____

Total Words: 1456

Even for Richard Nixon, it was an extraordinary and dubious venture. There was the ex-President, thoroughly disgraced in his own country, being treated in Peking as if he still occupied the Oval Office and Watergate meant nothing more than a fancy apartment building. With wife Pat at his side, Nixon waved from the door of his plane as in campaigns of old. He waded into excited crowds, shaking hands as if he were running for the Politburo. He discussed foreign affairs with Chinese leaders as if he were still Henry Kissinger's boss. The ex-President clearly relished the chance to play a role once again on the international stage. But in so doing, he profoundly embarrassed the U.S. and its policymakers at an extremely sensitive juncture in U.S.-Chinese relations.

The reaction back home ranged from annoyance to outrage. "If he wants to do this country a favor," Arizona Senator Barry Goldwater commented acidly, "he might stay over there." About the most gentle comment made in the wake of the trip came from an aide to President Ford. "You can't blame Nixon for hankering for some kind of resurrection," he said. Ford himself acknowledged that Richard Nixon's China trip was "probably harmful" to him in New Hampshire, and before the primary, most Administration spokesmen seemed to feel that Nixon's purpose was less to resurrect himself than to crucify Ford. Some even speculated that Nixon wanted to harm Ford in New Hampshire so that the ex-President could broker a deadlocked Republican convention this summer and tip the nomination to Texan John Connally, the lapsed Democrat. Whether that was true or not, it was clear that, whatever his ulterior motives, Nixon had allowed himself to be manipulated by Peking for the purposes of Chinese, and not U.S., foreign policy. Following by just 2½ months an unproductive trip to Peking by Ford and Secretary of State Kissinger, the Nixon visit had to be, as one Chinese diplomat put it, "a slap in the belly of Kissinger with a big wet fish."

There was an almost spectral air about the visit. Nixon arrived in Peking on a chill, foggy night aboard a white Chinese Boeing 707 that appeared on the airport tarmac like a phantom out of the mist. The former President and Mrs. Nixon walked down the red-carpeted ramp to be greeted by China's Acting Premier Hua Kuo-feng, Foreign Minister Chi'iao Kuan-hua and a group of 350 Chinese. There was no military guard to greet Nixon and his entourage of 20, including 15 Secret Service men (20 journalists were also along, among them *Time* Diplomatic Editor Jerrold Schecter, who was with Nixon on his previous trip to China). Nixon was whisked away in a black "Red Flag" limousine to the same government guest house in Peking where he stayed in 1972.

The trip came almost precisely four years after Nixon, then still President, had paid his first visit to inaugurate what both sides had hoped would be an era of U.S.-Chinese rapprochement. This year's trip also coincided with the 25th Communist Party Congress going on in "revisionist" Moscow. Clearly, the Chinese wanted to show their unhappiness over the slow pace of "normalization" under the Ford Administration and, more importantly, over Washington's support of the policy of détente with the Soviet Union. When Nixon was President, Mao & Co. evidently believed that he stood for a strong U.S. position against the Soviet Union. With Ford and Kissinger, however, the Chinese believe, rightly or wrongly that the U.S. has become dangerously "soft" on the Russians.

During his four days in Peking, Nixon met with Acting Premier Hua four times for a total of ten hours. He had an hour and 40 minute audience with Chairman Mao, finding him "alert, in good humor, and gracious."

In many respects, it was a vastly changed Nixon who toured China. His shoulders were more stooped, his gait slower. He favors the left leg, on which he was operated for phlebitis in 1974, and wears an anti-embolism stocking on it to keep fluids from accumulating. Nixon was accompanied by his own U.S. Navy medical corpsman who took his blood pressure at least twice a day, and a top doctor from Peking Hospital was also assigned to him during the visit.

The ex-President tired visibly toward the end of the trip; yet in Kweilin, a city famous for its landscapes of jagged hills and misty waterways, he was able to walk up some 300 yds. of steep stone steps to visit the Reed Flute Cave, apparently with no ill effects.

There were moments of the same old lame humor and banality. After touring an agricultural exhibit in Peking, the former President quipped: "We'll make an even trade. We'll send you technology if you send us the pretty girls who showed us around today."

PARTLY SANDBAGGED: In his more weighty public remarks, Nixon, inadvertently or not, did exactly what the Chinese would have wanted. At the opening banquet, hosted by Hua Kuo-feng, he seemed to paraphrase China's own foreign policy position by saying: "There are, of course, some who believe that the mere act of signing a statement of principles or a diplomatic conference will bring lasting peace. This is naive." Many believed that Nixon was alluding to the Ford Administration's signing of the Helsinki declaration with Moscow, an act strongly condemned by China. Nixon denied that interpretation. "My God," he said, through Aide Jack Brennan, "I've used that statement a dozen times before, and I used it in a general context. There is no such thing as instant peace. It could also apply to the United Nations Charter or the Shanghai communique or any international document." Nonetheless, coming in the midst of specifically anti-détente remarks by the Chinese, Nixon's statement lent itself to the interpretation that it was a slap at Ford's policy—and thus precisely fitted Peking's mood.

The next night the Nixons were invited to a soiree presented by the Performing Arts Troupe of China, at which Mao's wife, Chiang Ch'ing, served as host. When the troupe finished a song promising the liberation of Taiwan, Chiang Ch'ing jumped to her feet and applauded wildly. Nixon half rose and applauded perfunctorily in turn. When he was told later that a news account described him as having stood and applauded the song, Nixon angrily replied through an aide: "Like hell I did! It was just a gentleman-to-a-lady gesture. I stood up for a lady who was standing, not for the song." Nonetheless, though Nixon presumably did not want to endorse Peking's position on Taiwan, he had allowed himself to be at least partly sandbagged on a crucial issue. The inclusion of the Taiwan song was hardly an accident.

Nixon returned Peking's hospitality with a lavish dinner for his hosts in the Great Hall of the People. The Chinese, however, refused to allow him to pay for the ten-course banquet (including "eight-jewelled Pigeon" stuffed with lotus root and virgin mushrooms, cream-of-chestnut puree, and other delicacies).

In his toast during the banquet, Nixon proclaimed the importance of what he had started four years earlier. "We have not finished the bridge," he said. "There is much work to be done. But we are determined to complete it." Many would agree with that statement. Nonetheless, few last week thought that Nixon had helped U.S. interests in making it. There was widespread chagrin that the ex-President chose Peking as the place to get back into the headlines. The feeling, even among former conservative Nixon supporters, was that the ex-President had been guilty of a gross impropriety in going to China in the first place, and that he had compounded the offense by trying to usurp the foreign policy role reserved for the President and the Secretary of State.

NO SHAME. State Department officials were angered by some of Nixon's foreign policy pronouncements. Ohio's Democratic Congressman Wayne Hays claimed that Nixon had gone to China "to hurt President Ford in New Hampshire." Syndicated Columnist David Broder angrily foreswore a promise made to himself not to write another word about Richard Nixon. "There is nothing, absolutely nothing, he will not do in order to salvage for himself whatever scrap of significance he can find in the shambles of his life," wrote the normally even-tempered Broder. "Nothing shames him." The harshest attack came from Goldwater, who claimed that Nixon had violated the Logan Act.

Despite all the adverse comment, the Nixon trip cannot simply be ignored in Washington. The ex-President, after all, is the first American to discuss policy with China's newly named Acting Premier Hua. He also received the most detailed briefing yet given to anyone on the meaning of the political campaign now sweeping China. Thus the Administration, as Henry Kissinger said last week, will definitely debrief Nixon after his return to the U.S.

In the anxious days before New Hampshire went to the polls, Kissinger said much the same thing—and the White House quickly fired off a classified cable to him in Latin America reprimanding him. Now, as a State Department official put it, "We've got to figure out a way of exploiting this resource—namely Nixon—without embarrassing the President." The problem is that the President has already been acutely and needlessly embarrassed.

Ending Time:

_____

WPM: _____

Comprehension Check: Nixon's. . . .

Directions: Complete each of the following statements by writing in or circling the correct answer.

1. Nixon's visit to China drew a reaction termed by the author as ranging from "annoyance to outrage." Reaction to the visit was _____

   _____.

2. From the tone of this article, did the author personally approve of Nixon's visit to China? Which words did the author use to give this feeling?_____

   _____

   _____.

3. ". . . a slap in the belly of Kissinger with a big wet fish. . ." meant:
   a. that Ford's present dealings with the Chinese were unacceptable and Nixon was still considered the Chief U.S. Spokesman.
   b. that Henry Kissinger had been vacationing at Cape Cod when he was hit by a wet fish caught by one of his guests.
   c. that Nixon deliberately visited China as a political "slap in the face."

4. Which events took place during Nixon's trip that caused the author to call it a "road show"?_____

   _____

   _____.

5. The author also implied that
   a. President Ford's opponents on the Helsinki Declaration personally sent Nixon to China to embarrass Ford.
   b. Nixon's comments during the opening banquet were a direct slap at President Ford's policy on the Helsinki Declaration.
   c. the Helsinki Declaration was totally unacceptable to the United States.

Comprehension Accuracy:

_____

Beginning Time:

_____

Total Words: 1855

Selection 5: Mood Maybe _____

A U.S. radio monitor in a little frame house in Oregon caught the first hint. The Japanese were interested in peace, the Domei broadcast said, provided that the prerogatives of the Emperor would not be "prejudiced." Then came two days of diplomacy, a few hours of false armistice, more waiting through an interminable weekend. Finally, on Tuesday, August 14, 1945, reporters were summoned to the Oval Room of the White House. President Truman glanced at the clock to make sure he was holding to the agreement of simultaneous announcement in Washington, London, and Moscow. At exactly 7 p.m. he began reading: Late that

SOURCE: From the CRUCIAL DECADE, by Eric Goldman. Copyright © 1956 by Eric Goldman. Reprinted by permission of Alfred A. Knopf, Inc.

afternoon a message had been received from the Japanese Government which "I deem . . . full acceptance of . . . unconditional surrender."

Across America the traditional signs of victory flared and shrieked. In Los Angeles, yelling paraders commandeered trolley cars, played leapfrog in the middle of Hollywood Boulevard, hung Hirohito from scores of lampposts. Salt Lake City thousands snakedanced in a pouring rain and a St. Louis crowd, suddenly hushing its whistles and tossing aside the confetti, persuaded a minister to hold services at 2 a.m. New York City, hardly unaccustomed to furor, amazed itself. With the first flash of V-J, up went the windows and down came the torn telephone books, the hats, bottles, bolts of silk, books, wastebaskets, and shoes, more than five thousand tons of jubilant litter. Whole families made their way to Times Square until two million people were milling about, breaking into snatches of the conga, hugging and kissing anybody in sight, greeting each twinkle of V-J news on the Times electric sign with a cheer that roared from the East River to the Hudson. The hoopla swirled on into the dawn, died down, broke out again the next afternoon, finally subsided only with another midnight.

Americans had quite a celebration and yet, in a way the celebration never really rang true. People were so gay, so determinedly gay. The nation was a carnival but the festivities, as a reporter wrote from Chicago, "didn't seem like so much. It was such a peculiar peace . . . And everybody talked of 'the end of the war,' not of 'victory.' " The President himself spoke with a mixed tone. When the crowds around the White House chanted, "We want Harry," he appeared beaming with Bess on his arm and proclaimed this "a great day." His face quickly sobered as he added warnings of an "emergency" ahead—a crisis "as great . . . as Dec. 7, 1941." At V-J, 1945, the United States was entering the newest of its eras in a curious, unprecedented jumble of moods.

Peace had not come to the nation with the soothing coo of a dove. Instead it came in swift hammer blows of news, smashing old sure standbys. Four months before the Japanese surrender, cerebral hemorrhage struck down Franklin Roosevelt, a second father to millions of Americans during their worst depression and their worst war. Another three months and the British were sweeping out of office Winston Churchill, doughty symbol of steadiness to much of Western Civilization. Eleven days later, just before V-J, President Truman announced: "An American airplane (has) dropped one bomb on Hiroshima . . . It is an atomic bomb. It is a harnessing of the basic power of the universe."

Over all the victory celebrations, the fact of the atomic bomb hung like some eerie haze from another world. Americans tried to make jokes. The Japanese were suffering from atomic ache, people giggled to each other. Or when God made Atom, he sure created a handful for Eve. Americans were sententious. The bomb meant the end of civilization and atomic energy was certain to usher in a golden age of peace and plenty. Americans argued furiously. John Foster Dulles intimated that atomic bombs and "Christian statesmanship" were hardly compatible and scores of leaders answered hotly that a truly Christian nation ended wars as quickly as possible. Somehow neither the arguments nor the jokes nor the sententiousness meant much. People fumbled along, trying to comprehend the incomprehensible, to fit a sense of terrifying newness into their accustomed ways of thinking. And in almost every American mind, there was one corner that could respond to the words reported from a European prison cell. "A mighty accomplishment," the captured Nazi leader Hermann Goring said. "I don't want anything to do with it."

The sense of a scarifying future was accompanied by memories of the last postwar, jabbing, mocking memories. In the America of V-J, the story went around how Franklin Roosevelt had kept a picture of Woodrow Wilson hanging in the meeting room of the War Cabinet, frequently glancing toward it when he discussed the coming years, and everybody got the point of the tale. Woodrow Wilson also had led the United States to victory in a world war. Then came the hard times of 1920–1, less than a decade of prosperity, the brutal depression of the 1930's, and the furies of Word War II.

For one large section of the American people, memories were particularly disturbing. Cotton-pickers, professors, and secretaries, auto workers, writers, and the man who collected the garbage, they had given their minds and their hearts to the credo represented by Franklin Roosevelt. The cotton-pickers and the secretaries might speak of the "New Deal"; the professors and the writers were inclined to talk of "liberalism." Whatever the term, the groups joined in a zest for legislation in favor of lower-income groups, for questioning and nose-thumbing, for chopping away at the crust of social castes. Now that World War II was over, the liberals also shared an apprehension provoked by history. The least educated among them were acutely aware that the previous generation's "New Deal," the reformism of Theodore Roosevelt and Woodrow Wilson, had passed through World War I and come out Warren G. Harding.

Worriedly, yearningly, the liberal leaders were talking of sixty million jobs, the figure that Franklin Roosevelt had used in his vista of the postwar. Sixty million jobs, the argument ran, were a symbol of the full employment and social advances which could be; they were also a measuring-rod that would warn of oncoming disaster. And this time, a thousand New Deal commentators added, failure to solve America's domestic problems would mean something worse than hard times. As the end of Word War II neared, *Harper's Magazine*, certainly a restrained liberal journal, was running an article which argued that "the veterans are not going to accept unemployment with the bewildered docility which was characteristic of most of the jobless in the last depression . . . What action will result from that attitude . . .? Nobody knows, of course. But we have some hints, and they are hints which should make any American start worrying. One of them is the report of a historian who watched fascism rise in Italy and Germany after the last war."

In the eyes of many educated New Dealers, the national scene already included dangerously large areas of rightism. During the month of V-J, Bernard De Voto, a favorite of liberal readers, pointed to the dismissal of Homer Rainey from the presidency of the University of Texas. The situation was complex, De Voto wrote. But basically Rainey was dismissed because of his New Dealish opinions and his insistence on academic freedom for subordinates. The case resulted from a rapidly spreading doctrine of "Ruthless industry and finance," which equated both free inquiry and New Dealism with Communism.

This kind of argument, De Voto went on, "is a powerful sentiment, and one easily polarized by a rabble-rouser or an honest deluded man. The communists (so the argument runs) were responsible for the New Deal and they intend to inflict a labor dictatorship on us. . . . They want to destroy initiative and profit, business and freedom, the individual and the United States . . . Get rid of the communist professors—who are all homosexuals and New Dealers anyway—and everything will be all right once more. We will be back in the days before . . . the New Deal conspiracy was hatched, before labor unions had to be dealt with . . . before socialists and bureaucrats in Washington could tell us . . . what we had to do and whom we had to hire and how much we had to pay him, before the foundations of our society were undermined by atheism and bolshevism.''

De Voto was ready for a grim prediction. Free universities are "the central mechanism of democracy." Yet "as the waves of reaction gather strength in the years immediately ahead of the United States, this same attack will be made repeatedly, in many colleges, always by the same interests and forces, employing the same or equivalent means."

The anti-New Dealers, the people who more and more were coming to be called "conservatives," had their portentous reading too. Late in the war, the University of Chicago Press published *The Road to Serfdom*, by an Austrian-born economist, Friedrich A. von Hayek. The Press knew well the usual fate of scholarly treatises; it printed only two thousand copies. But Hayek had set his scholarship within a general proposition that caught perfectly the mood of much of American conservatism. Nazism, he contended, had not grown up in opposition to New Deal-type liberalism; such liberalism and Nazism came from the same roots. All Western Civilization had been relying increasingly on ideas of national economic planning, and the ideas, whether called liberalism, Nazism, socialism, or Communism, led inevitably to totalitarian serfdom. Hayek's volume was scarcely in the bookstores before the University of Chicago Press discovered that it had published not only a scholarly monograph but a manifesto for American conservatism. Hailed by anti-New Deal publications, purchased in quantity by a number of American corporations, *The Road to Serfdom* promptly made its way to the best-seller list and stayed on month after month into the V-J period. The severely intellectual Hayek, dumbfounded at the sales of the volume and half-protesting that he did not want to be a spokesman for any political group, found himself lecturing up and down the country to rapt anti-New Deal audiences.

The defeat of Winston Churchill by the British Labour Party shortly before V-J stoked the fears of American conservatives. Here was repudiation of a beloved national hero for a bluntly socialist regime; here was precisely the swing toward economic controls against which Hayek was warning. People in conservative commuter communities read the election headlines with "shock" to use the term of the *New Canaan* (Conn.) *Advertiser*. The Labour victory, *Business Week* added, brought worried reconsideration of the general strength of "New Deal" forces in and outside Britain. The most optimistic conservative survey could not fail to note one great fact. At V-J, the long-time trend toward controls over economic life had gone so far that no government in Western Civilization except Washington gave even lip service to free enterprise—and in the White House sat Franklin Roosevelt's chosen heir.

Some American conservatives were avid for an all-out effort to get rid of the New Deal and turn America back toward unregulated capitalism. Others acquiesced in what the New Deal had done but insisted upon drawing a stern line, beyond this not one step further. Both conservative groups often talked a formula that was decades old but now had a fresh significance and a new name, "welfare capitalism." Industry itself, the formula ran, should protect the welfare of its employees to such an extent that social legislation, and perhaps unions, would lose their appeal. Whatever the emphasis, conservatives joined with liberals in considering the postwar a battleground on which domestic issues of far ranging significance would be fought out, with results that could mean heaven or hell.

Comprehension Check: Mood Maybe

Directions: Place a T before each true statement. Place an F before each false statement.

_____ 1. This story began with the Japanese surrender, which ended World War II.

_____ 2. Americans almost celebrated too hard when the news of victory came, but something was different; it seemed as if everyone was going through the motions.

_____ 3. The atom bomb cast an eerie cloud over peace and the future.

_____ 4. The Liberalism and "New Deals" were pre-World War II hopes that were rudely dashed by a backlash of conservatism.

_____ 5. When Winston Churchill was replaced by the British Labor Party, American conservatives became more convinced than ever that the Liberal New Dealism was a threat.

Selection 6: One Woman's Liberation— From Fat, Fatigue and Apathy

I sit here now, thinking about what aerobics has done for me in terms of my figure (dress size down to size 8 from size 12), and my weight (down 10 to 12 pounds), my energy and sense of well-being, the luxury of eating what I please without worrying about calories and my freedom from tension and insomnia, and I feel rather smug.

But I also have to wonder how Ken must have felt 10 years ago when he was studying exercise physiology—knowing he intended to devote his life to this field, and knowing too that his wife couldn't care less about it. If he couldn't convince me of the health benefits and sheer pleasure that come from having a fit, conditioned body, how could he convince anyone else?

You may think you're indifferent to the subject of exercise, but you couldn't find anyone more tuned out than I was when Ken and I were married in 1959.

We're both natives of the Sooner State (we grew up 20 miles apart without crossing paths) and we also met in Oklahoma at the Fort Sill Army Base in Lawton. Ken had just finished his internship and was fulfilling his military obligation as a flight surgeon and I, fresh from the University of Oklahoma with a degree in sociology, had a job there as a recreation director with special services.

I come from a family that suffers from a disease common to 50,000,000 Americans: obesity. (Incredible as it seems, 25 percent of this country's popula-

SOURCE: From AEROBICS FOR WOMEN by Mildred Cooper and Kenneth H. Cooper, M.D. Copyright © 1972 by Mildred Cooper and Kenneth H. Cooper, M.D. Reprinted by permission of the publisher, M. Evans and Company, Inc., New York, N.Y. 10017.

tion is at least 15 pounds overweight.) My sister used to tip the scales at over 200 and my grandmother died weighing close to 300 pounds. I never had a weight problem while I was growing up because I was active—I played girl's basketball and in college I took the required physical education courses—but like many others my family certainly didn't encourage regular exercise as a way of life.

On the other hand Ken's family had always been exercise-conscious. His father is a dentist who instilled in him a deep appreciation of the value of preventive medicine, and his mother encouraged him in athletics. During his high school years he was Oklahoma state champion in the mile (time, 4:31) and when I met him at Fort Sill, running and jogging were as much a part of his daily routine as brushing his teeth. I viewed his concern with fitness as a mild eccentricity (but it certainly wasn't a deterrent when he proposed).

In those days before joggers had become a familiar sight, people who saw you running in a public area thought you were being chased or going to a fire. I was always being asked, ''Is your husband that nut who runs all the time?''

Truthfully, exercise to me was strictly for athletes and body-builders. I couldn't imagine anyone making a career of it. I used to wish Ken would go into pediatrics so I could say he was a baby doctor—everyone knows and respects that field.

Instead, he switched from the Army to the Air Force because of his interest in the aerospace program and eventually we were transferred to Boston so he could work on his master's in public health and doctorate in exercise physiology at Harvard.

If I nurtured any illusions about life in a big, conservative New England city influencing my husband against running in public, they were short-lived. I soon learned that I was up against the Boston Marathon. His determination to compete in this 26-mile foot race, staged every April for amateur runners, made him even more avid about his daily exercise. To train for it, he ran every day in every kind of weather, including -10 degree temperatures that actually froze his nostrils. Naturally, he'd wear his most beat-up old clothes, and most days he'd pass the same two newspaper boys doing their route. Once he heard one remark to the other, ''Hey, look, here it comes again.''

That pretty much expressed the way I felt when I'd see him. After running 10 miles, he'd ride his bicycle 8 miles to Harvard. I'd drive our car to work and turn my head when I passed him. I found the whole thing acutely embarrassing. (When the Boston Marathon was run, he placed 101 among 400 competitors.)

You might well wonder what earthshaking event converted me from such negativism about exercise. It was the swift and steady beating of my own heart.

After Ken finished his course work at Harvard we were stationed at Brooks Air Force Base in San Antonio, where he began to specialize in research relating to the particular exercise needs of the astronauts. I still wasn't exercising regularly, although I'd occasionally go bike riding with Ken. Our daughter Berkley was born and then I was totally housebound for the first time. I had that after-pregnancy dumpiness and dragginess. One night Ken and I were relaxing after dinner, watching television, and he said, ''Take my resting heart rate.''

So I checked his pulse—and got about 50 beats a minute. Then he counted mine and got 80 beats.

''Thirty beats' difference isn't so much,'' I said blithely.

''Oh, no? Think of it this way,'' said my cagey husband. ''While we're asleep tonight, your heart is going to beat ten thousand times more than mine will. Even though our hearts are pumping the same amount of blood, it takes your heart much more work and effort to do the job because you're not in condition. You're just going to wear out faster than I will.''

Do I need to elaborate on what went through my head, including visions of Ken, a widower, courting the woman who would become the second Mrs. Cooper—and Berkley's stepmother?

The combination of these dire thoughts with the fact that deep down inside I secretly admitted that Ken was right about the need for daily exercise and the benefits of it, finally persuaded me that I couldn't afford not to get into an aerobics conditioning program.

The next day I put Berkley in her stroller, hitched our dog on her leash and started pushing and pulling all of us over a mile-and-a-half course that Ken measured out for me around our neighborhood in San Antonio.

An exercise program has to be individual if it's to be successful. Fortunately, aerobics offers plenty of options: you can walk, jog, run, skip rope, climb stairs, swim, bicycle—do any number of activities or sports that stimulate your heart and lungs over a prolonged period of time. Several of the options weren't feasible for me because of Berkley or because they just didn't appeal. (I don't enjoy water sports. As a result, Ken and I have never shared one of his favorite recreations, water skiing, and I have an almost worshipful admiration for any woman who earns her aerobic points by swimming.)

I decided to make running ''my thing'' because it was handiest and I could take Berkley with me. At that time it was convenient for me to run in the late afternoon and that was when I seemed to need it most. I got through the day fine, but about four o'clock I'd find myself getting headachy, irritable and lethargic from being cooped up in the house.

The first few weeks were the very hardest because I was just starting and knew I couldn't expect results right away. It was like a diet, I'd think, ''I just can't do this.'' But somehow each day I'd manage to put on my track shoes and get me, my child and my dog on the road again. First I'd walk, and then I got to the point where on downhill sections I'd start jogging—it must have been quite a spectacle, me pushing Berkley in her stroller with her red hair standing up on end, and a fat blond cocker lumbering along behind.

On Sundays, Ken and I would run together. He'd put Berkley in the stroller and let me get to the top of the hill in front of our house and then they'd start out behind me. Little Berkley would yell ''Faster, faster, Daddy,'' and I'd hear them gaining on me even though I had a half-mile start. I felt insulted that they could catch me, so I started trying harder on my daily workouts during the week. In time, the effort paid off in far more than being able to outdistance my husband and daughter.

I became two sizes smaller. I've always been heavy through the hips and I took off 4″ in that area alone. My dress size went from 12 to 8.

I weighed less. You don't lose a lot of weight rapidly from exercising, but you do convert fat to lean muscle and you lose inches. This, combined with the fact that the exercise curbed my indulgent appetite, resulted in a weight loss of over 10 pounds. Of course, a reduced-calorie diet with exercise is marvelous; you burn up 100 percent fat. (If you fast without exercise, you burn about 50 percent fat and 50 percent muscle mass.)

My eating habits were automatically controlled. Although you may not lose weight on an exercise program by itself, you definitely won't gain. I love to eat, and what a pleasure to enjoy a dessert or between-meal snack and know I wasn't going to pay for it in pounds because I was burning them up!

At the same time, I found my desire for rich goodies was not as keen. When I came back from exercising, the thought of a piece of cream pie was nauseating, but sucking on a fresh orange was just great. Also, people who exercise regularly crave more fluids, and drinking a lot of fluids is a good way to control appetite.

I was less tense, more energetic and slept better. Exercise banished my end-of-the-day blahs. I built up a second wind and felt less tired in general. And I had no residual tension to keep me awake when I went to bed.

My resting heart rate decreased from 82 to 57 beats per minute. My entire heart/lungs/blood-vessel system became more efficient. This was evident not just from my lower heart rate; I actually breathed easier. Lungs are like balloons and most of us breathe out of the top half only. Getting air down into the lower half isn't easy at the beginning—it's like trying to inflate a new balloon for the first time. But after you're conditioned, you feel a real difference in the ease of air flow in and out.

My self-image was definitely enhanced. Even if you couldn't document everything that happens to a person physiologically as a result of aerobics, which you can, the psychological benefits are worth everything. I know I don't lose a pound or an inch every time I run, but I know how good I feel when I do something to improve myself and my figure. In one area of my life, at least, I have discipline. No matter what else happens during the day, I can say to myself, "Well, I got my exercise in."

I was aware of my husband's pride in me. Before I started exercising, I'd watch a woman come up to Ken and say, "Dr. Cooper, I'm running a mile in such-and-such a time." The admiration that would come into his eyes really made me jealous. Now I can hear the pride in his voice when he tells other people what I've accomplished in my aerobics program.

As I said before, exercise is individual, as individual as the make-up you choose for yourself. It's got to fit your needs, your desires, what you're best at—walking, swimming, cycling, whatever.

Once you get into it, you're hooked: the smaller dress sizes, the good feeling about your body, your husband's pride, even the way other people envy your self-discipline.

Eventually, when Berkley started nursery school, I switched my exercise program to mornings so I could do it while she was being taken care of. Even then, after some conditioning, I never dreamed I'd ever be able to run a mile nonstop. It wasn't even my goal. I'd start off jogging, then walk a while, then jog a while. And every day I'd jog to the same point before I got tired.

One day I was jogging along, planning what to have for dinner, and when I looked up I'd passed the point where I always stopped before—yet I was still running and I was not fatigued.

Now this is the aerobic training effect. One day it's just there. What you couldn't accomplish the day before suddenly becomes a snap.

So every day I set little goals for myself—getting beyond a certain house, and so on. And every day I inched my way to running a mile nonstop, and it was the greatest feeling in the world to know I could do it. It's a fact that most people—men included—can't run a mile. If you happen to mention that you can, people look at you and marvel. Being able to excel at something unusual does wonders for your self-esteem.

For example, one day I went out to the air force base where Ken was testing some young WAF's of 18 or 19. He was running them on a mile test and said, "Why don't you run with them?"

I was 32 or 33 then, at least 10 years older than those girls, and it was a challenge. I started running with them and after the first quarter-mile, scads of them began to poop out—in fact, my 16-year-old niece ran with us and she finished last. I came in second. Can you imagine what it felt like to know, at my age, I was in better shape than those dewy young recruits?

Shortly afterward, a man-woman running event was held at the base—the woman would run the first mile, then pass the baton on to the man and he'd run the next 2 miles. Ken and I won first place in our age category. Another triumph that meant more than merely winning!

Ending Time:

_____

WPM: _____

Comprehension Check: One Woman's Liberation. . . .

Directions: Place a T before each true statement. Place an F before each false statement.

_____ 1. Aerobics deals with the science of physical exercise of the body.

_____ 2. The author did not share her husband's interest in aerobics until several years later.

_____ 3. Because the husband's chosen field of work was not an established one, his author/wife was embarrassed and held his work in low esteem.

_____ 4. Unexpected benefits are derived from a good regular physical exercise program.

Comprehension Accuracy:

_____ 5. When designing a program of physical self-improvement, be sure to set small goals for yourself in order to help maintain your progress.

_____

Beginning Time:

_____

Total Words: 608

Selection 7: Namibia: A Wealth of Minerals Waiting to Be Tapped

Twice a week, a French DG-8 air cargo plane lifts off from an airstrip in Windhoek, South Africa. Its cargo 44-gal. drums of uranium oxide "yellowcake" bound for France. Each day, De Beers' Consolidated Diamond Mines in South-West Africa yield up roughly 6,000 carats, 98% of them gem quality. Uranium, diamonds, copper, cadmium, and other valuable minerals go far toward explaining the world's interest in South-West Africa, a harsh, sparsely populated, sunstruck land now in transition from South African control to independence as the new nation of Namibia.

Politics of that transition remain highly dubious. South Africa yielded to Western pressure in October and reluctantly agreed to hold U.N. supervised elections in Namibia next April. But Pretoria is pressing ahead with its own plans to hold elections for an interim government in early December. That could lead to the creation of a South African client state and the intensification of the decade-old guerrilla war being waged by the South-West Africa People's Organization (SWAPO).

Foreign reserves: Pretoria's willingness to court international wrath and possible economic sanctions demonstrates Namibia's vital role in South Africa's economic calculus. Although economic statistics have not been separately published for Namibia since 1970, South African economist Sue Collett estimates that the country contributed a net $460 million to Pretoria's foreign reserves in 1977—equivalent to half of South Africa's year-end total. Namibia's exports last year were $805 million, yielding a surplus of $173 million. Gross domestic product was $1.15 billion. South Africa has been administering the area since it was wrenched from German colonizers during World War I, and Namibia's foreign earnings have all gone into South Africa's own reserves. There is no escrow account to get the new country launched. "They have been pinching our earnings for years," complains John Kirkpatrick, Windhoek leader of the splinter Namibian National Front.

Those earnings could soon be phenomenal. Under the aegis of the six mining groups that dominate its economy (De Beers, Rio Tinto Zinc, General Mining, Newmont, AMAX, and Falconbridge), Namibia is well en route to becoming the world's seventh largest minerals exporter. Rio Tinto Zinc's $300 million Rossing mine has already set off a uranium based boom. Beginning next year, that mine and others will ship 5,000 short tons of uranium to Minatone—owned jointly by Pechiney Ugine Kuhlmann and Companie Francaise des Petroles, British Nuclear Fuels Ltd., and others. But SWAPO is committed to nationalizing the resource.

Consolidated Diamond Mines (which extracted more than $200 million worth of stones in 1977 from South-West Africa) would face more stringent government controls, too, and threats of nationalization, if SWAPO wins the U.N.'s April election. For one thing, the new country could gain millions in revenues by controlling diamond mine taxations, although it might lose many South African subsidized services.

That prospect is bound to be upsetting for De Beers, which drew fully 22% of its $733 million in 1977 profits from Namibian operations. Nor would Pretoria be pleased to sacrifice its 61.5% tax bite of South-West African diamond mine income. But if South Africa's intentions for the territory are in doubt, a host of companies are ready to move in should the political situation warrant.

Easy credit: Most eager are the Germans. Indeed 25,000 descendants of the pre-1915 colonists still speak German as their principal language. Now, with Bonn's blessing, the Kreditanstalt Fur Wiederaufbau of Frankfurt is studying multibillion-mark loans to the new nation. As a developing country, Namibia would be eligible for easy, 30-year, 2% credits. Cape Town financial executive Gideon Nel estimates that up to $750 million in German capital is "just out there hovering" until the course of Namibia's independence is clear.

A number of international mining companies, among them Union Carbide

Corporation, also are interested in Namibia once the ground rules are drawn. But the growing anxiety over whether independence will come in an orderly way has spurred a capital outflow of roughly $115 million this year. So far, South African administrative and defense spending (more than $400 million) has more than made up for that. And the 9,000-man U.N. transition team, due to arrive next year, will spend an estimated $250 million to $300 million enough to set off an inflationary spiral.

Ending Time:

Political stability is vital if Namibia's great economic potential is to be realized. Whether December's election or the one in April can establish that sort of tranquility remains to be seen.

WPM: _____

Comprehension Check: Namibia . . .

Directions: Complete each of the following statements by writing in or circling the correct answer.

1. The two most striking characteristics of the nation, Namibia, are

    a. _____

    _____

    b. _____

    _____

2. The country that has played the "godfather" role for Namibia has been
    a. Germany.
    b. South Africa.
    c. England.

3. The word that best describes the political situation in Namibia is
    a. established.
    b. mercurial.
    c. transitional.

4. Nationalization of the mining industry in Namibia is not a concern for the corporations that conduct the everyday mining activities.
    True   False

5. Why might Namibia find that Germany may be its best friend?

Comprehension Accuracy:

_____

_____

_____

Beginning Time:

_____

Total Words: 3728

Selection 8: Male and Female _____

The controversy over the origin of sex differences—whether innate or learned—has raged for centuries and the last word is still to be said. Evelyn Goodenough

Pitcher does not take a stand on the issue, though her studies of preschool children indicate that psychological sex differences exist from a very early age and that parents unconsciously encourage them. This essay was first published a decade ago before the present rebirth of feminism, explaining perhaps the author's complacent view of women's status. Commenting on the mother's role, Pitcher remarks, "She knows that the worlds of both sexes are hers!"

How early do young children play a distinctive sex role, and how do parents accent sex differences in young children? Evidence from a recent study of mine suggests that by two and through ages three and four, boys and girls have strikingly different interests and attitudes, which their parents steadily influence and strengthen.

The influence is inescapable. In my study, fathers and mothers who were questioned agreed that women are more indirect, illogical, circuitous in their thinking than men. Men's thinking was considered to be more analytical, definite, precise, abstract, direct. "Men have a quantitative, analytical, objective interest in things," was a typical remark. The woman's mental approach was described to me as "cunning and deceptive, intuitive, subjective." Be a listener at a women's luncheon and note the subjects of conversation; do the same with a group of men. Eavesdrop on a woman's telephone conversation; listen to a man's. It has long been a byword that men like to talk about business, politics, and the mechanisms of their cars, while women commonly talk about their friends, their hats, and their children. Is this true?

If men and women are really thus different in their thinking, or if they are believed to be, how would this influence the development of young children? How can we find out? I devised a simple experiment which allowed me to take boys or girls, one at a time, into a room to play with a box of brightly colored plastic chips the child had never before seen. During the ten-minute period I recorded everything said, and thus had some tangible record of the way the child was thinking.

The forms and problems the game presented seemed to fascinate the boys, so that they kept talking about the chips, wondering about their use, how they could be arranged, where they had come from. If the boys' remarks left the immediate situation, they rarely went far away.

The whole business intrigued the girls much less. Like women bored by men's conversations, after a few minutes they would look up and say, "I'm going to a party tomorrow," or, "We have blue wastebaskets at our cottage at the beach." Their digressions included comments about planting seed, birthday parties, Christmas, friends, gifts, clothing, visits to doctors, pictures on the wall, quarrels with brothers, conversations with mothers. The tendency of the female to jaywalk in conversations was amply illustrated by the little girls.

Had the parents themselves presented different models of thinking to their children and thereby influenced the way the children thought? And what about different kinds of interests in boys and girls? Did parents expect the girl to be more "intuitive, subjective," and the boy to be more "analytical," with an "objective" interest in things?

To find out about this, I questioned parents about what they thought made their little girls feminine and what characterized masculinity in the little boys.

Both fathers and mothers clearly regarded it as feminine to be interested in pretty clothes, domestic habits, families, or babies, or for a girl to identify herself with women. They expected a girl to be more social, more interested in herself and in other people than a boy would be. They reported of their girls, "She looks at people's faces and observes their expressions. She observes relationships," or, "She wins by guile; she has bright playful ideas calculated to win and attract attention." In addition, the girl—never the boy—is marked as especially feminine because of her coquetry, in such remarks as "seductive, persuasive," and "She cuddles and flatters in subtle ways." It would seem that by noticing such social awareness and coquetry in the little girls, parents encourage the development of precisely these traits.

In contrast, parents regarded it as masculine to be interested in objects or ideas, not persons. Parents commented often on the boys' preoccupation with bulldozers, trucks, cement mixers. The boy, as the parents reported him, was not only interested in objects but in making them work.

Would young boys and girls actually show such a difference in interest in people or objects as parents seemed to expect? To answer this question, I again devised a simple test. I gave a child a paper and pencil and asked him to make something. Any parent will know that with a child from two to four I got usually meaningless scribbles, often slightly formed but still hardly recognizable as drawings. Clearly, nothing could be learned from the marks themselves; the point was to ask the children what they had drawn and then to record their intentions.

The result was significant and fascinating. Over 50 percent of the girls drew, or said they had drawn, persons, while only 15 percent of the boys did so. In just as great disproportion boys were drawing things, such as a car, a park, a bench, an egg, a train, a tree. The girls' drawings also showed a marked interest in the family, in babies, in clothing, in domestic activities, which was not apparent in the boys' drawings. When asked what they had drawn, girls made such remarks as, "Susie on roller skates, sleeping"; "Just a girl, with snaps instead of buttons"; "A man with an orange shirt, white hair, like Grandpa. He's barefoot in the grass, because it's summer." Usually boys would only name the object.

The impression that the greater interest of women in persons and the greater interest of men in things and processes begin at an early age was confirmed also by the stories children made up in response to the simple request, "Tell me a story." Here are some typical examples:

Two-year-old Girl

Once there was a little kitty cat, and he scratched. Then the Mommy spanks the kitty. Then the kitty doesn't cry. He scratches the Mommy. The Mommy puts him in jail, but he has friends and he can peek at them. More friends come, but they're going to be naughty friends and spank the kitty. He scratches them and cries because he doesn't like naughty people.

Two-Year-Old Boy

A camel, and he went down the mountain, and he fell down. Then he fell down in a hole. Then a bear came and saw, but he shoot the bear. Then he jumps on the bear. Then he ride on the horse and go, "Giddyup, giddyup," up the mountain.

Three-Year-Old Girl

A little girl, gone to a party. Her got dressed up. Her came back home and got spanked 'cause her been a naughty boy 'cause she got into Mommy's ink. And she spilled it all over the floor, over the rug, and over the floor. Then she went to bed.

Three-Year-Old Boy

A broken train was going down a hill. And it splashed right in the water. The engine driver got wet. A big wolf came along. And the Indians came too, and ran into the water. A big Indian was very mad and chased the engine driver, and the fight. The Indian wins, and the engine driver is dead.

Analysis of some 360 stories collected from children of from two to five years revealed that girls tend to present people more vividly and realistically and to identify themselves with the personalities and experiences of others. Direct conversations are often quoted in the girls' stories, and people are more individually conceived and characterized by their names. The boy, on the other hand, speaks with significantly greater frequency of things. He seems especially fascinated by vehicles of transportation and machines, and talks about rockets, boats, cars, trucks, ambulances, fire engines, covered wagons, parachutes. He is interested in mechanical gadgets, too, such as the cement mixer and typewriter, and in such elements of nature as sun, ice, rain, snow, and hurricane. The girl's interest in objects is more likely to be in personal or household equipment, or in productive nature—leaf, tree, flower. She mentions relatively few vehicles of motion.

Among the people most prominent in the girls' stories are parent figures, and the girl is much more likely than the boy to express emotions about the parental figure, particularly the mother.

If the boy is experiencing intense reactions to his mother and father, he rarely expresses them directly. From the stories, it would seem that the girl's personal awareness and personal identity are sharpened by seeing the mother doing things all day with which she can identify. The boy, on the contrary, especially one whose father goes away to a business or profession all day, sees little he can copy or take to himself. Under the circumstances, it is not surprising that he is less aware of himself as a person than the girl. The girl usually knows in great detail what it is to be a mother. The boy more often discovers masculinity and identifies himself with it in a general way—in the policeman, fireman, soldier, Indian. These are the masculine roles he can comprehend and play at imitating as he cannot do with his father's role as factory worker, executive, lawyer, or scholar.

It also seems that the girl's early identification with her mother may influence her ideas about morality, for she is over and again more personally and maternally involved in her judgement of what is good or bad than is the boy. The girl seems not to be the more moral of the sexes, but the more personally concerned with morality. Even at an early age she moves in her traditional role of guardian of domestic morality. She can be emotionally and personally involved as she identifies both with the mother who must punish naughtiness and with the child who is naughty. The badness the girl reports is usually minor and spiteful—tearing dresses, ripping trousers, snatching candies, spilling milk or ink, cracking things, scattering crumbs. The girl is skilled in planning punishment at once devastating, personally rejecting, and humiliating.

Considering the amount of aggression and destruction in the three-year-old boys' stories, relatively little is labeled naughty. For the most part, the gamut of physical aggression is described, atrocity is piled on atrocity, and there seems no particular reason why it should start or stop. For all this aggression, the boy most often mentions two forms of punishment—spanking and jailing. Clearly, the expression of aggression is more common than the consideration that aggression should be punished.

It is the boy rather than the girl who seems to move into a concern for the larger social aspects of goodness and badness. He sees the possibility of good and evil in the same person and specifies that standardized kinds of good and bad characters, such as witches or police, might have other qualities. For boys the arena of evil is more often out of the house. It is the boy who matches forces of good and evil in organized warfare, who sees a responsibility for saving people or fighting from a sense of duty.

All these data from children would be consistent with the observation that questions of social or personal morality among adults are largely regulated by women, while men generally formulate the problems of law, labor, or diplomacy. Children in this study suggest that such differences are already identifiable in the years two through five.

Although almost as many girls as boys speak of aggression, it tends to be much more violent with the boys than with the girls. One almost feels and hears the reverberation of crashing, shooting, and pounding as general catastrophe reigns. Boys have much more shooting in their stories, and often use the word "fight," suggesting an adversary and a definite concern as to who will win. They biff and butt, roll on the ground, punish with their hands, puke and whiz, lasso and tie up, poison and hook with rope ladders. They use oral aggression freely, in addition to swords, knives, bows and arrows.

Girls show in their stories a relatively more prosocial, adultlike aggression. Among the girls, even shooting is not so likely to be synonymous with violence or death. The girl seems, indeed, more sensitive to the personal implications of death, and more likely to see death as a reversible process, with persons disappearing and returning. The boy seems more likely to deny the reversibility of death. His greater expansiveness in ideas, on the other hand, may lead him to be more receptive to abstract considerations of the finality of life or of a life hereafter, as the following story shows:

> Once there was a terrible crocodile with sharp teeth. He saw a person, ate him up, and he got fatter, fatter, and fatter. He threw up and died. He was underground. He couldn't get up, 'cause he was dead. He went back to seed; he has a little seed like you have a baby in your stomach. And he grew up to be a crocodile again, because he was planted in the ground and up came a crocodile again. And that's the end.

In considering such a theme as food, or eating, which includes the providing, preparing, or partaking of food and drink, data from the stories show that it is obviously the girl who markedly identifies with the female role of cook and hostess. The girl mentions specific meals and is interested in the eating of food as a social occasion, and in the preparation of food. The boy is not so likely to mention specific foods; breakfast, lunch, and dinner are likely to be just in the routine of the day.

The girl's interest in food again suggests the female's loving concern with details, her tendency to utilize experience in the enhancement of self. Similarly, mention of clothes or apparel is not only more popular with the girls, but among them is treated with more attention to detail, to color, to suitable costume. The girl is also likely to comment on general appearance, to perceive greater subtleties of emotional tone in characters—"a nice smile," "a stern voice," whereas the boy tends to a more generalized description of persons or references to being "mad" or "glad."

A concern with friendship and pleasure from interpersonal relationships, a mention of friend or friendship are more frequent among the girls. It is the girl, not the boy, who refers to love, courtship, and marriage. Already, in the early years, the female is attentive to the predatory task of ensnaring a husband. A memorable example is the story from a four-year-old girl which seems to express the association of feminine sexuality and the sea, which appears so often in myths:

> Once there was a fish named Flower. She went down in the water and said, "Oh, my gosh, where's my lover?" She went down in the cellar where my house is. She saw a big father fish which had a sword in his nose. She ran away from the house and hid in another house. She ran up the water and flapped out. She ran away. She went to another house in a deep, deep river. She saw her own home which had her lover in it. They kissed each other. That's the end.

These stories from children bring out the different emphases expressed by boys and girls in fantasy themes. Such differences must in part have arisen from the different ways in which society makes demands or presents opportunities to children of different sexes.

I have already made reference to the parent interviews as providing evidence of cultural demands and expectations; a closer scrutiny of the material comparing the father's interviews with those of the mother reveals a curious differential in parents' sex-typing.

Both fathers and mothers allow what appears to be tomboyishness in girls during the early years, while they try to discourage what might be feminine behavior in their sons. Their attitude seems to reflect the general pattern in America, where our culture tends to grant the female the privileges of two sexes: with impunity she can dress like a man; she can at will interchange the "little boy look" with cloying femininity. She can use any name—her own or her husband's—enter any job, any area of education, or she can make a career of motherhood. She can be independent or dependent, or both, as and when she pleases.

The male has no corresponding freedom. He is increasingly expected to help in the home, but this is largely because the woman without servants demands such help. Deviations in dress, appearance, or job that reflect the feminine are immediately suspect. If a man is actually feminine in his instincts, even homosexual, he must never appear to be so.

It was impressive to observe to what extent the father more than the mother was responsible for sharpening such differences. There were clear indications that fathers especially tended to emphasize what seemed to be an exclusive masculinity in their sons. "He gets mad if I tease him about his interest in anything girlish and therefore babyish," said one father about his two-year-old son. And another mother remarked, "On Halloween a boy can't wear anything feminine. The idea of lipstick horrifies a father."

A direct question followed such observations as those I have just mentioned, and brought out the same contrast between father and mother. A father, when asked if he would be disturbed by aspects of femininity in his son, said, "Yes, I would be, very, very much. Terrifically disturbed—couldn't tell you the extent of my disturbance. I can't bear female characteristics in a man. I abhor them." But a mother said, "Jimmy is not as masculine. But he'll grow up to be considerate and kind. Gentlemanly, rather than masculine." Another father was distressed and scornful at signs of his son's femininity. "He's always interested in flexing his muscles. Perhaps he has to prove that he's masculine—that's why I call him feminine." The same boy's mother admitted that at one time she was very much concerned about her son's femininity, but reasoned thus, "I am aware these people make splendid contributions to the world. I'd try to help. I would turn all my energies to producing a good environment for him."

A father was also more likely to appreciate femininity in his daughter. One mother reported her husband's pleasure when she put their six-month-old daughter into a dress for the first time. "That's much nicer than these old pajamas," said the father. Another mother reported that her husband blanched when he found she had cut her daughter's long hair. "Promise me that you will never, never cut it again," he said.

Still another father taught his son how to react to femininity in his baby sister. "His attitude toward his sister is masculine, very big-brotherly. I've impressed him with this—to be careful, treat her nice, 'Oogle-google' with her." The same boy's mother remarked, "My husband talks in a high voice to the little girl, in a deep bass voice to Jimmy." Other remarks show that there is a tendency for the father to grant his daughter a special, privileged place: "It is so inevitable to spoil a first child, I'm glad my first child was a girl," and, "I'd be stricter with a boy than with a girl, perhaps because my own father was stricter with me. Mary (daughter) once asked me (the father) which of my 'girls' I liked best—her or her mother. One is always conscious that there is a little sex factor between a little female child and her father."

Indeed, half of the little girls' fathers pointed out their daughters' coquetry in a way to show that they were themselves personally intrigued. Ten different fathers made the following remarks, describing their daughters:

"Very conquettish. Gallantry and consideration work with her."

"Seductive, persuasive, knows how to get me to do things she can't get her mother to let her do."

"Inclined to be coy and a little seductive."

"A bit of a flirt, arch and playful with people, a pretended coyness. Sometimes she seems like a Southern girl—may be a little flirt when she gets older."

"Soft and cuddly and loving. She cuddles and flatters in subtle ways."

"Engages in outward display of affection."

"Her coyness and flirting, 'come up and see me sometime' approach. Loves to cuddle. She's going to be sexy—I get my wife annoyed when I say this."

"Certain amount of flirtatiousness to most everyone, especially strangers. Occasionally with me too. Little shy looks and smiles—attention-getting devices. I am probably completely taken in by her."

"She is extremely loving, always coming around hugging and kissing. She loves to play with me at night. I always heard that girls look more to their fathers than to their mothers."

"A soft person, lovable, affectionate."

Such statements suggest that there may be some general truth about father-daughter relationships in the remark of one father: "Femininity cannot be divorced in my mind from a certain amount of sexuality." Such an attitude of the fathers must be presumed to be conditioning their little daughters in this aspect of femininity.

Again, in contrast, only half of the mothers mentioned the flirtatious character of their daughters at all, but when they did so, showed no such personal involvement. Where the father said, "She flirts with me," the mother, in one way or another, said, "She flirts with her father or with other people."

Only sparse examples could be gathered from the interviews to indicate that the mother was playing an active part in encouraging her son to a more masculine role insofar as interaction between the sexes, or the cultivation of manly custom, is concerned. Mothers are as likely to take their sons to a tea party as to visit a railroad yard, and are as likely to give their daughters overalls as dresses. The fathers appeared more likely to view the boy as a male trapped in a world of women and needing to guard his uncontaminated masculinity from association with the female sex.

Of course, the impact of this expectancy of the child appears in his everyday behavior. In children's drawings, we noticed that a boy drew a boy, whereas girls would draw either girls or boys, almost indifferently.

Thus, it would appear that the father has much greater interest, and hence influence, than the mother in accentuating differences between boys and girls. He likes the little girl to be a little girl and enjoys her femininity, but expresses himself with intolerance about any show of femininity in his son. The mother, however, seems more like a mother animal, treating the babies in her litter with little distinction. Perhaps the mother can afford to be relaxed, since she knows that the worlds of both sexes are hers. She has no real need to promote the purity of either, except insofar as she wishes to please her husband and go along with general cultural mores.

It seems from the evidence I have here presented that boys and girls are from early age subjected to influences that would develop different characteristics. However, the parents interviewed were apparently unaware that they were doing or saying anything directly to foster in their children interest or lack of interest in people. They were probably influencing their children in two ways. First of all, by subtle rewards and punishments, if only those of tone of voice, they perhaps registered approval or disapproval as situations arose. Second, we assume that the girl tends to imitate the mother and the boy the father by reproducing their kinds and sources of interests.

The question arises whether parents really create such distinctions as I have described in otherwise undistinguished personalities. Or do parents—and all our cultural influences—just develop and accentuate tendencies that children are born with? Of course, it is impossible to come to any firm conclusions about whether or to what extent psychological sex differences are innate or learned or both. But however the differences arise, it is clear that they exist from a very early age in children in our society, and that we might do well to consider such differences in planning children's education.

Ending Time:

_____

WPM: _____

Comprehension Check: Male and Female

Directions: Complete each of the following statements by writing in or circling the correct answer.

1. "Male and Female" considers whether the differences between the sexes is innate or learned but does not give a definite answer.

   True   False

2. The differences between boys and girls in interests, attitudes, and behaviors are most noticeable in the teenage years.

   True   False

3. The research procedures used for gathering young children's perceptions of the world around them was _____

   _____.

4. The thinking of men is viewed as more logical, analytical. Identify three adjectives most frequently associated with women's thought patterns.

   _____, _____, and _____.

   Are these terms sex biased? Yes _____ No _____

Comprehension Accuracy:

_____

5. Conditioning by parents seems to be quite strong in helping boys be boys and girls to be girls.

   True   False

Make sure you have plotted your words per minute and comprehension accuracy scores on the Reading Progress Chart for Unit 4 on p. 181.

EVALUATING YOUR PROGRESS

It is now time to evaluate your high-powered speed progress. From the Reading Progress Chart on p. 181 can you detect a rise in the number of words you are reading per minute? Remember, the first goal of high-powered speed training is increased speed. You must first establish a fast new rate. You must replace old plodding patterns with a new pattern that you will use in all your pleasure reading materials.

Home Practice

Obviously eight practice exercises are not enough to guarantee that you have established a consistent fast speed for pleasure reading. It is time for you to set up home practice sessions of approximately thirty minutes to an hour per day. The objective for this practice is to continue to increase speed until you reach your desired limit. (See Unit 1 for your Pleasure Speed Reading Goal.) A paperback or other novel of your choosing would be most appropriate for this practice.

Using an Alarm Clock Graph

Several excellent procedures are available to help you maintain consistent practice and growth. One is to increase the number of pages you can read within a specified time limit, for example, one hour. Your goal for the next day's practice

is to read more pages than you did the previous day. Set an alarm clock or a timer
for one hour and read until it signals to stop. Then record the number of pages you

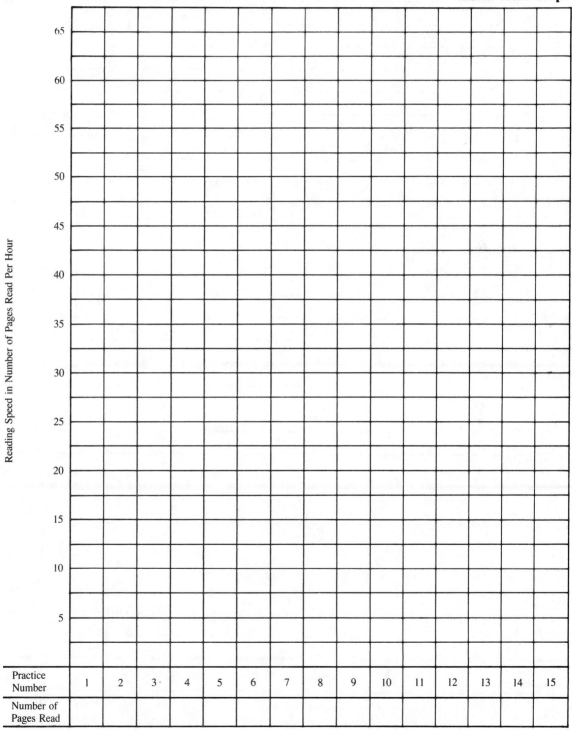

Alarm Clock Graph

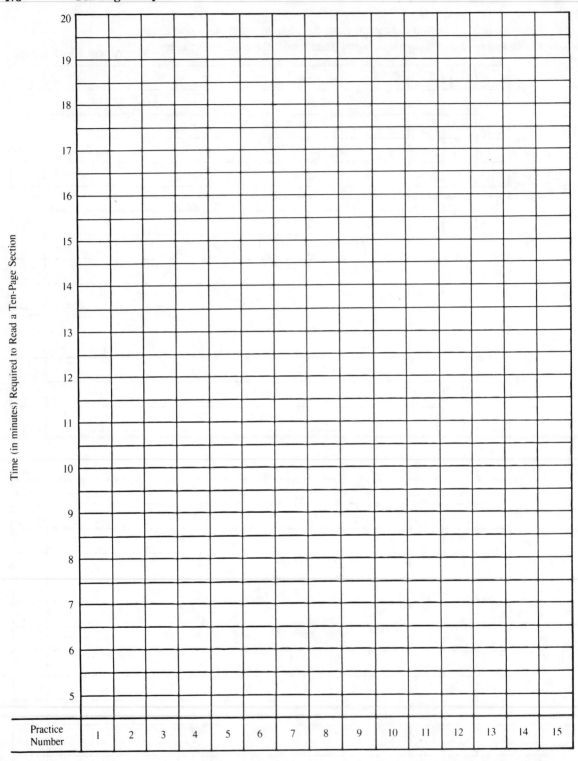

SOURCE: From Ellen Lamar Thomas and H. Alan Robinson, IMPROVING READING IN EVERY CLASS, Second Edition. Copyright © 1977 by Allyn and Bacon, Inc., Boston. Reprinted with permission.

have completed. You should keep a daily record of your progress. The chart on page 177, recommended by Thomas and Robinson, is a good one to use.

Using the Ten-Page Graph

Another way to record your own speed practice at home is the ten-page goal. You record your beginning time; then read ten pages. After noting your finishing time, you determine how long it took to read the ten pages. Plot your time on the Ten-Page Graph. Next, read ten more pages, trying to reduce the time. You must practice daily if you use this technique.

Using the Push-Card Pacer

Many other possibilities for home practice are available. The push-card pacer is a very useful one. The student uses a 4×6 notecard in this manner described by Thomas and Robinson:

1. Students place the card above the line to be read. They then move it down the page, forcing themselves to keep ahead. Or they may prefer to place the card just below the line to be read, exposing the reading matter line by line and "chasing" the card down the page.
2. Students push the card down the page more rapidly than they think they can comprehend. They may be surprised at the speed attainable without loss of comprehension.
3. This suggestion is given: "You now have a lifetime 'portable reading pacer.' If you really want to pick up speed, use it with easy newspaper and magazine content and light, fast-moving books."[1]

Remember that speed reading techniques are like sterling silver tableware. They grow more beautiful, refined with use.

If you truly want to read faster and more efficiently, you must force yourself to use the techniques you are mastering in *all* of your reading. All materials should be previewed—even the simplest magazine article. Obviously previewing study materials saves valuable time when you know what you are looking for as you read. Reading by phrases in all materials brings speed and understanding.

As you begin to develop your speed reading skills, try to follow these suggestions:

1. Set aside a particular time of the day just for speed practice. Fifteen to thirty minutes per day is recommended. (This can be your usual reading—study or pleasure.)
2. Preview everything. Then read in phrases. You will find yourself becoming more comfortable with your new speeds as time goes on.

These same techniques that you are developing to improve your pleasure reading speed will help you as you begin to strengthen your study reading rates, the subject of Unit 5.

NOTE TO UNIT 4

1. Ellen Lamar Thomas and H. Alan Robinson, IMPROVING READING IN EVERY CLASS, Second Edition, pp. 173 and 176. Copyright © 1977 by Allyn and Bacon, Inc., Boston. Reprinted with permission.

Answer Key:
Unit 4

Selection 1: Only One Came Back, p. 144

1. a   **2.** c   **3.** a   **4.** b   **5.** b

Selection 2: Teaching Your Body to Work Better, p. 147

1. True   **2.** a   **3.** help the person learn to control himself, learn self-regulation
4. False   **5.** True

Selection 3: Firebuilding, p. 150

1. True   **2.** master fire building techniques   **3.** c   **4.** True   **5.** Choose
any three of the following: canned heat
                       paraffin
                       newspapers
                       tablets
                       charcoal briquets

Selection 4: Nixon's Embarrassing Road Show, p. 155

1. Negative, not positive   **2.** No, ulterior, exploiting, lame humor, spectral, sandbagged, banality, chagrin, resurrection, etc.   **3.** a   **4.** Given red-carpet treatment,
briefed him when wouldn't cooperate with Ford or Kissinger, stood for lady.   **5.** b

Selection 5: Mood Maybe, p. 158

1. True   **2.** True   **3.** True   **4.** True   **5.** True

Selection 6: One Woman's Liberation . . ., p. 162

1. True   **2.** False   **3.** True   **4.** True   **5.** True

Selection 7: Namibia, p. 166

1. a. huge monetary assets from mining that do not come to them now   **b.** it is not
yet a separate nation, elections will determine this   **2.** b   **3.** c   **4.** False
5. the willingness of the German government to extend credit if Namibia should need it

Selection 8: Male and Female, p. 168

1. True   **2.** False   **3.** through examination of the children's conversations and
drawings   **4.** cunning, intuitive, perceptive, subjective; Yes   **5.** True

Reading Progress Chart: Unit 4

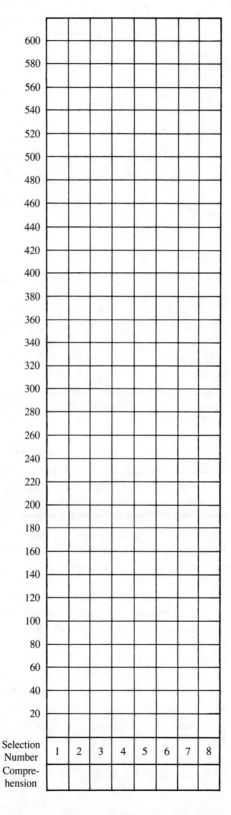

UNIT 5

Study Reading: Increasing Efficiency

Organizing your day to allow time for both work and pleasure is the goal of every student. Your success in balancing the two depends on whether you have devised time-saving shortcuts. Efficient study means spending no more time than is necessary to learn the material thoroughly. A critical part of studying is the amount of time you must spend doing assigned readings. It can be laborious; it can be time-consuming. But by learning and applying three groups of techniques to your reading, you can rapidly improve both your speed and efficiency in studying. These techniques include identifying organizational structure in both the selection and the paragraph, identifying and organizing details, and identifying signal words for speed.

Because efficient study reading is a complex task requiring the use of many separate skills, you should always preview before you read. As you preview, remember that identifying structure and organizing details helps you quickly spot the main ideas of a selection and establish the purpose for the reading. If you can identify signal words, you will be able to speed over unimportant details but slow down for major points. Each of these techniques will be discussed in this unit.

Study reading is more difficult than easy pleasure reading. Therefore, mastering reading techniques that improve your efficiency in studying will develop more slowly also. You will need much practice before you can perform these techniques easily and without visual aids or other help. However, if you patiently apply these procedures to your reading, you will soon notice improvements in your efficiency and comprehension—the reading goals of all good students.

IDENTIFYING ORGANIZATIONAL STRUCTURE

Successful reading of study or factual material depends on your ability to recognize the overall framework or organization of longer, complex selections. Smith has identified five such organizational patterns: Sharing-Experience, Question-Answer, Imparting-Information, Opinion-Reason, and Substantiated-Facts patterns.[1]

Identifying the organizational structure is similar to previewing. Whereas previewing alerts you to the information to be gained, finding the organizational structure alerts you to the manner in which the information is presented and offers an easy "how to read" blueprint. You can quickly detect the organizational pattern of a selection as you preview.

The Sharing-Experience Pattern

The Sharing-Experience pattern is a direct description. The writer frequently uses personal references such as "I," "me," "my," which encourage the reader to identify with the characters. This pattern is most often found in human interest stories. Although this pattern is seldom used in detailed study materials, you should be able to recognize it. The following is an example of the Sharing-Experience Pattern:

"My main hunting grounds have been in Kenya and Tanzania," said Dr. Perdue, when I reached him at his Bettsville, Maryland, station, "but I've gathered botanicals on almost every continent."

"My latest trip was the most successful," he said. "With two African assistants and a carryall truck, I got some 1,700 plant samples to be screened for anticancer activity. After fifteen years of experience, I also had my first adventure in the wilds."[2]

The Question-Answer Pattern

You can identify the Question-Answer pattern very easily. A direct question is asked. The material that follows is an answer to that question. Once you locate the question, you read to answer the question. Material irrelevant to the question may be skimmed over. The following paragraph is an example of this organizational structure:

Still, isn't it possible to go straight through a book at the rate of 10,000 words per minute? Conceivably it is, if the book is light fiction. The late Erle Stanley Gardner, during his mystery-writing days, published some eighty novels in which Perry Mason, the attorney-at-law, is the hero. Suppose you were a Perry Mason fan and had read a number of books. You would know the usual plot structure well: the preliminary set-up; the fact that Perry defends the murder suspect; the climactic courtroom scene in which he battles the hostile district attorney; and finally, the ending, with the confession of the real murderer, whose identity he has apparently known all along.[3]

Question
Answer

The Imparting-Information Pattern

A writer's use of the Imparting-Information Pattern can signal slow reading rates for the speed reader. Because, in detailed study reading, a writer may be packing a lot of information into a short amount of space, you the reader may have difficulty sifting through the facts. The relationships of many subtopics to the main idea may not be clearly drawn. If this is the case, you should outline or diagram the information to strengthen your retention and recall. Here is an example of this pattern:

The structure of present-day British English and American English—the difference between them is chiefly in certain idiomatic expressions, forms of spelling, and pronunciation—*is not hard to understand.* The heart of the structure of both is the simple sentence. Long and complicated sentences are only developments of this.[4]

Statement

Fact
Fact

The Opinion-Reason Pattern

An author who uses the Opinion-Reason Pattern may make a blunt statement and explain by adding fact upon fact to lend credence to the original statement. You may often detect that the presentation is somewhat biased or slanted. Vocabulary— use of sarcastic or emotionally "loaded" words—will signal to you the author's real feelings. Because of the ostensibly straightforward presentation of the Opinion-Reason Pattern, your reading speed can usually be rapid. However, it may be a good idea to re-examine the author's position by reading the information a second time at a moderate rate. The following paragraph is an example of this pattern:

Opinion   *A short and simple sentence in which you know all the words is not likely to stop you as you read.* You take it in easily and go right on to the next sentence.

Reasons   If this is also short and simple, you keep moving ahead. If it contains an unfamiliar word, you either guess the meaning or make a note to look it up later. In any case your reading continues.[5]

The Substantiated-Facts Pattern

The Substantiated-Facts pattern is the most frequently used pattern for textbook materials. A central thought or main idea is developed; a statement of fact is made. The author then uses other material to identify and expand this idea. Many important details are given. All are necessary and must be remembered. However, you should be aware that the central idea may not always be identified at the beginning of the selection. You will have to fit details together until you can locate it.

In the teaching method known as programmed instruction, textbooks are specially designed to provide students with a learning experience by presenting them with a question or a statement that requires an immediate response. The response is immediately checked for accuracy against the correct answer before the student can continue in the book. The check reinforces the student's learning.

The subject matter is broken up into small units called "frames," beginning theoretically where the student is or at a lower level, so that he can easily reach the point where new learning takes place. Steps follow in a sequential fashion.

There are two principal techniques: linear and branching. In the linear technique the units are arranged in a single ordered sequence of a stimulus-response type. Answers that require recall ability may be supplied by choosing one out of several multiple-choice items. The correct response is hidden until the student completes his own answer.[6]

Practice Identifying Structure

Use the selections at the end of this unit, pages 221–26, to practice previewing a selection. Note its content and identify its overall organizational structure.

For each of the selections in this unit, do the following:

1.   Before reading, preview the selection. (Refer back to Unit 2 if you need to review previewing.) On the lines provided, jot down what you found about the topic.
2.   Quickly glance through the article. Note how the selection is designed. Which organizational pattern is being used? Write your answer at the end of the selection.

Congress: Where The People Speak

I. Congress' Powers

_____

_____

_____

_____

_____

_____

II. Makeup of Congress

_____

_____

_____

_____

III. Congress Votes

_____

1. It levies taxes.
2. House seats are apportioned among the states on the basis of population.
3. It may remove officials for high crimes.
4. Different versions of bills can be passed requiring a ''conference agreement.''
5. Americans of all callings have served in the Congress.
6. Lobbyists may pressure congressmen for their own special interest legislation.
7. It can declare war and approve treaties.
8. There are two branches, the Senate and House.
9. A bill clearing one house is sent to another.
10. Each state elects two members to the Senate.
11. It may subpoena witnesses and compel testimony.
12. The House ''roll-call'' for approving legislation is done electronically.[7]

Identifying Main Ideas in Paragraphs

Now that you have sharpened your awareness of main ideas as opposed to supporting details, you can use your skill for identifying the information given in single paragraphs. Since longer selections are composed of many smaller paragraphs, you must be careful not to yield to the temptation to read sentence after sentence until the whole selection has been read. Instead, you must demand that each paragraph tell you something directly. When approaching a paragraph, read it as if it were the only material to be read. Look first for the person, place, thing or condition that is being described. Second, determine what this person, place, thing, or condition did, or what was done *to* it or what property it has that makes it worth being discussed.[8]

Keeping these two ideas in mind, read the following paragraph. Determine what is being discussed by finding the noun or noun phrase that identifies the main idea. Then find the group of words that describes this idea or what was done to it.

Paragraph 1

In the strictest concept of measurement, some kind of scale along which equal units can be indicated and on which the position zero corresponds to "just nothing" of whatever is being measured is regarded as a necessity. Thus it is with a yardstick. The user has confidence that one inch anywhere along the scale is exactly equal for all practical purposes to an inch arbitrarily chosen along any other point of the scale. Moreover, zero inches has for him rational significance as corresponding to the absence of any length whatever. With such a measuring instrument, one length can meaningfully be expressed as a multiple of another length. Thus it makes sense to say that a stick ten inches long has twice the length of a stick five inches long.[9]

1. What is the basic idea discussed in the paragraph?
2. What is its significance or special characteristic?
3. Where did you find the key/topic sentence?

If you analyzed the paragraph carefully, you noted that the key idea was that in measurement, a scale which indicates equal units and has a zero position which corresponds to "just nothing" is a necessity. Its significance or special characteristic is that, with such a measuring instrument, length can be expressed meaningfully as a multiple of another length. The first sentence identified the key idea.

Paragraph 2

Interior decorators have long recognized that modern buildings with their severe and simple lines must introduce some softening effect if architectural design is not to appear stark, cold and uninhabited. This is why we find murals or paintings on bare walls, fountains or futuristic art in entrance halls, period furniture and statuary in corridors. Here is where specimen foliage plants can add warmth and a breath of nature alive, thereby enriching the empty vastness of such edifices, making employees and visitors alike feel welcome and more comfortable.[10]

1. What is the basic thought in this paragraph?
2. Which elements of design are used to add this warming effect?
3. Where did you find the key sentence?

The basic premise of this paragraph is that in modern buildings architectural design must add a softening effect or the buildings would appear stark, cold and not lived in. Such things as paintings, fountains, furniture and plants help achieve this softening effect. The first sentence, again, identifies the basic idea.

Paragraph 3 ▬▬▬▬▬▬▬▬▬▬▬▬▬▬▬▬▬▬▬▬▬▬▬▬

One puzzling aspect of animal domestication is why it occurred in the first instance. Today we find many of the domesticates' traits of obvious advantage, but most of these traits were present in only rudimentary form in the wild animals from which the domesticates were derived. It was in the domesticated state that cattle began to give substantial quantities of milk, that sheep became very woolly, that chickens laid eggs in large numbers. The inclusion of these animals within man's cultural shield, in the man-made artificial environment, made possible greater variability and subsequent selection for desired traits. Logically, the earliest domestication must have been for a readily available meat supply, for the flesh was always present whatever else was present or lacking.[11]

Underline the most important idea.

1. Man has always derived great benefits from his associations with animals.
2. Wild animals possessed the same desirable characteristics in earlier times as they do now.
3. Why man domesticated the animal in the first place is a puzzle to the author of this paragraph.

If you chose 3, you are correct.

Paragraphs That Have No Main Idea

As you read longer selections you must become aware of paragraphs that may not have a central theme or idea. Smith has identified four such paragraph constructions: the one-sentence paragraph, a paragraph with several ideas of equal importance, a paragraph with two ideas of equal importance, and a series of paragraphs.[12]

The One-Sentence Paragraph

The only way to deal with this type of paragraph construction is to note the one basic thought in the paragraph. Just add that idea to the others you are gathering and continue reading. Examine the following example:

If a radio astronomer from a planet circling a nearby star happened to be listening to our solar system, he would hear the sun and possibly the giant planet Jupiter which also transmits radio signals.[13]

Several Ideas of Equal Importance

A more complicated construction is the paragraph that enumerates several ideas of equal importance. Since all the ideas presented are stressed equally, you must decide for yourself what the overall theme is. What would you identify as the main theme of the following paragraph?

Astronomers reckon the Milky Way galaxy is about 12,000 million years old. We do not think that all the planets in our galaxy will be the same age. If the process of evolution is taking place on other planets, it might be happening more quickly or more slowly than it does on earth. This means that, if there are other inhabited worlds, some will still be at the equivalent of the dinosaur stage, while others will be far in advance of our civilization. These advanced civilizations would be very interesting to discover. Their inhabitants might live in what we would think of as a science-fiction world, with all kinds of mysterious powers and knowledge.[14]

What did you identify as the main theme? It might read: The ages of the planets in the Milky Way galaxy probably are not the same.

Two Ideas of Equal Importance

A third type of paragraph construction is one in which two ideas of similar value and importance appear. The following is an example. The two main ideas are italicized.

> *Some people have even suggested that, if we did receive a message from another world, we should not reply.* These people think it would be risky to reveal ourselves to the rest of the universe. They fear an invasion from outer space by creatures who might see us as a hopelessly primitive life-form to be kept as amusing pets, or, still worse, they might carry humans away to their home planet to serve up to their friends as exotic tasty delicacies. *On our planet, contact between two races of men with different ways of life has almost always resulted in the domination of the weaker by the stronger.* This is a very pessimistic suggestion and is the result of judging unknown intelligent beings by our own deplorable standards. Anyway it is too late. A message has already been sent.[15]

Both main ideas are of equal value. There is little point in trying to decide between them. It would be better to combine both ideas in a statement that shows their relationship, such as, "Because the stronger race always seems to dominate the weaker one when the two come in contact, it would be wise not to answer a message from outer space with its unknown races since they may be stronger than we."

A Series of Paragraphs

The fourth construction occurs in a series of paragraphs. Each succeeding paragraph may develop a concrete idea, but suddenly one is just a maze of details with no identifiable theme. Waste no time trying to figure it out. You must push on to other more important paragraphs. Normally this type of paragraph is just a continuation of the point made in the previous paragraph or paragraphs. It is not important enough to linger over.

Practice Identifying the Main Idea

You are now ready to practice finding the main idea in each of the following paragraphs. Practice on paragraphs 4 through 6. Remember to try to read each paragraph faster than the last one.

Paragraph 4 ─────────────────────────────

> An abrasive personality is one that rubs us the wrong way and makes us want to scream or sets our teeth on edge to such an extent that we find ourselves trying to avoid contact with him. One person may be abrasive because of his pompousness, another because of a rasping voice that never ceases, another

because he does not exemplify what he exhorts others to do—and he is always exhorting! Some describe their most abrasive acquaintance as "one who has all the answers." Coping with abrasiveness is like chasing a phantom, but perhaps some of the following will at least help you live with the abrasive one in your classroom.[16]

Select the key idea:

1. Abrasive people exhibit many unsavory traits.
2. The paragraph provided many suggestions for dealing with abrasive classmates.
3. An abrasive personality is one we avoid because the person rubs us the wrong way.

If you chose 1 you are correct.

Paragraph 5

The bluffer knows he's not going to succeed forever. He's the great pretender, the staller for time, the fantasizer. In the classroom he pretends to know the answer when he doesn't, to have more information than he in fact has, and to have skills that he hasn't. "Insecure" describes him. He has a poor self-image. He is more brash and outspoken than the habitual liar, with whom he differs in that he's pretty sure that if he can delude someone (teacher, parent, priest, classmate) just this once, he can correct his deficiency and no one will be the wiser. A characteristic comment is, "I bluffed my way through that class, but now I'm really going to study." He needs help in sound ways of learning and retaining information so that he won't feel compelled to bluff.[17]

Select the key idea:

1. The bluffer needs to be helped.
2. The bluffer feels insecure for he knows his lack will soon be known.
3. The bluffer is a really brave person.

If you chose 2 you are correct.

Paragraph 6

To be labeled devious is highly uncomplimentary, for it implies manipulation and deception. The devious student has lost trust in adults. He feels that he can deal with them best through chicanery. He expects adults to respond adversely to his wily ways, perhaps because some have conveyed to him that they think he's sneaky and crooked. He may even want them to think so, so that his negative view of adults can be confirmed. Adults working with the devious student have the task of convincing him that he can achieve his goals via more direct routes.[18]

Select the key idea:

1. To be devious means to be deceptive.
2. The devious student has lost trust in adults.
3. Devious students can be shown other ways of dealing with people.

If you chose 2 you are correct.

Applying Speed as You Find the Main Idea

Now that you have had sufficient practice in finding main ideas, you need to apply time constraints to help you accomplish the task more efficiently. Paragraphs 7 through 10 are provided for your practice.

Directions:

1. Record your beginning time in the space provided. (Use the exact hour, minute, and second.)
2. Read the paragraph. Be sure to use the phrase reading skills you learned earlier in Unit 2.
3. Record your finishing time in exact minutes and seconds. Subtract your beginning time from your ending time. Record this total amount of time in minutes and seconds in the space provided.
4. Circle the letter before the statement that most accurately explains the main idea. Three statements are listed below each paragraph.

Beginning Time:

_____

Ending Time:

_____

Total Time:

_____

Paragraph 7

The story of Casey Stengle and the sparrow has been told in many variations. Usually it is warped around so that it becomes a piece of deliberate screwball behavior on the part of Stengle. Newspaper accounts of the incident, written in 1918 right after it occurred, would contradict these versions.[19]

1. Newspaper accounts in 1918 did not present the "Stengle and the Sparrow" story as screwball behavior.
2. The story of "Stengle and the Sparrow" has been told in many ways.
3. Many accounts of "Stengle and the Sparrow" written after 1918 picture this as an incidence of screwball behavior.

Answer: 2

Beginning Time:

_____

Ending Time:

_____

Total Time:

_____

Paragraph 8

Stengle was a great hero in the few years he played with the Dodgers; then he was traded to the Pirates. On that day in 1918 he came back to Brooklyn as a member of the Pittsburgh club. Technically he had now gone over to the enemy, yet the Brooklyn fans held him in such high esteem that it was a sure thing they would salute him with cheers on his return.

1. Stengle became the enemy of Brooklyn Dodger fans.
2. Stengle belonged to the Pittsburgh club.
3. Stengle was a great hero.

Answer: 3

Beginning Time:

_____

Ending Time:

_____

Paragraph 9

The fact appears to be that Mr. Stengle was as greatly startled as the fans had been when a bird flew out of his thatch. For the moment, however, he made no effort to disillusion his admirers, being content to let them think he had rigged the bird trick in their honor.

1. Mr. Stengle was startled by the bird.
2. Mr. Stengle knew the bird was there.
3. Mr. Stengle deliberately planned a dramatic display for the fans.

Answer: 1

Paragraph 10

Later on he told his story of what had happened. When he had gone to his position in right field in the first inning, he saw an injured sparrow wobbling along at the base of the wall. He walked over and picked it up and was trying to decide what to do with it when he noticed that the ball game had been resumed and he needed to get down to business. He quickly placed the stunned bird under his cap and went to work as an outfielder. He swore later on that he had completely forgotten about the sparrow when he came in from the field and went to bat. Nonetheless, the bird story has been widely repeated as an example of Stengle's showmanship.

1. Stengle later told the true story.
2. Even after Stengle told the true story, many believed that it was an example of his showmanship.
3. Stengle's tenderness toward other creatures was revealed.

Answer: 1

Checking Speed

Compute the time it took you to read each paragraph.

1. Find the total time it took you to read all five paragraphs. Record your total reading time below.
2. Now find the number of seconds it took you to read the paragraphs by multiplying your total time by sixty.
3. Divide the total number of words for the paragraphs by the number of seconds it took you to read the selection.
4. Multiply your answer by sixty to find your words per minute.

Total Time:_____ No. of Words:_____ × 60 _____
                       No. of Seconds   WPM

Refer to page 4 in Unit 1 if you need further help in computing your WPM.

Checking Comprehension

Now check your accuracy in finding the main idea. Allow a score of five for each correct answer. Multiply twenty by the number of answers you had correct. This will be your comprehension score.

Rate: WPM _____

Comprehension Score:_____

Total Time:

_____

Beginning Time:

_____

Ending Time:

_____

Total Time:

_____

ORGANIZING DETAILED STUDY MATERIAL

Now that you have learned to identify the central thought or main idea in single paragraphs, you are ready to develop some new skills in reading detailed study materials. All of these main ideas can quickly become unmanageable if they are not organized into a logical framework that helps the reader see their relationship to the overall discussion.

Two major avenues are open to you for developing your ability to organize detailed study materials into logical relationships for later recall—for example, for a paper or an exam. One is the diagram which helps you visualize the relationships between ideas;[20] the other is the written outline.[21]

Diagramming

Your major task in organizing the information you read is to visualize relationships among the facts presented. The diagram is a useful way to do this. Most paragraphs contain major details as well as minor details that explain the main idea or central theme of that paragraph. But let's concentrate first on major details that expand the main idea. Read the following paragraph to identify the main idea.

> Of the three levels of comprehension, literal comprehension is most used. That is because everyday reading skills, such as skimming and scanning telephone directories, catalogs, movie and television listings, and even reading the newspaper and favorite magazines, seldom require anything but literal comprehension. In addition, most training in reading courses from the early grades through college classes places a larger emphasis on literal recall than on critical or interpretive comprehension. This is not to say that there is no training in these areas, but an examination of materials and tests used in reading courses, as well as in other subjects, reveals a strong reliance on literal comprehension with more stress on recall than on forming judgments, evaluations, or personal reactions at the critical and affective levels.[22]

Did you recognize that the author felt that the level of comprehension most used is literal comprehension? There are three details related to this main idea. Find them and sum them up in as few words as possible in the space provided here:

1. _____

2. _____

3. _____

Your summary should read something like this:

1. Everyday reading skills seldom require anything but literal comprehension.
2. Training given in reading courses emphasizes literal comprehension.
3. Tests in reading and other subject areas place more stress on recall or literal comprehension.

Drawing a mental diagram of the information gathered during reading is not a skill that is mastered instantly. Writing your thoughts down is required in the beginning; however, after a time, the technique will come naturally to you and you will find yourself diagramming mentally rather than with a pencil. You will need practice as you move from one stage to another. Two different diagrams are available for use. The first uses a series of rectangular boxes connected by lines to show the interrelationships between ideas. The second uses a series of connected circles. See the figures on this page and on page 196 for diagrams of Exercise 5.3.

Directions: The following exercises are designed to develop your skill in analyzing paragraphs by perceiving the relationships between their component parts. No time limit is placed on your reading of the paragraphs, but don't dawdle. Work at a quick pace, just as fast as you can go. Your goal is to read rapidly for details. After you have finished reading the paragraph, fill in the two diagrams that accompany each one with the main idea and major details. The diagrams for Exercise 5.3 are partially filled in as an example.

□ Exercise 5.3 □

Thomas Jefferson's country estate, Monticello, illustrates its master's inventiveness as well as America's response to a new environment. Jefferson began building his "little mountain" home near Charlottesville in 1768 on land which his father had owned. The site overlooks the Blue Ridge Mountains in the west and the Virginia plains to the east, vistas which had intrigued Jefferson since childhood. Unable to find a competent architect in the colonies, the resourceful Virginian studied a few books, drew his own plans, and supervised most of its forty-one years of construction. Although he combined currently popular styles— laid out as an Italian villa, Monticello also has a Greek portico, a Roman dome, and colonial detail—Jefferson relied principally upon Andrea Palladio, the architect who had created the "Georgian" style in England. Taken together, Monticello's diverse design did much to launch the "classical revival" which swept the United States during the early nineteenth century.[23]

Complete the diagrams as indicated:

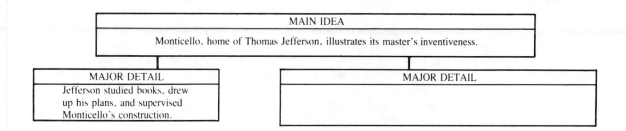

MAIN IDEA
Monticello, home of Thomas Jefferson, illustrates its master's inventiveness.

MAJOR DETAIL	MAJOR DETAIL
Jefferson studied books, drew up his plans, and supervised Monticello's construction.	

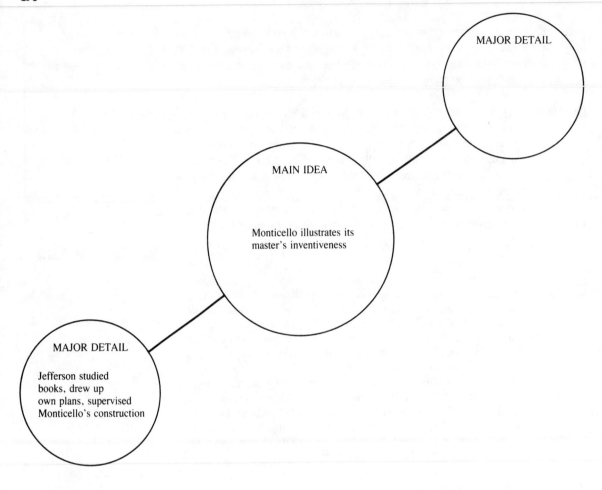

MAJOR DETAIL

MAIN IDEA

Monticello illustrates its
master's inventiveness

MAJOR DETAIL

Jefferson studied
books, drew up
own plans, supervised
Monticello's construction

☐ **Exercise 5.4** ☐

Mercantilism in Europe in the sixteenth–eighteenth centuries must be under-
stood in broad terms as an integral part of the transition from feudalism to
capitalism in Western society. Although the most articulate practitioner of
mercantilist policy was the French Finance Minister Colbert, and the most
successful practitioners were the English, mercantilism was not confined to any
one country. Although much of mercantilist theory did evolve around the
acquisition of gold bullion reserves as a prime object of national policy, it was
not simply a monetary program. Mercantilism rather describes a series of
strategies employed in various combinations which provided a bridge to the
industrial revolution and modern economic development.[24]

Complete the diagram:

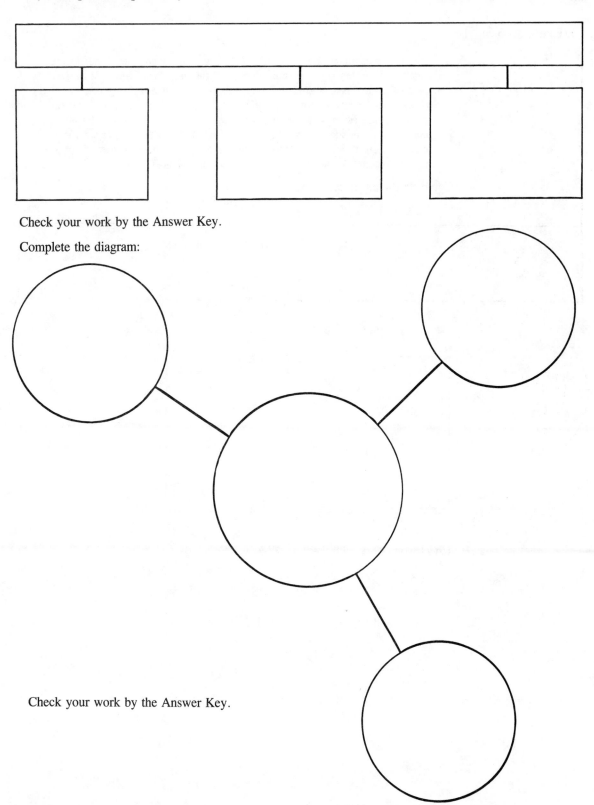

Check your work by the Answer Key.

Complete the diagram:

Check your work by the Answer Key.

☐ Exercise 5.5 ☐

It is a common observation that people tend to incline their heads to one side when "trying to make something out," that is, when faced by a difficult perception such as an abstract painting. It is as if they were trying to discover an *appropriate orientation* for the picture, one that gives it meaning, so that it can be recognized as something. This is the sort of activity which would seem to qualify as a heuristic perceptual technique. That there appears to be a significant conformity in people's judgement about which way is the right-way-up for an abstract picture . . . points to the basis of this technique.[25]

Complete the diagram:

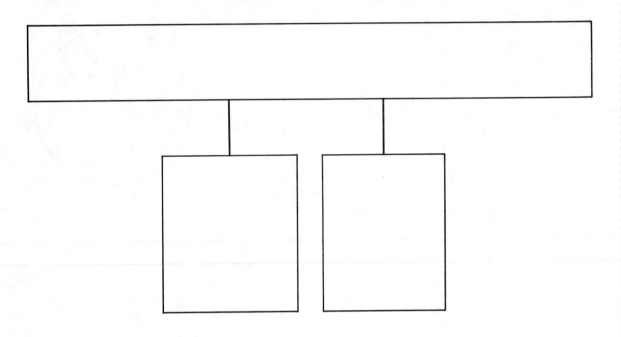

Check your work with the Answer Key.

Complete the diagram:

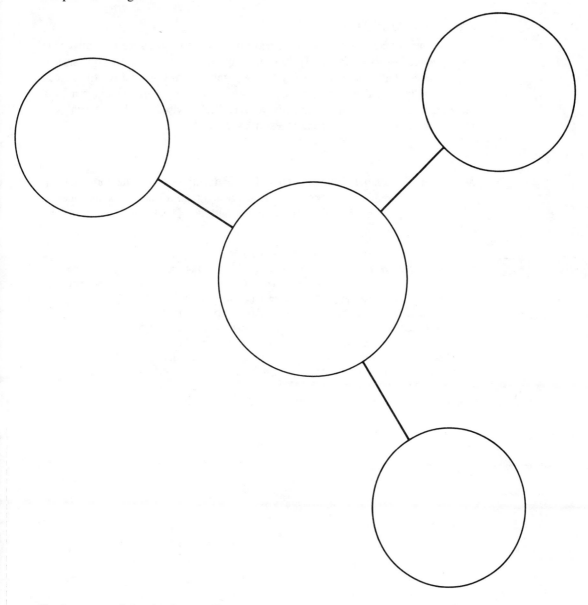

Check your work by the Answer Key.

Outlining

Identifying Major Details

The outline is another way to strengthen your ability to visualize mentally what you have read. This technique works especially well for the student who wishes to read detailed study materials quickly, yet remember what was read. Outlining can be especially effective if it is mastered simultaneously with the diagramming technique. Learning both strengthens your ability to visualize the material you read. Now apply these new techniques in Exercises 5.6 through 5.9.

☐ Exercise 5.6 ☐

Directions: Read the following paragraph and complete the diagram that accompanies it. Then use the suggested plan for headings and lines to change your diagram into an outline. Check your work by the Answer Key.

   It is said that mathematics began long ago in Early Egypt. The Nile River would flood on occasion and wash away all landmarks and monuments. People needed a way to know where their land was after these floods, so methods of earth measurement (later called Geometery) were invented. The Greeks, always thinking, picked up those techniques, developed them further, and added new ideas such as Algebra and Trigonometry. Math was off and running. It was used in oceanic exploration. It was interesting. It was fun. Mathematics was used to help learn about the ways in which the world worked, what it looked like, and how much things cost. Calculus, statistics, and income taxes were invented.[26]

Complete the diagram on page 201.

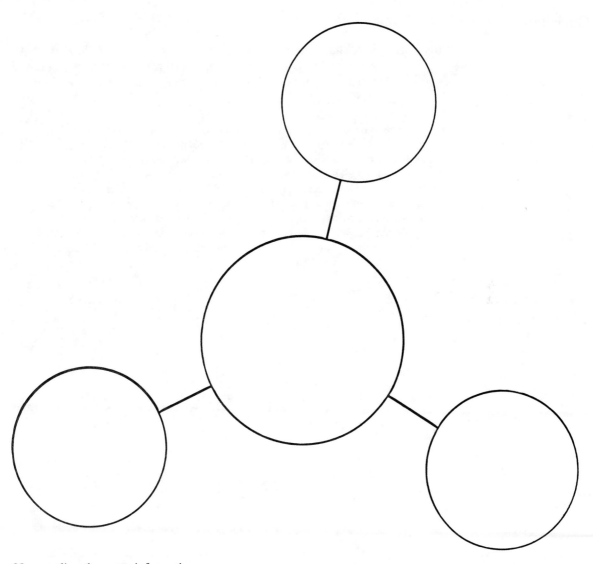

Now outline the same information:

Main Idea

_____
_____
_____
_____

Major Details

A. _____
B. _____
C. _____

☐ Exercise 5.7 ☐

Directions: Read the following paragraph and complete the diagram that accompanies it. Then use the suggested plan for headings and lines to change your diagram into an outline. Check your work by the Answer Key.

The incomes of families whose heads of household are prevocationally deaf fall below those of families in the general population. . . . The deaf families' median income is 84 percent as much as the United States average. For white deaf heads, the comparison is slightly more favorable—85 percent. But for nonwhite and female deaf heads of households the figures are worse. Nonwhite deaf males head households whose median income is 74 percent of that for nonwhite male heads in general. Similarly, white deaf female heads have median family incomes that are 74 percent of those for white female heads in general, and for nonwhite deaf female heads the comparison yields a rate of 73 percent for those who are deaf.[27]

Complete the diagram:

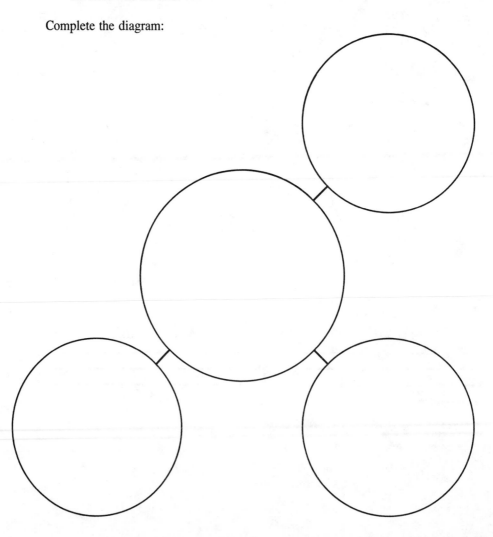

Now outline the same information:

Main Idea		*Major Details*

            A. _____

            B. _____

            C. _____

☐ **Exercise 5.8** ☐

Directions: Outline the main idea and major details in this paragraph without diagramming first. Check your work by the Answer Key.

Prior to the nineteenth century, an individual demonstrating unusual behavior that could not be explained was thought to possess an alien spirit or to be under the control of an outside force. Hence the person was classified as an *idiot* or *insane*. The development of the biological sciences during the nineteenth century permitted neurological and etiological anomalies to constitute a more refined classification system.[28]

Complete the blanks to show an outline of the paragraph:

Main Idea		*Major Details*

            A. _____

            B. _____

            C. _____

            D. _____

            E. _____

            F. _____

☐ **Exercise 5.9** ☐

Directions: Outline the main idea and major details in this paragraph without diagramming first. Check your work by the Answer Key.

The Civil War, often called the first "modern war," took a frightful toll in human lives. Submarines, ironclad ships, and torpedoes made their first appearance. More important to the average soldier, new designs in firepower also changed land warfare. Whereas the old smoothbore musket was a hit-or-miss type of weapon, the new rifles propelled a much more accurate, much deadlier missile. Although rifled cannons were not so much in evidence as infantry rifles, the old smoothbore cannons fired murderous cannisters filled with lead slugs, producing the same effect as gigantic sawed-off shotguns. Commanders adjusted slowly to these and other types of new military technology. Close formations and straightforward charges too often proved suicidal to the men in the ranks. Even in our age of B-52's, rockets, and "smart" bombs, Civil War casualty figures seem staggering. During a single day of fighting at Antietam the North lost over twelve thousand men and the South about an equal number. And other battles which lasted two or three days proved proportionately bloody.[29]

Main Idea		*Major Details*
	A.	
	B.	
	C.	

Identifying Minor Details

Finding only the major details that explain main ideas in a selection may be sufficient for some of your reading. But in careful study reading you may want to get *all* of the details in a page of text, both the major *and* the minor details that describe a main idea. You will find that minor details group themselves around a major detail just as major details group around the main idea. This, of course, is your key to making sense of the mass of facts in front of you. In Exercises 5.10 through 5.12, you will practice grouping minor details around major details and relating the separate parts to the whole—the main idea.

☐ **Exercise 5.10** ☐

Directions: Read the following paragraph and complete the diagram that accompanies it by filling in the minor details. Then use the suggested plan for headings and lines to change your diagram into an outline. Check your work by the Answer Key.

But once again, legal defiance was only a part of Britain's colonial problem. In some areas, enforcement of commercial regulations broke down almost completely. A Boston ship's captain, Daniel Malcom, drew a pistol on two revenue agents searching for illegal wine in his basement. Returning with the sheriff and a search warrant, the agents discovered the captain's house surrounded by a crowd of his friends, and the harried sheriff avoided a direct confrontation only by stalling for time until the search warrant expired. After the disgusted officials departed, Captain Malcom treated his protectors to buckets of smuggled wine. Such cases were not infrequent.[30]

```
+-------------------------------------------------------------------+
|                            MAIN IDEA                              |
+-------------------------------------------------------------------+
|        Legal defense was only a part of Britain's colonial problem. |
+-------------------------------------------------------------------+
                                 |
+-------------------------------------------------------------------+
|                           MAJOR DETAIL                           |
+-------------------------------------------------------------------+
| In some areas, enforcement of commerical regulations broke down almost completely. |
+-------------------------------------------------------------------+
                                 |
+-------------------------------------------------------------------+
|                          MINOR DETAILS                           |
+-------------------------------------------------------------------+
   |                    |                    |
+-------+          +----------+          +-------+
|       |          |          |          |       |
+-------+          |          |          +-------+
                   +----------+
```

I. (Main Idea)_____

_____

    A. (Major Detail)_____

    _____

        1. (Minor Detail)_____

        _____

        2. (Minor Detail)_____

        _____

        3. (Minor Detail)_____

        _____

☐ **Exercise 5.11** ☐

Directions: In the paragraph below there is a main idea as usual. Then there are two major details, each of which has one or more related minor details. Find these clusters of major and minor ideas and complete the diagram. Then use the suggested plan for headings and lines to change your diagram into an outline on page 206. Check your work by the Answer Key.

Intelligence plays a major part in determining what students will read. Generally, the areas of interest of more-intelligent students are on a slightly higher level than are those of less-intelligent students. Students with high IQ's read books that are more difficult and more adult. Mental age rather than the intelligence quotient appears to be the major factor and it seems to direct interest toward specific areas of content rather than toward reading as distinguished from other activities. Boys who score high on intelligence or aptitude tests (IQ 130 or more) read mystery stories, biographies, history, historical fiction, comics, scientific materials, sports, humor, and westerns; girls of above-average intelligence read historical fiction, modern novels, biographies, mystery stories, teenage books, sports, animal stories, science, history and books treating social problems.[31]

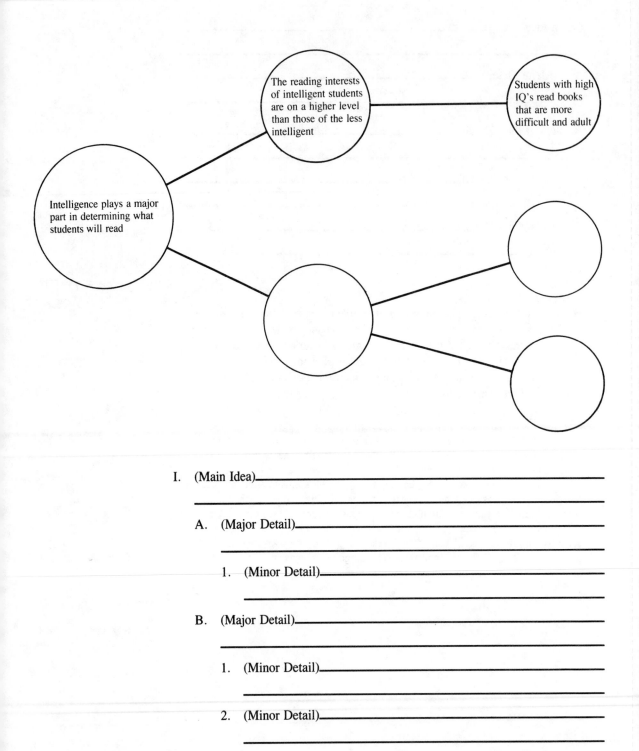

I.   (Main Idea)_____

_____

A.   (Major Detail)_____

_____

1.   (Minor Detail)_____

_____

B.   (Major Detail)_____

_____

1.   (Minor Detail)_____

_____

2.   (Minor Detail)_____

_____

□ Exercise 5.12 □

Directions: Read the following paragraph and complete the diagram that accompanies it. Then use the suggested plan for headings and lines to change your diagram into an outline. Check your work by the Answer Key.

There are two kinds of auditory deficiency: *intensity deafness* and *tone deafness*. A tone-deaf person cannot discriminate between pitches. Intensity deafness is of three types. (1) *Central deafness* is caused by damage to the auditory areas of the brain or by a neurotic conversion reaction (hysteria). (2) A *conductive loss* stems from an impairment in the conductive process in the middle ear. Either the eardrum is punctured or there is a malfunction of the three small ossicles or bones in the middle ear. This reduces the person's hearing ability, affecting the loudness with which a person hears speech, but if the loudness of the sound is increased, he hears and understands. A person with a conductive loss can hear his own voice through bone conduction. Thus, the voices of others sound much softer than his own. To compensate, he frequently speaks softly so his voice conforms to the voice of others around him. (3) *Nerve loss* stems from an impairment of the auditory nerve and affects clarity and intelligibility of speech. A person with such a loss hears the speech of others, but may not understand what he hears. The high-tone nerve loss prevents him from hearing and distinguishing certain speech sounds, especially such sounds as f, v, s, z, sh, zh, th, t, d, b, k, and g. Articulation generally is affected.[32]

Complete the diagram on page 208.

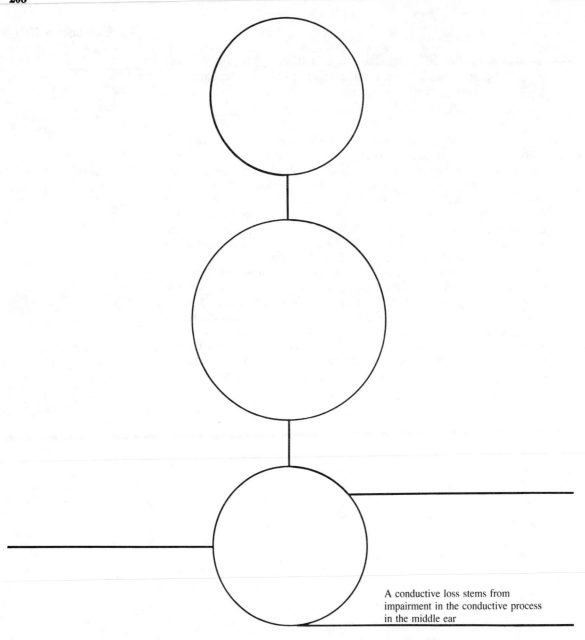

A conductive loss stems from
impairment in the conductive process
in the middle ear

Completing the Outline Without the Help of a Diagram

You are now ready to outline without the visual aid of diagramming. Practicing
on Exercises 5.13 through 5.15 will help you develop this skill.

□ **Exercise 5.13** □

Directions: The following paragraph is more difficult than the ones you have
been working with. First, find the main idea. Then find two other
ideas of next relative importance that are used in expanding on the

idea. Each of these two sub-ideas has several facts that cluster under it. In the space provided, group these details in relationship to the larger sub-idea to which it is related, and also in relationship to the total topic. If you read for the purpose of identifying this pattern, you should have no difficulty in filling in the outline. If you need to refer back to the paragraph for some of the details, feel free to do so. When you are finished, check your work by the Answer Key on p. 233.

One of these unexplained stories is the tale of the Kentucky Glowing Man. Late one evening in 1955 a farmer was standing outside his farmhouse in a remote part of Kentucky when he saw a flying saucer land behind some trees. He went inside and told his family. Nobody would believe his story. An hour later the family were alerted by one of their dogs which was barking angrily. Two men went outside to investigate and they found what they later described as a small glowing man with large red eyes walking towards the house. This strange sight scared the farmers, but as they were carrying rifles they began to shoot their luminous intruder. A metallic sound told them that they had hit their target and they stopped firing, but the glowing man seemed unharmed and simply "floated away into some trees." The two men went back into the house and bolted all the doors. A few moments later the glowing man peered in through one of the farmhouse windows. The two farmers rushed outside to chase him off, but their visitor had vanished. They searched all around the outbuildings, and suddenly one of the men felt a tap on his head. He looked up and saw a claw-like hand reaching down towards him from a low roof.[33]

I.   What is the main idea?_____

_____

_____

What are the two major sub-topics or major details? What are the minor details under each sub-topic?

A.   (First large sub-topic)_____

_____

(Related details)

1. _____

2. _____

B.   (Second large sub-topic)_____

_____

(Related details)

1. _____

2. _____

3. _____

C.   (Third large sub-topic)_____

(Related details)

1.   _____

2.   _____

3.   _____

□ **Exercise 5.14** □

Directions: In this paragraph, find the two ideas of next relative importance
that expand the main idea. Each of these two sub-ideas has several
facts clustered under it. Group these details in relationship to the
larger sub-idea to which it is related, and also in relationship to
the total topic. Check your work with the Answer Key at the end of
this unit and correct your outline if necessary.

Words permit the writer to share experiences with the reader. The reader
does not see nor experience directly the object, person, place, sensation, or
event of which the author writes. He sees or experiences them through the
symbols that stand for them and evoke his perception of them. There is no direct
or invariable connection between the symbol and referent, the datum, object,
event, or sensation. Verbal symbols at best are inadequate substitutes for direct
experience. In fact, language does not represent objects but, rather, concepts that
the mind has formed of them. Communication through reading is most difficult
when the reader's experience is inadequate. And the degree of accuracy of
perceptions depends greatly upon the number and variety of experiences that the
reader has had.[34]

I.   (Main Idea)_____

_____

A.   The reader does not see nor experience directly the object, person, place,
sensation, or event of which the author writes.

1.   _____

2.   _____

B.   Verbal symbols are at best inadequate substitutes for direct experiences.

1.   _____

_____

_____

2.   _____

_____

_____

3.   _____

_____

_____

☐ **Exercise 5.15** ☐

Directions: Read the following paragraph and outline by yourself with no help at all. Remember: First, you must read and decide on relationships of ideas. Second, make your own outline complete with Roman numerals, letters, and numbers. Third, correct the outline by referring to the Answer Key at the end of this Unit.

In 1664 Charles' brother, the Duke of York, later King James II, received a broad grant encompassing the Dutch colony of New Netherland. Seizing the opportunity to oust England's hated rival from North America, James quickly dispatched a small expeditionary force. After stopping in Boston to secure additional troops, the fleet's commander sailed into New Amsterdam's inviting harbor and demanded surrender of the settlement. Peter Stuyvesant, New Amsterdam's feisty, one-legged governor, threatened a fight but yielded when citizens refused to follow their unpopular leader. Without a single shot being fired, Peter Minuet's twenty-four-dollar bargain fell to the Englishmen, and they immediately renamed the city and colony New York, in honor of the Duke. The new proprietor eased the transition to English rule by guaranteeing Dutch inhabitants fair treatment, tolerating their religion, and recognizing the validity of their inheritance customs. Many old Dutch families continued to dominate New York's society and politics into the eighteenth century, and the city was North America's most cosmopolitan center, containing Dutch, English, French, Swedish, African, and Jewish people. James' goals in New York were primarily political and strategic, rather than economic, and he imposed only a low annual assessment—called a "quitrent" (not a rent but a feudal fee)—on colonial landholders.[35]

Your Outline

From Written to Mental Outlining

☐ Exercise 5.16 ☐

Directions: At this point you probably will not need to write the outline of the paragraph in order to sense the relationships between its parts. However, an intermediate step taking you from writing outlines to mentally grasping the basic structure may be needed. Therefore, for the following paragraph, write the numbers and letters that indicate different parts of an outline right into the paragraph itself. Check your work with the Answer Key at the end of this unit and correct your work if necessary.

A false notion, held by many, is that certain items or events in and of themselves serve as positive reinforcers for all individuals. Common examples of these assumed "reinforcers" include words of praise, smiles, and certain sweets (such as the ubiquitous candy-coated, chocolate bits). We already stated that reinforcers are defined by their effect upon an individual's behavior—the "acid test" is whether the object or event when made contingent upon a behavior causes an increase in that behavior. If this is not the outcome, a positive reinforcer has not been selected. What is reinforcing to one individual may not be to others because of past experiences or personal preference. For example, many youngsters initially do not like carbonated beverages; with repeated tastes, however, they learn to like them. Some children learn to fear water, although most learn to enjoy it. The reinforcing value of some events depends partially upon an individual's mental abilities. This can be illustrated by an adult's verbal praise and cash rewards which are reinforcing only if the individual has respectively some basic understanding of the language and the currency system involved.[36]

☐ Exercise 5.17 ☐

Directions: Using the same method as in Exercise 5.16, label this paragraph. Use the Roman numeral I for the main idea and the letters A and B for the major details. The arabic numerals 1 and 2 should be used for minor details.

Creative writing is simply an act of personal authorship. It is defined as the act of recording one's ideas in words and sentences. The term *creative* is intended only to express the idea that these words and sentences are the personal product of the child's experience and imagination. The product itself may be a letter, a story, a poem, a report, an observation, or an account. Others may judge it to be unique or mundane, dull or scintillating, thoughtful or careless, beautiful or ugly, worthy or unworthy, original or imitative. It may be fictitious or factual, expository or narrative, imaginative or documentary. It matters not how others may choose to characterize it. Any act of personal authorship should be regarded as intrinsically valuable and creative.[37]

☐ Exercise 5.18 ☐

Directions: If the use of outlining symbols is not your favorite technique for organizing details into logical relationships, another technique may be used—that of underlining. In the following paragraph, use a single underline to mark the main idea. Use two underlines to identify major details and three underlines to indicate minor details.

Perhaps one of the more interesting aspects of intelligence of a high order is the ability to be creative. This rare talent causes people to see the world in a different fashion. They are able to draw on their experiences as a source of new ideas, and are able to project those ideas back into the world. Obviously, a consideration of creativity is colored by the discipline or activity to which it applies. Creativity in some processes largely rejects form and structure as an aesthetic principle. This Dionysian aesthetic is seen in many contemporary art forms which have largely abandoned the traditional intent to communicate. It is also seen in some marginal forms of literature, whose major theme has generally been the intent to give insight into reality by communicating. This desire to be creative within conventions and to communicate uses form and structure as aesthetic principles, and brings fresh ideas in a form largely comprehensible to others. Undoubtedly, there are many personality and life-style correlates to these modes of creativity, and to whatever blends of these, and alternatives, are found.[38]

☐ **Exercise 5.19** ☐

Directions: Try underlining the following paragraph as you did for the one in Exercise 5.18. Check your work by the Answer Key at the end of this unit.

The second type of writing system is what has usually been called "phonetic" . . . In this type of system, the separate written symbols have no semantic value (i.e., no meaning) in themselves, but correspond only to sounds made in uttering the words in the spoken language. For this purpose, the total number of symbols required by any one language is relatively small (between twenty and forty), and is known as an "alphabet." Only in an alphabetic writing system can there be any question of spelling, i.e., combining written symbols in a conventional order to represent words. In some languages—Finnish and Turkish, for instance—there is an almost complete one-to-one correspondence between the written symbols and the sounds of the language; that is to say, each significant sound can be consistently represented by the same letter or combination of letters. This situation remains possible only so long as (a) the total number of significant speech-sounds used in the language is not more than can be represented by the available letters or combinations of letters in the alphabet, and (b) the pronunciation of the language does not change, or (if it does change) does so with complete consistency. For various reasons, in most languages these conditions seldom prevail for very long together. Neither of them has been true for the English language.[39]

It is now time to see how much you are able to grasp without diagramming, outlining, or other aids. For Exercises 5.20 and 5.21 follow this procedure:

1. Preview the material. In the preview you are looking only for the information that interests you. You are not trying to grasp all the small details at this time.
2. Read carefully the material that interests you, speeding quickly over the remaining information. Give yourself no more than ten seconds.
3. Read the entire selection carefully.
4. Check your comprehension and reading rate.

☐ Exercise 5.20 ☐

A learner can be considered to have mastered the essentials of any phonemic system of writing when he is able to respond to each of the written signs by overtly making the corresponding sound. If the learner knows the meaning of the spoken words so produced, these sounds may be said to serve as "vehicles" from the written signs to the writer's ideas. At a more advanced stage, however, the reader is able to understand the message without any "overt" utterances, i.e. merely by "looking" at the printed signs, even if he is encountering some of the words in their written form for the first time. In this case, what sort of "vehicles" take the reader from the printed signs to the writer's ideas? In an alphabetic system of writing, the configuration of any word as a whole is largely a coincidental product of the shapes of the written signs associated with certain speech-sounds; it does not in itself provide any clue to meaning. If—to take an imaginary example—we were to encounter the word *ditter*, we could get no help as to its meaning from knowing words that look like it, such as *bitter* or *dither*. We might perhaps be able to deduce from its context whether it was a noun or an adjective or a verb. But what we could do at once with reasonable certainty is to pronounce it. In a completely phonemic language such as Finnish, Turkish or Serbian, it is possible to pronounce any word at sight. And in any alphabetic language, it seems that the learner first has to translate individual signs into some elements of inner speech; they have been described as "partial responses" . . . , or "auditory sensations" . . . evoked by the visual perception of letters.[40]

If a language is completely phonemic, name the one thing that the reader can do almost immediately as he reads. Check your answer by the Key.

Comprehension Check

Directions: Complete each of the following statements by writing in or circling the correct answer.

1.   An *alphabetic* language means _____

     _____

2.   Visual perceptions precede auditory perceptions in the reading process.
     True   False

3.   An awareness of _____ permits one to quickly determine the pronunciation of a word.

4.   Being able to pronounce a word does not always signal its meaning.
     True   False

5.   The auditory sensations experienced by a reader play which role in facilitating

Comprehension Accuracy: meaning?_____

_____   _____

Debilitating definitions of mental retardation and assignment of classificatory levels of retardation have led to the stigmatization and placement of individuals in programs accentuating their deficiencies and attenuating their chances of tapping their full potential to acquire the complex physical, mental, and social schemata of their age mates. The enervating effects of such misfortunes were forewarned as early as 1905 by the father of the testing movement, Binet, who said, "It will never be to one's credit to have attended a special school" (Binet & Simon, 1905). Perhaps more devastating than attendance in special schools or classes has been participation in a potpourri of programs negatively stereotyping the children into a homogeneous group rather than recognizing their heterogeneity and carefully constructing learning environments conducive to the development of each individual's potential.[41]

Comprehension Check

Directions: Complete each of the following statements by writing in or circling the correct answer.

1.   The author of this selection believes that _____ has led to the placement of retarded persons in programs that accentuate their deficiencies.

2.   Who is the "father of the testing movement"? _____

3.   The author presents evidence supporting the effectiveness of special schools and classes.

   True   False

4.   What are two important things that special schools could encourage, but don't?

   a. _____

   b. _____

5.   Problems stemming from labeling were recognized before the early 1900s.

   True   False

IDENTIFYING SIGNAL WORDS

All words in the English language are not key message bearers. Some function just to hold ideas together. Such are the signal words found in all your reading materials. Signal words warn you what to expect. If you heed them, you will read much more rapidly and intelligently. They help you get to the point of what you are reading.

Reading uses two types of signals for speed—those that signal straight ahead and those that clue you to turn around. Such signals also act as your guide to gathering the meaning as the author presents it. Some common signal words are given in Table 5.1.

Table 5.1:   *Signal Words*

Straight-Ahead Signals

and	more	and so
also	moreover	therefore
furthermore	more than that	accordingly
likewise	thus	consequently
in addition to	so	as a result
first	concluding	finally
second		in conclusion

Turn-Around Signals

but	otherwise	despite
yet	although	in spite of
nevertheless	however	on the contrary
still	not	rather
	notwithstanding	

SOURCE: Nila Smith, *Read Faster and Get More From Your Reading* (Englewood Cliffs, N.J.: Prentice-Hall, Inc., 1958), pp. 51–53; and Jane Bracy and Marian McClintock, *Read to Succeed* (New York: McGraw-Hill Book Co., 1975), pp. 88.

Straight-Ahead Signals

Straight-ahead signals show that the writer is continuing with the explanation of an idea. Because such words indicate the repetition or elaboration of a main idea already introduced, you will usually be able to speed up your reading when you recognize these signals.

The most commonly used straight-ahead signal is *and*. It tells you that ideas are of equal importance or belong in a particular sequence. As an example, read the following sentence. Underline the signal words that say go straight ahead.

Our family bought peaches, and apples, and grapefruit at a roadside stand.

And was the signal; it indicated that the words in the sentence were items in a sequence.

Now read the following sentence about flowering plants. Underline the signal word.

Most flowering plants smell good and are really beautiful to the eye.

In this sentence, the signal word *and* connects ideas of equal importance.

There are other straight-ahead words that also indicate, "there is something else, follow along." Among these are *more, moreover, more than that, likewise, also, furthermore,* and *in addition to.* The following paragraphs in Exercise 5.22 are provided to help you become aware of straight-ahead signals which say that something else follows.

☐ Exercise 5.22 ☐

Directions: Underline the words in the following paragraphs that give you the straight-ahead signal.

1.   The secret of Chinese cooking? First of all, thousands of years of

2. practice,'' says Luke. ''And selecting the proper food that's good for the body for the proper season.''[42]

2. This points up a central problem of photographing wildlife in depth. In addition to the blind you need a gimmick—something that you know the animals will come to, so that you don't have to chase after them. On Machias Seal Island, a rock above a puffin's nest served as such a gimmick. From observation I knew that he liked to rest up there, and that's what I zeroed in on, waiting for him.[43]

3. The restaurant's chef, Luke Chan . . . , takes all day to prepare a winter melon. ''First, I have to find the right melon from a market,'' he explains. ''The skin must be just the right color. Then I hollow it and fill it with lotus seeds, mushrooms, chicken, and other ingredients. I carve the dragon (on the outside of the melon) with a skewer, in relief, by scraping away the skin around it. Thereafter it steams for eight hours. For our New Year the dragon symbolizes good luck, prosperity, and authority. . . .''[44]

Some straight-ahead signal words are more commanding than others and frequently indicate the heart of the paragraph. Something of significance is coming. These words include:

furthermore	first	therefore
thus	likewise	accordingly
so	second	and so
consequently	third	finally
as a result	concluding	in conclusion

☐ **Exercise 5.23** ☐

Directions: In the following paragraph, underline once the signal words that give clues for other items in a sequence or for ideas of equal value. Then circle one of the more commanding straight-ahead signals.

Initially, we felt strange in the habitat—not because we were underwater; that adjustment comes quickly—but because we were constantly watched. Our actions and conversations were monitored by TV cameras and microphones transmitting to the command van ashore. Likewise, we could glance at our own screens and see the watch director on duty. At first, this around-the-clock surveillance gave me a hair-prickling sensation.[45]

Signals such as *finally, as a result, concluding,* and *in conclusion* are extremely important because they signal that the author is coming to a stopping point or is summarizing an idea.

☐ **Exercise 5.24** ☐

Directions: Underline the stopping signals in the following paragraphs.

1. The absence of organized political parties also hindered the Confederate government. Lacking the level of party loyalty—the Confederacy never developed a two party system—Davis found it more difficult than Lincoln to control his cabinet. Davis went through no less than six secretaries of war; five attorneys general, and four secretaries of state. Unlike Lincoln, Davis possessed no party machinery with which to fight obstructive state leaders,

and he simply had to suffer the opposition and abuse from independent state chieftains such as Brown and Robert Toombs in Georgia. Finally, the lack of party organization impeded efforts to inform and mobilize the Confederate electorate. Lacking the party hoopla which had surrounded Jacksonian politics, Confederate elections apparently generated little excitement and failed to stimulate voter interest.[46]

2.   The Turks and Afghans were nomadic warriors from central Asia. A semibarbaric people, they were capable of united action under daring leadership. They had adopted Islam and they had been strongly influenced by Persian culture. As a result, they often combined great cruelty with an appreciation of beauty and culture. In establishing control over the Ganges Valley and the Punjab, they destroyed Hindu and Buddist temples, but later covered the land with buildings of exquisite design, combining the best of Moslem and Hindu architecture. They also brought with them the typically Turkish practice of taking children from their homes and educating them as military or administrative officials.[47]

Note the impact of the statements following the signal "as a result" in the latter paragraph.

Turn-Around Signals

Following straight-ahead signals is easy because such writing has a clear sense of progression. As a reader, you just add more and more information to your present stock. However, writing that contains many turn-around words, words that signal ideas that are contrary to or in opposition to the ideas that preceded it, is more difficult to follow. A reader is more likely to lose his train of thought. Therefore, turn-around signals are more important than the straight-ahead signals.

The most frequently used turn-around signals are:

but	otherwise	not	in spite of
yet	although	notwithstanding	on the contrary
nevertheless	however	despite	rather

☐ Exercise 5.25 ☐

Directions: In the following paragraphs, draw a box,   , around each turn-about signal.

1.   Only the strict policy of the Dutch government, which prevented peasants from selling or alienating their land, saved the Javanese from what would otherwise have been their certain fate—the tenant-farming and share-cropping pattern that was to develop in the Philippines. Nevertheless, a very prolific, poor, and backward peasantry became characteristic of Java, while peasants on the outer islands remained landowners and enjoyed greater prosperity.[48]

2.   Tamerlane marched with a great army down the Khyber Pass from Afghanistan plundering as he went. His armies entered Delhi in December 1398, and he was proclaimed "Emperor of Hindustan." But in the next year, having gained an enormous booty, Tamerlane led his forces toward

the Himalaya Mountains, then westward to the Indus River, and on into central Asia.[49]

3.   There was also a language problem. Because most of the Filipinos still spoke one of the hundreds of different languages of the islands, the sensible course seemed to be to teach in English rather than in Spanish or a Filipino language. But the peasant children seldom mastered English. In spite of these drawbacks, popular education was further advanced in the Philippines than elsewhere in Southeast Asia.[50]

Practice Identifying Signals

□ Exercise 5.26 □

Directions: In each of the following paragraphs, locate the signal words. Circle each straight-ahead signal. Place a box around each turn-around signal. Check your answers in the Answer Key at the end of this unit.

Example: Mary and Beth are both attractive and have pleasing personalities. Therefore, one would expect both girls to be popular among their age mates. However, they do not get along well with their peers.

1.   English belongs to the Germanic language family, but it has borrowed many words from other language groups. Like the romance languages of French, Spanish, Italian, and Portuguese, English traces more than half of its vocabulary to Latin. Therefore, if you know a few morphemes of Latin origin, you will be able to break up and build up thousands of words.[51]

2.   The first English dictionary was compiled in 1755 by Samuel Johnson— an eccentric, pedantic, hard-working scholar. Today, the *Dictionary of the English Language* seems full of errors and inconsistencies, more a reflection of the compiler's personality than of the English language. Yet this dictionary provided Englishmen with the first authoritative guide to their language. With only six copyists to help him, Dr. Johnson compiled two large volumes of words in nine years. His source was literature, not life. Consequently, his dictionary uses literary quotations in support of its definitions. Dr. Johnson's major achievement was the standardization of spelling and meaning. Imperfect as it was, the *Dictionary of the English Language* laid a solid foundation for the dictionary you use today.

3.   Most writing that tells what happened makes use of the time arrangement. Events recorded in this manner may be reports of your own actual experiences, historical records, and, most frequently, news stories. On the other hand, the events may be fictional, as in some poems and in most other stories.

   The term narrative is often used to describe the kinds of writing just noted. The process in general is called narration. Perhaps you have thought that *narrative* or *narration* apply only to make-believe events. However, these terms suggest a series of events arranged according to time. Therefore, both real and fictional happenings may be arranged in this way.

4.   Through the power of suggestion, more soft drinks, french fries, and gas are sold. No group uses words more effectively to influence the common man than advertisers. Advertisers are hidden persuaders who sell, not lipstick, soap, and perfume, but a dream, a hope, and an adventure. Note the words in ads, and you will see power at work—enough power to sell over four billion dollars worth of cosmetics a year. . . .

5.   Old Mr. Mason stopped shuffling along the sidewalk. He bent down very slowly, carefully bracing himself with his cane. Finally, his gnarled fingers reached what he was after. He straightened painfully and in the glare of the noonday sun examined the quarter he had retrieved from the scorching concrete.

6.   In response to his question, Mrs. Brown told the grocer that she had had a very nice time on her vacation in Montana. Furthermore, when he asked her how the children had enjoyed the trip, she admitted that Sam and Charles had to be dragged away from the ranch, while Andy wanted to bring one of the horses home with him.

7.   Right now you may be thinking that imaginative writing is just fine if you happen to be a copywriter or a poet. Naturally you are not as free to use your imagination in factual writing—especially when you are restricted not only in your choice of subject but also in your development of that subject. Nevertheless, factual writing can challenge your power to imagine . . .

8.   Although there are many levels of pitch, only four are used to show differences in meaning. . . .

9.   The eggs were too hard; otherwise, the breakfast was good.

10.   My cousin is going to Europe this summer; moreover, she will visit four different countries during her stay.

Test Yourself on Signal Words

How well do you remember the signal words? Place the initials *SA* before each straight-ahead signal listed below. If the signal is a ''turn'' signal, place a *T* before it.

Signal Words

_____	in spite of	_____	however
_____	also	_____	yet
_____	still	_____	likewise
_____	and	_____	consequently
_____	furthermore	_____	thus
_____	but	_____	although
_____	moreover	_____	so

APPLYING WHAT YOU'VE LEARNED

It is now time to apply all of the paragraph techniques you have learned to the reading of entire selections. Read Selections 1 and 2 as quickly as possible. Use your newly developed speed skills to find the main idea of each paragraph, remembering to speed over those unimportant paragraphs in which no central thought is developed. Time your reading. Then check your comprehension. Record your scores on the reading Progress Chart for Unit 5 on p. 237.

Selection 1: Daffodils Go Au Naturel

Beginning Time:

Total Words: 957

> "Ten thousand saw I at a glance,
> Nodding their heads in sprightly dance . . ."

William Wordsworth's poem about daffodils describes exactly what many of us would like to see on our own property: masses of fragrant daffodils heralding spring, growing more numerous and lovely every year with little effort on our part.

By buying the right varieties, ones that self-multiply with vigor, you can have a naturalized planting of daffodils in your yard. To achieve that effect, it's not necessary to own an acre of meadow or a large expanse of open woodland. Daffodils look splendid when naturalized in a small rockery, beside a pond or stream, or on a berm. Even a patch of lawn under a silver birch or similar tree makes a good site for naturalizing daffodils.

But it is a mistake to believe that a daffodil planting will thrive uncared-for. It's true that daffodils are among the most carefree of all flowering bulbs. And small clumps in beds and borders around the house often do take care of themselves, blooming faithfully year after year. But daffodils planted in naturalized settings do require careful treatment, especially where they must break through a surface of sod before blooming. Otherwise, instead of more and more flowers each year, you'll get fewer and fewer until they stop blooming altogether.

One attribute of daffodils is the fact that they will naturalize in lawns. Many other flowering bulbs, such as tulips and hyacinths, have a hard time competing against the grass.

Another good quality of daffodils is their pest resistance. Naturalized plantings of crocus and tulips can be wiped out by rodents before they ever have a chance to bloom. Daffodils are poisonous to these pests.

Daffodils make excellent cut flowers, and cutting the flowers will in no way harm the bulbs or next year's display. Large naturalized plantings can provide armloads of flowers for indoors and still leave plenty for outdoor display.

BUYING AND PLANTING

Special naturalizing "mixtures" and "collections" of daffodils are offered by bulb companies. I feel that you should examine these carefully before choosing them, because the best naturalized effects are produced by planting separate colors in drifts rather than making a hodge-podge with too many different varieties.

The important factors for naturalized plantings are a sunny, well-drained location plus a regular feeding and soil conditioning program.

Start out with good soil. Daffodils love to grow in soil that's rich in leaf mold or similar organic material. Garden compost and peat moss are good substitutes. Daffodils also need plenty of phosphorus mixed in with the soil before planting. Phosphorus encourages bulb growth. As a source of phosphorus, bone meal is suitable for use when planting small areas, but becomes too expensive for plantings on a large scale. Where large areas are involved, less-costly superphosphate is a more sensible choice.

Mix these two ingredients—the organic material and the superphosphate at the rate of equal parts by weight. Dig the mixture thoroughly into the soil at the rate of 100 lbs. per 1,000 bulbs at time of planting (unless of course you are planting daffodils in an established lawn).

After this initial planting, normally done in fall between September and December, the bulbs should be fed with superphosphate twice a year—in spring before the bulbs bloom and again in fall before the ground freezes.

When you plant, space the bulbs 6 inches apart, and plant them at least 4 inches deep (measuring from the top of the bulb). To avoid a regimented pattern—which looks most unnatural for a naturalized planting—scatter the bulbs gently on the ground like broadcasting seeds, and plant them where they fall.

Naturalizing daffodils in grass is best done at the edge of a lawn or bordering a fence or wooded area. That's because the grass must not be mowed where the daffodil are planted until the middle of June when the daffodil leaves have all died down. Cutting the daffodil leaves prematurely will prevent the following year's flowers from developing. These unmowed areas can become quite unsightly unless the daffodils are confined to a special area on the sidelines.

If you want to plant your daffodils in the center of a lawn anyway, you can do that by lifting out a square of sod, loosening the dirt in the hole, mixing in a little organic material and bonemeal, then planting the bulb. Replace the sod.

VARIETIES FOR NATURALIZING

Species: Hoop petticoat daffodil (Narcissus bulbocodium) is a common sight in the alpine meadows of Switzerland. These tiny daffodils have funnel-shaped cups resembling raised hoop petticoats, and pointed petals. Hoop petticoats are among the earliest blooming daffodils.

Cyclamineus hybrids: February Gold is a golden-yellow with a long trumpet. Dove Wings has white swept-back outer petals and a pale yellow trumpet. Beryl appears to be in a constant swirl of motion with its turned-under white petals and golden-yellow trumpet. All of these are miniatures.

Triandrus hybrids: These have flowers that appear in clusters and hang downwards. The variety Thalia is a gleaming pure white.

Poeticus narcissus: This group is characterized by large white petals and tiny, red-rimmed eyes. The variety Actaea is outstandingly beautiful.

Large Cup: The variety Aranjuez is extremely vigorous, sporting large yellow petals and a crimson-edged, ruffled cup. Rushlight is a distinctive variety because of its primrose-yellow petals and primrose cup with a white base. Routlette is a large white with an enormous yellow cup rimmed with coral.

Small cup: Apricot Distinction stands out in any crowd of daffodils. The apricot-buff petals surround a solid scarlet cup that's as prominent as a stop-light.

Trumpet: The old-favorite varieties Beersheba (white) and King Alfred (yellow) are still dependable and generally less costly than more recent introductions. But if you can afford the best then choose Spellbinder, one that exhibits unusual lemon petals and a two-tone white and lemon trumpet.

Ending Time:

WPM:

Comprehension Check: Daffodils Go Au Naturel

Directions: Complete each of the following questions by writing in or circling the correct answer.

1. Daffodils are noted for their
   a. ability to grow and spread without any outside assistance.
   b. pest resistance as the bulbs are poisonous to rodents.
   c. long-lasting ability as cut flowers.

2. The one mineral needed by daffodils planted in natural settings is _____
   _____.

3. Daffodils' hardiness and self-multiplication qualities are present in all varieties.
   True   False

4. Although daffodil bulbs are planted from September to December, they
   herald _____.

5. The hoop petticoat daffodil grows as far away as the alpine meadows of Switzerland.
   True   False

Comprehension Accuracy:

_____

Selection 2: Porsche ——————————————————————

Beginning Time:

_____

Total Words: 479

Once there were nearly a score of small European firms that built sports cars—largely as a labor of love. Today, high wage costs and government-imposed design requirements have overwhelmed these legendary creators of auto exotica. They are either out of business (like Facel Vega and Jensen), able to produce only a handful of units annually (like Aston Martin and Maserati), or tiny divisions of huge corporations (like Ferrari, now owned by Fiat).

Then there is Porsche. Tiny by auto industry standards, it flourished on a unit volume—35,000 cars last year—that wouldn't keep most auto companies alive for a single month. In its fiscal year ending last July, this family-owned German business had annual revenues of over $500 million. The Stuttgart-based firm's bread and butter is its racy, rear-engined 911—on the market since 1964 and still moving briskly. The price: a minimum of $25,000, but over $50,000 for a turbo-charged version that can zoom from a dead stop to 60 mph in less than six seconds.

Still, Porsche isn't resting on the 911's market victories. Its third generation owners stepped aside five years ago in favor of professional outside management, and two new models introduced since then have broadened the company's base considerably. The 928 is a luxury sedan, available with automatic transmission, that competes against Mercedes and BMW; the 924 is a $15,000 sports car intended to challenge cheaper Italian and Japanese models.

"With high-price cars like ours, we must sell all over the world to maintain production volume," says Heinz Branitzki, who runs Porsche's financial operations and came to the company from the Carl Zeiss optical firm. At the moment, however, Porsche's problem is too much foreign business. Over 50% of its production goes to the U.S.—half of that to California, where sleek Porsches look just right in Beverly Hills driveways. The dollar's decline squeezes those margins, and Branitzki aims to limit his exposure by boosting sales at home and in Japan, which is already a major Porsche market.

Despite its unique success, tradition prevails at Porsche. Top-of-the-line models are largely hand-built by workers in blue overalls emblazoned with the company name. And Porsche still gets a 50-cent royalty for every Volkswagen "Beetle" that is built; founder Ferdinand Porsche designed it for VW in 1936. Several years ago, in fact, VW's Audi division and Porsche seemed about to merge. But Porsche backed away, though the two still share dealers in the U.S.

Ending Time:

At the moment, thanks to the demise of many competitors, Porsche easily sells all the cars its cramped factory can build. Branitzki, however, isn't about to cut customer waiting times and push production beyond 40,000 units a year. "That would cost us $50 million for expansion," he says, "and I'd rather have a bit of money in the bank. Look at our revenues—four times what they were four years ago. Give us a while to consolidate."

WPM: _____

Comprehension Check: Porsche

Directions: Complete each of the following questions by writing in or circling the correct answer.

1. Porsche is unique among auto industries because _____

_____

_____.

2. The scope of Porsche's market is
   a. contained within the European nations.
   b. worldwide.
   c. mainly Japan.

3. Professional outside management is spurned by the owners of the Porsche auto industry.

   True   False

4. The major buyer of the Porsche is _____

_____.

Comprehension Accuracy:

5. Porsche limits the number of cars that it makes per year and at present refuses to expand.

   True   False

_____

Read Selection 3, "The Satellite." What is the main idea? When you have finished reading, refer to the article to complete the outline that follows.

Selection 3: The Satellite ━━━━━━━━━━━━━━━━━━━━━━

Beginning Time: _____

━━━━━━━━━━━━━━━━━

Total Words: 733

The man-made satellite seems destined to become both a most powerful tool of science and a dominant instrument of national policy. It has several advantages over sounding rockets and high-altitude balloons. The scope of its observations is many times greater, and the period of time these observations cover is of much greater length. Moreover, data such as those which revealed that the earth is not a slightly flattened sphere but somewhat distorted in the shape of a pear cannot be acquired by any other method yet devised.

The satellite is also a symbol of scientific and industrial strength. In its present stage of development, it can be regarded as a first stepping stone to adventure beyond the earth's atmosphere. Its development can proceed in either of two directions. In the hands of a nation ambitious for power, it can become a means for controlling the destinies of the world. In the hands of a nation dedicated to a program of peace it can become a scientific laboratory without an equal, a vantage point for policing the universe, and a possible embarkation center for those who venture into interplanetary commerce.

Future progress in the construction of manned satellites and space vehicles will depend upon a strong national effort. A manned satellite or spaceship can be launched and maintained only by a nation having first-class scientists and technical personnel. Contributing to its development are highly skilled personnel employing first-rate facilities over a wide range of basic sciences such as chemistry, mathematics, metallurgy, and physics. These skills and facilities also must be supported by the proper attitude of a nation's people. The fabricating of space vehicles and satellites must be regarded as first objectives, and taxpayers must be willing to spend the vast amounts of money and energy their development requires.

Orbital Velocity

In its present stage of development, the man-made earth satellite is simply the instrument-carrying section of a research rocket. The research rocket must be powerful enough and sufficiently controlled in flight so that it can place such an instrument section in orbit. We know that the highest velocity that the earth's gravity can produce is 6.965 miles per second, or 25,074 miles per hour. From this information we correctly conclude, for all practical purposes, that the speed at which an object must travel to escape from the earth is also 25,074 miles per hour. Strictly speaking, no object can escape the force of attraction of another. This force of attraction varies directly with the product of the mass of such bodies and inversely with the square of the distances between them. Hence, gravitational force equals GM_1M_2/r^2, where G represents the universal gravitational constant, M the mass of a body, and r the distance between the bodies.

Satellites balance gravity with centrifugal force; they do not escape the earth's gravitational field. Circular orbital velocity varies with the distance of a satellite from the earth. (The circular orbital speed at any altitude above the earth's surface is equal to about seven-tenths the escape speed at such altitude divided by

━━━━━━━━━━━━━━━━━━━━━━

SOURCE: Reprinted with permission from the National Aeronautics and Space Administration.

the square root of 2.) In order to establish an orbit 350 miles from the earth, a satellite need have a speed of only 16,950 miles per hour; to establish an orbit 4,000 miles from the earth, a satellite need have a speed of only 10,320 miles per hour. Explorer I, the first satellite launched by the United States, had a perigee (nearest distance) 229 miles above the earth, an apogee (farthest distance) 1,587 miles above the earth, and an average speed of 17,420 miles per hour. A manmade earth satellite orbiting at a distance of 1,075 miles from the earth would have a speed of 15,800 miles per hour.

Launching the Satellite

Because of its great size, a rocket used to place a satellite in orbit must be launched vertically. Early in its flight it should be caused to tilt so that it accelerates under power in a long slanting climb, followed by a ballistic ascent. Just as it reaches its apogee, it should receive its final burst of power; otherwise, its nose would tilt toward the earth and the rocket's final state would reenter the atmosphere. Once the satellite-carrying stage of the rocket reaches its orbital height and is given the proper velocity, it maintains an orbit indefinitely without further fuel expenditure unless it is routed through an atmosphere where air friction slows it down and eventually decays its orbit.

Ending Time:

_____

WPM: _____

"The Satellite"

I. Importance of the Satellite

    A. _____

    B. _____

    C. _____

II. _____

    A. Man-made satellites are placed into orbit by a research rocket.

    B. _____

III. _____

    A. _____

    B. Early in the flight it should be caused to tilt so that it accelerates under power in a long slanting climb, followed by a ballistic ascent.

    C. _____

    D. _____

NOTES TO UNIT 5

1. Nila Banton Smith, *Read Faster and Get More From Your Reading* (Englewood Cliffs, N.J.: Prentice-Hall, Inc. (1958), pp. 205–9.

2. Lannelle Aikman, "Nature's Gifts to Medicine," *The National Geographic*, 146, No. 3 (Sept., 1974), p. 427.

3. John Waldman, *Reading with Speed and Confidence* (New York: Random House, 1972), p. 153.

4. Waldman, p. 105.

5. Waldman, p. 104.

6. Waldman, p. 258.

7. "Congress: Where the People Speak," *U. S. News and World Report*, 9 May 1977, pp. 49–51. Used by permission.

8. Smith, p. 89.

9. Dorothy A. Wood, *Test Construction* (Columbus, OH.: Charles E. Merrill Publishing Co., 1961), p. 10.

10. A. B. Graf, *Exotic Plant Manual, Fascinating Plants to live with—their requirements, propagation and use*, 2nd ed. (East Rutherford, N.J.: Roehrs Co., 1970), p. 817. Used by permission.

11. Robert F. G. Spier, "Technology and Material Culture," in *Introduction to Cultural Anthropology*, ed. James A. Clifton (Boston: Houghton-Mifflin Co., 1968), p. 142.

12. Smith, pp. 97–98.

13. Peter Ryan and Ludeh Pesek, *UFO's and Other Worlds* (London, England: Puffin Books, 1975), p. 41. Used by permission.

14. Ryan and Pesek, p. 41.

15. Ryan and Pesek, *UFO's*, p. 44.

16. Myrtle T. Collins and Dwane R. Collins, *Survival Kit for Teachers* (Santa Monica California: Goodyear Publ. Co., Inc., 1975), p. 35. Used by permission.

17. Collins and Collins, *Survival Kit*, p. 35.

18. Collins and Collins, p. 60.

19. Paragraphs 7 through 10 are taken from Ira L. Smith and H. Allen Smith, *Law and Inside, A Book of Baseball Anecdotes, Oddities, and Curiosities* (Doubleday & Co., Inc., 1949), pp. 212–13. Used by permission.

20. Jane Bracy and Marian McClintock, *Read to Succeed* (New York: McGraw-Hill Book Co., 1975), pp. 146–50. And Nila Smith, *Read Faster* (Englewood Cliffs, N.J.: Prentice-Hall, Inc., 1958), p. 109.

21. Smith, *Read Faster*, pp. 117–20.

22. W. Royce Adams, *Developing Reading Versatility* (New York: Holt, Rinehart, and Winston, 1977), p. 7.

23. David Burner, et al., *America: A Portrait in History* (Englewood Cliffs, N.J.: Prentice-Hall, Inc., 1974), I, pp. 184–86.

24. Burner, *America*, p. 81.

25. Brian J. Fellows, *The Discrimination Process and Development* (Oxford, England: Pergamon Press, 1968), p. 163.

26. Staff of the Texas Instruments Learning Center, *The Great International Math on Keys Book* (Dallas, TX: Texas Instruments, Inc., 1976), p. i.

27. Jerome D. Schein and Marcus T. Delk, Jr., *The Deaf Population of the United States* (Silver Spring, MD.: National Association of the Deaf, 1974), p. 99.

28. Martha E. Snell, *Systematic Instruction of the Moderately and Severely Handicapped* (Columbus, OH.: Charles E. Merrill Publishing Co., 1978), p. 3.

29. Burner, p. 304.

30. Burner, p. 99.

31. Emerald V. Dechant and Henry P. Smith, *Psychology in Teaching Reading*, 2nd ed. (Englewood Cliffs, N.J.: Prentice-Hall, Inc., 1977), p. 181.

32. Dechant and Smith, p. 138.

33. Ryan and Pesek, pp. 20–21.

34. Dechant and Smith, pp. 38–39.

35. Burner, p. 42.

36. Snell, p. 75.

37. Ronald L. Cramer, *Writing, Reading, and Language Growth* (Columbus, OH.: Charles E. Merrill Publishing Co., 1978), p. 1.

38. Thomas E. Jordan, *The Exceptional Child* (Columbus, OH.: Charles E. Merrill Publishing Co., 1962), p. 305.

39. Radomir Gaspar and Dalid Brown, *Perceptual Processes in Reading* (London: Hutchison Educational Ltd., 1973), p. 2.

40. Gaspar and Brown, pp. 30–31.

41. Snell, p. 9.

42. William A. Allard, "Chinatown, the Gilded Ghetto," *National Geographic*, 148, No. 5 (Nov., 1975), p. 637.

43. Frederick K. Truslow, "Businessman in the Bush," *National Geographic*, 137, No. 5 (May, 1970), p. 650.

44. Allard, p. 637.

45. Sylvia A. Earle, "All-Girl Team Tests the Habitat," *National Geographic*, 140, No. 2 (Aug., 1971), p. 291.

46. Burner, p. 300.

47. Michael B. Petrovich and Philip D. Curtin, *India and Southwest Asia* (Morristown, N.J.: Silver Burdett Co., 1970), pp. 49–50.

48. Petrovich and Curtin, p. 105.

49. Petrovich and Curtin, p. 51.

50. Petrovich and Curtin, p. 109.

51. David A. Conlin, et al., *Our Language Today 8* (New York: American Book Co., 1966). Each of the paragraphs in this exercise is taken from this source, pp. 156, 135, 24, 162, 116, 116, 113, 80, 87, and 87, respectively.

Answer Key: Unit 5

Exercise 5.1, p. 185

1.
I. Ways to Travel
   A. car
   B. buses
   C. dog sled
   D. Amtrak
   E. trains
   F. submarine
II. Tools Used for Work
   A. combine
   B. sewing machine
   C. Drill

2.
I. Appearances
   A. pleasant
   B. attractive
   C. obese
   D. demure
   E. repulsive
II. Actions
   A. depart
   B. appear
   C. advance
   D. approach
   E. move

3.
I. Words Having the Same Root
   A. colorful
   B. coloring
   C. colored
   D. discolored

II. Pertaining to a Lack of Concern
   A. disloyal
   B. passive
   C. unwilling
   D. delaying

III. Taking Small Bites
   A. nibble
   B. mince
   C. pick
   D. taste

Exercise 5.2, p. 186

I. 1, 11, 7, 3
II. 2, 5, 8, 10
III. 4, 6, 9, 12

Exercise 5.3, p. 195

Monticello, home of Thomas Jefferson, illustrates its master's inventiveness.

Jefferson studied books, drew up his plans, and supervised Monticello's construction.

Monticello's design combined from many popular styles revived classical architectural style in the United States.

Exercise 5.4, p. 196

Mercantilism in 16th to 18th century Europe was an integral part of the transition from feudalism to capitalism in Western society.

Mercantilism was not confined to any one country.

Mercantilism was not simply a monetary program even though acquisition of gold bullion reserves was seen as a goal of national policy.

Mercantilism was a series of strategies employed in various combinations to bridge the way to the industrial revolution and modern economic development.

Exercise 5.5, p. 198

People incline or tilt their heads to one side as if to make something out when faced by a difficult perception such as an abstract painting

They seem to be trying to discover an appropriate orientation for the picture, one that gives meaning so that it can be recognized.

This behavior is identified as a heuristic perceptual technique.

Exercise 5.6, p. 200

Main Idea:
Mathematics began long ago in Early Egypt.

Major Detail A:
Geometry was invented to measure land or the earth.

Major Detail B:
The Greeks further developed the Egyptian ideas and added new ideas such as algebra and trigonometry.

Major Detail C:
Mathematics expanded greatly adding such areas as calculus, statistics and others.

Exercise 5.7, p. 202

Main Idea:
The incomes of families whose heads of household are prevocationally deaf fall below those of families in the general population.

Major Detail A:
The deaf families median income is 84 percent as much as the United States average.

Major Detail B:
For white male heads, the comparison is slightly more favorable—85 percent.

Major Detail C:
For nonwhite and female deaf heads of households the figures are worse.

Exercise 5.8, p. 203

Main Idea:
Before the nineteenth century, people who were very different from others were said to be insane or were an idiot.

Major Details:
1. *Any one exhibiting very unusual behavior before the nineteenth century was thought to be possessed by an alien spirit.*
2. *Developments in the biological sciences permitted a more refined way of classifying these people.*

Exercise 5.9, p. 203

Main Idea:
The Civil War took a frightful toll in human lives.

Major Details:
A. New weaponry and war machines changed the way the war was fought.
B. Commanders adjusted slowly to these changes.
C. Civil War casualty figures seem staggering.

Exercise 5.10, p. 204

Legal defiance was only a part of Britain's colonial problem.

In some areas, enforcement of commercial regulations broke down almost completely.

Daniel Malcolm, a Boston ship's captain drew a pistol on two revenue agents searching for illegal wine in his basement.

The sheriff avoided a direct confrontation only by stalling for time until the search warrant expired.

Such cases were not infrequent.

I.   (Main Idea) Legal defiance was only a part of Britain's colonial problem.
   A.   (Major Detail) In some areas enforcement of commercial regulations broke down almost completely.
     1.   (Minor Detail) Daniel Malcolm, a Boston ship's captain drew a pistol on two revenue agents searching for illegal wine in his basement.
     2.   (Minor Detail) The sheriff avoided a confrontation by stalling until the search warrant expired.
     3.   (Minor Detail) Such cases were not infrequent.

Exercise 5.11, p. 205

The reading interests of intelligent students are on a higher level than those of the less intelligent.

Students with high IQ's read books that are more difficult and adult.

Intelligence plays a major part in determining what students will read.

Mental age rather than IQ appears to direct interest toward specific areas of content rather than toward reading as distinguished from other activities.	Boys with high IQ's read books of a certain type content.

Girls with above-average IQ's have specific content interests. |

I. (Main Idea). Intelligence plays a major part in determining what students will read.

    A. (Major Detail) The reading interests of intelligent students are on a higher level than those of the less intelligent.
        1. (Minor Detail) Students with high IQ's read books that are more difficult and adult.

    B. (Major Detail) Mental age rather than IQ appears to direct interest toward specific content rather than toward reading as distinguished from other activities.

        1. (Minor Detail) Boys with high IQ's read books of a certain type content.

        2. (Minor Detail) Girls with above-average IQ's have specific content interests.

Exercise 5.12, p. 207

Main Idea
There are two kinds of auditory deficiency: intensity deafness and tone deafness. | A tone-deaf person cannot discriminate between pitches.

Intensity deafness is of three types. | Central deafness is caused by damage to the auditory areas of the brain or by a neurotic conversion reaction.

A conductive loss stems from impairment in the conductive process in the middle ear.

Nerve loss stems from impairment of the auditory nerve and affects clarity and intelligibility of speech. |

I. (Main Idea) There are two kinds of auditory deficiency: intensity deafness and tone deafness.
    A. (Major Detail) A tone-deaf person cannot discriminate between pitches.

    B. (Major Detail) Intensity deafness is of three types.

        1. (Minor Detail) Central deafness is caused by damage to the auditory areas of the brain or by a neurotic conversion reaction.
        2. (Minor Detail) A conductive loss stems from impairment in the conductive process in the middle ear.
        3. (Minor Detail) Nerve loss stems from impairment of the auditory nerve and affects clarity and intelligibility of speech.

Exercise 5.13, p. 208

I. A strange being really showed himself to some farmers in Kentucky.

    A. A farmer saw a flying saucer land behind some trees.
        1. He told his family about it.
        2. They didn't believe him.
    B. An hour later one of the dogs barked angrily
        1. Two men went to investigate and found a small glowing man with large red eyes.
        2. They were armed yet they were scared.
        3. They fired and hit the little man, but he was unharmed and simply floated away.
        4. They went back into the house.
    C. A few moments later the small man looked in a window of the farmhouse.
        1. The farmers rushed out to chase him off but he vanished.
        2. They searched all outbuildings.
        3. One of the men felt a tap on his head, he looked up to see a claw-like hand reaching down towards him from a low roof.

Exercise 5.14, p. 210

I. Words permit the writer to share experiences with the reader.

    A. The reader does not see nor experience directly the object person, place, sensation, or event of which the author writes.
        1. He experiences them through symbols that stand for them and evoke his perception of them.
        2. There is no direct or invariable connection between the symbol and the referent.
    B. Verbal symbols are at best inadequate substitutes for direct experiences.
        1. Language represents concepts that the mind has formed of them, not actual objects.
        2. Communication through reading is most difficult when the reader's experience is inadequate.
        3. The degree and accuracy of perception depends greatly upon the number and variety of experiences that the reader has had.

Exercise 5.15, p. 211

I. The Duke of York (later King James II) received a broad grant encompassing the Dutch colony of New Netherland.
    A. James sent an expeditionary force to oust the Dutch, England's hated rival.
        1. The fleet sailed into harbor and demanded surrender.
        2. Stuyvesant, New Amsterdam's governor, refused and threatened to fight but yielded when the citizens did not back him.
    B. English renamed the colony New York in honor of the Duke.
        1. England eased the transition to English rule by guaranteeing Dutch inhabitants fair treatment.
        2. Many old Dutch families dominated New York society and politics into the 18th century.
    C. James' goals for New York were primarily political and strategic rather than economic.

Exercise 5.16, p. 212

I. All individuals do not respond positively to the same things as is commonly believed.

    A. These reinforcers or things such as sweets, smiles, praise are defined by their effect upon behavior.
        1. If these reinforcers cause an increase in the desired behavior, they are positive.
        2. If these reinforcers cause the opposite effect, they are not positive.

    B. What is a reinforcer for one person may not be such for another.
        1. Past experiences and personal preferences affect this.
        2. A person's mental abilities determine to an extent what will serve as a reinforcer.

Exercise 5.17, p. 212

I. Creative writing is an act of personal authorship.

    A. It is defined as the act of recording one's ideas in words and sentences.
        1. The words and sentences are the personal products of the child's experiences and imagination.
        2. The product may be a letter, story, poem, etc.

    B. Others may judge it variously but that does not matter.

    C. It may be fictitious or factual, etc.

    D. Any act of personal authorship should be regarded as intrinisically valuable and creative.

Exercise 5.18, p. 212

Perhaps one of the more interesting aspects of intelligence of a high order is the ability to be creative. This rare talent causes people to see the world in a different fashion. They are able to draw on their experiences as a source of new ideas, and are able to project those ideas back into the world. Obviously, a consideration of creativity is colored by the discipline or activity to which it applies. Creativity in some processes largely rejects form and structure as an aesthetic principle. This Dionysian aesthetic is seen in many contemporary art forms which have largely abandoned the traditional intent to communicate. It is also seen in some marginal forms of literature whose major theme has generally been the intent to give insight into reality by communicating. This desire to be creative within conventions and to communicate uses form and structure as aesthetic principles and brings fresh ideas in a form largely comprehensible to others. Undoubtedly there are many personality and life-style correlates to these modes of creativity, and to whatever blends of these, and alternatives, are found.

Exercise 5.19, p. 213

The second type of writing system is what has usually been called 'phonetic' . . . In this type of system, the separate written symbols have no semantic value (i.e. no meaning) in themselves, but correspond only to sounds made in uttering the words in the spoken language. For this purpose, the total number of symbols required by any one language is relatively small (between twenty and forty), and is known as an ''alphabet.'' Only in an alphabetic writing system can there be any question of spelling, i.e., combining written symbols in a conventional order to represent words. In some languages—Finnish and Turkish, for instance—there is an almost complete one-to-one correspondence between the written symbols and the sounds of the language; that is to say, each significant sound can be consistently represented by the same letter or combination of letters. This situation remains possible only so long as (a) the total number of significant speech-sounds used in the language is not more than can be represented by the available letters or combinations of letters in the alphabet, and (b) the pronunciation of the language does not change, or (if it does change) does so with complete consistency. For various reasons, in most languages these conditions seldom prevail for very long together. Neither of them has been true for the English language.

Exercise 5.20, p. 214

1. that the speech sounds made in the language are represented by written symbols
2. True   **3.** alphabetic sound-symbol system of the language   **4.** True
5. Recognized words are built. Through these the reader detects the author's meaning.

Exercise 5.21, p. 215

1. debilitating definitions of mental retardation and assignment of classificatory levels of retardation   **2.** Binet   **3.** False   **4.a.** heterogeneity of retarded individuals
b. carefully constructed learning environments that are conducive to the development of each individual's potential.

Exercise 5.22, p. 216

1. First of all, and   **2.** In addition, and   **3.** First, then, and, and, thereafter

Exercise 5.23, p. 217

Initially,   and,   likewise,   and,   At first

Exercise 5.24, p. 217

1. Finally   **2.** As a result, also

Exercise 5.25, p. 218

1. Nevertheless   **2.** But   **3.** But, in spite of

Exercise 5.26, p. 219

1. but   Therefore

2. and   Yet   not   consequently   and

3. and   on the other hand   and   However   Therefore

4. and   not   but   and

5. and   Finally   and

6. Furthermore   and   while

7. but   Nevertheless

8. Although

9. otherwise

10. moreover

Test Yourself, p. 220

T	in spite of		T	however
SA	also		T	yet
T	still		SA	likewise
SA	and		SA	consequently
SA	furthermore		SA	thus
T	but		T	although
SA	moreover		SA	so

Selection 1: Daffodils Go Au Naturel, p. 221

1. b   **2.** phosphorus   **3.** False   **4.** the Spring season   **5.** True

Selection 2: Porsche, p. 223

1. they are a family owned business and are quite small   **2.** b   **3.** False
4. the U.S., California in particular   **5.** True

Selection 3: The Satellite, p. 225

   I.   A.   Scope of its observations is many times greater than high altitude balloons and
                sounding rockets.
          B.   The period of time these observations cover is of much greater length.
          C.   It symbolizes scientific and industrial strength.

  II.   Orbital Velocity
          B.   Satellites do not escape earth's gravitational field but balances gravity with
                centrifugal force.

 III.   Launching the Satellite
          A.   A rocket used to place a satellite in orbit must be launched vertically.
          C.   As it reaches its apogee it should receive its final burst of power.
          D.   Once the satellite carrying stage of the rocket reaches its orbital height and is
                given the proper velocity, it maintains an orbit indefinitely.

Reading Progress Chart: Unit 5

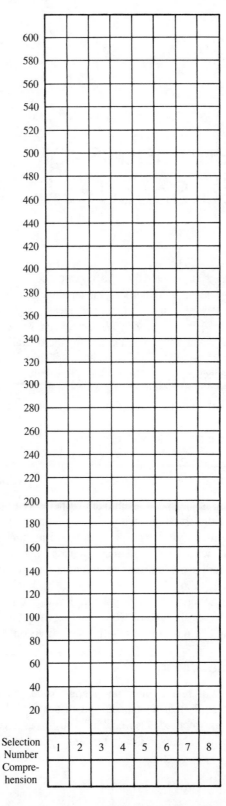

UNIT 6

Additional Techniques for High-Powered Speed

The speed at which you read depends entirely on the type of material you are reading and on your purpose for reading. Detailed or study materials require that you closely examine all facts and ideas; easy pleasure reading can be read less closely and more quickly. *High-powered speed* can be used with both types of material when you are searching for the overall ideas in a reading. For example, sometimes you may need to locate a specific fact or a particular date. Reading the entire selection is clearly not the quickest way to obtain this kind of information. *Skimming* and *scanning*, two rate-adjustment techniques you will learn and practice in this unit, are the most efficient ways you can examine a selection without reading every word. They are invaluable high-speed techniques if you are to become a flexible reader.

SCANNING

Scanning is the speed technique that helps you locate a bit of specific information very rapidly. It could involve finding a name, date, place, or statistic. Or it might involve identifying a general setting in a short story. Scanning is the technique you use when you read maps, charts, tables, or graphs. It is the main skill researchers use when they examine various sources to locate information about a specific topic.[1]

Scanning requires two skills of you, the reader. The first is that you recognize the specific type of word that identifies the item. The second is the use of a different eye movement pattern, vertical vision.[2]

Strengthening Your Vertical Vision

If you will recall, your peripheral vision, so helpful in acquiring the phrase reading skills that demanded you to see what was on either side of the spot at which you focused, also enabled you to perceive what was above or below that same point. The exercises in this unit for developing your scanning skills will help strengthen your use of vertical vision as well as your ease in selecting key words to use in your search.

Vertical vision can be illustrated by the following technique.[3]

Look at the following column of three figures. Focus on the middle figure. Now, without moving your eyes, read the figure above the middle figure. While still looking at the middle figure, read the number below the middle.

12:15
12:30
12:45

□ **Exercise 6.1** □

Directions: Focus on the center of the columns until you locate the name indicated; concentrate on it. Then let your vertical vision help you read the names written above and below the name you located.

Now try this same technique as you find each of these names in the following lists:

1. Walt Disney   3. Johnny Cash
2. Laura Ingalls   4. Barbra Streisand

Heddy Lamar	Marlin Perkins
Farah Fawcett	Gabe Cotter
Doris Day	Frederick Newman
Steve Austin	Barbara Walters
Barnaby Jones	Laura Ingalls
Johnny Carson	Bonnie Franklin
Major Boyington	Vinnie Barbarino
Hawkeye Pierce	Tony Baretta
George Scott	Peter Faulk
Louise Jefferson	Marty Robbins
Barbra Streisand	Johnny Cash
Julie London	Roy Clark
Hotlips Hulihan	Debbie Boone
Samantha Stevens	Anita Bryant
Mary Hartman	Annette Funicello
Mark Twain	Carol Burnett
Walt Disney	Dick Van Dyke
Lorne Green	Jerry Clower

Vertical vision is most frequently used in combination with horizontal vision while reading materials such as tables, charts, and graphs. The vertical vision is used to locate the item quickly while horizontal vision is used to identify details. Your skill in changing from one type of visual movement to the other will determine how rapidly you will scan.[4] Exercise 6.2 will involve changing from the use of vertical to horizontal eye movements. *Read the entire set of directions before you begin work.*

☐ Exercise 6.2 ☐

Directions: Look at the telephone number at the top of the column of numbers. Remember to focus on one number and use vertical vision to see the other two. Let your eyes follow down the column until you have located the correct prefix. Now using horizontal vision make a sideward glance to determine if it is the exact number. If it is not, continue using vertical movement to locate another prefix with the same numerals, glancing sideways to see if it is the number above the column. Continue until you have found the same number. Do this for all columns.

1. *756–1985*	2. *757–5394*	3. *758–8653*	4. *757–3709*
757–3988	756–1833	756–0431	759–9333
759–2255 • Focus here	757–5555	757–2688	758–8411
758–7313	758–7564	758–6009	757–4563
757–4111	759–1141	759–1166	759–2231
756–0677 •	757–5394	758–7292	756–2020
758–6691	758–6833	756–1929	758–8899
758–8653	756–2492	758–8653	759–2246
756–1985 •	757–3511	757–4387	756–7484
756–0543	759–9010	759–1124	757–3709

It is now time for you to scan actual reading materials that use a combination of visual movements for locating specific information. In order to scan successfully in such materials you must know two things before you begin—one, the name of the information you are seeking and two, the organization of the material to be examined.

☐ Exercise 6.3 ☐

Directions: Suppose you are interested in buying a good used car for transportation to and from campus. Underline the key word you will look for in the following advertisement. Yes, it is *used car*. Examine the following newspaper ad carefully. What types of information are provided?

1. Does this dealer carry used cars?_____

2. In which part of the ad are they described?_____

3. What four pieces of information are provided for almost all of the cars in

    this ad?_____

4. You are interested in purchasing either a Ford LTD, a Toyota Corolla, or a Jeep CJ-5. These are key words you will use as you scan. Notice that you will scan this ad by first using vertical vision to locate the make of car in the second column of information. Work in groups of three as you did in Exercises 6.1 and 6.2. When you locate the particular make or type of car, shift your vision to horizontal movements, glancing sideways to note the price, then

glancing sideways in the other direction to note the year or model. Scan for one type of car at a time. Now, scan the advertisement for the following information.

	Has in stock	Year	Description	Cost
Ford LTD	————	———	—————————————	———
Toyota Corolla	————	———	—————————————	———
Jeep CJ-5	————	———	—————————————	———

NATIONAL AUTOFINDERS, INC.

AUTO-BROKERS
NATIONAL AUTOFINDER

1980 924 PORSCHE, turbo, 6,000 mi., loaded, must sell. . $20,850
1980 TORONADO, like new, loaded $10,600
1977 CHRYSLER LeBARON, loaded, silver, priced to sell $3650
1978 PONT. Trans Am, ¼ spd., air, am/fm, t-top, low mi. . $5895
1976 FORD LTD 4 dr., vinyl roof, air, nice inside and out. Special $1995

1980 TOYOTA Corolla, 5 spd. SR-5 Liftback, am/fm sunroof, low mi. $6995
1978 TOYOTA Celica Liftback, auto., air, am/fm, ... $5495
1981 JEEP CJ-5, AM/FM stereo tape, 24000 mi. $7550
1975 CUTLASS SUPREME, 2 dr., AM/FM stereo tape, air, auto. $2500
1975 TOYOTA WAGON, 76,000 mi, clean $3000
1980 MERCEDES 240 Diesel, air, AM/FM, like new. . $19,995

GOODMAN TOYOTA

Open Weeknights til 9

3100 N. Blvd. 876-5900

SOURCE: "National Autofinders, Inc.," Advertisement, *The News and Observer*, Raleigh, N.C., 1 June 1981, p. 8.

Many reading activities such as finding a telephone number in the directory, locating a word in a dictionary or a topic in an encyclopedia, and using an index require that you use scanning skills. To be able to scan such materials you must have excellent alphabetizing skills as well. Exercises 6.4, 6.5, and 6.6 are provided as practice.

□ **Exercise 6.4** □

Directions: Examine the index on page 242. Notice its organization.

1.   Only topics whose names begin with letters ——————— are listed.

2.   The topic to be located is *Birth weight*. Will it be found on this page of the Index? ———————.

3.   The key detail here is the first letter *B*. Find the list of words beginning with this letter. Scan in groups of three until you find *Birth weight*. Now using a sidewise glance, identify the page on which this topic is discussed.

Index

Abrams, J. C., 5, 229
Accountability, 18
   checks, 308, 314–315, 318, 319, 360
Achievement, levels of. *See also* Fernald
     techniques, stages 1–4; Stauffer,
     remedial techniques, stages 1–4
   expectancies, 287
   in remedial programs, 286
Actions, 3, 307, 363
Adams, R., 21
Adjustment, pupil, 303, 342, 315. *See*
    also Attitudes; Self-acceptance;
    Self-esteem; Therapy
Aides, 356
Allport, G., 3, 13
Anderson, R., 4, 358
Anoxia, 211
Astigmatism, 181
Attention, 229
Attitudes, pupil, 255, 261, 287, 294,
    310, 311, 325, 332, 337, 341
Audiometer, 184
Auditory discrimination, 35, 46, 330
Auditory perception
   factors, 189–192
   measures of, 191
Averages, 122, 123

Barnard, D. P., and DeGracie, J., 60
Barrett, T., 46
Basal readers, 339, 341
Bateman, B., 19
Beery-Buktenica Test, 187
Beldin, H. L., 56

Bender, L., 46
Bender Visual-Motor Gestalt Test, 186
Bettelheim, B., 2, 13, 251, 279
Betts, E., 56, 250, 279, 285, 334
Beuchlar, J., 8
Birth weight, 210
Blanchard, P., 233
Blankenship, E., 185
Bleismer, E., 111
Bond, G., and Tinker, M., 179
Boring, E. G., 164
Bormuth, J., 158
Bortnick, R., and Lopardo, G., 159
Brain damage, perinatal types of, 213
Brandt, R., 361, 366
Bryan, T., 23
Burke, 351
Buros, O., 149

California Achievement Test, 142
California Teachers Assoc., 11, 13
California Test of Mental Maturity,
   176
Carroll, J. B., 189
Carver, R., 107
Case staffing, 301, 303, 304, 313–314,
   316, 322
   form, 302–303
Causes (or factors), 273, 281. *See*
    also Emotional causes; Etiologi-
    cal factors; Pedagogical causes;
    Physiological conditions; Psycho-
    logical conditions in instruction
   constellation of, 281

SOURCE: Russell G. Stauffer et al., *Diagnosis, Correction, and Prevention of Reading Disabilities* (New York: Harper & Row, Publishers, 1978), p. 368. Used by permission.

□ **Exercise 6.5** □

Directions: In your study of events leading to World War II, you have become aware of Hitler's concept of the role of war in politics and that he was ready to initiate a war to establish German supremacy when the time was right. Scan the "Contents" from *Hitler* on page 244 to find which sections would most likely treat this idea in depth. *Remember*, first scan the entire "Contents" to determine which sections directly discuss Hitler's concept of war. Then scan listings *within* that section to find those that may explain the information in more detail. Use your horizontal vision to find the page number for the material you seek. Answer the following questions about the "Contents."

1. Does the book *Hitler* discuss the war?_____

2. Which section(s) treat this topic?_____

_____

3. On which book pages will you be able to find this information?_____

_____

After you have located the answers to these questions, scan the "Contents" again. Notice that the author prefaces several major sections with an interpolation, or explanation. These will verify your choice of major sections dealing with Hitler's concept of war. Answer the following questions when you have scanned the "Contents":

1. Will the information about Hitler's concept of war most likely be explained

   most clearly by the major chapters or the author's prefaced explanations?

_____

2. Identify and list the particular section which seems to best treat the topic.

_____

3. On which page is it found?_____

☐ **Exercise 6.6** ☐

Directions: Scanning the telephone directory for a particular number involves vertical and horizontal eye movements and alphabetizing skills. After examining the organization of the page from the Phone Book on page 245, answer the following questions:

1. How many different sets of names can be found on this page?_____

2. Which ones?_____

3. Now you are ready to locate the number of Kenneth W. Smith. The *S* in Smith is your key element. Vertically scan the S's for Smith. *Sm* is the key. Good. Now you must go to Kenneth—K is the key. Vertically scan the K's for Ken—Kenneth. Now use a sidewise glance to find his number. What is

   it?_____

Contents

SOURCE: Joachim C. Fest. *Hitler*. New York: Harcourt Brace Jovanovich, Inc., 1973, pp. v, vi. Reprinted by permission.

R

R & N Swine Farm Hwy 258 747-8311
Rackley Shelton E 208 SE 4th 747-2291
RADFORD & SAULS INSULATION CO RFD 2 **747-8211**
Radford Ben RFD 3 747-3979
Radford Cornelius RFD 3 747-3207
Radford Elbert Maury NC 747-3820
Radford James T 312 SE 3rd 747-2709
Radford Junius A 747-3616
Radford Kenneth 207 Lakeside Dr 747-3212
Radford Linwood E 210 Lakeside Dr 747-3869
Radford Linwood Earl Jr RFD 4 747-2787
Radford Melvin Maury NC 747-3065
Radford Melvin Cnty Rd 1146 747-5072
Radford Patrick C RFD 4 747-5860
Radford Preston RFD 3 747-3116
Rainbow Grill restrnt Hwy 13 747-2433
Rainbow United Methodist Church Parsonage RFD 4 747-2668
Ramsey Moses H Jennifer Ln 747-5468
Rand Wade Oil Co Inc Hwy 258 S 747-5040
Randolph Joe James 209 James 747-2700
RANDOLPH W H BARBECUE **747-3813**
Randolph William H 747-3629
Ray Charles RFD 2 747-5797
Ray James 324 Pine Shoal Dr 747-2543
Ray Nathaniel RFD 2 747-3832
Ray Thelma D RFD 2 747-3323
Ray Willie Mae RFD 3 747-3940
Rayford R Ben 409 Greenridge Rd 747-5171
Reason Preston 212 Lakeside Dr 747-5494
Redd Sam 307 SE 3rd 747-3300
Reddick S Guy Maury NC 747-2268
REDWOOD GARDEN CENTER & NURSERY Maury NC **747-2162**
Reid Annie Ruth RFD 4 747-2116
Reid Luby 747-5060
Reid Mattie RFD 2 747-5785
Rhodes Michael RFD 4 747-2669
Rice Bertha 3rd Hookerton 747-8212
Richardson Joe RFD 3 747-5607
Riley Brent RFD 4 747-8332
Robbins Roberta H Mrs RFD 1 747-2629
Roberson Dorothy RFD 1 Maury 747-2974
Roberson Leonard Earl 105 Frances 747-2771
Roberson Lucille S RFD 4 747-8266
Roberts James A 12 California Dr 747-2037
Roberts Phyllis RFD 3 747-2061
Robinson Floyd Maury NC 747-5528
Rodgers James RFD 1 Walstonburg 747-3559
Roebuck William Shines Cross Rds 747-3760
Rogers Bryant RFD 4 747-2832
Rogers David RFD 1 Hookerton 747-3278
Rogers Thomas RFD 1 747-2978
Rogers Virginia C Mrs Hookerton NC 747-2307
Rose David Hookerton NC 747-2569
Rose John A RFD 3 747-2132
Roundtree Frances RFD 1 Hookerton 747-3295
Roundtree Jesse RFD 2 747-2776
Rouse Albert L Jr RFD 1 La Grange 747-2530
Rouse Annie RFD 1 747-2747
Rouse Berry RFD 4 747-5689
Rouse Bobby RFD 4 747-5770
Rouse James C RFD 4 747-5704
Rouse James T Cnty Rd 1202 747-3318
Rouse Jessie Lee Maury NC 747-2249
Rouse Martha J RFD 4 747-2096
Rouse Marvin RFD 3 747-5304
Rouse Milton RFD 1 Hookerton 747-3062
Rouse Phil RFD 1 747-2737
Rouse Preston A RFD 4 747-3141
Rouse Raymond R RFD 1 Hookerton 747-3104
Rouse Robert RFD 1 Hookerton 747-2714
Rouse Sandy embalmr 747-5075
Res 747-2522
Rouse Steve RFD 4 747-8196
ROUSE SUPPLY CO Hwy 13 **747-3782**
Rouse T C 210 Oak 747-3540
Rouse's Millwork & Cabinet Shop RFD 4 747-5704
Rowe Clarence Mrs RFD 3 747-5274
Rowe Phillip RFD 3 747-2947
Rowe Wilton O Cnty RD 1205 747-5904
Ryder Everett RFD 2 747-2080

S

Sara's Beauty Salon RFD 2 747-5132
Sasser Carl 747-5895
Saul Elverta RFD 4 747-5826
Sauls Alma RFD 4 747-3155
Sauls Andrew RFD 4 747-5345
Sauls Billy G RFD 2 747-5459
Sauls George 207 Hart 747-8120
Sauls Hattie RFD 4 747-5576
Sauls Kat Hwy 91 747-5289
Sauls Lyman RFD 2 747-2334
Sauls Ned D Cnty Rd 1204 747-2278
Sauls Ted RFD 3 747-2637
Sauls Virginia 115 Eastover Dr 747-5087
Sauls William T RFD 2 LaGrange 747-8319
Schaffer Logan RFD 1 747-5558
Schertzinger George OD
Snow Hill Medical Center 747-8149
Res 522-3562
Scott Joe RFD 1 La Grange 747-5309
Scott Linda RFD 4 747-5273
Serv All Store grocr RFD 1 747-2688
Serve-Well Super Mkt 747-3733
Seymour Carl E RFD 2 747-5631
Seymour Kathryn Mrs Cnty Rd 1128 747-2105
Seymour Raymond A Cnty Rd 1128 747-2206
Shackelford Ossie T CPA Greene 747-5159
Shackleford Ava D 134 W Harper 747-2048
Shackleford Cecil Cnty Rd 1247 747-5130
Shackleford Dwain Hookerton NC 747-5049
Shackleford Erva RFD 3 747-5976
Shackleford F H RFD 2 747-5740
SHACKLEFORD F H & SON FARM CENTER farm supls Hookerton NC **747-2595**
Shackleford F H Jr RFD 1 Hookerton 747-2390
SHACKLEFORD FERTILIZER CO Hookerton NC **747-3368**
Shackleford James RFD 1 Hookerton 747-2743
Shackleford James Jr 611 W Harper 747-2182
Shackleford James T Cnty Rd 1002 747-3969
Shackleford James T Jr 230 Pine 747-5609
Shackleford Jerry Hookerton NC 747-3818
Shackleford Lester Sr 710 W Harper 747-3118
Shackleford Rita Rose RFD 2 747-5925
Shackleford Roger D RFD 1 747-2087
Shackleford William RFD 4 747-3554
Shackleford's Grocery 709 Kingold Blvd 747-2621
Sharpless John F RFD 4 747-8278
Sheaffer Evelyn RFD 2 747-8217
Shepard Willie RFD 1 747-5063
Sheppard Mary W RFD 1 Hookerton 747-2802
Sheppard Robert Maury NC 747-3696
Sheppard Sarah Mrs RFD 1 747-2697
Sheppard Shirley Ann RFD 1 Hookerton 747-8261
Sherrill Eugene RFD 2 Walstonburg 747-3788
Sherrill J E Cnty Rd 1315 747-2340
Shine Fire Dept Emergency Only 747-3888
Shine's Hair Stylist bty salon Shines Cross Rds 747-2411
SHINES SHOPPING CNTR genl mdse Shine's Cross Rds **747-3289**
Shingleton Bobby RFD 4 747-3106
Shingleton Brooks RFD 2 747-5923
Shirley Alton E Walstonburg NC 747-3263
Shirley Bertha 408 School 747-3970
Shirley Bessie Mrs Walstonburg NC 747-2146
Shirley Charles Hillview 747-3837
Shirley Cora Cnty Rd 1247 747-3974
Shirley George Cnty Rd 1225 747-2374
Shirley J W Walstonburg NC 747-2562
Shirley James L Walstonburg NC 747-3967
Shirley John B Shine Community 747-3977
Shirley Lena S Mrs Walstonburg NC 747-3068
Shirley Ray RFD 2 Walstonburg 747-2267
Shirley Roger RFD 2 747-5240
Shirley Rosa Miss Walstonburg NC 747-2345
Shirley Sudie 118 W 3rd 747-3674
Simmons Elijah RFD 2 747-2477
Sims Issac 228 Pine 747-3208
Sims Lozetta RFD 2 747-2086
Skinner Doc A Maury NC 747-2322
Skinner Effie W Mrs Maury NC 747-2222
Skinner Randall E RFD 2 747-2667
Skinner Robert E RFD 2 La Grange 747-2991
Skinner Ronnie RFD 1 747-2237
SKYLAND CHEVROLET INC Hwy 13 S **747-5818**
Slater John RFD 1 La Grange 747-2736
Slater John C RFD 1 Hookerton 747-3057
Small Jim L Cnty Rd 1106 747-5495
Smith D Emerson Indian Head Dr 747-2687
Smith Danny RFD 3 747-5956
Smith Donald Morgan RFD 2 La Grange 747-5496
Smith Dyke RFD 2 La Grange 747-2387
Smith Frederick Lee Walstonburg NC 747-3022
Smith James Albert Hwy 102 W 747-2233
Smith John W RFD 2 747-5464
Smith Johnnie C RFD 3 747-2026
Smith Kenneth W RFD 3 747-5856
Smith L H 747-3509
Smith Lanie RFD 2 747-5983
Smith Lee Hwy 102 W 747-5033
Smith Linda J RFD 2 Walstonburg 747-2645
Smith Lloyd Jr RFD 3 747-5335
Smith Lorraine C RFD 3 747-2482
Smith Mary RFD 2 Stantonsburg 747-8160
Smith Maryleen Mrs Hwy 102 W 747-2218
Smith Michael RFD 3 747-2079
Smith Nathaniel Lakeview Ests 747-5319
Smith Nollie Jr RFD 2 La Grange 747-3994
Smith Phil A RFD 3 747-3343
Smith Robbie RFD 3 747-3972
Smith Robert C RFD 3 747-8263
Smith Rosa M Hookerton NC 747-5061
Smith Rudolph RFD 3 747-5290
Smith S W Ramblewood Apts 747-2995
Smith Shirley T RFD 3 747-8269
Smith Sophelia M RFD 3 747-5017
Smith T Jerry RFD 2 Walstonburg 747-5139
Smith Willie H RFD 2 La Grange 747-2509
Smith Zell C RFD 3 747-5364
Snipes David 1303 NE 4th 747-2446
SNOW HILL APPAREL CO INC Hwy 258 S **747-8200**
Snow Hill Fire Dept 747-3888
SNOW HILL MEDICAL CENTER 302 N Greene **747-2921**
SNOW HILL METAL CRAFTS INC Hwy 258 S **747-2863**
SNOW HILL MILLING CO Hwy 58 S **747-3405**
Snow Hill Pentecostal Holiness Church Parsonage Eastover Dr 747-2596
SNOW HILL PHARMACY N Greene **747-3885**
SNOW HILL PLUMBING-HEATING & AIR CONDITIONING CO Hwy 258 By-Pass **747-3408**
If no answer dial 747-5629
SNOW HILL SUPPLY CO fertlzr 311 SE 2nd **747-3455**
Snow Hill Tape Corp US 13 W 747-3698
Snow Hill Town of
Town Office 747-3647
Police Department 747-3647
SNOW HILL TV SERVICE 406 E 3rd **747-3011**
Sowers Harry Mrs RFD 2 747-2359
Sowers Norman Hillview 747-3307
Sowers Willie V Cnty Rd 1128 747-2273
Sparrow William C RFD 4 747-3702
Speaker Kathy D Hookerton NC 747-5620
Speaker Letha RFD 1 Hookerton 747-5906
Speight Allen RFD 1 Walstonburg 747-5665
Speight B M Hookerton NC 747-2129
Speight Bertha Lee 111 Carver 747-5476
Speight Booker T Hwy 258 N 747-2365
Speight Chip Arba Community 747-2012
Speight Clarence Hookerton NC 747-3774
Speight Clarence Ray RFD 2 747-5802
Speight Fred 747-3311
Speight George 103 Circle Dr 747-5569
Speight John RFD 1 Walstonburg 747-5665
Speight John Thomas Jr Hwy 102 E 747-3157
Speight Lawrence Ray RFD 1 747-3889
Speight Lizzie Lee RFD 1 747-5279
Speight McCoy RFD 2 Walstonburg 747-5643
Speight Mildred R Dixon Cnty Rd 1300 747-5775
Speight Robert Cnty Rd 1127 747-5325
Speight Robert Jr RFD 3 747-3720
Speight Walter RFD 4 747-5068
Speight William H Hwy 102 E 747-5323
Spencer Clara Mae Hwy 13 W 747-3257
Spencer James William RFD 1 Hookerton 747-8345
Spikes Hubert Maury NC 747-3194
Spivey C E Mrs Maury NC 747-3353
Spivey R L Maury NC 747-5455
SPOTLIGHT PROMOTIONS INC entrtainmnt bur Maury NC **747-5401**
SPRUILL MASONRY INC 1102 Arba Rd **747-2780**
St James United Presbyterian Church 308 W Harper 747-2432
Stalling Eddie Lee Hwy 91 W 747-3700
Stallings Exterminating Co Hookerton NC 747-5788
Stallings P H Hookerton NC 747-5788
Stallings Roy Mrs 211 Oak 747-5263
Stallings Tom Jr RFD 2 747-8242
Stallings Tony H RFD 1 Hookerton 747-3102
Stallings Willie E Hookerton NC 747-5711
Stancil Larry O RFD 1 747-2710
STANDARD-LACONIC THE newspapr 223 N Greene **747-3883**
Stanton Rother S Mrs 747-3669

SOURCE: Carolina Telephone & Telegraph Co., "The Phone Book," Greenville, N.C., 1979, p. 138.

Scanning Practice

Exercises 6.7 through 6.10 are provided for your practice in scanning. You should approach the scanning task in this manner:

1. Examine the organization of the material. What information is given? How is it placed on the page?
2. Read the directions to identify the information for which you will scan.
3. Decide how you will scan for this information. Can the information be found simply by using your vertical vision? How many times must you scan vertically before you can use your horizontal vision?
4. Record the time when you start the exercise.
5. Scan the material using the procedure devised in Step 3 above.
6. Record your ending time.

Do this for each of the following exercises. Try to scan selections at increasingly rapid rates.

☐ Exercise 6.7 ☐

Directions: Scan page 247 from a telephone directory for the number of Jeffrey Hamm. What is Mr. Hamm's number?_____

Beginning Time: _____

Ending Time: _____

Scanning Time: _____

H

H & H DEVELOPMENT CORPORATION
Hookerton NC **747-3471**
Haddock A H Hookerton NC 747-3965
Haddock Walter RFD 1 Hookerton 747-8230
Hagan H J phonogrphs Maury NC 747-2141
  Res Maury NC 747-2141
Hagan L R Hookerton NC 747-8110
Hagan Sallie P 105 Lakeshore Dr 747-3546
HALF AND HALF GRILL Maury NC **747-5358**
HALF AND HALF SELF SERVICE grocr
  Maury NC.......................**747-2611**
Hall Annie F RFD 2 747-3578
Hall Bert M Forest Hl Acres 747-5605
Hall Caiolus E Harper 747-3238
Hall David Maury NC 747-2248
Hall Georgia D 747-5316
Hall James RFD 1 747-8356
Hall Joe RFD 1 747-2973
Hall Lena B W Greene 747-3150
Hall Odell RFD 3 747-2665
Ham & Albritton Fertilizer Co 747-2647
Ham Allen 106 Corbett 747-5836
Ham Alton Lewis RFD 3 747-5367
Ham Bobby G RFD 1 747-2632
Ham Carrie G RFD 3 747-3748
Ham Durwood E Cnty Rd 1202 747-3680
Ham Earl Mrs RFD 3 747-3661
Ham Edward 1308 SE 2nd 747-5236
Ham Howard Shine Community 747-5095
Ham Inez H Mrs RFD 3 747-5418
Ham J B 747-3691
Ham James H Hwy 258 S 747-3925
Ham Johnny L Gray's Trlr Pk 747-8309
Ham L B Shines Cross Rds 747-2231
Ham Lloyd Grocery Hwy 91 S 747-2211
Ham Lloyd Mrs RFD 4 747-5371
Ham Lonnie RFD 3 747-2353
Ham Lyman E 1305 SE 2nd 747-3553
Ham Otis Cnty Rd 1146 747-5381
Ham Robert Hwy 91 W 747-3173
Ham Roland RFD 3 747-8308
Ham Roland K RFD 4 747-2858
Ham Woody Cnty Rd 1400 747-5729
Ham's Margaret Beauty Salon RFD 3 ..747-2353
Ham's Swap Shop Shine Cross Rds 747-3710
Hamm Billy RFD 4 747-2720
Hamm Bruce G Jr Maury NC 747-5811
Hamm Carl Cnty Rd 1300 747-5581
Hamm Horace Cnty Rd 1300 747-2376
Hamm J C Cnty Rd 1205 747-3864
Hamm J W 111 W 3rd 747-3533
Hamm Jeffery RFD 1 747-2882
Hamm Royce Hwy 258 N 747-5657
Hamm Steve RFD 1 747-5513
Hammond Edward J RFD 1 747-8225
HAPPY JACK INC pet supls Hwy 258 S ...**747-2911**
Hardee Mary Mae Maury NC 747-2765
Hardee Richard C Maury NC 747-5951
Hardin Benjamin A Maury NC 747-2030
Hardison Beadie Mrs Hwy 91 W 747-3876
Hardison Bruce Cnty Rd 1248 747-5158
Hardison Charles H RFD 1 747-3075
Hardison Douglas Elwood RFD 4 747-3039
Hardison James RFD 4 747-2701
Hardison Jimmy Lee Sr RFD 1 747-5173
Hardison Maynard 1003 Indian Head Cir .747-3532
Hardison N F N Hines Ext 747-3764
Hardison William A RFD 4 747-3121
Hardy A T Cnty Rd 1103 747-5660
Hardy Allen RFD 1 Hookerton 747-2604
Hardy Diane J RFD 1 747-3622
Hardy Gene RFD 2 747-5741
Hardy H Steve RFD 1 747-3058
Hardy Herbert W Judge Maury NC 747-5848
Hardy Hubert (Buck) Maury NC 747-3184
Hardy James H 747-3523
Hardy James H Jr Maury NC 747-2303
Hardy James H Sr Maury NC 747-5952
Hardy John 303 W Harper 747-3229
Hardy John C 118 W Greene 747-5573
Hardy Lillian RFD 1 Hookerton 747-2741
Hardy Paul RFD 1 La Grange 747-2891
Hardy Ruby Mae Cnty Rd 1222 747-5183
Hardy William RFD 4 747-2560
Hardy Wilma F 203 W Greene 747-5162
HARDY'S APPLIANCE elec applncs
  208 Greene **747-2638**
Harper Albert L Shine Community 747-2247
Harper Ben T Greenridge Rd 747-3632

Harper Blanie RFD 1 Hookerton 747-3694
Harper Bynum Jr 209 Harper 747-3391
Harper Bynum Service Station RFD 1 : .747-3333
Harper Charles.....................747-3326
Harper Chuck 309 W Greene 747-5694
Harper Edna Earl Lakeview Ests 747-5015
Harper Edward E RFD 1 Hookerton 747-5591
Harper Gloria 704 Welch 747-2768
Harper Harold RFD 3 747-2994
Harper Harry RFD 3 747-2693
Harper J H Mrs 208 W Harper 747-3527
Harper Jimmie 305 W Greene 747-3584
Harper Jimmy Henry RFD 3 747-5700
Harper John Edward 308 Hines 747-5029
HARPER JOHN S INSURANCE AGENCY
  227 N Greene **747-5815**
Harper John S Mrs 747-3537
Harper Junious RFD 2 747-5058
Harper Lyman RFD 2 747-2352
Harper Matthew L Hookerton NC 747-3802
Harper Phillip RFD 1 Hookerton 747-5038
Harper Randall RFD 3 747-2803
Harper Richard S Cnty Rd 1328 747-3195
Harper Theresa Hookerton NC 747-5590
Harper Travis RFD 2 747-5196
HARRELL & HOLDEN STORE hdw **747-3685**
Harrell A J Mrs 203 NW 3rd 747-3436
Harrell Alton F RFD 1 747-3135
Harrell Claude J Hwy 58 N 747-3346
Harrell David 404 Liberty Av 747-3401
Harrell Elma D Maury NC 747-5461
Harrell Elmer E RFD 4 747-2893
Harrell Gene Ramblewood Mbl Hm Pk ..747-2470
Harrell Gregory RFD 4 747-8129
Harrell H L Rev RFD 3 747-2090
Harrell James T RFD 2 Walstonburg ...747-2474
Harrell Larry 1007 Indian Head Ests ..747-5310
Harrell Melvin Wooten's Cross Rds 747-3025
Harrell Percy RFD 4 747-5846
Harrell Percy H 105 Greene 747-5954
Harrell Pete RFD 2 Walstonburg 747-5008
Harrell Ruby S Mrs 508 SE 3rd 747-5970
Harrell Tommy RFD 1 747-5267
Harrell Walter Richard Hwy 91 W 747-3794
Harrell's Jean Beauty Shop Hwy 58 N ..747-3346
Harris A M RFD 3 747-2965
Harris Albert L RFD 2 747-8255
Harris Bobby Hwy 91 N 747-5735
Harris Donald E RFD 1 747-3082
Harris Donnie H RFD 1 747-2537
Harris Frank Hwy 91 N 747-3791
Harris George M Forest Hls 747-3573
Harris J H RFD 3 747-3776
Harris Marvin C Jr 211 Lakeside Dr ..747-5009
Harris Russell C RFD 4 747-5834
Harris Ted RFD 4 747-5341
Harrison Addie S Mrs RFD 2 747-5661
Harrison Albert Lee Cnty Rd 1109 ...747-3917
Harrison Blaney Arba Community 747-5764
Harrison Bunyan RFD 1 La Grange ...747-2108
Harrison Carson RFD 1 La Grange ...747-8128
Harrison Charles D 1017 Long Shore Dr .747-2157
Harrison Ed RFD 2 747-3521
Harrison Ellsworth Arba Community ...747-2680
Harrison Emma L RFD 1 La Grange ...747-5126
Harrison George H RFD 2 747-5245
Harrison Gregory RFD 2 747-2748
Harrison Guy RFD 2 747-3946
Harrison H Elton RFD 1 La Grange ...747-5813
Harrison Heber RFD 1 La Grange 747-2313
Harrison J L RFD 2 747-5897
Harrison Jarvis RFD 4 747-3707
Harrison Joel S 82 California Dr 747-5978
Harrison Kathryn 107 Greenridge Rd ..747-5776
Harrison Kenneth RFD 1 La Grange ...747-3291
Harrison Kenneth Tile Contractor
  701-D SE 2nd 747-2663
Harrison Larry RFD 2 747-3457
Harrison Lloyd RFD 2 747-5730
Harrison Lula RFD 4 747-2480
Harrison Milton Mrs RFD 2 747-2112
Harrison Phillip 747-5109
Harrison Rosa Arba Community 747-2243
HARRISON UPHOLSTERY SHOP 208 Oak . .**747-3388**
Harrison Wate RFD 2 747-5529
Harrison Zeb R RFD 2 747-3829
Harry's Restaurant Greene 747-5744
Hart Bill Ford Inc 127 SE 2nd 747-2966
Hart Bill II RFD 4 747-2028
Hart Delma Shine Community 747-2246
Hart Dewey W Hookerton NC 747-2755
Hart Donald E 1312 SE 2nd 747-5256

Hart Evon RFD 4 747-2919
Hart George W Jr 747-3558
Hart J B Jr Cnty Rd 1140 747-5493
Hart L M Arba Community 747-3110
Hart Mable RFD 3 747-2548
Hart Margaret Mrs 210 SE 4th 747-5673
Hart R E RFD 3 747-5351
Hart Ricky RFD 2 La Grange 747-2339
Hart Sarah C Mrs 201 Harper 747-3692
Hart Steve RFD 4 747-2219
Hart William P Indianhead Ests ...747-3240
Hart's Virgil Grocery Hwy 13 W ...747-3027
Hastings Ford Inc 3013 E 10th
  Greenville NC Long Distance.....758-0114
Hayes Austin T RFD 3 747-2021
Hayes Richard A RFD 3 747-8152
Head Bailey RFD 3 747-3253
Head Billy Cnty Rd 1140 747-5560
Head Buster RFD 3 747-5362
Head James 109 Edgemont Dr 747-5589
Head Jim Hwy 58 747-5377
Head Larry Hookerton NC 747-5178
Head Tommy RFD 3 747-3515
Head Wadeus Store Cnty Rd 1201 ..747-3070
Head Zeb Cnty Rd 1209 747-2149
Head's Bailey Grocery Hwy 13 W ..747-2304
Head's Kermit Cabinet Shop RFD 3 .747-5691
Heath Alma Miss RFD 4 747-3085
Heath Alvin RFD 1 747-2589
Heath Arthur RFD 3 747-3055
Heath Bennie J 107 NW 4th 747-5297
Heath Bobby Gene Hookerton NC ...747-5530
Heath Carroll 1024 Indianhead Dr ..747-2722
Heath Dennis RFD 4 747-5678
Heath Donna Lynn Greenridge Rd Ext .747-5041
Heath Douglas 211 Eastover Dr 747-5593
Heath E Raeford RFD 1 747-2252
Heath Edna Maury NC 747-5128
Heath Essie Miss 756 E 3rd 747-3024
Heath Geneva Walstonburg NC 747-2187
Heath Gerald Cnty Rd 1240 747-3013
Heath J C RFD 4 747-3431
Heath J H 747-3513
Heath James RFD 3 747-5507
Heath Jerry B RFD 3 747-5608
Heath John Walstonburg NC 747-5342
Heath Lyman RFD 4 747-5736
Heath Lyman Jr RFD 1 747-3308
Heath Nellie Mrs 305 SE 3rd 747-5157
Heath R A 106 NW 4th 747-3149
Heath R Veston Greenridge Rd Ext ..747-3841
Heath Randy RFD 1 Walstonburg ..747-3835
Heath Robert RFD 1 Walstonburg ..747-5047
Heath Robert Cnty Rd 1246 747-5395
Heath Roy L Cnty Rd 1247 747-2377
Heath Stella McCoy Cnty Rd 1104 ..747-2100
Heath Tommy Walstonburg NC 747-3276
Heath Walter L RFD 1 747-3462
Heath William M Hwy 91 S 747-3752
Hedgepeth Joe Hookerton NC 747-5090
Hedgepeth Linnie Ray Hwy 13 N ..747-5757
Heitman Bertha 308 W Greene 747-2887
Hemby Jimmie RFD 1 La Grange ..747-2127
HENDRIX-BARNHILL CO farm eqpt
  Memorial Dr Greenville NC 752-4122
Herring Alfonza RFD 2 La Grange ..747-5050
Herring Blanche T RFD 3 747-2311
Herring Guy Walter Cnty Rd 1110 ..747-2614
Herring J Carson Mrs 102-A Greene .747-3662
Herring J W RFD 3 747-5188
Herring L F Jr RFD 3 747-5702
Herring Lee Mrs...............747-3479
Hicks H Maynard 747-3644
High Charles M 1309 SE 2nd 747-8316
Hilco Inc Hookerton NC 747-3471
Hill Albert M 105 Bruce 747-3427
Hill Alvin D RFD 1 Hookerton ...747-3061
Hill Arthur RFD 3 747-2288
Hill Betty RFD 3 747-3196
Hill Beulah RFD 3 747-5552
Hill Britt Cnty Rd 1427 747-3831
Hill Callie Mrs RFD 2 747-5637
Hill Carl 104 Crestwood Dr 747-5527
Hill Clarence E 108 SW Hines ..747-5102
Hill D W Hookerton NC 747-3251
Hill Drew 701 SE 3rd 747-3179
Hill Edward V Maury NC 747-3168
Hill Envid RFD 3 747-5543
Hill Eula Grace Cnty Rd 1427 ..747-3547
Hill Evelyn Miss RFD 2 747-5129
Hill Floyd 307 Liberty 747-5077
Hill Frank Hwy 91 S 747-3761

SOURCE: Carolina Telephone & Telegraph Co., "The Phone Book," Greenville, N.C., 1979, p. 134.

Monday television

Schedules compiled by
TV Data Inc.
Glens Falls, N.Y.

② WUND, Columbia
③ WWAY, Wilmington
③ WTKR, Norfolk, Va.
⑤ WRAL, Raleigh
⑤ WTTG, Washington, D.C.
⑥ WECT, Wilmington
⑦ WITN, Washington, N.C.
⑨ WNCT, Greenville
⑨ WOR, New York
⑩ WAVY, Portsmouth, Va.

⑪ WTVD, Durham
⑫ WCTI, New Bern
⑬ WVEC, Norfolk, Va.
⑰ WTBS, Atlanta
㉕ WUNK, Greenville
㊴ WUNJ, Greenville
(ESP) Entertainment & Sports
(HBO) Home Box Office
(HTN) Home Theater Network
(NIK) Nickelodeon

(SHO) Showtime
(SPN) Satellite Program
(USA) USA Network
• • • •
(CC) indicates closed captioning
(R) indicates rerun

Movie ratings:
★ — poor
★ ★ — fair
★ ★ ★ — good
★ ★ ★ ★ — excellent

Daytime

5 a.m.
⑰ Mission: Impossible
(ESP) Professional Rodeo
5:04 a.m. ⑨ News

5:30 a.m.
⑥ Zane Grey Theater
⑦ Sergeant Bilko
⑨ Daniel Boone
⑨ Rookies
(SPN) Movie (Time Approximate)

6 a.m.
③ Jim Bakker
⑤ Panorama
⑥ Carolina in the Morning
⑦ Almanac
⑨ Carolina Today
⑩ My Three Sons
⑫ Jimmy Swaggart
⑬ Good Morning News
⑰ Hollywood Report
6:10 a.m. ③ Down to Earth

6:30 a.m.
③ Newsmakers
⑤ Country Morning
⑨ News
⑩ Tidewater Today
⑪ Summer Semester
⑫ Pop! Goes the Country
⑬ Good Morning Tidewater

7 a.m.
③ ⑤ ⑫ ⑬ Good Morning America
③ ⑪ Morning With Charles Kuralt
⑤ New Zoo Revue
⑥ ⑦ ⑩ Today
⑨ Richard Simmons
⑰ Funtime
(ESP) Sports Center
(SPN) International Byline

7:30 a.m.
⑤ Great Space Coaster
⑨ Jim Bakker
(SPN) Medicine Man
7:45 a.m. ② ㉕ ㊴ A.M. Weather

8 a.m.
③ ⑪ Captain Kangaroo
⑤ Porky Pig
⑨ Morning With Charles Kuralt
⑰ Lassie
(ESP) NASL Soccer
Los Angeles Aztecs vs. Vancouver Diplomats
(NIK) Dusty's Treehouse
(SPN) A Little Leeway
8:05 a.m. ② ㉕ ㊴ Over Easy

8:30 a.m.
⑤ Fred Flintstone and Friends
⑨ Meet the Mayors
⑰ My Three Sons
(NIK) Pinwheel
(SPN) The Women's

Channel
8:35 a.m. ② ㉕ ㊴ School TV Update

9 a.m.
② ㉕ ㊴ Sesame Street (CC)
③ Jim Bakker
③ ⑪ Donahue
Phil Donahue examines the cases of young Mexican Americans who were regularly victimized by members of the McAllen, Texas Police Department.
⑤ Hour Magazine
Gary Collins is joined by parapsychologist Dr. Thelma Moss for a look at the world of the supernatural; Pat Mitchell visits the home of Glenn Ford and his wife Cynthia; Dr. Lorraine Stern dispells myths about raising children.
⑤ Leave It to Beaver
⑥ Donahue
Guest: Senator Jesse Helms (R-N.C.).
⑦ Mike Douglas
⑨ Joe Franklin
⑨ Captain Kangaroo
⑩ Richard Simmons
⑫ Donahue
⑰ Family Affair
(SPN) Susan Noon

9:30 a.m.
⑤ My Three Sons
⑩ Bullseye
⑰ I Dream of Jeannie
(SPN) Fran Carlton Exercise

10 a.m.
② ㉕ ㊴ Thinkabout
③ The Real McCoys
③ Morning Connection
⑤ Time for Uncle Paul
⑤ The Ghost and Mrs. Muir
⑥ ⑦ ⑩ Las Vegas Gambit
⑨ Romper Room
⑨ ⑪ The Jeffersons (R)
⑫ John Davidson
Guests: Bob Hope, Robert Duvall, Roger Moore, Rita Coolidge.
⑬ Movie
★ ★ ½ "The Outsider" (1962) Tony Curtis, James Franciscus.
⑰ Movie
★ ★ ★ "About Mrs. Leslie" (1954) Shirley Booth, Robert Ryan.
(ESP) Sports Center
(SPN) Movie
★ ★ "Chandu of the Magic Isle" (1940) Bela Lugosi.
(USA) C-Span Congressional Hearings
10:15 a.m. ② ㉕ ㊴ All About You

10:30 a.m.
② ㉕ ㊴ What on Earth?
③ Family Feud
③ $50,000 Pyramid
⑤ Edge of Night
⑤ Chico and the Man
⑥ ⑦ ⑩ Blockbusters
⑨ ⑪ Alice (R)

11 a.m.
② ㉕ ㊴ Energy

③ ⑤ ⑫ Love Boat (R)
③ ⑨ ⑪ The Price Is Right
⑤ Medical Center
⑥ ⑦ ⑩ Wheel of Fortune
⑨ Straight Talk
(ESP) Gymnastics

11:30 a.m.
② ㉕ ㊴ Word Shop
⑨ Jim Burns
⑦ ⑩ Password Plus
(SPN) Picture of Health
11:45 a.m. ② ㉕ ㊴ Story Bound

1 p.m.
② ㉕ ㊴ Readalong
③ ⑤ ⑫ ⑬ All My Children
③ ⑨ ⑪ The Young and the Restless
⑤ Mike Douglas
⑥ ⑦ ⑩ Days of Our Lives
⑨ Movie
★ ★ ½ "Tea for Two" (1950) Doris Day, Gordon MacRae.
⑰ Movie
★ ★ ½ "Sangaree" (1953) Fernando Lamas, Arlene Dahl.
(ESP) All-Star Soccer
(SPN) School of Country Living
1:10 p.m. ② ㉕ ㊴ Matter of Fact

1:30 p.m.
② ㉕ ㊴ Trade-Offs
(NIK) Dusty's Treehouse
(SPN) Paul Ryan

2 p.m.
② ㉕ ㊴ What on Earth?
③ ⑤ ⑫ ⑬ One Life to Live
③ ⑨ ⑪ As the World Turns
⑤ I Love Lucy
⑥ ⑦ ⑩ Another World
(ESP) Auto Racing
(NIK) Vegetable Soup
(SPN) Financial Inquiry

2:30 p.m.
② ㉕ ㊴ Zebra Wings
⑤ Mayberry R.F.D.
(NIK) First Row Features
(SPN) The Gourmet

3 p.m.
② ㉕ ㊴ Big Blue Marble
③ ⑤ ⑫ ⑬ General Hospital
③ ⑨ ⑪ Guiding Light
⑤ Bugs Bunny and Friends
⑥ ⑩ Texas
⑦ Bullseye
⑨ Bonanza
⑰ Funtime
(SPN) It's a Great Idea

3:30 p.m.
② ㉕ ㊴ Villa Alegre
⑤ Tom and Jerry
⑦ Leave It to Beaver
⑰ The Flintstones

(NIK) Studio See
(SHO) The Odd Couple
(SPN) The Women's Channel

4 p.m.
② ㉕ ㊴ Sesame Street (CC)
③ ⑬ Edge of Night
③ Merv Griffin
⑤ Batman
⑥ Hollywood Squares
⑦ The Munsters
⑨ Movie
★ ★ ½ "Strange Cargo" (1940) Clark Gable, Joan Crawford.
⑨ ⑪ One Day at a Time (R)
⑨ John Davidson
Guests: John Schneider, Jenilee Harrison, Fred Travalena, Stephen Macht.
⑫ Powww!
⑰ The Addams Family
(ESP) College Golf
(NIK) What Will They Think of Next?
(SPN) Fran Carlton Exercise

4:30 p.m.
③ ⑤ The Flintstones
⑤ Good Times
⑥ Six Million Dollar Man
⑦ Wild, Wild West
⑨ Gunsmoke
⑪ John Davidson
Guests: Bob Hope, Robert Duvall, Roger Moore, Rita Coolidge.
⑫ Emergency
⑬ Happy Days Again
⑰ Hazel
(ESP) College Lacrosse
"Division I Championship"
(NIK) Livewire
(SPN) Movie
★ ★ "Sing While You're Able" (1938) Toby Wing, Pinky Tomlin.

5 p.m.
② ㉕ ㊴ Mister Rogers
③ Happy Days Again
⑤ Beverly Hillbillies
⑤ The Brady Bunch
⑬ All in the Family
⑰ Ozzie and Harriet
(USA) C-Span Call-In (Tentative)

5:30 p.m.
② ㉕ ㊴ Electric Company (R)
③ Good Times
③ To Tell the Truth
⑤ Andy Griffith
⑤ I Love Lucy
⑥ Cartoons
⑦ All in the Family
⑨ ⑩ MASH
⑫ Get Smart
⑬ News
⑰ Beverly Hillbillies
(HBO) Movie
"Skatetown U.S.A." (1979) Scott Baio, Greg Bradford.
(NIK) Video Comics
(SHO) Crossbar
5:45 p.m. ⑥ News

SOURCE: "Carolina People," *The News and Observer*, Raleigh, N.C., 1 June 1981, p. 16.

Directions: Scan the local television listings on p. 248 to answer the following questions. Note your beginning time.

Beginning Time:

_____

1. Are the morning programs listed?_____

2. Is the late, late show shown after midnight listed?_____

3. Which station(s) will broadcast the International Byline?_____

4. Is the soap opera "Edge of Night" shown more than once on this particular day?_____

Ending Time:

_____

5. Which channel will show the movie, "Strange Cargo?"_____

Scanning Time:

_____

_____ When?_____

Record your ending time and compute entire scanning time.

Directions: Scan the classification index on p. 250 for the want ad section of the newspaper. Place your responses to each scanning immediately below the question. Note your beginning time.

Beginning Time:

_____

1. Could you find information in this newspaper about real estate loans?_____

_____

2. Under which number would you find Antiques?_____

_____

Ending Time:

_____

3. Do the numbers refer to pages or do they refer to classification numbers?

_____

Scanning Time:

_____

4. Under what number are motorcycles classified?_____

Record your ending time and compute entire scanning time.

The News and Observer
Raleigh Times

WANT ADS
PHONE

821-4112

Convenient Classification Index

SOURCE: "Want Ads," *The News and Observer*, Raleigh, N.C., 2 June 1981, p. 1.

Scanning Reading Selections

Now you are ready to use your scanning skills to practice on entire reading selections. As you work through Selections 1 through 8, remember that scanning is *not* reading. You are looking only for the answer to a question. All other material is passed over. You are looking only for a word, number, or idea. If you keep this image of the word or the idea clearly in mind, the item you are looking for will stand out more sharply than the others. Thus you can find the item quickly.[5]

While scanning reading selections, you must be willing to skip large amounts of material. You should work with a single purpose in mind—a key word or phrase—searching for one item at a time. As you scan the following articles, use this procedure:

1. Record your beginning time.
2. Read the first statement to determine exactly what you will search for as you scan. Underline the key word that you will use in your search.
3. Quickly glance over the selection until you spot the key word. Read only that sentence carefully. Do not read any farther.
4. Place a T in the blank before the statement if it is true. If it is false, place an F in the blank.
5. Go immediately to the next statement and repeat the procedure. Do this for each statement relating to the article. Record your ending time. Then

compute your total scanning time for the article. Move to the next article and do the same. Scan all articles in the group of selections provided.

6. Compute your total scanning time for a particular group of selections and record.[6]

Selection 1: Roses Prized for Ages as Medicine and Food ⸺   Beginning Time:

Directions: Scan the following article to determine the truth or falsity of these statements. Use a T for True, F for False.

⸺ 1.   Roses predate man on earth by about 40 million years.

⸺ 2.   Cut roses that start to wilt or develop weak stems cannot be revived.

⸺ 3.   Many helpful hints on how to grow roses are provided.

⸺ 4.   Roses have never been used as a food for man.

One of the symbols, tokens and signs used by man since the beginning of recorded time, and one of the most prevalent, has been the rose. This is not surprising since fossils found in the western United States prove that the rose predates man by about 40 million years.

The rose has been cultivated for over 5,000 years. It was valued as a medicine and food long before its use as an ornamental flower began. The Greek physician Hippocrates was among the first to use rose extract as a medicine.

Roman Emperor Nero once spent the equivalent of $100,000 for roses to decorate a single night of revelry. In the Trojan War, Achilles wore roses on his shield; Hector on his helmet. And the 30-year War of the Roses ended when the feuding families of Lancaster (whose insignia was a red rose) and York (with its white rose) were joined by marriage, and the Tudor rose—with red and white petals—became the national flower of England.

Roses are versatile, beautiful and easy to care for. They bloom from April to November. Here are some hints for growing fine roses:

- Choose a sunny spot for planting.
- Don't crowd too many plants together. Easy access to each plant is a must.
- Plant in a hole 18–20 inches in diameter with the bud onion (thickened portion at the top of the root) above the soil.
- Water roses frequently. Water should reach full depth of the roots.
- Nourish plants with food which contains a balanced combination of nutrients designed for sturdy plants and abundant blooms.
- Don't be afraid of pruning; it's necessary to encourage new growth. Trim dead leaves, limbs and weak or damaged twigs.
- Cut a third of last year's new growth on a 45 degree angle above each leaf bud.
- Don't forget to spray. It's an important part of rose care to insure pest-free plants. Spray in the evenings so the combination of pesticide and heat won't burn the leaves.
- Don't neglect winter protection. Cover the bud onion (at stem base) with eight inches of soil. After soil freezes, place straw or leaves on it.

With this type of care, you should have a garden full of beautiful blossoms to adorn your yard or to cut and bring inside. With proper care, cut roses can be made to last from three to seven days.

Whether you get cut roses from your garden or from a sweetheart, when you get them inside hold them under water and use a sharp knife or snips to cut back the stems by one half to one inch in a diagonal direction. Remove any foliage that will be below the water line of the container you want to use.

Let the stems soak for several hours in warm water (100 to 110 degrees), to which an aspirin and a couple tablespoons of sugar, or a chemical preservative, has been added. The aspirin and sugar or preservative will arrest bacterial action and extend flower life. Put the flowers in a cool place for this conditioning period.

Use the same water to fill a vase at least eight inches full and arrange the roses as you like.

If you have a rose that starts to wilt or develop a weak stem, don't throw it away. It can be resuscitated.

Ending Time:

_____

Scanning Time:

_____

Beginning Time:

_____

While holding the stem underwater, cut about one inch from the stem base. Then submerge the entire rose—bloom, stem foliage and all—under water for 20 minutes or so. The water should be about 100 degrees F. Be sure to straighten the angle of the head while it soaks.

For a long stem rose, a couple of inches of water in the bathtub will accommodate nicely. When revived, the rose can be replaced in its vase.

Selection 2: *Playboy* Visits Down Home to Find "Girl Next Door" —

Directions: Scan the following article to determine the truth or falsity of these statements.

_____ 1.   *Playboy* will feature a southern woman in its 25th Anniversary edition coming in January.

_____ 2.   *Playboy* conducts its interviews away from big cities.

_____ 3.   This stop on *Playboy's* tour is the only one to be made.

_____ 4.   The Miss January centerfold will be paid $25,000.

If you have something you'd like to get off your chest, Playboy magazine may want to talk with you.

A crew from the Chicago-based men's magazine will be in Columbia and the Raleigh-Durham area next month, holding interviews and taking photos of women who think they might be suitable as Playboy centerfolds.

"You have a lot of good-looking ladies down there in the South. Oh, yes," says David Salyers, Playboy public relations director.

And it's those women, in or out of college, that Playboy hopes to display in its 25th anniversary edition in January.

Playboy, Salyers says, is combing the country for the woman who personifies the Playboy image of women:

"They are very fresh and very young. . . . It's the girl next door."

Playboy is willing to pay generously for its Miss January—$25,000 for the centerfold. Centerfolds in other issues receive $10,000.

Carolinians can interview beginning April 3 at the Carolina Inn in Columbia and April 10 at the Governor's Inn in the Research Triangle Park between Raleigh and Durham. The interview crew will stay about a week in each place, Salyers says.

Playboy representatives will spend 15 minutes with each woman, explaining what Playboy is looking for and trying to gauge how the interviewee feels about the project. An initial "bikini shot" will be made with a Polaroid camera.

"We don't want it to be like a modeling call," Salyers says. "In a modeling call, like when they're looking for a model for an auto commercial, they'll bring in 15 or 20 beautiful women, but they don't use any time with them.

"They're just waving their hands, saying 'No, honey, we don't need a redhead. Out. Out. Out.' Well, we're dealing with people's egos, and they shatter easily."

Salyers says the Columbia and Raleigh interviews were part of a 20 city tour.

"In addition to the fact that we're looking specifically for a 25th anniversary centerfold, we hope to find a number of other Playmates for on down the road."

Salyers says Playboy conducts interviews away from big cities for several reasons:

• "In most markets that aren't a Chicago or New York or Los Angeles, people are still sort of fascinated with Playboy. They say 'Gee, what do they look like? Do they have green hair?' So we get a good turnout."

• Playboy wants newcomers as nude models. "If she has ever been published in the nude before, we won't use her," Salyers says.

• Playboy finds the well-publicized interviews help build circulation. Playboy sells about 90,000 issues each month in North Carolina and about 40,000 issues in South Carolina. The magazine has a total circulation of about 5 million.

Salyers says some feminist groups opposed Playboy's trips to some Midwestern college campuses.

"There were some girls who were really irate. But the girls who came out to pose, their ideas towards the radicals (demonstrators) was, 'Hey, mind your own business. Don't try to coerce me, thank you.' "

The interview teams in the Carolinas probably won't meet much resistance, mainly because the upcoming visits have received little publicity.

Don Oldhan, treasurer of the Association of Women Students at UNC, said he would bring the subject before his group, but the protest would probably be little more than a "strongly worded newspaper ad."

Ending Time:

_____

Scanning Time:

_____

Selection 3: Want to Buy a Nice Swimming Pool? _____

Beginning Time:

_____

Directions: Scan the following article to determine the truth or falsity of these statements.

_____ 1. Swimming pools are classified as in-ground or above-ground structures.

_____ 2. Homeowners cannot install pools themselves for a savings.

_____ 3. The coming of summer starts homeowners to thinking about pools.

_____ 4. The firm from which a pool is purchased should have a proven track record for service and quality.

With summer just around the corner, many homeowners' fancies are turning to water—the kind in a pool in the backyard.

Homeowners concerned with increasing their property values and enjoyment may want to think about adding an in-ground pool.

"An in-ground pool retains its value and increases the resale value of the home by the value of the pool," said Bob Siegel of Pacific Pools in Charlotte. "Above-ground pools are worth absolutely nothing on the resale value of the house because they are not considered permanent structures."

The classification of in-ground or above-ground is determined by the type of wall structure and how it's located in the ground. There are basically three types of in-ground pools, with some subclassifications of one type.

The first type is the one that most people are familiar with—the all concrete, or gunite pool. The gunite pool lasts longest and is the strongest type. Models range in cost up to $14,000.

The second type is the fiberglass wall with a concrete bottom. These are priced from $6,000 to $10,000.

The third major type is the vinyl-lined pool. There are four kinds, ranging in cost from $2,000 to $7,500. Properly installed, a vinyl-lined pool should last 10–15 years. The difference in the kinds is the material from which the walls are made. Walls are made of metal, wood, fiberglass, and polymer foam. The fiberglass and polymer are considered better because they are completely inert in the ground. Over a period of time, metal and wood walls can corrode.

Otis Johnson of Johnson Pool Builders in Charlotte says that the most popular pools sold are rectangular.

"Anytime you get away from straight lines, it costs more," Johnson said. "If you decide to get a kidney shaped pool, you'll pay more because of the increased labor, and have less water to swim in."

Having someone install a pool is not the only way to have it done. There are many pool kits on the market that anyone with the least mechanical ability can install in a few days.

"It only takes about four or five working days for two people to install a vinyl-lined pool," said Siegel. "It's not easy to mess up either."

As an example of the savings available if you install the pool yourself, Siegel said the cost of a 16 × 32-foot vinyl-lined pool with polymer foam walls and complete pump and filter system installed is $5,000. If you install it yourself, the same pool would cost you $3,000—complete.

Whether you have someone else install your pool or plan to do it yourself, both Johnson and Siegel said to be extremely careful of the bait-and-switch schemer who'll get into your home with a promise of a heck of a deal and end up selling you a turkey of a deal.

Make certain the company you are dealing with is a reputable firm with a proven track record, both gentlemen said.

"One year we had a fellow come to Charlotte, sell over a hundred pools and then go bankrupt," said Johnson. "The people that bought pools from him were left holding the bag with no valid guarantee."

"Absolutely check with the BBB before signing anything," said Siegel. "Be very leery of anyone who advertises pools at very low prices. There are some real charlatans in this business." . . .

So, if you decide you want a pool, be very careful whom you buy it from. Don't allow yourself to be high-pressured into something you don't want.

Ending Time:

_____

Scanning Time:

Selection 4: Grasshoppers: They're Kinky, Really Kinky —————————

Directions: Scan the following article to determine the truth or falsity of these statements.

————— 1.   The researcher chose the Chicago area to observe his grasshoppers.

————— 2.   "Flicker fusion" makes grasshopper observation difficult for man.

————— 3.   A chemical called glycerin enables some grasshoppers whose bodies are frozen solid in winter to survive and resume normal activities in spring.

————— 4.   When grasshoppers mate, the females dance to attract the males.

Grasshoppers live in a world all their own, and for 15 years Robert Willey has done his best to join them.

"Trying to think like a grasshopper is very important," says Willey, a biologist at the University of Illinois Circle Campus.

Sometimes grasshoppers aren't quite sure what they are thinking. An expert in grasshopper mating, Willey has seen them try to mate with sticks, thermometers and the edges of cardboard cartons.

He has seen male grasshoppers court each other instead of a female, only to stop at the sound of a chipmunk chirp, which they mistook for the call of a female grasshopper.

At times, the grasshoppers are sure of themselves; humans may still be puzzled as they gaze through a time warp from our slow-motion world into the lightening-fast cosmos of the insects.

Grasshoppers rub their hind legs together 60 times a second to communicate. Willey makes high-speed films and tapes to be slowed later for "prolonged replays" perceptible to humans.

The notion of "flicker fusion," or how many distinct movements a creature can perceive before they blur, gives some idea of the gulf between man and grasshopper. We see up to 16 distinct movements a second, while they can distinguish 200.

Quiet Kissers

"They'd find it difficult watching movies," Willey says.

Humans are such slow, lumbering objects to grasshoppers that they usually ignore Willey as he observes them in the Colorado Rockies, sometimes only inches away.

They may annoy him more than he bothers them, especially when Willey encounters species that can be heard up to half-a-mile away.

"It reaches the threshold of pain when they hover in front of me, clicking at their own reflection in my glasses," he says.

Willey's favorites, the Arphia genus, are somewhat quieter with their kissing, barking and drummer-like noises. Grasshoppers abound in the Rockies, and he often tracks individuals by painting colored spots on their backs to follow their activities with binoculars.

"You have to do it right," he says. "If they are too bright, birds will spot them and eat your specimen. If they aren't bright enough, you can't see them."

Arphia grasshoppers are among the few species to spend their winters as young nymphs rather than as eggs.

Arphia grasshoppers may freeze solid over the winter, becoming crystallized all through their bodies, but the glycerin in their cells allows them to survive the cold and resume usual activities and attain maturity when spring warmth arrives.

Oooh, Dance for Me

Females demand that males fly into the air to dance for them before mating. This is dangerous for the males, who are likely to become bird's lunch during the show.

Sometimes the males form "chorus lines," dancing together.

"We're not sure what chorusing means," he says. "It may be a way for females to bring males together so they can pick a mate they like, or it may be a way to confuse predators.

"I've seen robins go into a chorus, trying for a meal. They go first for one, then another, uncertain which to choose."

Another unanswered observation is courting of males by each other. It is unclear whether these fellows are "gayhoppers" or merely confused.

"When it happens in nature, it probably means confusion," Willey says. "But it may also be a learned behavior. I've seen it happen in the lab when males have been kept together, never seeing females. Others have noticed this also, but it's hard to replicate."

Ending Time:

_____

Scanning Time:

_____

Beginning Time:

_____

Selection 5: Greenhouse Can Increase Delights of Horticulture ____

Directions: Scan the following article to determine the truth or falsity of these statements.

_____ 1.   Heating is the least expensive operating cost in a greenhouse.

_____ 2.   Greenhouse enthusiasts consider a greenhouse to be a valuable asset to their property.

_____ 3.   Keeping nighttime temperatures at the 50° level in greenhouses is undesirable.

_____ 4.   Greenhouses provide a stable environment for plants.

Many gardening enthusiasts consider greenhouses a valuable asset to their horticultural activities.

Greenhouses provide a stable environment for plants by maintaining a controllable amount of light, providing proper humidity, optimizing temperature and limiting exposure to disease and pests.

For many gardeners, the convenience a greenhouse affords is equal to the relaxation of puttering with plants and the farming of a home-grown harvest.

In choosing the size of a greenhouse, the type and size of desired foliage and required upkeep should be kept in mind.

Persons with limited space might consider a small, inexpensive window greenhouse. These are installed inside or outside a window frame and hang over the window like an air conditioner.

A design that offers more space is the tri-walled greenhouse. Three green-house walls are connected to an existing structure, usually the rear of a house or a garage. This model offers considerable savings because of the existing wall.

Freestanding greenhouses are the most expensive. They provide more space than the tri-wall structures, and foliage placed in them grows straighter and faster due to increased light.

Greenhouses can be purchased as a whole, in assembled sections or as models designed for do-it-yourself installation. Ambitious gardeners may want to build from scratch using scrap wood, glass and plastic.

All installations require electrical plumbing and heating work. A heater, ventilator and plant benches add value to greenhouses.

Heating is the largest greenhouse operating cost. Greenhouses attached to a heated building can save 20 percent fuel costs over free-standing types. General savings in heating bills are accomplished by stretching a layer of plastic over the entire greenhouse interior, omitting only ventilator openings.

Ending Time:

_____

Fuel costs can be further minimized by choosing plants tolerant to low nighttime temperatures of approximately 50 degrees. Plants requiring higher temperatures should be placed near the heater and heating cables.

Scanning Time:

_____

Selection 6: Oil Spill Is No Holiday for Resorts ━━━━━━

Beginning Time:

_____

Directions: Scan the following article to determine the truth or falsity of these statements.

_____ 1.   An American supertanker is responsible for the oil spill off the coast of Brittany in France.

_____ 2.   The Brittany coast is a very popular and famous tourist attraction.

_____ 3.   Part of the appeal of this region is heated seawater as a cure for rheumatism and other ills.

_____ 4.   There were no problems finding seafood in the area.

The smelly oil-laden waves pounding 70 miles of Brittany coastline are blackening prospects for the summer vacation season, but tourism operators say it is too soon to measure the consequences.

The March 16 wreck of the American supertanker Amoco Cadiz on rocks just off Brittany's scenic coast spilled more oil into the ocean than any similar disaster in history. Many vacationers canceled plans for holidays in one of France's most popular tourist regions.

Of particular concern is the town of Roscoff, normally packed from April through October with 300 visitors a day "taking a cure"—baths in heated seawater for rheumatism and other ills.

Operators of the two spas in Roscoff took opposite views on the image of a seawater cure on the edge of a bay covered with oil.

"We are installing complicated filtering equipment and will be ready to open as usual early next month," said Dr. Jean Lefranc of the Ker Lena Center. "We had anticipated such a disaster and studied the necessary equipment.

"But the other center has decided not to open until May, and to our knowledge is not using the filters. It has written to its clients canceling their earlier cures."

The region north of Portsall, known for its seafood, reported cancellations of up to one-third of its reservations for Easter.

"Seafood is a problem," said a restaurant owner at Aber-Wrac't. "I just can't find any shell-fish in the area, even from the south, and that's what our guests come here for.''

Traffic jams clogged narrow roads near the wreck last Sunday, and police planned to close roads this weekend.

But after protests, officials decided to relax controls and allow in anyone with a country house or a hotel reservation.

Ending Time:

_____

Scanning Time:

_____

Beginning Time:

_____

Selection 7: Praise Julia, Pass the Haute Cuisine _____

Directions: Scan the following article to determine the truth or falsity of these statements.

_____ 1.   Mrs. Child, the French Chef, has had 15 successful years on TV.

_____ 2.   "The French Chef" is shown on Sundays by the Charlotte TV networks.

_____ 3.   No new series of TV is being planned for the near future by Mrs. Child.

_____ 4.   Mrs. Child, the French Chef, does not indeed have to diet herself.

"Is the public tired of Julia Child?" D'Etta Leach, public television producer at Charlotte's WTVI, asked recently on the air. The station during March, is testing responses to present offerings and trying to raise $75,000 from viewers for further programs (to date, the station has raised $58,965).

Immediately the studio phones began to ring. Ms. Leach quickly learned that Charlotteans, indeed, still love "The French Chef."

A few days later I had a chance to chat by phone with Mrs. Child in Boston and catch up on her activities. I had just watched a segment of "The French Chef" . . . where she lifted two lids from steaming pans of coq au vin and chicken fricassee and clanged them together exuberantly over her head, like cymbals. Condensed water from the lids splashed down the front of her blouse.

She welcomed the TV viewers as she nonchalantly mopped her front with a towel.

"I don't know why I did that," she says with a laugh. "It was silly."

She remembered one welcoming gift last time she was in Charlotte, in 1974—a fancy wrapped package of grits. She graciously thanked the giver and remarked about the many users of grits and the similarity with Italian Polenta.

"Little did we know how popular grits would become," she says, chuckling.

Her culinary knowledge, her unflappability, her naturalness have certainly won and kept the fans over 15 years, since she began her TV programs. She's the same person, charming, diplomatic and, yet, likely to tell it like it is in matters of food. Some people in her Charlotte audiences recall she verbally spanked a local department store, during a cooking demonstration, over the quality of their knives.

These days Mrs. Child is putting finishing touches on a fall series, "Julia Child and Company"—her first new series in five years for public TV. Recipes for the programs will appear in a cookbook, also called "Julia Child And Company."

Mrs. Child's new series, filmed on a new set somewhat like her own kitchen, will focus on meal management—planning and coordinating the dishes so they come out of the oven at the right time. Some of the programs: low calorie banquet, dinner for two, indoor-outdoor barbeque, VIP lunch, Sunday night supper and dinner for the boss.

"The idea is to use the background you have and take off on your own," Mrs. Child says. "This time we don't have to teach people how to chop carrots."

After all those cooking sessions with creamy, rich dishes, does she have to diet?

Yes, she does it all the time, she says.

Ending Time:

_____

Scanning Time:

_____

Selection 8: Pack Up Your Ski Togs

Beginning Time:

_____

Directions: Scan the following article to determine the truth or falsity of these statements. Mark a T for a true statement or an F for a false one.

_____ 1.   The bikini is no longer the number one swimsuit style.

_____ 2.   Nylon is the top selling swimsuit fabric.

_____ 3.   American women on the average buy a swimsuit every year.

_____ 4.   The way swimsuits are sold in America keeps many women from buying more often.

Shed a tear, Suzy Chaffee. It's no longer re-e-e-al Chapstick weather!

It is . . . thank heaven, at last . . . real swimsuit weather.

Knowing what type of suit to buy is fairly easy: The no-nonsense action-cut maillot ("my-oh") is this year's fashion look. And just because it's cut like a racing suit doesn't mean it isn't sexy. This maillot is so lightweight and unconstructed it leaves only stretchmarks to the imagination.

The second best-selling suit is the bikini—no, it's not about to go out of fashion—and the smaller the bikini the more fashionable.

In addition, there are one-piece strapless blousons, maillots that plunge to the navel and ride high on the hip, standard two-piece styles and even a few suits with skirts. All come in tropical colors and prints.

The next item, finding the most flattering suit for you, can be a much more difficult matter, agree swimsuit designers.

Catalina's senior designer . . . gives these tips: Try on many styles, even ones you think you don't like. Look for fashion and good fit through the bust, waist and hips. Straps should be comfortable, and if you actually intend to swim, versus sun, the suit should be made for movement.

A survey by Du Pont, which manufactures Lycra, the top-selling swim fabric, showed American women buy only one swimsuit every four years. (Only girls aged 14–17 buy more: one suit purchase every three years.)

"The thing that's always puzzled us," says Du Pont's Richard T. Brigham, "is that with the increase in leisure time and the number of swimming pools, swimsuit sales haven't gone up."

In contrast, European women buy a suit a year, in part because they're less critical, more accepting of their bodies, say American designers. The attitude of a slender Charlotte woman who said, "I don't want to hear about suits; I need one from chin to toes," typically American.

Says Catalina's Edith Thais; "In Europe you see some of the biggest gals at the beach, and they're enjoying the water. You think they'd have to go to Omar the tentmaker to get their suit, and it doesn't slow them down a bit. It's a mental attitude."

The way suits are sold is another factor, manufacturers suggest. They can't be returned, you have to strip to try 'em on, and then you can take only so many into the fitting room. And, as Richard Brigham from Du Pont suggests, "You get the feeling when you talk to women that there's about a five-minute period that's the right time to buy a swimsuit. If you come before they're not in the stores."

Indeed, most stores stock suits in the dead of February—when everyone looks fat and ghastly green under florescent fitting room lights. By July what's left has been picked to death and is on sale. The Catalina firm, for one, is trying to remedy this by coming out with a new line of suits for early summer delivery. It remains to be seen if stores will be interested.

Edith Thais predicts women will become better swimsuit customers when they begin to consider suits as a fashion item instead of just any old thing to be worn at the beach. Adds Brigham, "Once a woman is married, has children and less money to spend on herself, the swimsuit gets pushed to the background. If she can make her swimsuit last, she will."

Ending Time:

Designers hope the growing accessory business will help give swimwear more importance.

Scanning Time:

Cole of California's chief designer Marc Vigneron designed a full-length strapless coverup "that looks marvelous over a bandeau maillot. I've seen it out at dinner in the most formal settings. But I've never seen it at a swimming pool."

Now compare your scanning times for Selections 1 through 8. Your total time should be no more than five minutes. Do you feel more comfortable finding facts at an extremely high rate of speed?

SKIMMING

Now that you have learned and practiced scanning, you are ready to master skimming, the most complicated of the high-powered speed techniques. *Skimming* is an overview of a selection. It is used to gain a general impression of a selection when you, the reader, do not actually intend to read it more completely later on. (This is how skimming differs from the *previewing* technique you mastered earlier in your training. In previewing, you *do* intend to read the article.) Skimming is important in helping you build broad background knowledge about a topic through consulting many varied sources. For example, skimming is an invaluable skill for newspaper and magazine reading.[7]

Skimming involves the use of all cues for gathering information that you can call on. You must use your knowledge of previewing to become acquainted with the selection, establishing your purpose for reading. As you read you must apply your skill of identifying the writing style or pattern used by the author to locate quickly the main idea and its major supporting details. You must also apply paragraph reading techniques as well as the use of signal words and key words relating to the main idea. Skimming also requires the use of vertical vision accompanied by skipping large sections of content.

The new skills involved in your learning to skim are perfecting your skill in quickly locating key words and applying your vertical vision to actual reading selections.

Identifying Key Words

The basic message in a selection is carried by its nouns, verbs, adjectives, and adverbs. Words such as *a, an*, and *the* are not crucial to meaning. Neither are the pronouns *I, me, my* or prepositions such as *to, from, on, at*. Many other words are also unnecessary to the basic message. Selections 9 and 10 are keyed for you.

Selection 9: Udderly and Odderly ——————————————

Directions: Skim the following story giving yourself thirty seconds to complete the article. Check your comprehension when you are finished. Check your work by the Answer Key at the end of this unit.

Udderly and Odderly Otter are taking ＿ liberated approach ＿ caring ＿ their new family.

＿ two otters, ＿ ＿ at ＿ Western North Carolina Nature Center ＿ Asheville, have been sharing ＿ duty ＿ caring ＿ ＿ two ＿＿＿＿ offspring.

Animal experts say ＿ ＿ very unusual ＿ ＿ mother otter ＿ allow ＿ male ＿ approach ＿ pups. Mother ＿ ＿ handle ＿ care ＿ ＿ young themselves, ＿ behave violently ＿ males ＿ ＿ close ＿ ＿ pups.

＿ Odderly, ＿ male North American river otter, ＿ ＿ allowed ＿ ＿, ＿ mate, ＿ take ＿ active part ＿ ＿ nursery routine.

"＿ otter pups ＿ born, ＿ ＿ normal procedure ＿ separate ＿ male ＿ female," said naturalist ＿ ＿, "＿ ＿ ＿ case, ＿ ＿ separated Udderly ＿ Odderly, Udderly left ＿ babies, ＿ out ＿ door ＿ wouldn't go back ＿ them ＿ I let him (Odderly) ＿ in."

Experts decided ＿ even though Odderly ＿ ＿ loan ＿ Louisiana ＿ breeding purposes, he ＿ ＿ allowed ＿ remain where ＿ was. Leslie said ＿ ＿ happening ＿ ＿ "international zoo history."

Ronnie Allen, ＿ cares ＿ ＿ animals ＿ ＿ center, said "＿ first ＿ Udderly ＿ tired ＿ caring ＿ ＿ pups, she ＿ leave them ＿ Odderly ＿ ＿ went ＿ ＿ swim.

"He ＿ go ＿ ＿ cubbing room ＿ ＿ around ＿ pups ＿ ＿ mother did ＿ ＿ offered milk," Allen said. "＿ he ＿ nudge ＿ ＿ stroke ＿ ＿ move ＿ ＿ ＿ ＿ she would do."

＿ problems ＿ beset ＿ ＿ family.

Odderly ＿ ＿ behaving ＿ ＿ traditional manner, ＿ Udderly ＿ not permit ＿ near ＿ cubs. Leslie ＿ waiting ＿ see ＿ he ＿ ＿ allowed ＿ ＿ ＿ cubbing area.

＿ ＿ difficulty ＿ ＿ experts aren't ＿ ＿ ＿ long ＿ ＿ otters ＿ ＿ birth ＿ conception, and there's ＿ chance Odderly isn't ＿ ＿ father ＿ ＿ pups.

＿ pair ＿ ＿ encouraged ＿ breed ＿, ＿ ＿ experts ＿ watch ＿ ＿ signs ＿ ＿ unusual family behavior.

———————————————

Source: "Udderly and Odderly," *The Daily Reflector*, Greenville, N.C., 9 Apr. 1978, p. A-11. Reprinted by permission of The Associated Press.

Comprehension Check: Udderly and Odderly

Directions: Complete the following statements by circling the correct ending.

1.   Udderly and Odderly
   a.   are zoo keepers.
   b.   are a pair of otters.
   c.   are a pair of oxen.

2.   Animals like Udderly and Odderly leave caring for the young
   a.   to the male.
   b.   to other members of the family.
   c.   to the female.

3.   Udderly is liberated in the sense
   a.   that she permits the male near her pups.
   b.   that she leaves the housebuilding to her mate.
   c.   that she lives in the zoo.

4.   Odderly's first behavior toward the pups
   a.   was quite wild and most threatening.
   b.   was the same as that manifested by the mother.
   c.   was rather passive, taking no interest at all in them.

5.   If an animal possesses unusual behavior characteristics, these may be passed to a new generation of the same animal
   a.   through close habitation.
   b.   through no known procedure.
   c.   through breeding.

Comprehension Accuracy:

_____

Selection 10: Wife-selling ━━━━━━━━━━━━━━━━━━━━━━━

Directions: Skim this article as you did for Selection 9. Check your comprehension.

__ early __ __ century, selling __ wife __ __ swift, __ safe way __ unloading __ unwanted __ unfaithful spouse __ England.

It __ __ __ __ __ disgusting, barbarous, outrageous __ deplorable practice, __ __ __ words __ __ critics.

__ it __ had __ __ advantages.

__ __ __ __ __ anthropologist says __ "... __ served __ __ __ way __ restructuring __ family—__ __ __ divorce."

Writing __ __ __ __ Samuel Pyeatt Menefee __ wife-selling __ no more traumatic than __ divorce hearings, less expensive __ __ singles bar __ offered __ participants __ __ start __ conjugal life.

"__ __ not __ __ form & __ divorce, but __ valuable __ method __ giving __ husband __ __ separation __ insured __ support __ __ wife __ created a __ __ social relationship __ __ purchaser."

━━━━━━━━━━━━━━━━━

Source: "Wife-selling," *The Daily Reflector*, Greenville, N.C., 9 Apr. 1978, p. 4–11. Reprinted by permission of The Associated Press.

Interest __ wife-selling __ rekindled __ in Britain __ __ television adaptation __ Thomas Hardy's novel, *The Mayor of Casterbridge*.

Menefee __ __ found __ 200 __ instances __ __ __ early times __ __ __ 20th century.

__ Divorce Act of 1857 made divorce __ feasible __ all, Menefee said, __ "__ advantage __ __ __ was __ __ __ __ terminated __ __ marriage, __ __ provided __ market __ social exchange__no woman __ deserted without someone __ provide __ her. __ appears __ __ been __ rationale behind __ general, __ otherwise inexplicable, assent __ __ wives __ __ __ transactions."

__ __ 18th __ __ 19th __ sales, __ woman __ __ sold __ __ cattle market. Payment __ __ based __ __ weight.

__ __ __ link __ livestock sales __ __ halter __ __ wife's neck or waist, Menefee said.

"Bridled __ __ __, __ woman __ __ led __ market __ __ turnpike gate, __ established possession __ legalized __ sale."

He __ __ sales occurred __ __ reasons. __ significant number __ __ wife's adultery.

Husbands __ sold directly. __ Joseph Thompson __ __ __ __ urged __ purchasers __ "avoid troublesome wives __ __ __ __ mad dog, __ __ lion, __ loaded pistol, cholers . . ."

Menefee said __ wives consented __ __ sold, __ some __ driven __ market __ cudgels __ lured __ __ false pretenses.

Menefee's research uncovered __ wife __ turned __ tables __ __ spouse __ suggesting __ __ sell better __ __ different town. __ then __ him shanghaied __ __ __ cruise, __ her __ __ home __ possessions.

Feminists __ opposed __ practice __ __ stones __ weighted socks __ disrupt __ sales, Menefee said. __ __ caused __ auctioneer __ seek protection, __ __.

Wife-selling __ __ __ misdemeanor __ England __ __ __ 19th century. __ __ punishable __ up __ two years __ prison.

__ __ __ 20th century sales __ __ __ pubs instead __ markets __ agreements __ commonly __ private contract. __ came __ light __ __ support cases __ __ __ family squabbles.

Comprehension Check: Wife-selling

Directions: Complete the following statements by circling the correct ending.

1. In England wife-selling was considered

   a. as disgusting, barbarous, and outrageous.
   b. to have many social advantages.
   c. to be a form of slavery.

2. Wife-selling was recently brought to public notice in England

   a. because of a TV adaptation of Thomas Hardy's novel, *The Mayor of Casterbridge*.
   b. because of a recent court suit involving a wife-selling incident.
   c. because of the Anglican Church's official declaration of policy on wife-selling.

3. Wife-selling was practiced in England

    a. by the very wealthy.

    b. by those too poor to secure a divorce.

    c. by both rich and poor.

4. Feminists existed in England during the wife-selling period and

    a. bitterly opposed the practice, even disrupting some sales.

    b. were bitterly opposed to the practice, but took no action.

    c. were quite accepting of the practice, not taking any action.

5. Wives involved in the sale

    a. were usually bitterly opposed to the practice and had to be forced to participate.

Comprehension Accuracy:

    b. were accepting but usually found ways to abort the sale.

    c. were usually accepting of the situation but many were forced against their wishes.

Now you are ready to skim materials in which all unimportant words are included. Skim Selection 11 at top speed, reading only key words. Give yourself two minutes. No more. Then check your comprehension.

Total Words: 1782

Selection 11: History

Very little is known of the Roman occupation, when their colony of Palmaria was equal in status to Pollentia in the north of the island. Both these towns were destroyed by the Goths and Vandals, and what was to become the capital of the island was not to reassume a historical identity until the eighth century, when the Saracens invaded and renamed it Medina Mayurka. During the four centuries of Moorish rule the city was enclosed by four concentric walls, with its citadel, the Almudaina, functioning as the residence of the Wali, or governor.

When King Jaime of Aragon landed on the island in the autumn of 1229, he had at first intended to take Palma by storm before the Muslims, who had retreated behind its walls, could have had time to rally. However, unforeseen delays made a siege inevitable. The city was then bombarded by engines of war which recycled a variety of missiles including, it is said, the severed heads of Muslims who had been caught in the act of attempting to cut off the invading army's water supply. The assault reached its climax the last day of December, 1229, when the walls were breached and the Christian army swarmed in, headed, it is rumoured, by the mystical figure of Saint George, the patron saint of Catalonia, resplendent in white armour. Chroniclers report that 20,000 Muslims were killed in the fighting. There was in fact a repetition of the wholesale massacre of the city's Muslim population which had been perpetrated in the Catalan-Pisan crusading operation of 1114–15.

The implementation of the Carta de Poblacio—the written constitution—of 1230 created the basis for Palma's stability, and the city acquired further prestige upon the arrival of Jaime II, Majorca's own king, to take up residence in the rebuilt Almudaina Palace. With trade booming, the Catalan noblemen who had

SOURCE: Hazel Thurstone, "History," in *The Travellers Guide to the Balearics: Majorca, Minorca, Ibeze & Formentera* (London: Jonathan Cape, Ltd., 1979), pp. 90–94. Used with permission.

been granted country estates as recompense for their military services took advantage of the situation by moving in from the country to the city, where they involved themselves with shipping and commerce, and hived off a mass of their profits into the building of fine churches in thanksgiving and to the glory of God, while priority was given to the splendid new cathedral.

When in later centuries recession set in, the nobility reinvested in land, but made the mistake of adopting the role of absentee landlords more interested in levying taxes and collecting rents than in either the welfare of their dependents or the husbandry of their land. To a large extent popular disaffection was directed against the Jews who acted as agents, bankers, and tax collectors. The Palma ghetto was sacked in 1391, and another rising of insurgents protesting their wrongs occurred between 1450 and 1452. There were further civil disturbances in 1521, when a peasant rebellion was fortified by Palma craftsmen who took up arms, occupied public buildings and forced the viceroy to flee the country. He was strong enough to return two years later to enforce the rules of law. When a small party was admitted to the city for parley, power was seized treacherously, and the ringleaders of the rebellion executed. By that time, in the sixteenth century, Majorca's traditional markets had, for one reason or another, dwindled almost to the point of collapse, and one-third of the city was uninhabited and falling into decay. These were days of fear and uncertainty, made none the more comfortable by the rising power of the Church, invested in the Inquisition.

But human error and vagary were not exclusively responsible for the troubles of Palma's citizens. They also repeatedly suffered punishment by natural causes—in epidemics which further decimated the population, and recurred well into the nineteenth century in the form of yellow fever and cholera . . . and in earthquakes, and as if this were not enough, the city underwent what was perhaps its worst disaster in the flooding of La Riera, the seasonal torrent which flows down from the mountains to empty into Palma Bay. At the turn of the thirteenth century, the watercourse had divided the city roughly into two parts, the upper and lower, or east and west. Though Jaime II had recognized flooding to be a hazard, and had drawn up plans to divert the river, these had not been implemented. The consequence was that in October 1403 a great spate demolished a large part of the lower section of the city. The death toll amounted to more than 5,000, with, of course, a commensurate destruction of property. Though some subsequent measures were taken to control the river, it was not until 1623 that its course was turned, so that the flow was diverted into the moat outside the city walls. The river—dry in summer—is nowadays bordered by Paseo Mallorca until it reaches its outfall immediately west of the Club Nautico. Also, and of even greater interest from a town-planning point of view, the original course of the river has for a length of 1½ km. been converted into two broad and dignified boulevards—Via Roma (otherwise La Rambla) and El Borne, whose formal name is the paseo Generalissimo Franco—which lead eventually to Paseo Sagrera and the waterfront.

The walls, too, had given trouble at various stages of history. Their original circumference encompassed an area containing the eventual site of the Almudaina Palace, the cathedral and some distance north. A second wall was added in the ninth century to take in much of the upper town lying to the east; and later, in the twelfth century a third wall was hastily erected to act as a defence against the Catalan-Pisan crusading operation. Though it was breached on that occasion, it was rebuilt by a Muslim labour force brought in from Anduluz immediately after the victorious Christians had retired from the island. During pre-gunpowder days these walls had been strong enough to withstand assault, except when there was treachery within the gates. However, in 1560 it was decided that they were inadequate, and should be strengthened. The fortifications were based on the original Moorish layout. The work continued sporadically for centuries according to the availability of funds, and it is ironic to know that the strengthened walls were to be manned once only in their history. This was in 1715, when the city withstood a siege for seventeen days only, in spite of its reinforced defence system. . . . It is significant that by the beginning of the nineteenth century many of the walls and battlements were already crumbling—notably the seaward line.

These ancient and patched-up walls, which had contained and withstood so much action throughout the centuries, suffered ignominious demolition in 1873, when it was decided that they would be better removed so as to allow space for growth of the city, and incidentally to make it more hygienic. This was done in the face of opposition by traditionalists. Present-day visitors may well search in vain for remnants of the old lines of defence; nothing is left that is of great consequence, with the exception perhaps of the Almudaina Arch to the south-west of the palace, and much of this is a reconstruction. However, it will interest dedicated map-readers to observe that the city's ring road, consisting of sections named variously as Avenida this and that, encloses the bulk of the older built-up area in a series of angles. This line defines the original outer fortifications. The seaward defences, too, have been almost entirely scrapped in a major scheme of land reclamation aimed at further protection against flooding, and as an extension of the port area. These works have created the Ronda Littoral which carries fast-moving traffic to seaward of the old quarter of the town, the cathedral and the Almudaina Palace to join, without interruption, the coastal trunk road leading west out of the city.

During the years when Majorca existed in isolation as a mere part of a Spanish province, lassitude set in. This was reflected particularly in Palma. The largest island of the Balearic group was far less affected by, and involved in, world affairs than Minorca, which was of considerable strategic importance to the warring European powers. Nevertheless, in spite of depression and poverty the eighteenth and nineteenth centuries had brought some improvement to Palma both in planning and in general smartening up. In fact, the concentration of the landed gentry in the metropolis, though it was at the expense of the countryside, caused the building and maintenance of a great many grand town houses whose architecture owed much to Italian taste and the Renaissance, and which are of inestimable value today.

In the same way that the bombing of cities in the second World War in northern Europe created space for modern traffic-free development, the re-routing of the Riera presented the opportunity for reorganizing the medieval, haphazard pattern of the congested streets. The two new boulevards that were built were additionally provided with ornamental stonework, such as the fountain of Las Tortugas (the tortoises) in what is now known as Plaza Pio XII, and a series of benches, as well as traffic islands with ample space for trees, shrubs and formal borders. El Borne was lit by gas as early as 1859, before the introduction of an electric power station in 1902, the year, incidentally, when the city's first hotel, the Gran, was opened. The hotel-building explosion was slow at the beginning, but was hastened somewhat by the inauguration of a fast steamer service to Barcelona in 1911, and as a presage of the future—the first crossing of the channel by aeroplane from Barcelona in 1916. Though it is possible to become temporarily disorientated in Palma—usually because intriguing narrow streets tempt one to depart from a set course—the geography very soon becomes imprinted upon one's memory if one thinks in terms of boundaries. To begin with, there are the harbour installations to the south, alongside which the coast road pursues an uninterrupted course, overlooked by great buildings and, later, by grand hotels. The ancient town behind may be divided into two: known as the upper and lower. Reference to the map will show that these are contained by the tangential avenues created by the removal of the outer walls. The two sections of the town will then be seen to be separated by the El Borne, which is a good example of traditional Spanish town planning with its trees and parterres and a double flow of traffic—not exclusively wheeled, because it is here that the evening paseo, or ritual walkabout, may be seen to advantage from pavement cafes and restaurants. El Borne continues north, becoming Calle San Jaime until, near the church of Santa Magdalena it meets Via Roma, again with its central island, plane trees, flower stalls and ornamental shrubs. Incidentally, this thoroughfare's name is of recent origin, given to commemorate the island's allegiance to the Nationalist cause during the Spanish Civil War when Mussolini's air force was stationed near by. Two plaster statues of Romans stand guard at the southeastern end. El Borne and Calle San Jaime meet at Plaza Pio XII roundabout, where from the deeply arcaded Avenida General Mola one can reach the central Plaza Mayor by a flight of steps below the little-used Teatro Principal. The theatre backs on to this spacious pedestrian plaza, beneath which there is an equally roomy car park. From here onwards to the northwest and the south, the street patterns are irregular. Deep inside this quarter will be found the greatest number of the medieval churches and palaces which are such an important characteristic of this city. Though some sort of pattern radiating from Plaza Mayor may be discerned on the map, in practice this is difficult to follow. However, distances are not great, and no harm will come from blind wandering until some recognizable landmark is reached.

Comprehension Check: History

Directions: Answer each of the following statements by writing in or circling the correct answer.

1. This selection is a simple factual account of the ancient history of Palma.
   True   False

2. The slaughters of the Muslim populations of Palma were motivated
   a. by desire for extensive military conquests.
   b. by the religious fervor of the Christian conquerors.
   c. by migrating European colonists seeking farmland.

3. Other disasters such as _____, _____, and _____ plagued the Palma of earlier times also.

4. The walls of Palma gave way to _____

_____

_____.

5. As with Palma, stability has come to many countries with the advent

   a. of the implementation of a written constitution.
   b. of the institution of a strong defense system.
   c. of the church's ascendancy to power.

Skimming Vertically

Skimming vertically may be done by either of two methods: one, centering your focus in the middle of the material while noting key words within range above and below the focal point[8] and two, using a Basic-Z pacing technique.[9]

Using a Center Focus

For centering the focus, pull your finger down the center of the column or page, two lines at a time. Focus between the two lines just above your finger. Take in key words above and below the focus, glancing to the right or left only if you must. Continue this procedure as you skim the entire selection.

Using a Basic-Z

When using the Basic-Z pacing technique, your index finger slides underneath the first line of print; don't point, slide the finger. Your eyes should follow immediately behind your finger noting key words only. When you reach the end of a line, slide your finger quickly to the beginning of the next—never stopping. Your eyes will follow.

Try both of these methods on Selection 12. Use centering the focus on the first column, the Basic-Z on the second. Which do you prefer? Begin again, using the preferred pattern. Allow yourself only ten seconds to complete the article. Test your comprehension by answering the questions at the end of the article.

Total Words: 817

Selection 12: Dictionary Documents Dialects _____

In Kentucky, a hill billy is a hill-billy, but in Maine, he's a hayseed.

In Georgia, he's a cracker, but in New York State, he's a backwoodsman.

In the "American" language—or English as it is spoken in America—there are at least 479 differing things one can call a person of conspicuously rural origin according to Raven McDavid, who has spent decades collecting such terms.

McDavid, a professor emeritus at the University of Chicago, has toiled since the 1940's gathering words and pronunciations for his "Linguistic Atlas of the United States," which, when it is finished, will be a virtual library of all the dropped r's, mispronounced vowels, ain'ts, cain'ts, and tain'ts in the country.

It will document for Americans, who tend to think they all speak alike, just how differently they sound to a trained ear.

Not only do the words used by Americans vary vastly from community and state to state, but the pronunciations vary drastically, even from one

SOURCE: Susan J. Smith, "Dictionary Documents Dialects," *The Daily Reflector*, Greenville, N.C., 26 Oct. 1980, p. C-8. Reprinted by permission of The Associated Press.

city neighborhood to another, says McDavid, editor-in-chief of the atlas.

"There are at least 18 different dialects in Charleston (S.C.) alone," he says.

In Charleston, if they tell you to go sit on the piazza, they are inviting you to sit on what is called a porch in Kentucky and a stoop in the Hudson Valley, McDavid says.

In Baltimore, policemen don't hit people with their nightsticks, they hit them with their espatoons. In the Minneapolis area boys don't flip each other with rubber bands, they do it with rubber binders. In Savannah, Ga., and Philadelphia, when they speak about the pavement they mean the sidewalk, not the street, according to McDavid.

There's no end to the variation because each community develops its own local expressions and pronunciations based on its history, McDavid says.

Despite the common myth that there is "pure American" spoken somewhere, that's not true, McDavid says.

"It used to be thought that there was Eastern, Southern and General American," he says. But field workers conducting research for the Linguistic Atlas have discovered there is a great deal of differentiation in the "General American" or catch-all, category.

People from Northern Indiana do not talk like people from Southern Indiana, and neither group talks like folks from Oklahoma or Nevada. That's because dialects—like customs, culture, and modes of government tend to follow lines of settlement, McDavid explains.

One of the widest belts of Southern-influenced speech follows Daniel Boone's historic Wilderness Road westward from Virginia and the Carolinas into Tennessee, Kentucky, Southern Indiana, Southern Illinois and Missouri, McDavid explains.

However, you can't predict the way a person will speak based solely on his home town, McDavid says. Linguistic Atlas researchers have found people who say "warsh," generally a Southern pronunciation for "wash," as far north as Vermont, he says.

Some of the mixing of dialects is due to mass communication, urbanization and the speed and frequency with which Americans travel, he says.

If America had not come into being at a time of improved means of communication and travel, differences in speech around the country would be much more marked, he says.

"If we had a serious energy shortage in this country that lasted 50 years, it would affect our language, because people couldn't travel," he says.

However, he adds, television is not the great leveler of language that some people think—largely because people do not talk back to the television set. A Bostonian who hears the Midwestern accent of Walter Cronkite on the nightly news is still going to talk like a Bostonian.

How long before this awesome dialect-gathering project is complete? McDavid can't predict, except to say it will be several years, probably more than a decade.

That's because of the size of the United States, the huge amount of time needed to interview people, edit the findings, and, to some extent, funding difficulties, he says.

The atlas is being published by sections of the country. The New England states and the upper Midwest are the only sections already in print.

Years are spent on each region because it takes that long to analyze a region, choose interviews, make up questionnaires, do the interviews and edit the results.

Responses are plotted out on maps. When there are enough similar responses, a dialect area is plotted out. In addition to the maps, each volume of the atlas has information about the region's history, culture, settlement, population and geography.

The atlas was started in 1929 by the American Council of Learned Societies under the leadership of Hans Kurath, a linguist who is now retired but who was the editor-in-chief of the New England portion of the atlas.

McDavid, who holds a doctorate in Milton from Duke University, started as a field worker in his native South Carolina, then ended up doing one-fourth of the interviews on the Atlantic seaboard. McDavid has been editor for 28 of the 49 years that research on the atlas has been conducted.

"Now I have to carry the bucket on my shoulder," he says of the atlas. Asked where he got that expression, he laughs.

"Ah don't know," he says.

Comprehension Check: Dictionary Documents Dialects

Directions: Complete each of the following statements by writing in or circling the correct answer.

1. Raven I. McDavid was the initiator of the first linguistic atlas.

   True   False

2. Development of the linguistic atlas will
   a. proceed according to different sections of the country.
   b. have a design based on a town-by-town analysis.
   c. proceed for a total country format as a general American language has been readily identified.

3. An interesting observation of linguistic researchers who are analyzing data for the atlas is that
   a. a person's background has relatively little influence on his or her speech patterns.
   b. television is not the great speech leveler as was thought earlier.
   c. the speech of most Americans is relatively homogeneous.

4. There are 479 different words by which Americans call people who _____

   _____.

5. The American language would be affected in which manner if there was an energy shortage that would last as long as 50 years?_____

   _____.

Skimming Page-Wide Materials

You are now ready to try your hand at skimming page-wide materials using vertical eye movements. Follow this procedure for skimming Selections 13 through 17:

1. Determine the pattern or style of writing used by the author.
2. Preview the selection underlining the main idea and major points (subheadings) explained about it. Determine your purpose for the reading.
3. With your purpose in mind, skim the material under one subheading at a

time. Skim rapidly to find information about that point or subheading. Then skim to find out about the second. Do this for each subheading.[10]

4. Give yourself only 30 seconds to skim.
5. Answer the questions in the Comprehension Checks at the end of each selection. Check your work in the Answer Key at the end of this unit.

Selection 13: Tips For Cold Weather Driving ———————————   Total Words: 1220

There's a great deal to be said about driving in the snow—but very little of it is good. A substantial number of motorists face two to four months a year traveling by car in winter conditions—ice, slush, sleet, drifts and worse. Even with the best equipment and the most skillful drivers, the undertaking can be inconvenient, costly and, on occasion, dangerous. But there are some simple rules that can significantly reduce the overall unpleasantness. They are relatively inexpensive, especially when compared to the cost of a tow truck, the hourly rates for a mechanic or body repairman—or a stint in the hospital.

1. *Get the right extra equipment.* If there is one immediate, direct way to immobilize yourself in snow, it is with the wrong tires. The neatest compromise for all except the worst winter weather is a full set of quality steelbelted radial tires. These are so good in most winter conditions that many states legally accept them as snow tires. Moreover, they're excellent on ice, wet pavements and mud as well as pure snow. They wear like iron—25–30,000 miles with proper care—and can be used year-round. For even better traction and steering in really heavy snow country you might consider radial snow-tread tires, whether on the driving wheels or on all four wheels. If there's a great deal of ice on the highways in your area, consider adding studs (although they are noisy and might be illegal in your state). Or, if you seek the ultimate in traction and are willing to live with the noise, harsh ride and general inconvenience of a military light reconnaissance vehicle, use old-fashioned tire chains. But the best overall compromise involves radials—four conventional tires in climates with light to medium snowfalls; radial snow tires in heavy snowbelts.

You should equip your car with several other items, including at least two *strong* windshield scrapers. Also pack a can of de-icer fluid for quick windshield clearing, a can of dry gas, a roll of paper towels for wiping mud and road salt off headlights (which can cut your headlight power by half), a shovel (for you know what), a blanket and, in the event you are stalled for any length of time, a small first-aid kit and a few highway flares.

Two accessories that aren't cheap but can be invaluable in bad weather are a CB radio for signalling trouble and a set of quartz-halogen auxiliary driving lights, which will add tremendous range to your vision, especially in fog or blowing snow.

2. *Winter driving is not like summer driving; it's harder.* Ice and snow are slippery, which is why we need additional traction with radial tires, and why certain driving techniques are necessary to keep you out of the snowbanks. These techniques can be condensed into one word: *featherlight.* Because you're operating on extremely slippery surfaces, a very dainty touch must be used with the

steering, brakes and accelerator. Any severe movement is bound to break traction and send the car skidding. Therefore, the snow driver is advised to (1) *accelerate easily,* to keep the wheels from spinning; (2) *turn gently,* so the front wheels won't pull the car into a skid, and (3) *apply the brakes as if you were stepping on an egg* to prevent the wheels from locking up and skating along the slippery surface.

Winter driving takes greater anticipation than in other seasons. Trips have to be planned more carefully, the automobile must be more completely equipped, and the actual act of controlling the automobile demands that the driver allot extra distance for slowing, turning and accelerating.

An excellent way to get the feel of your car's behavior on ice and snow is to do some private maneuvering in a deserted corner of a shopping center parking lot. When there's plenty of room to flail around without hitting anything, take your car out and lock up the brakes, make some hard, sudden turns and try accelerating quickly. You'll feel the wheels spinning and locking up under various conditions. You'll discover how the car wants to slide and spin when you make sudden alterations in course. These reactions will be evident at speeds of no more than 25–30 mph, and will give you a solid impression of how much distance you need to brake as you approach a red light, or how careful you must be not to spin the driving wheels when trying to extract yourself from a snowbank. The object of winter driving is to keep the wheels *rolling*—providing traction at all times under braking and acceleration (locked wheels while breaking is taboo, as are spinning wheels while accelerating).

3.   *Treat a winter drive like a military campaign.* Travel in the snow requires planning and forethought. Attentiveness to the weather forecasts is necessary, but remember that winter air is extremely unstable and difficult to predict. Killer blizzards have repeatedly appeared on days when the Weather Bureau expected flurries. Expect the worst when you leave home.

A good idea is to join an automobile club such as the American Automobile Association or another that's well-represented in your area. They'll start your stalled car, tow you out of snow-banks, advise you about travel conditions and so on, for modest annual dues which are worth every cent.

Whenever possible, keep your gas tank full. With rear-wheel-drive cars, the extra weight of the gasoline (which weighs a bit over 6 pounds per gallon) helps traction. Moreover, the added engine running time can be invaluable. For example, if you were to get stuck in a massive freeway jam-up, creeping along in blinding snow, the last thing you need is to run out of gas.

Be prepared to walk. Too many drivers leave home totally at the mercy of their car heaters. They dress lightly, knowing that a cozy automobile will transport them through the cold outside. But if an emergency should occur, they're completely vulnerable to chills, frostbite or, not uncommon, freezing to death before help arrives. Do not leave home without enough heavy coats, hats, gloves and boots to keep all the passengers warm during extended periods outside.

Should you ever have the misfortune to be caught in a blizzard, do the following: (1) Immediately use your CB radio (if you have one) to call for help. (2) If you can safely do so without danger of being hit by oncoming traffic, put out flares. (3) If you can get a ride in another vehicle or reach a nearby house, do so. However, do not blindly strike out cross-country if you have no idea how far away a refuge might be. In the zero visibility of a major blizzard, navigation on foot is impossible, and in this situation it's better to stay with your car. (4) If you have no choice but to remain in your car, run the engine sparingly, only long enough to maintain minimal heat levels. Keep a window cracked at all times to permit the entry of fresh air. Otherwise, death by carbon monoxide becomes almost a sure thing.

All this sounds pretty grim, but it isn't meant to discourage the winter driver. For many Americans, such travel is an utter necessity. Still with a little bit of forethought and preparation, the experience can, in the words of the weatherman, be "downgraded" from severe storm warnings to the threat of flurries.

Comprehension Check: Tips for Cold Weather Driving

Directions: Complete each of the following statements by writing in or circling the correct answer.

1. The author feels that the driver can make a real difference in determining whether winter driving is just unpleasant or is highly dangerous.

   True   False

2. The "right equipment" for winter driving includes _____
   as the most basic item.

3. "Featherlight" is a term identified by the author for describing _____

   _____

   _____.

4. An excellent way to get the feel of your car's behavior on ice and snow is
   a. wait until such weather occurs and drive extensively.
   b. do some private maneuvering in a deserted corner of a shopping center parking lot.
   c. have an expert winter driver guide you.

5. Because of the unpredictability of winter weather, the author recommends that you prepare ahead of time just as if you were engaging
   a. in a military campaign.
   b. in a fight with an unknown assailant.
   c. in a friendly tug-of-war.

Comprehension Accuracy:

_____

Selection 14: Anthropology's Contributions to Marketing _____

Total Words: 2713

WHAT THE ANTHROPOLOGIST KNOWS

The anthropologist is specifically trained to study national character, or the differences which distinguish one national group from another. He should be able to provide measures for distinguishing the the subtle differences among a Swede, a Dane, and a Norwegian; or between a Frenchman and an Englishman; or a Brazilian and an Argentinian; or between a typical resident of Montreal and one of

Toronto. The anthropologist is also a specialist in the study of subcultures. He would be able, in a city like New York, to differentiate the patterns of living of such disparate but rapidly homogenizing groups as Puerto Ricans, Negroes, Italo-Americans, Jews, Polish-Americans, and Irish-Americans.

Because almost any large community consists of a variety of subcultures, this awareness of subcultural trends can be especially useful. A more subtle area of special interest to anthropologists is the silent language of gesture, posture, food and drink preferences, and other nonverbal cues to behavior.

Related to this is the anthropologist's professional interest in languages and symbols. He might, for example, be especially concerned about why a particular shape has special significance as a symbol in a society, or how the structure of a language or a regional speech pattern was related to how people think.

Another area of concern to the anthropologist, because of its symbolic meanings has to do with "rites de passage" or the central points in a person's life at which he may ritually be helped to go from one status to another, for example, birth, puberty, or marriage.

Taboos represent a continuing area of interest to the anthropologist. Every culture has taboos or prohibitions about various things, such as the use of a given color, or of a given phrase or symbol. The anthropologist is aware of the larger values of a culture, which represent the substratum of custom which is taken for granted and the violation of which represents a taboo.

The anthropologist's method is primarily the exposure of his highly developed sensitivity to the area in which he is working, via observation and extended interviews with informants. Projective tests have also been widely used in anthropological studies. The anthropologist can bring a wealth of insight to marketing situations.

USE OF ANTHROPOLOGY IN MARKETING

There are at least three kinds of situations in which the knowledge of the anthropologist has been employed in marketing: specific knowledge; awareness of themes of a culture; sensitivity to taboos.

Specific Knowledge. Here are a few cases in which the specific knowledge of an anthropologist was applied to marketing situations.

A manufacturer of central heating equipment was planning to introduce central heating to an area which previously had used other heating. Since people generally grow up to accept a certain approach to heating which they take for granted, introduction of the new central heating posed marketing problems in coping with deeply imbedded consumer resistance to what would be an innovation. An anthropologist was able to draw on his knowledge of the folklore and symbolism of heat and fire in order to suggest methods of presenting the new system, so as to make it as consonant as possible with the connotations of heat, even though the nature of the heating method had changed radically. There was considerable consumer resistance to the central heating, but it decreased substantially after the first year.

In addition to a marketing problem, the introduction of central heating also posed problems of public policy which the manufacturer had to overcome before he could obtain approval for the introduction of the heating equipment. The area was one which suffered from a declining birth rate, and officials were concerned about the extent to which central heating might cause the birth rate to decline further, because of their belief that heated bedrooms would cause a decline in sexual activity and ultimately in births.

The anthropologist was able to point to some cultures in which the birth rate had declined and some in which it had not done so after the introduction of central heating. The anthropologist's data made it possible for the manufacturer of the central heating equipment to discuss its probable effects realistically with the appropriate officials.

Another field in which the anthropologist has specific knowledge that other social scientists are not likely to have is that of clothing and fashion. The only empirical study of the fashion cycle in women's clothing which has successfully been used for predictive purposes by clothing manufacturers was conducted by anthropologists. In marketing situations, the anthropologist has often been able to combine his special knowledge of the needs of the body for clothing of various kinds at different ages, his sensitivity to what technology makes possible and his awareness of fashion.

For example, an anthropologist was consulted by a leading manufacturer of overalls for young children, a product which had remained unchanged for decades. He examined the product in the light of the special needs of children who wear overalls, the growing use of washing machines to launder the overalls, their relative frequency of laundering, and contemporary technology. He suggested that the overall straps have a series of sets of metal grippers instead of buttons, thus making it possible to use different sets of grippers as the child grew instead of tying or knotting the straps. Noting that the straps often fall off the shoulders when children played, he suggested that the shirts which children wore under the overalls have either a loop for the straps to pass through or a synthetic fastener which faced matching material on the strap, so that the shoulder of the shirt could be pressed against the strap and remain attached to it until shoulder strap and shirt were pulled apart.

He also recommended that the seams of the overalls, previously single stitched, be doubled stitched like those of men's shirts, which have to withstand frequent launderings. The double-stitched overalls would be less likely to come apart as a result of frequent launderings in a washing machine. These recommendations were adopted, and within a few years substantially changed and expanded the nature of the overall market for young children. The children's parents were more pleased with the overalls because they lasted longer and looked better on the children, and they were far more functional than before.

The special knowledge of the anthropologist has been called into play where there are special subcultural groups to which the marketer wishes to address himself. One beer manufacturer wished to extend his market share among Negroes in a large eastern city in the United States. He was advised about reaching this group by an anthropologist who was familiar with the special subculture of Negroes, and who pointed to the profound effects of Negroes' caste membership on their purchasing behavior. The ambiguity of their role has led many Negroes to be especially aware of articles that have status connotations and of whether a brand symbolizes racial progress. Examination of the manufacturer's marketing program by the anthropologist led to several recommendations for change. The manufacturer began to help in the support of several major social events related to the arts in Negro communities, and to stress that the beer was a national brand with quality-control procedures. He changed the content of his advertising in the direction of enhancing its status and quality connotations. These changes were all directed toward improving the status connotations of the beer to Negroes.

Guidance on related problems with respect to the Puerto Rican and Jewish markets has also been used constructively. Since 35 to 40 percent of the population of the United States consists of minority subcultures, the anthropologist's contributions may be considerable.

Another situation had to do with the selection of specific symbols for various purposes. A major manufacturer of women's products was uncertain about whether to continue using the Fleur de Lis emblem on his package. Anthropological analysis of the symbol suggested that its association with French kings and other cultural connotations of maleness made it more masculine than feminine. The anthropologist's recommendations were confirmed by subsequent field testing.

In a related case, a manufacturer of women's cosmetics conducted an anthropological study of the comparative symbolism in our culture of women's eyes and mouth, which suggested that the eye tends to be experienced as more nurturing. This knowledge of the differences between the special meanings of eye and mouth could constructively be used in marketing the products, and especially in advertising. The advertising explicitly and implicitly mentioned the role of the eye in protection of the woman. It stressed the role of the mouth as the organ which both symbolically and literally gives love. This replaced the manufacturer's previous advertising, in which both eye and mouth were treated in the same way, as organs which could be made beautiful.

Awareness of Themes. The anthropologist has functioned in situations in which he can use his special understanding of themes of a culture, oftentimes taken for granted.

A major chain of candy shops was suffering a decline in sales. A marketing-research study had established that the brand was usually bought as a gift, either for others or as a gift for the purchaser. The chain was unable to develop any ways of using this finding that was not hackneyed. Anthropological guidance on the symbolism of gift-giving enabled the chain to develop merchandising, packaging, and advertising formats for the gift theme. Anthropological study of the connotations of the major holidays suggested themes for window displays and advertising of the candy in conjunction with the holidays. The chain's marketing strategy was revised on the basis of the anthropological interpretation and clarification of the marketing research study. Anthropologists are the only social scientists who have systematically studied gift-giving and gift-receiving.

Another example of anthropological interpretation of a marketing research study was provided by a shirt manufacturer. The study had established that women buy more than half of men's shirts in a particular price range. The anthropologist was able to interpret this finding in the light of several anthropological studies of the relations between husbands and wives in America. The manufacturer had been thinking of placing advertising for his men's shirts in selected women's magazines. The anthropologist was able to point to a number of studies of husband-wife relations which suggested growing resentment by men over the extent to which women had been borrowing and buying men's clothing, and which suggested that the proposed advertising campaign might not be propitious.

Another anthropologist's special sensitivity to the "rites de passage" helped a shoe manufacturer whose sales were declining because of aggressive foreign and domestic competition. The anthropologist was able to point to the extent to which shoes represent major symbols of our going from one stage of life to another, and to assist the manufacturer in developing methods for using the relationship between shoes and "rites de passage."

A landmark along the road of an infant becoming a child usually is found between the ages of 4 and 6 when he can tie his own shoe laces. The manufacturer developed some pamphlets and other instructional material for parents on how to help children to learn to tie their shoe laces. Distribution by local retailers contributed toward making parents favorably aware of the brand's line for children in this age group.

The teenager signalizes her entrance into a new social world by her first high heels. Window displays and advertising which explicitly stressed the new social activities of the teenager wearing her high heels, and naming specific shoe models after teenage social events ("The Prom") contributed toward associating the manufacturer's name with the excitement of the new world symbolized by the high heels.

Older people see the wearing of special "old people's shoes" as the ultimate reminder that they are becoming old. The manufacturer was able to redesign his line for older people so that it retained its special health features but still looked as stylish as any adult shoe, and had no visible stigma of "old people's shoes."

Sensitivity to Taboos. Marketers may unwittingly violate a taboo, whether cultural, religious, or political, especially in selling overseas. Blue, for example, is the color for mourning in Iran and is not likely to be favorably received on a commercial product. Green is the nationalist color of Egypt and Syria and is frowned on for use in packages. Showing pairs of anything on the Gold Coast of Africa is disapproved. White is the color of mourning in Japan and, therefore, not likely to be popular on a product. Brown and gray are disapproved colors in Nicaragua. Purple is generally disapproved in most Latin American markets because of its association with death. Feet are regarded as despicable in Thailand, where any object and package showing feet is likely to be unfavorably received.

The anthropologist can cast light on taboos and on their opposite: favored colors and symbols. The reason for the people in a country or an area liking or not liking a particular color or symbol may be a function of political, nationalist, religious, cultural, or other reasons.

SOME APPLICATIONS IN CANADA

Canada represents a special opportunity for the application of anthropology in marketing situations. Twenty-nine percent of the country's entire population is in French-speaking Quebec, and over half of this number know no English. Canada thus offers a changing kind of bilingual and culture contact situation with major cross-cultural differences for anthropological analysis.

Both the farm community and the industrial community of Quebec have been studied by anthropologists. The re-evaluation of the nature of Quebec family and community life sparked by Dean Phillipe Garigue of the University of Montreal and a team at Laval University has led to renewed interest in Quebec on the part of anthropologists. Their studies have produced considerable information on styles of life in Quebec which should be translatable into marketing data on pricing policies, colors, package size, flavor and taste of various food items, texture of fabrics, automobile symbolism, product scents, and related subjects.

Specific Knowledge. Perhaps the most frequent occasion for the anthropologist to demonstrate specific knowledge in Canada has to do with language. One laundry-soap company had point-of-sale material on its soap describing it as extra strong and the best one to use on especially dirty parts of wash ("les parts de sale"). After sales of the soap had declined, an anthropologist who was called in by the company pointed out that the phrase is comparable to the American slang phrase "private parts." This kind of mistake might have been avoided if anthropological guidance had been available before sales declined.

Some products do not sell well in Quebec because the English name may be almost unpronounceable to a French speaker, or the name of the product may be meaningless even when translated idiomatically. Even the English spoken in Montreal differs somewhat from the English spoken in Toronto, creating potential hazards for the marketers who may not know, for example, that a "tap" in a "flat" in Toronto is likely to be a "faucet" in a Montreal "apartment."

Awareness of Themes. A study done by an anthropologist for a food manufacturer demonstrated the relationship between the purchases of certain food items and the gradual decline of the wood-burning stove which used to be a staple of Quebec farm kitchens. The wood stove would almost always have a stew pot ("pot au feu") simmering all day. Various ingredients were put into the pot to provide flavor. With the introduction of gas and electric kitchen ranges, it not only became relatively expensive to keep the stew pot going but the simmering could not be sustained because the pot would tend to boil rather than simmer.

This change was accompanied by some radical adjustments in food consumption which were of great relevance to food marketing. The manufacturer was able to begin distribution of canned soups and stews which soon found a very large market and rapidly replaced the "pot au feu."

Taboos. Alertness to taboos was illustrated by an anthropologist's suggestion to a manufacturer of canned fish for changing a series of advertisements which were appearing in Quebec magazines and newspapers. The same advertisement was run repeatedly. The advertisements showed a woman in shorts playing golf with her husband. The caption read that the woman would be able to be on the golf links all day and still prepare a delicious dinner that evening if she used the product. Every element in the advertisement represented a violation of some underlying theme of French Canadian life; the wife would not be likely to be playing golf with her husband, she would not wear shorts, and she would not be serving the particular kind of fish as a main course. In this case, the anthropologist was consulted *after* the series had been running for a while.

THE MARKETER AS AN ANTHROPOLOGIST

A good case could be made for the thesis that marketing researchers do more anthropological research on modern cultures than do anthropologists. Marketing researchers are studying national character, subcultures, themes, and ways of life. The kind of information which marketing research studies seek on how people live and what products they use represent first-rate material for the cultural anthropologist.

The questionnaire, panel, audit, sales analysis, and other methods of modern marketing differ in degree but not in kind from the trained observations of the anthropologist, but there is no reason why the two methods cannot complement each other. Greater communication between these two fields can and should lead to mutual enrichment of both.

Comprehension Check: Anthropology's Contributions

Directions: Complete each of the following statements by writing in or circling the correct answer.

1. The anthropologist's major work is _____

   _____.

2. Marketing refers to

   a. the purchasing of the raw materials for production.
   b. the selling of goods to prospective buyers.
   c. the manufacturing of goods for public consumption.

3. The anthropologist's knowledge of subcultures proves to be of little value to manufacturers since groups such as Negroid, Puerto Rican and Jewish peoples comprise such a small segment of the consumer market.

   True   False

4. List the three situations in which the anthropologist's knowledge is most valuable to marketing.

   a. _____

   b. _____

   c. _____

5. The marketing researcher shares common interests with and uses work methods similar to those of the anthropologist, but concentrates on _____

   _____.

Comprehension Accuracy: _____

Selection 15: Tool-using Bird: The Egyptian Vulture _____

Total Words: 592

The midday heat seemed intensified by the blackened ground and smell of smoke, aftermath of one of the periodic grass fires that sweep east Africa's plains.

As my husband Hugo and I bounced along in our Land-Rover, we saw few signs of life, though grass would soon appear and the herds of antelopes would

SOURCE: Baroness Jane Van Lawick-Goodall, "Tool-using Bird: The Egyptian Vulture," *National Geographic Magazine* (May, 1968), pp. 631–41. Reprinted by permission of the publisher.

move back to feast on the succulent shoots. We were on a wildlife photographic safari, with National Geographic Society support, in the Serengeti National Park of northern Tanzania, and we were headed for country we had never seen before.

Suddenly Hugo noticed vultures plummeting down in the far distance, and we swerved to see what had attracted them. How well Hugo's sharp eyesight would be rewarded!

At first we saw only a confusion of vultures gathered round about 20 ostrich eggs, squabbling over the contents of some that were broken. The nesting ostriches apparently had fled the grass fire as it swept near them.

But our attention was abruptly riveted by an extraordinary action among the vultures.

"He's using a tool!" Hugo and I exclaimed almost with one voice.

Amazed, we watched an Egyptian vulture, a white, yellow-cheeked bird about the size of a raven, pick up in his beak the stone he had just thrown down. The bird raised his head and once more threw the stone at the ostrich egg lying on the ground before him.

It was true! We were watching that seldom-recorded phenomenon—the use of a tool by an animal. And we were, as far as we know, the first scientifically qualified witnesses to this extraordinary talent of the Egyptian vulture.

Gradually we sorted out the different vultures. The company included the usual gathering of white-backed vultures and Ruppell's griffons, some hooded vultures, a few huge lappet-faced vultures, and just two of the small white Egyptian vultures.

As we watched, the second Egyptian vulture picked up a stone in his beak and moved toward an egg. With excellent aim the bird threw the stone with a forceful downward movement of head and neck. He pecked at the shell, as though feeling for a crack, then picked up the stone again and flung it. This time he missed the egg, but the third time he scored another hit. Three minutes later a direct hit cracked the shell, and after a few more throws, the vulture buried his beak in the rich, nutritious yolk as it spilled onto the ground.

Three of the larger vultures immediately rushed in and drove the stone-thrower away. Others joined them, and soon the egg was lost beneath a mass of feathers. In a few moments there was nothing left save the broken shell and a damp patch on the earth.

As for the provider of the feast, he was walking toward another egg, head in air, stone in beak. "Crack!"—the sound told us of the success of his first throw.

No Other Species Seen Cracking Eggs

We soon noted that only the Egyptian vultures were able to fracture the ostrich eggs.

By the time we left Ngorongoro Crater, we felt that our research was off to a good start. We knew that stone throwing was the normal response of many Egyptian vultures to egg-shaped objects that could not be picked up. This was manifestly true even when such an object was larger than any living bird's egg, and even when it was red or green.

We had seen, too, that none of the vultures paid the slightest attention to a white cube about the size of an ostrich egg—which suggests that shape may be the major factor that stimulates stone throwing.

Comprehension Check: Tool-Using Bird

Directions: Place a T before true statements; place an F before false statements.

———— 1.   All types of vultures use tools for securing their food.

———— 2.   Ostrich eggs seem to be a common food for the Egyptian vulture.

———— 3.   The Van Lawicks were the first scientists to observe and record the tool-using habit of the Egyptian vulture.

———— 4.   If one stone did not break the egg, the Egyptian vulture found another and tried until he succeeded.

———— 5.   The Egyptian vulture ate very little of the egg that he had broken since numbers of other different vultures invited themselves to dinner.

Comprehension Accuracy:

————————

Selection 16: Public Relations ————————————————

Total Words: 1969

Many years ago, Ebbinghaus wrote "Psychology has a long past, but only a short history."[1] It seems to the writer that no more appropriate an expression to describe public relations could be found. The long past of public relations is easy to substantiate, as Cutlip and Center have effectively done:[2]

> "Efforts to communicate information to influence actions likewise can be traced from the earliest civilizations. Archeologists found a farm bulletin in Iraq which told the farmers of 1800 B.C. how to sow their crops. This effort was not unlike today's distribution of farm bulletins by our U.S. Department of Agriculture. Much of what is known of ancient Egypt, Assyria, and Persia was recorded in efforts to publicize and glorify the rulers of that day. Much of the literature and art of antiquity was designed to build support for kings, priests, and other leaders. Vergil's *Georgics* represented a persuasive effort to get urban dwellers to move to the farms to produce food for the growing city. Demosthenes used publicity to oppose the imperialist schemes of Philip of Macedon. The walls of Pompeii were inscribed with election appeals. Caesar carefully prepared the Romans for his crossing of the Rubicon in 50 B.C. by sending reports to Rome on his epic achievements as governor of Gaul. Historians believe *The Commentaries* were written by Caesar as propaganda for Caesar."

The short history of public relations is also easily demonstrated. For one thing, an exceedingly high proportion of present-day public relations practitioners came from a variety of other fields. Predominant among these fields are journalism, advertising, and publicity. In this sense, most public relations practitioners today have one thing in common: They really didn't intend to get into the

————————

[1]Hermann Ebbinghaus, quoted in E. G. Boring, *A History of Experimental Psychology* (New York: Appleton-Century-Crofts, 1929), p. vii.

[2]Scott M. Cutlip and Allen H. Center, *Effective Public Relations* (3rd ed.; Englewood Cliffs, N.J.: Prentice-Hall, Inc., 1964), p. 17.

field—at least when they were young and obtaining their formal education. They couldn't. For most of them the option of planning and preparing for a career in public relations—in the sense that one would plan and prepare for a career in law or medicine—was not possible.

For this reason, the practitioners in the field, along with the whole discipline of public relations itself, just "grew like Topsy," without a common body of knowledge or without evolving any theory to guide their problem-solving efforts; hence the short history that public relations must contend with today. This situation is the fault of no one and was probably unavoidable.

In addition to the fact that most public relations practitioners today came from a variety of other fields, the educational backgrounds of today's public relations practitioners are quite varied. A great many have only high school education. Others have college education. A comparatively few have advanced degrees, and they are from a mixture of fields. The point to understand is that, unavoidably, their formal education, whatever the level, was not obtained with a career in public relations in mind. They couldn't; as was noted earlier, they had no opportunity to "plan" to go into the field of public relations.

Some Important Implications of This Heterogeneous Make-up

Because of the heterogeneous make-up of public relations practitioners from both the standpoint of previous work experiences and formal education, it is certainly understandable that there are so many interpretations as to what public relations is and is not.

For some, public relations is hardly distinguishable from straight publicity. This subgroup approaches every problem in public relations with essentially the same formula—get your story to the public by using every conceivable publicity-type stunt possible. For others, public relations is a management function, part and parcel of the total job of running a corporate body. This interpretation subsumes almost every conceivable activity that a company (or any other type of organization, for that matter) might engage in under the heading of public relations.

In addition to heterogeneity concerning what public relations is and is not, there are also widespread differences concerning how one learns to be a public relations practitioner. To many practitioners, public relations is strictly an art—what's more, an art that cannot become anything that faintly resembles a science, or at, the very least one more rigorous in execution than is true at the present time. Furthermore, for these same public relations practitioners, public relations is something that you have to learn "by experience." If there is one thing they are sure of, it is that you can't *teach* public relations. It is too intuitive, too varied, too complicated.

The major implication that must be seen clearly at this point is that however understandable the reasons may be for the heterogeneity in training, definitions, and previous experiences, the bulk of present-day public relations practitioners are a species of vanishing Americans, a species that might be called *Homo in Publicus Relationibus Indoctus*—the untrained man of public relations. The demands that will be placed on the public relations practitioner in the future will be such that many present-day practitioners will not be able to measure up. The fact that their previous training and experiences are haphazard and were not obtained with a career in public relations in mind will render these people unable to cope with the demands that management will place on them. The public relations man of the future (one might even say the near future) will have to demonstrate increasingly what effects his programs are having. This one demand alone will presuppose a lot. It will require that the public relations practitioner be conversant with social and behavioral science research in a very broad sense. It will require that the public relations practitioner of the future be capable of executing some of the necessary research himself. For more complicated problems, it means that he will have to understand the research done by the outside consultant and be able to read lengthy, technically written research reports and relate the findings contained in them to organizational public relations programs.

Demands will also be placed on the public relations practitioner of the future that will require him to be conversant with communication theory as well as practice. He will be expected to interpret all developments in communication theory and research in the light of his organization's communication needs.

In short, the public relations practitioner of the future is going to be expected to be aware of all pertinent developments in the social and behavioral sciences that have relevance for solving public relations problems. At the same time, he will be expected to possess enough knowledge of social and behavioral science theory to be able to decide correctly whether this or that particular social science technique can be used by him to further his communication objectives.

The End Result of These Demands

It is because of these demands that the present untrained man of public relations will become extinct. What's more, he *should* become extinct for the good of the discipline of public relations. As long as any speciality can be engaged in by a broad spectrum of individuals with a wide variety of backgrounds and training then that speciality is in danger of being replaced.

This does not mean that there are no present-day public relations practitioners who are going to survive. On the contrary: a new species, now mostly in evolution will mature, and very soon. Two main streams of individuals will feed into the supply of this new species of public relations practitioner. One stream will be a certain proportion (what proportion no one could possibly predict) of present-day practitioners who will avail themselves, in a variety of ways, of specialized education in the social and behavioral sciences and research. The other main stream, and the most important from the standpoint of the long-range future of public relations, will be the young individual desirous of a career in public relations and who will have received training at the college level designed for public relations.

Public Relations Is Not Alone in This Evolutionary Dilemma

This evolutionary chain of events is not peculiar to public relations practitioners or to the field of public relations itself. Two specific examples of other fields are included here to support the above contention that an evolution is taking place in public relations and that it is also taking place in other fields. One example is general: the field of business administration; the other one is specific: the field of purchasing. Let us examine both of these illustrations briefly for the light they shed on the evolution going on in public relations.

Preparation for a career in business administration, particularly in graduate schools of business administration across the country, has undergone dramatic changes in the past few years. One of the characteristics of these changes is that preparation for becoming a businessman is recognized as one in which the candidate must acquire a *broad* appreciation of the social sciences as they apply to business. Likewise, business curricula across the country are increasingly introducing courses in such areas as research, mathematics, and understanding the application of computer systems to business problems.

One of the major guiding convictions behind such changes in business education is the realization that business management in the future has to become increasingly rigorous. It is not enough to have "business experience." It is not enough to make decisions on the basis of personal experience, hunch, intuition, or any other subjective basis one might name. Rather, business decisions are being based increasingly upon all sorts of research data, mathematical projections, surveys, and so on. This is true regardless of whether one is speaking of sales, production, personnel management, or any other facet of business. Businessmen of the future will have to know a lot of specific information from the social and mathematical sciences, to say nothing of situations where a knowledge of the physical sciences will also be required. So much for the general example.

More specifically, one can look at one small segment of business and find that the same thing is true. Consider the purchasing agent and the revolutionary changes the field of purchasing has undergone during the past twenty years.[3] The time was when a person became a purchasing agent after having done a wide variety of other things. Like most public relations practitioners today, the purchasing agent did not take any particular training to become a purchasing agent—for the most part such training did not exist. He drifted into the field from sales, from personnel, or from a wide variety of other backgrounds. In time, however, the job of the purchasing agent became an increasingly critical one in an organization. Such questions as the flow of raw materials, how much to stockpile, how to predict shortages, how to relate purchasing behavior most advantageously to economic changes in the society at large became of vital importance. (Here again, the analogy to public relations fits. At first, public relations was not recognized as being vital to the normal operation of any company. Today, the public relations function is widely accepted.)

While the job of the purchasing agent became increasingly critical, another important event took place in a parallel sense, so to speak. During World War II and afterward, a number of engineers somewhat disenchanted with engineering and looking for different challenges began to become interested in the problems dealt with in purchasing. Naturally, they looked at the problems in the light of their own previous training (just as purchasing agents from sales or personnel had done) and found that one segment of their training was particularly suited for purchasing problems—their mathematical background. Almost overnight, the field of purchasing was revolutionized by such developments as the application of "operations analysis" to purchasing problems. Today the picture is clear for the old-time purchasing agent. He must learn these new techniques or suffer the consequences from the standpoint of being able to do an effective job. Likewise, the picture is clear for the young people desirous of entering the field of purchasing. Their training will become increasingly specific, rigorous and designed for the field of their interest.

---

[3]These observations are based partly on the results of a comprehensive survey conducted by Harbridge House, Inc., Boston, for the National Association of Purchasing Agents in 1957. The author was a consultant to Harbridge House at that time and directed the survey.

In both of these examples, we see other fields undergoing revolutionary changes. The implications of these changes for the general field of business, and the specific field of purchasing, is precisely what the author is attempting to argue for in the field of public relations. Revolutionary changes in approach, in training, and in use of techniques are taking place; these changes are comparatively simple but have profound implications for all those in the field of public relations. Those established in the field must do what it is often said that "old dogs" cannot do: namely, learn new ways of behaving. Those interested in coming into the field must recognize these revolutionary changes and prepare themselves accordingly from an educational point of view.

Comprehension Check: Public Relations

Directions: Complete each of the following statements by writing in or circling the correct answer.

1. The major purpose for all public relations efforts is _____

    _____

    _____.

2. The ancients were well-acquainted with public relations techniques.

    True   False

3. Public relations specialists of the recent past were characterized by
    a. their rise through the ranks to their present positions.
    b. their specialized training by public relations programs offered in major universities.
    c. the heterogeneity of their educational levels and actual work experiences.

4. Solving the public relations problems of the future will require specific

    knowledge of _____ and _____.

5. Because revolutionary changes are taking place in the business world, the author wrote this selection to alert interested persons to the changing requirements of today's public relations agents.

    True   False

Comprehension Accuracy:

_____

Selection 17: The Best Small Cars _____

Total Words: 2255

I like small cars. Even in the halcyon, gas-glutted days when almost every American drove around in chrome-encrusted arks almost as an act of patriotism, I maintained a fascination for nimble, undersized automobiles. I and others carped that domestic automobiles were profligate wasters of space and energy, but those complaints were met with patronizing head-pats from the Detroit car builders and assurances that the flow of oil from the Middle East was as perpetual as the morning sun.

Of course, now all that is obsolete. Today everyone, with the exception of Greyhound Bus Lines, is converting to downsized cars. That great American status symbol, the six-passenger family sedan with vinyl roof and power-everything, is about to become as extinct as the passenger pigeon. We are entering a new era of automotive consciousness—an era of higher efficiency that has gripped so many aspects of our lives since we are finally realizing that the earth-vat of petroleum is running dry. The emerging generation of compact cars from Detroit and abroad are, in many cases, vastly superior to their larger successors in everything except size, weight and sheer garishness. These new cars are a direct contradiction of the old Yankee nostrum that bigger is better.

Some of them are wonders of efficiency. They use front-wheel drive, which permits all the mechanical gadgetry (engine, transmission, etc.) to be stuffed in the nose of the car in a tidy, compact package. This leaves much more room in the overall length of the car for passenger space. As a bonus, front-wheel drive augments traction on mud, snow and ice, and helps stability in cross-winds and high-crowned secondary roads. These new cars carry brilliantly designed small powerplants with advanced components to aid mileage and reduce exhaust pollutants. And while they can't carry six passengers or haul your outboard cruiser, the family Labrador retriever and the entire Little League team, they will transport a family of four and an amazing amount of luggage with ease. Better yet, they are cheap to own and operate. While the Environmental Protection Agency (E.P.A.) mileage figures are about as reliable as movie ratings and Amtrak schedules, there's no debating that careful operation will produce around 30 miles per gallon with many of the smaller models.

Let's discuss small car values in terms of sensible outlays of dollars. In the present market, it's practically impossible to find a broad-based small car for under $5,500. By "broad-based" I mean a vehicle that has a sufficient level of comfort and carrying capacity. It also has the power to remove it from the category of the Spartan, underpowered roller-skates that dominate the cheapest segment of the market. I am referring to a *small* car, but not a *miniature* one; a machine that can serve a wide spectrum of drivers, whether they are single or have families.

It might be noted that until recently women were considered to be an eccentric minority by most automobile manufacturers. Men were the "serious" car buyers. Women, it was believed, could be bought off with a few strips of chrome, a splash of garish paint and a yard or two of exotic upholstery fabric. The Hausfrau was the shopper and errand runner, deserving, at best, a cheap second car, while the man of the house had sole possession of the front-line family vehicle. Today, like so many musty, chauvinistic notions about women, the theory of the "eccentric minority" is as obsolete as wagon wheels and rumble seats. The needs of men and women in the world of automobiles are parallel. Everyone who drives is faced with the same spectres of high costs, low energy, congestion, pollution and the increasing overall aggravation of traveling from Point A to Point B in relative ease and safety.

To qualify for "Best Buy" status, I believe that this new generation of small cars should contain certain essential components. (1) Front-wheel drive is a must, for the reasons I've previously mentioned. Any small car without it is cutting corners in terms of efficiency. (2) A "third-door" or hatchback is required—combined with a fold-down rear seat. This produces a vast, easily accessible luggage compartment that in some cases can accomodate more bulk than the trunk of a full-sized car. (3) The vehicle should be solidly built, with quality materials that are resistant to rattles and corrosion. (4) A reasonable list of options should be available, including either two- or-four-door models (three- and five-doors, if we include the hatchback). (5) Mileage figures of at least 25 miles to the gallon should be easily attainable under *realistic*, normal driving conditions. (6) The car should be sufficiently modest in external dimensions (an overall length of less than 15 feet) so that it can be easily parked and maneuvered in tight quarters. (7) The seats, insulation, sound-deadening, rear-passenger leg room and ventilation should permit the car to be used on long trips without the travelers being left with the feeling that they made the journey on a Harley-Davidson. (8) Parts and service for the car must be readily available throughout the country. (9) The price should not exceed $7,000, even when loaded with options. (10) Its value on the used-car market ought to remain at a level where it can be readily sold or traded-in by the owner without fiscal loss. (11) The car should have brisk acceleration for urban driving conditions, and cruise easily and quietly in the 55 mph range on the open highway. (12) The automobile should be expected to run 50,000 miles with only minor mechanical repairs and maintenance. In other words, it should have reliability of the first magnitude.

Three automobiles best qualify for this select group, in my opinion. Naturally every self-proclaimed expert—including your service station attendant, local meter maid, high school shop teacher and grocery boy will readily provide you with a different list of "best" small cars, but suffice it to say that my conclusions have been reached after thousands of miles of hard driving in all the candidate vehicles. Certainly there are numerous models—the Toyota Corolla, Dodge Omni and Colt, Plymouth Horizon and Champ, Datsun 210 and 310, Mazda GLC, Honda Civic, Subaru DL, Ford Pinto and Fiesta, Chevrolet Chevette,—which others may say belong in such a selection, but I consider each to have sufficient shortcomings to disqualify it as a "Best Buy!" Many of these cars are simply too small. Others, like the Pinto, Fiesta and Chevette, are due for replacement by new versions. Others are noisy and underpowered as well as having below-average resale value.

While all lists of this nature are extremely subjective and compromises at best, I think the trio of automobiles I have chosen qualifies best when measured against my list of one dozen criteria. They are not perfect vehicles, but then, no such device exists. However, they are useful and enjoyable for a reasonable price, and that is why they are here.

Honda Accord: This car is universally acclaimed. Automobile experts have been dazzled by its overall excellence since its introduction in 1976. Except for a slightly larger engine (eliminating its sole deficiency: modest horsepower), a more luxurious LX model and a four-door introduced last year, the Accord remains essentially unchanged. One element sets off the Accord from its competition: It is exquisitely handcrafted and assembled. The finishing on the automobile rivals anything to be found on a $30,000 Mercedes-Benz. And this beauty is not skin-deep. The Accord is one of the most reliable cars on the road, with no endemic mechanical weaknesses.

In terms of economy, anyone driving the standard five-speed manual transmission model (a three-speed, automatic is optional) should expect at least 30 miles to the gallon on regular gas. The Honda's special CVCC engine needs no catalytic muffler and therefore does not require the more expensive unleaded gasoline.

But perhaps the most endearing features of the Accord are its thoughtful little details like the dashboard coin compartment (with clip for paper money) for tolls; the internal release latch for the rear hatchback to eliminate fumbling for the lock in pouring rain; the superb ventilation system; the washer-wiper system for the back window; the full instrumentation; the fully adjustable seats; the excellent internal lighting, and so on. These small and at first insignificant components, are the very elements that enhance the appeal and overall utility of the Accord. Combine them with the superb workmanship, reliability, wide option list (air-conditioning, etc.) and you have the absolute state of the art in a small car capable of transporting four adults in genuine style and grace. The waiting list for the Accord is long and the price is rather stiff (in the $6,000–$6,500 range depending on the dealer markup, options, etc.), but these factors are more than offset by the many advantages of the car.

Volkswagen Rabbit: In terms of overall design, there is very little to separate the Accord from the VW Rabbit. Both are advanced front-wheel-drive, four-cylinder cars of similar size, with similar performance and carrying capacity. The Rabbit comes from a company long known for building automobiles with high standards of quality, backed by an outstanding service policy. And for those concerned about balance of payments and a general "Buy American" approach to consuming, the gasoline-powered Rabbit is manufactured by Americans in Volkswagen's new plant in Pennsylvania.

A diesel-powered version of the two- and four-door Rabbit has been selling like mad since it was introduced last year, and the recent gasoline shortage has only increased demand. However, I am inclined to favor the gas model for the following reasons: (1) The diesel is about $400 more expensive. If we accept the fact that diesel fuel is about 10 cents a gallon cheaper than gasoline and further accept the E.P.A. estimated mileage for the two cars—25 mpg for the gasoline Rabbit, 40 mpg for the diesel—then we can calculate that it would require nearly 30,000 miles of extra travel to translate the extra initial cost into fuel savings. (2) Diesel engines are noisier, smellier and less powerful (the gasoline Rabbit produces 72 hp, while the similarly sized diesel generates a modest 48), which means less of a margin of safety in terms of acceleration. (3) Only a small percentage of service stations sell diesel fuel, and during the recent oil crunch more severe shortages of diesel fuel were experienced than of conventional gasoline. (4) Long-range government policies regarding the pollution effects of the diesel engine are not yet clear. If the government chooses to severely control the diesel with regard to its exhaust emissions, the benefits of the engine might be reduced, thereby cutting its appeal in the marketplace. For these reasons, I personally recommend the gasoline-powered Rabbit.

Like the Accord, the Rabbit is available both as a two- and four-door. A number of trim packages are listed and the car can be fitted out to a state of rather high luxury. But it betrays some of its Germanic background by remaining somehow more spartan and severe than the Accord. Many of the Accord's standard equipment features are options on the VW, although the Rabbit enjoys a clear advantage in terms of automatic transmission. It is simply a better unit than the Honda on all counts.

Making a choice between the Accord and the Rabbit is totally subjective. Both are reliable vehicles capable of transporting four adults in comfort and economy. However, I lean slightly to the Honda because of its excellent detailing, superb workmanship and little "extras" that seem to be hidden everywhere on the automobile. This in no way diminishes my high regard for the Rabbit. Depending on your personal preferences, both the Volkswagen and the Honda could be legitimately described as "first among equals."

Chevrolet Citation: General Motors was the first of the American car builders to enter the small, front-wheel drive jousts with a domestically built car when it announced its new line of so-called "X-Body" lightweights in the spring of 1979. These cars, which include the Chevrolet Citation, the Pontiac Phoenix, the Oldsmobile Omega and Buick Skylark, are essentially identical except for external body styling, trim and interior decor. They are substantially larger cars than the Honda and Rabbit, with more powerful 90 hp four-cylinder engines standard (an optional 115 V-6 is available as well). Moreover they can carry five adults, whereas the Accord and Rabbit have a maximum capacity of four. In a pure engineering sense, the Citation and its other GM brothers are not comparable to the VW and Honda because of their larger size and greater power, but in terms of the price—which can be $500—$1,000 cheaper, depending on options—and overall usefulness to the driving public, they fall into the same category.

The Citation, with its front-wheel-drive and its rear hatchback, folding rear seat, etc., is a very roomy automobile. In fact, Chevrolet engineers say it has more interior space than the mid-size Malibu line and almost as much trunk space as the full-size Impalas.

With its standard four-cylinder, 90 hp engine and four-speed manual transmission, the Citation should give the prudent driver somewhere between 25 and 30 miles to the gallon. That, plus a wide list of options, a decent price in today's inflated marketplace (a *stripped* Citation can be purchased for about $4,300, although $5,000 is a more realistic price for a reasonably equipped model, while a fully loaded car can cost as much as $7,000) and an excellent basic design make the Citation an outstanding buy in my opinion. To be sure, it does not embody the craftsmanship of the Honda or the sturdy, one-piece feel of the Rabbit, but the Citation is the opening wedge of a whole new generation of smaller, more efficient American cars, and it deserves, and enjoys, wide support.

Three small cars: one American, One German, one Japanese. All superior expressions of contemporary automobile design. Others might debate that my selection is too small—that additional cars should be added, but I doubt that anyone who understands the basic qualities of automobiles would dispute the fact that this trio belongs on any "Best" list anyone might compile.

Comprehension Check: The Best Small Cars

Directions: Complete each of the following statements by writing in or circling the correct answer.

1. American tastes in the cars they drive have changed dramatically.

   True   False

2. Until recently, women's driving needs were considered as being _____

_____

by automobile manufacturers.

3. The author has little respect for miniature-sized cars; he appreciates a small car that is more suitable for the driving needs of many types of people.

True   False

4. The author considers three small cars to be in the "best-buy" bracket. These

are_____

_____

Comprehension Accuracy:

_____

5. In order to trust the opinions of this author, one would need to know about his experience with small cars.

True   False

NOTES TO UNIT 6

1. Charles C. Walcutt et al., *Teaching Reading, A Phonic/Linguistic Approach to Developmental Reading* (New York: Macmillan Publishing Co., 1974), p. 323.

2. George D. Spache and Paul C. Berg, *The Art of Efficient Reading* (New York: Macmillan Publishing Co., 1978), pp. 52 and 68.

3. Nila Smith, *Read Faster and Get More From Your Reading* (Englewood Cliffs, N.J.: Prentice-Hall, Inc., 1958), p. 261.

4. Smith, pp. 261–62.

5. Smith, pp. 261–62.

6. Spache and Berg, p. 52.

7. Spache and Berg, pp. 52 and 68.

8. Smith, p. 9

9. Ben E. Johnson, *Learn to RAPID-READ* (Indianapolis, IN: Howard W. Sams & Co., Inc., 1973), p. 20.

10. Spache and Berg, p. 53.

Answer Key:
Unit 6

Exercise 6.3, p. 240

1. Yes   **2.** They are identified by model year.   **3.** Model year, name of car, description of condition, and price.

4.

Has in Stock		Year	Description	Cost
Ford LTD	Yes	1976	4-dr., vinyl roof, air. . . .	$1995
Toyota Corolla	Yes	1980	5-spd., SR-5 Liftback. . . .	$6995
Jeep CJ-5	Yes	1981	AM/FM stereo tape, 24,000 mi.	$7550

Exercise 6.4, p. 241

1. A,B, and C   **2.** Yes   **3.** 210

Exercise 6.5, p. 242

First Scanning: **1.** Yes   **2.** VI, VII   **3.** 503–753
Second Scanning: **1.** explanations   **2.** Interpolation III, The Wrong War   **3.** p. 631

Exercise 6.6, p. 243

1. 2   **2.** R and S   **3.** 747–5856

Exercise 6.7, p. 246

747–2882

Exercise 6.8, p. 249

1. No   **2.** No   **3.** 17   **4.** Yes   **5.** Channel 9 at 4 pm.

Exercise 6.9, p. 249

1. Yes   **2.** 19   **3.** Classification Number   **4.** 60

Selection 1: Roses, p. 251

1. T   **2.** F   **3.** T   **4.** F

Selection 2: Playboy, p. 252

1. T   **2.** T   **3.** F   **4.** T

Selection 3: Pool, p. 253

1. T   **2.** F   **3.** T   **4.** T

Selection 4: Grasshoppers, p. 255

1. F   **2.** T   **3.** T   **4.** F

Selection 5: Gardeners Find, p. 256

1. F   **2.** T   **3.** F   **4.** T

Selection 6: Oil Spill, p. 257

1. T   **2.** T   **3.** T   **4.** F

Selection 7: Praise Julia, p. 258

1. T   **2.** F   **3.** F   **4.** F

Selection 8: Pack Up, p. 259

1. T   **2.** F   **3.** F   **4.** T

Selection 9: Udderly and Odderly, p. 261

1. b   **2.** c   **3.** a   **4.** b   **5.** c

Selection 10: Wife-selling, p. 262

1. b   **2.** a   **3.** b   **4.** a   **5.** c

Selection 11: History, p. 264

1. False   **2.** b   **3.** epidemics, earthquake, floods, riots   **4.** urban expansion, broad streets in later centuries   **5.** a

Selection 12: Dictionary Documents Dialects, p. 268

1. False   **2.** a   **3.** b   **4.** are of conspicuously rural origin   **5.** It would narrow the range of words used in a particular area because of lack of exposure to new and different words for the same ideas.

Selection 13: Tips for Cold Weather Driving, p. 271

1. True   **2.** snow tires or radials   **3.** how the driver guides the car: applies brakes, turns, accelerates, etc.   **4.** b   **5.** a

Selection 14: Anthropology's Contributions, p. 273

1. contrasting one national group with another   **2.** b   **3.** False   **4. a.** specific knowledge, **b.** awareness of themes, **c.** sensitivity to taboos   **5.** modern cultures, especially how people live and which products they use

Selection 15: Tool-using Bird, p. 279

1. F   **2.** T   **3.** T   **4.** T   **5.** T

Selection 16: Public Relations, p. 281

1. to persuade others to do as one desires   **2.** True   **3.** c   **4.** mathematics and social sciences   **5.** True

Selection 17: The Best Small Cars, p. 285

1. True   **2.** eccentric because she did only ''errand-running'' driving and was impressed more by looks than quality   **3.** True   **4.** Honda Accord, Volkswagen Rabbit, and the Chevrolet Citation   **5.** True

Supplementary
Selections for Unit 6

EVALUATING YOUR HIGH-POWERED SPEED READING

This section should be completed *only* if you did Unit 4, "High-Powered Speed." If you did only Units 1 and 2 and moved to Unit 5, then *skip this section*. To maintain high-powered speed you must practice consistently, daily. The three selections that follow are provided not for practice but to help you determine whether you are growing in your high-powered speed skills. Read each selection as quickly as you can. Time yourself. Check your comprehension by the Answer Key on p. 298. For each reading, plot both scores on the Reading Progress Chart on p. 299.

Selection 1: Scallops See With a Hundred Eyes ━━━━━━━

Beginning Time:

━━━━━━━━━━━

Total Words: 388

When at rest, the great scallop lies on its larger, slightly curved shell with the flat, smaller valve uppermost. With its valves agape, it shows the pinkish mantle and a fringe of feathery tentacles that can detect subtle chemical changes in the water.

One of nature's most startling sights, however, is the Atlantic bay scallop's double row of eyes—bright-blue beads, as many as a hundred, strung between the tentacles like Christmas-tree ornaments. . . . Some of the eyes are larger than others, but all are equipped with lens, retina, and optic nerve. When disturbed, the scallop closes its shell, often leaving a tiny crack through which the rows of unblinking eyes peer out.

Somewhere nearby, the scuba diver will find clusters of tiny kites whose lines seem to have been tangled in slender bushes. These are young scallops that have tethered themselves to hydroids by a web of threads known as the byssus, which they have spun somewhat as spiders do.

Mollusks that spin spider webs? Strange as it seems, many shells familiar in collections once rode at anchor at the end of a byssus. The scallop eventually breaks away from its byssus, but other bivalves, notably the familiar blue mussel, Mytilus edulis, spend their adult lives spinning and tying guy lines to rocks and stones, and to each other.

Europeans devour mussels by the tons as the strains of "Molly Malone" remind us. And harvesting a mussel entails cutting it out from its sturdy web of byssus mooring lines. I spent hours one afternoon peering into the water near a

SOURCE: Paul A. Zahl, "The Magic Lure of Sea Shells," *National Geographic Magazine* (March, 1969), p. 396. Reprinted by permission of the publisher.

Pacific Coast wharf and watching mussels move, extremely slowly, by paying out their byssus webs and working their way along like mountaineers.

The artists of the byssus-spinning bivalves are the pen shells of the Mediterranean, Pinna nobilis, whose silky thread was the "cloth of gold" of the ancient world. Artisans of the city of Tarentum (modern Taranto in Italy) were famous for this rarest of all fabrics. Procopius mentions that Emperor Justinian presented to the satraps of Armenia robes spun of byssus threads.

Across the instep of the Italian boot from Tarentum, a Roman market stands partially submerged in the sea at Pozzuoli. The land on which the market was built has subsided, and then risen again. Visitors today can see strange pits in the solid marble pillars. The holes were made by the "rockeater," a small mussel called Lithphaga, while the foundation was under water.

Ending Time:

_____

WPM: _____

Comprehension Check: Scallops See. . . .

Directions: Complete each of the following statements by writing in or circling the correct answer. Check your work by the Answer Key on p. 298.

1. The "cloth of gold" so famous in the ancient world was made from threads woven by mollusks.

    True   False

2. A bivalve refers to an animal that has a one-piece shell.
    True   False

3. The mollusk and the spider have one thing in common:

    a.   both belong to the same biological classification.
    b.   both are native to Italy.
    c.   both can spin thread.

4. The byssus is another name for _____.

5. The author's major objective for writing "Scallops See With a Hundred Eyes"

    was _____

Comprehension Accuracy: _____

_____   _____.

Beginning Time:

Selection 2: Science Town Plans Russia's Tomorrow _____

_____

Total Words: 382

If Bratsk symbolizes Siberia's leap into the future, Novosibirsk, Russia's largest city east of the Urals, may be called the place where the future has already arrived. We went to this last stop of my Siberian tour by train, an express that would roll on to Moscow.

Nivosibirsk was founded where the Trans-Siberian tracks bridge the Ob

Source: Dean Conger, "Siberia: Russia's Frozen Frontier," *National Geographic Magazine* (March, 1967), pp. 341 and 344. Reprinted by permission of the publisher.

River. Many factories moved there for safety during World War II and the town boomed to a population of 800,000. Now 1,029,000 live here. But the jewel of Novosibirsk actually lies 25 miles out of town on the shores of a reservoir called the Ob Sea. This is Akademogorodok, generally referred to in English as Science Town. It looks nothing at all like other communities in Siberia.

Andreo Trofimuk, deputy director of the entire development, talked to us:

"This city was only an idea on paper in 1957," he said. "Now we have the Siberian Department of the Academy of Sciences and twenty separate scientific establishments concerned with nuclear physics, chemistry, biology, geology, and economics. The city resulted from the need to realize the potential of Siberia—its rivers, forests, and the resources under the ground.

I toured the nuclear physics laboratories with one of the chief scientists, a humorous, softspoken man who talked with enthusiasm of his early years with Igor Kurchatov, who helped develop the Soviet nuclear bomb.

"I consider nuclear physics the greatest achievement of contemporary science," he told me. "It is the duty of men to use this knowledge for peace."

As we peered into a particle accelerator, he continued: "The colliding electrons and positrons here generate energy that, particle for particle, is several thousand times greater than that of the H-bomb. New fuels can be developed that will be a billion times hotter than contemporary fuels. With such fuels, man can go to faraway planets. Not many people realize how close we are to such energy."

"Doesn't all this power you are unleashing frighten you?" I asked.

"Why should a man be frightened by being armed with a rifle in the jungle? For man, nature is the jungle and this energy is our rifle."

The man and the institute were enormously impressive, but as we walked through a laboratory, I noticed that the Russians, like me, have still not solved the problem of how to make the linoleum lie flat.

Ending Time:

_____

WPM: _____

Comprehension Check: Science Town. . . .

Directions: Complete each of the following questions by writing in or circling the correct answer. Check your work by the Answer Key on p. 298.

1. Novosibirsk is known as Russia's Science Town.

   True   False

2. World War II prompted Russia to move its most respected scientists to Siberia for protection.

   True   False

3. Russia's Science Town was designed for the purpose of

   a. protecting its most reputable scientists.
   b. realizing the true potential of its Siberian north.
   c. building bigger and more powerful nuclear bombs.

4. The chief scientist who guided the author's tour through one of the physics laboratories was

    a. enamoured with nuclear power and its potential.
    b. most impressed by the number of industries that had located in Siberia.
    c. incensed over the lack of consumer goods to be found all over Siberia.

5. With all of the advanced scientific ''know-how'' present in Science Town, the author noticed the linoleum still would not lie flat.

    True   False

Comprehension Accuracy:

_____

Beginning Time:

_____

Total Words: 506

Selection 3: Six Changeable Sections of the Disciplinary Picture ▬

Probably one of the most serious errors we can make as teachers is to believe that one set of procedures can be used exclusively in coping with problem students or for that matter in teaching one's class. Even more erroneous is the practice of lifting successful procedures from one community or environment and attempting to trasplant them in their entirety to another community. True, some parts may fit both environments but a complete interchangeability is highly unlikely. The six variables which follow should be carefully analyzed before disciplinary action is decided upon.

1. *The gravity of the offense*. The nature and seriousness of the offense is the first consideration in determining how to respond. There is a vast difference between talking in class and defacing school property. Likewise the reasons for these actions are usually quite different. While punishments should differ, they must fit the offense.

2. *Student attitude*. There are some students you may not be able to salvage. Their home life and past experiences may have taken too great a toll which your relationship will not be able to overcome. This doesn't mean you should stop trying. However, you may have to work towards a goal which is lower than you had hoped. Conversely, the adolescent who is open-minded offers the best opportunity for your counsel.

3. *Number of offenses*. If this is the first time you have had difficulty with a student it may call for a lighter approach. Should it be one in a series of incidents, it brings an entirely different set of circumstances into consideration. Again, the seriousness of the offense has an important part to play. Numerous offenses may signal a new approach by teacher and student alike.

4. *Parental attitude*. It is helpful to understand the thoughts of parents about the student's behavior. They may be completely opposed to the way you are handling the situation or they may not care at all. Should they be extremely lax in discipline at home it will pose special problems for you. Together you will be able to approach the problem with greater chances for success.

5. *Your personality*. The personalities of teachers are as diverse as those of students. Many ways of saying and doing things are attuned to the particular

Source: DISCIPLINE IN THE SECONDARY SCHOOL by Louis E. LaGrand. © 1969 by Parker Publishing Co., Inc. Published by Parker Publishing Co., Inc., West Nyack, New York 10994.

personality of the individual. For you to copy another's approach may point out to students that you are "out of character."

6. *The reason for misbehavior*. The list of causes of misbehavior is a long one and in many cases a number of causes is the basis of a particular act. But to understand *why* the individual acted as he did can affect the punishment to be meted out. The youngster who is goaded into a deed and the one who commits an act out of malice may deserve punishments which differ in degree.

These six variables make the use of disciplinary procedures an individual process. Couple these with differences in community life and the overall attitude of the school administration and you have a hodge-podge of influences which demand careful calculation in a long-term approach.

Ending Time:

_____

WPM: _____

Comprehension Check: Six Changeable Sections. . . .

Directions: Complete each of the following statements by circling the correct answer. Check your work by the Answer Key on p. 298.

1. A synonym for discipline could be
    a. punishment.
    b. control.
    c. reward.

2. The number of causes of disciplinary problems was the major theme of this article.
    True   False

3. The one overriding factor that governs the disciplinary action to be taken is that
    a. each case must be dealt with individually.
    b. common offenses should be punished in the same manner each time.
    c. the chief authoritarian, the principal, should always be advised of the action.

4. The teacher should give no consideration to parental interaction when devising a disciplinary plan of action.
    True   False

5. The author feels that not all students are salvageable but that responsibility rests on the teacher to devise an appropriate method for dealing with them.
    True   False

Comprehension Accuracy:

_____

Answer Key: Supplementary Selections

Selection 1: Scallops See With a Hundred Eyes, p. 293

1. True **2.** False **3.** c **4.** the thread that holds many mollusks or bivalves
5. to acquaint the reader with some unusual characteristics of mollusks

Selection 2: Science Town. . . ., p. 294

1. False **2.** False **3.** b **4.** a **5.** True

Selection 3: Six Changeable Sections. . . ., p. 296

1. b **2.** False **3.** a **4.** False **5.** True

Reading Progress Chart: Unit 6

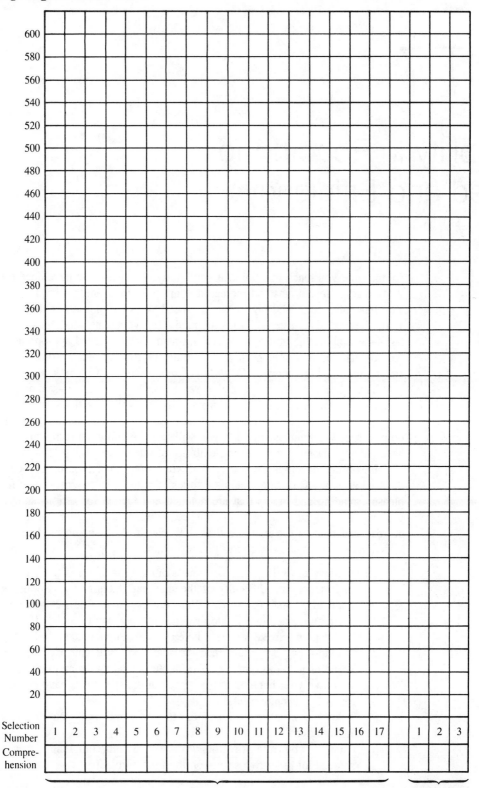

| Selection Number | 1 | 2 | 3 | 4 | 5 | 6 | 7 | 8 | 9 | 10 | 11 | 12 | 13 | 14 | 15 | 16 | 17 | | 1 | 2 | 3 |

Comprehension

Unit 6: Selections

Supplementary Selections

UNIT 7

Flexibility in Reading for Speed and Efficiency

By the time you reach this point in your study, you will have developed efficient study reading techniques and increased your speed for reading difficult materials. You have also cultivated high-powered speed skills for pleasure or light reading. With these skills mastered, you are ready for your final and most important task—developing the ability to select and read with the speed appropriate for the type of material and your purpose for doing the reading. As we discussed much earlier, this skill is known as *flexibility* of rate or speed of reading.

You have actually developed several speeds of reading—scanning, skimming, high-powered pleasure reading speeds, as well as efficient study reading speeds. Each is designed to meet a special reading need. In this unit you will learn no new speed techniques. Instead, you will learn to apply the techniques that you have already mastered to develop flexibility of rate or speed.

Flexibility develops as you read if you apply an appropriate speed to the material at hand. This unit contains a series of reading selections—some for light pleasure reading and others that are detailed and factual for serious study. Your task will be to identify the appropriate speed at which a particular selection should be read and then to use that speed as you read it. You should read each of the selections in this unit according to this procedure:

1. Preview the selection. Use your skimming techniques to determine the importance and difficulty of the material. Identify the overall topic or main idea. Ask yourself, ''What do I want to find out as I read this particular selection?'' Don't read if you don't know. If there are subheadings, make a mental note of each. Preview again quickly.
2. Decide how you should read the selection. Will you use high-powered speed or will you employ efficient study reading techniques?
3. Jot down your beginning time. Read at the speed you have chosen.
4. Record your ending time.
5. Take the comprehension quiz to see how well you absorbed the information.
6. Compute your rate of reading (WPM) and your comprehension accuracy score. Plot these two scores on the Flexibility Chart on page 343.

VARYING SPEED ACCORDING TO A STATED PURPOSE

Just to be sure you are ready to become flexible in varying your speeds of reading, try changing the speed at which you read according to the purposes stated immediately before Selections 1 through 3.

Directions: Read the following selection to determine how American tennis star Arthur Ashe feels about America. Read the article at a very high rate of speed. Time yourself. Check your comprehension by answering the questions at the end of the article. Plot both your speed and comprehension accuracy on the Flexibility Chart on p. 343.

Selection 1: What America Means to Me ————————————

Beginning Time:

———————————————

Total Words: 452

In 1967 when I was 23 years old, the United States was playing a Davis Cup tennis match against Ecuador in Guayaquil. We were expected to demolish the Ecuadoreans, probably 5–0. Instead, at the end of the second day, with the last two singles matches yet to be played, we were down 2–1. Well, I played the fourth match, and lost—giving Ecuador an unbeatable 3–1 lead. All of a sudden, the sky was filled with hats, bottles, seat-cushions, rackets, balls, handkerchiefs— anything not permanently tied down—and the air was overflowing with thunderous cheers, screams and shouts. People cried with joy in this small South American country, because their tennis team had defeated the United States.

What is it about America that arouses such passions? After all, we're only five percent of the world's population. Why does the rest of the world react so? My answer to this question explains what being American means.

Being American means that I'm blessed with freedom of speech, freedom of the press, freedom to move about whenever and wherever I wish. It means I'm blessed with public schools, the freedom to worship or not to worship, to assemble with, marry, associate with whomever I want. You may say, "So what?" Well, three-fifths of the world cannot.

Being American means that more is expected of me when I'm abroad. I'm supposed to spend more, know more, see more, win more, help more, share more. Again, "So what?" Well, I believe too many of us have an "I've got mine, you get yours" philosophy. Half of the world's peoples are malnourished.

Being American means we're King of the Mountain. We're envied, and we're resented. Envied because we're first most of the time. Resented because we're supposed to be the best, and sometimes we are and sometimes we aren't.

Being American means CARE packages, the eradication of smallpox, the World Bank, emergency food relief for Bangladesh, walking on the moon. We can justly be proud of this. I certainly am.

Being a black American means being perennially hopeful. Hopeful that one day we will be able to live any place we can afford. Hopeful that we may one day not have to worry whether race is a factor when applying for a job—or worse, have to explain to our children why more black Americans are not found in our history books.

And lately for me, being American implies a commitment, a commitment to excellence, to broadmindedness, open-mindedness, But, most important in 1976,

SOURCE: Reprinted by permission of *Reader's Digest* (January, 1976), pp. 119–20.

Ending Time:
a commitment to enlightened leadership, because, for all the world's criticism, we have much to offer. And inasmuch as "leadership" implies constructive change, let us, as Americans, take the lead in changing our world for the benefit of all mankind.

WPM: _____

Comprehension Check: What America Means to Me

Directions: Complete each of the following statements by circling the correct answer.

1. "What America Means to Me"
    a. was written by a black American.
    b. was written by an American Indian.
    c. was written by an American of European descent.

2. The author was competing
    a. in the Boston Marathon.
    b. in the Davis Cup tennis match.
    c. in the Summer Olympics in Ecuador.

3. The U.S. may be number one
    a. but this position has created enemies as well as friends.
    b. however, this is only true in military strength, not usually in sports.
    c. but this does not mean that the U.S. should try to save the world.

4. Being an American in the author's view
    a. means sharing privileges such as freedom of movement and speech.
    b. means total discrimination in all areas if you are a black American.
    c. means acceptance of the role of "savior of the world's masses."

5. Broadmindedness and openmindedness
    a. in America means being forced to accept the white man's point of view.
    b. in America signals acceptance of all Americans and commitment to building a better world.

Comprehension Accuracy:
    c. in enlightened America means doing one's own thing and leaving others alone.

Directions: Selection 2 provides accurate factual data on a topic usually treated humorously—fleas. Read quickly to see what the article can tell you about fleas. Record your time. Check your comprehension and compute your rate and comprehension when finished. Plot your scores on the Flexibility Chart at the end of this unit.

Beginning Time:

Selection 2: There's No Fleeing the Flea

Total Words: 1464
During the past three decades, our family has given bed and board to raccoons, foxes, skunks, ferrets, squirrels, woodchucks, spider monkeys, marmo-

SOURCE: Reprinted by permission of *Reader's Digest* (January, 1978), pp. 11–16.

sets, mice, guinea pigs, and more dogs and cats than anyone should remember. In theory, one should be able to have such an army of pets and not have fleas, but both logic and my own long experience indicate that this is a very remote possibility.

Yet pet owners persist in denying the inevitable. Protests of flealessness are made in the same manner with which some parents would deny that their children have cavities, rickets or watch trashy TV. Having fleas, it seems, is like having crabgrass or ring-around-the-collar. It is considered a sure sign of moral turpitude.

Up to a point, it is possible to keep one's flea population down, and therefore only the slovenly are supposedly plagued by them. In practice, however, fending off fleas requires almost superhuman fastidiousness. The view that fleas bother only slobs overrates human abilities and badly underrates those of fleas. Not only do these little beasts wildly outnumber all pets and pet owners, but they also have developed a lot of sophisticated equipment and tricky moves.

One thing the fleas have been doing for a long time (at least 40 million years; fossilized fleas have been found in amber deposits from the Oligocene period) is spreading out and diversifying. A British Museum report (1958) and the *Encyclopedia Britannica* (1976) claim there are 1600 species of fleas. The *Encyclopedia Americana* (1976) says 11,000 species.

Whatever the number, all fleas belong to an order of insects called Siphonaptera, which means "wingless siphon". This is a good description of your basic flea. Adults feed exclusively on warm blood, and they do so by drilling their sharp, flexible siphons into the skin of their victims and sucking out blood. Externally, fleas are oblongish, neckless, smooth-flanked creatures well shaped to slip through an underbrush of fur, feathers or thermal underwear. On their feet is a fine collection of claws which enable them to cling tenaciously when they come to a glade of inviting skin and decide to browse.

Fleas are generally five millimeters long and about as flat as an animal can be. Any dog who has tried to nip a flea between his teeth, any person who has tried to pinch one between fingernails, knows all about the lateral compression of fleas. It is hard to do anything to a flea, but it is even harder to catch one to begin with, because they are the best of all jumpers. The world flea records for the long jump and high jump are respectively 13 feet and 8 inches. If fleas were as big as men and retained this prowess, they could long-jump some 500 feet and high-jump 300.

Among the fleas, there is a fairly large group that has another trick. These are the sticktight fleas and the chigoe fleas (sand fleas, sometimes erroneously called chiggers). Instead of hopping around, they simply burrow into an inviting and sheltered patch of skin and stay put. They are a special nuisance for birds and barefoot beachcombers, under-the-toe-nail being a favorite den.

As a rule, fleas mate on the body of a warm-blooded host. In many species (including Pulex irritans, the "human flea"), the male does not mate until he has had a long, truly satisfying drink of blood. Then he goes looking for a female. Considering how tiny a flea is and how large, say a Great Dane is, this may be quite an adventure. Stalking through thickets of fur or feathers, the male eventually comes upon the object of his affection.

But the fleas are not especially fertile by insect standards. A female lays her one or two dozen eggs at a time, and perhaps 500 during her productive life. These white, oval eggs roll off the body of the host animal and collect, usually under rugs or in other dust-catching spots. They hatch into small maggot-like larvae which munch away on vegetable matter and animal wastes. Then the larvae spin cocoons, from which emerge the adult fleas.

Fleas are relatively long-lived (up to 2½ years) but, although they survive a wide range of environmental conditions, they don't thrive in extremes of heat, cold, aridity or wet. They are most fertile when temperatures remain between 65 and 80 degrees and the humidity hangs at about 65–70 degrees. An alert student will immediately note that a place which ideally suits these requirements and also provides quantities of warm blood is the modern family dwelling.

A great many hot-blooded creatures have their own kind of fleas. In addition to human fleas there are dog, cat, poultry, bat, rat, mouse and rabbit fleas (not a complete list by any means). However, these flea preferences have led to a lot of false optimism. When a dog or cat flea must eat to live, it will do so on whatever is handy, including you.

Once a flea bites, proteins are injected into the tiny wound, causing allergic swelling, irritation and itching. But, given our nimble fingers, large areas of hairless skin, and habit of sluicing down with water, we humans are reasonably well equipped to cope with fleas. Other animals are not so fortunate. A cat or dog, for example, is seldom able to rid itself of these parasites by its own exertions. Besides suffering the torments of the damned, a flea-rich pet can develop a severe allergic reaction, or scratch the bites until great sections of his hide are raw and bloody, creating ideal places for infections.

Historically, the worst thing fleas have done—along with rats—is help spread the bubonic plague. Biting an infected rat, the flea sucks up the one-celled plague bacillus. This little monster remains within the flea and eventually kills it. The bacilli congregate in and eventually clog shut the flea's stomach valve. He begins a kind of feeding frenzy, biting and sucking determinedly, if unsuccessfully, and when he tries to feed on a human he gives his victim a dose of plague.

The flea is host for some other microscopic internal parasites. And there is a kind of mite which clings to the flea, just as fleas travel around on the rest of us. The famous lines of Jonathan Swift are not bad natural history:

> So, naturalists observe, a flea
> Hath smaller fleas that on him prey;
> And these have smaller still to bite 'em.
> And so proceed ad infinitum.

Much human ingenuity has been devoted to coping with these insects. Women used to carry flea sticks, elaborately carved ivory rods with which one could dig elegantly about under voluminous garments. Flea collars, swatches of fur or feathers to entrap fleas, were also popular among medieval gentry. When these neckpieces became full they would be given to a servant who would take them outside and dispose of the fleas. The flea collar remains with us in the form of dead, glassy-eyed minks and foxes worn around the shoulders as fur pieces.

Contemporary authorities recommend a two-pronged effort against the insects. First, we should attempt to make the environment as unattractive to fleas as possible. A prime order of business is dusting, vacuuming, sweeping and shaking so as to mechanically dispose of as many eggs, larvae and cocoons as possible. The bedding used by pets should be cleaned on a weekly basis, if necessary, and sprayed or dusted with an insecticide. For household use, the U.S. Department of

Agriculture recommends preparations which contain methoxychlor, malathion, ronnel or pyrethrum, so long as the manufacturer's precautions are followed.

The second step is to go after the adult insects. Your veterinarian can advise a spray, powder or soap, which, if applied repeatedly, will keep down fleas. Or he may suggest a device that has been on the market for about a decade—a modern flea collar for pets, impregnated with insecticide.

From the time of the ivory flea stick to the poisoned flea collar, our relationship with fleas has been essentially an adversary one. Oddly enough, however, we have often found fleas to be entertaining. Up until a few decades ago, flea circuses were popular attractions at carnivals, fairs, and fun arcades, with harnessed fleas pulling miniature carriages or waltzing together or fighting duels with tiny swords.

Fleas also seem to have a great appeal for poets, philosophers and essayists. Shakespeare and Alexander Pope, among many others, had a lot to say about fleas, especially when they were dealing with the theme that all is vanity and men are not so highfalutin as they pretend—that they are, in fact, only a quick lunch for insects.

And when, in a proper mood, you stop to think about it, fleas may be among the most talented and dependable creatures with which it is possible to share a house, a rug or a pet. Certainly through the centuries they have given abundant proof that they like us for ourselves.

Ending Time:

_____

WPM: _____

Comprehension Check: There's No Fleeing. . . .

Directions: For each of the following questions, write in the correct answer.

1. How does the author secure and hold your attention: _____

_____

_____

2. List five facts you learned about fleas from your reading.

   a._____

   b._____

   c._____

   d._____

   e._____

3. The selection states that Americans consider having fleas to be a sign of moral turpitude. What does "moral turpitude" mean?

_____

_____

   Name three other commonly assumed signs of moral turpitude in America.

   a._____

b._____

c._____

4. Fleas have always been considered as adversaries, but human ingenuity has prevailed. The best example (as given in the story) of this is:

_____

Comprehension Accuracy:

5. Write a two- or three-word phrase to describe the flea as the author sees it.

_____

Directions: Suppose that your journalism class must examine four sources that discuss techniques that professional writers use when they prepare articles for publication. Selection 3 discusses the design and approach for such writing. Carefully examine this selection for the most efficient procedures to use in such writing.

Beginning Time:

Selection 3: Design and Approach ———————————————

Total Words: 2903

The organization of an article may vary with the logic of the writer's argument, with the requirements of the subject or discipline, or with the regulations of an editor. Good organization is simply arranging data in the way that will best communicate a given subject to a specific audience.

There are two types of logical reasoning common to professional articles: inductive and deductive. Inductive reasoning is used to arrive at new principles from known data; the writer goes from experience to general rules. Deductive reasoning, on the other hand, is not creative; it is the application of accepted rules to specific cases. Here the writer finds the right rule for the instance and then applies it correctly. . . . Either type of reasoning is acceptable in writing, but *the types must be kept separate*. A reader will be confused by logic that proceeds from the general to the particular and then reverses itself.

Logic within an article must be unidirectional, and logical organization exists when the reader is led by an inexorable progression of facts to an inevitable conclusion. Organization based upon such a progression does not permit too frequent a use of analogies and statements by authorities. Good articles are never a patchwork of comparisons and quotations; data alone are important.

The requirements of a subject or discipline affect organization for a different reason. *Most scientific and human situations are predictable*. For this reason, standard practices in communication have evolved that give similar situations similar treatment. Indeed, it is safe to say there could be no communication in science without agreement upon terminology and categorization. Organization in scientific writing is frequently a reflection of a specific method.

The predictability of the reader also affects organization. Because almost all readers have colossal self-esteem, they approach professional articles with an attitude of "What's in it for me?" They feel that their time is valuable. They want to be informed; they do not read articles for amusement. This situation forces

SOURCE: John H. Mitchell, *Writing for Professional and Technical Journals* (New York: John Wiley & Sons, Inc., 1968), pp. 1–8. Copyright © 1968. Reprinted by permission of John Wiley & Sons, Inc.

writers to present a meaningful title and summary at the outset. The reader is attracted only when he finds something pertinent to him in the title and summary. He remains attracted unless the tone of the writer offends him in one of two ways; that is, unless the writer offends him either by a lack of seriousness or by "talking down" to him. Facetious writing marked by witticisms and whimsical asides will repel a reader who wants only to be informed. Patronizing writing which labors the obvious and proceeds with a "John has two apples; he gives Mary one" sort of logic will so antagonize a reader that he will unconsciously set up an emotional block to any further communication. Few readers completed a recent article which actually began: "There are five living economists of importance, and we think. . . ."

Style and mechanics are important to organization because they are the invisible elements of organization. Style constitutes the theory, and mechanics are the application of the theory. Style involves tone, taste, and word handling; mechanics involves conventions. The conventions of language may be found in scores of reference books and style guides. Style, however, is subjective. It refers to the total effort that goes into the research and production of a given piece of writing. . . .

The attainment and restraint which . . . characterize style are inherent in professional writing. Patterns of logic and reasoning are preoccupied with exactness and brevity, and exactness requires the use of professional terminology or "jargon." The objections to jargon rise essentially from readers untrained in a discipline. These objections are valid when they are levelled at writing in mass media that attempts to popularize an esoteric area. They are invalid, however, when levelled at professional articles written for trained and professional readers. Exactness in writing is difficult to achieve unless the accepted terms of a discipline are applied. The writer of professional articles can assume an intelligent audience and can use the exact or jargon terms; only when he coins new terms does he need to define them.

This is not to say that a writer may use all the catchwords, trite words, stock responses, unthinking approaches, and automatic assumptions that exist in every discipline. "Good" jargon words read like the cards of a poker hand; only one interpretation is possible. Poker is a game with nice mathematical rules and fairly predictable probability only when a nine is a nine and a three is a three. Making those nines and threes wild changes the predictability. It is the confusion resulting from the change that sometimes makes players—and readers—drop out.

Techniques exist for determining readability, and almost all are preoccupied with brevity and exactness. The Flesch Check System, the Dale-Chall Formula, and the Gunning Fog Index are most significant. All have limitations; the first two can only be applied to writing *post facto*, and the Gunning Index involves only principles. Gunning's "Ten Principles of Clear Writing," however, are widely accepted and have become the decalogue governing the immense amount of writing done within the Department of Defense.

1. Write to express, not impress.
2. Make full use of variety.
3. Keep sentences short.
4. Use the familiar word.
5. Prefer the simple to the complex.
6. Avoid unnecessary words.

7. Put action in your verbs.
8. Write the way you talk.
9. Use terms your reader can picture.
10. Tie in with your reader's experience.

It should be noted that Gunning's Principles aim at clarity in writing. They would be adequate if communication were a science, if words were exact, if writers and readers were entirely predictable. None of these situations pertains.

A final aspect of style involves the extent to which *content* determines organization. A writer should always present his ideas in a written form that will reflect their logical relationship. For example:

- An unqualified observation requires a *simple sentence*.
  Propagation of rust-resistant white pine by grafting is feasible.
  The propeller failed at 5200 rpm.
  The rate of flow varies inversely with temperature.
- Coordinate ideas expressed in comparison, contrast, or balance require a *compound sentence*.
  Propagation of rust-resistant white pine by grafting is feasible, but processing costs are prohibitive.
  The propeller cavitated at 4200 rpm, and it failed at 5200 rpm.
  The rate of flow varies inversely with the temperature; it varies directly with the pressure.
- Subordinate ideas require a *complex sentence*.
  When cost is not important, propagation of rust-resistant white pine by grafting is feasible.
  Although the plane was put through a suitable warm-up period, the propeller failed at 5200 rpm.
  When J–4 fuel is used, the rate of flow varies directly with the temperature.
- Coordinate ideas, either or both of which are qualified, require a *compound-complex* sentence.
  When cost is not important, propagation of rust-resistant white pine is feasible, but processing costs are prohibitive except for certain ornamental plantings.
  Even after a suitable warm-up period, the propeller failed at 5200 rpm, however, when ground effect was absent, it cavitated at 4200 rpm.
  When J–4 fuel is used, the rate of flow varies directly with temperature; but when a solid propellent is used, temperature has no effect.

By extension, written elements other than the sentence should reflect logical organization. Paragraphs, subsections, sections, and chapters should all be constructed to show an easy and obvious logic.

A cliché about writing says, "Grammar involves right and wrong, and rhetoric involves better or worse." The generality is reasonably accurate; certainly the principles of grammar and mechanics distinguish right from wrong. Because rhetoric involves better or worse, it is essentially a matter of style. The preceding paragraphs discuss the theories on which a good writing style is based, but there remains something to be said, however arbitrary it may seem, about the application of those theories within the framework of accepted principles of grammar.

Simplicity, to Whitehead, is the fundamental characteristic of style. Variety should be used only to relieve a particular passage. Whitehead would have disapproved of the preceding paragraph. That paragraph contains a simple, a compound, a complex, and a compound-complex sentence. It uses too much variety. The present paragraph uses only simple sentences. It needs variety for relief.

Clarity is involved when a writer follows the advice of Gunning and Whitehead and prunes a sentence to its simplest form. The following condensations, which delete the vague phrases *there may be, it is possible to state, in the case of,* and *it has been decided that*, increase the strength of the sentences and achieve some dignity in simplicity. (In most of these condensations an *active* verb replaces the *passive* verb of the original version. A change from passive to active construction usually produces greater clarity and simplicity in a sentence.)

There may be overspeeding of the propeller if there is a rapid increase of power.
The propeller may overspeed with a rapid increase of power.

It is possible to state that the completion of the reaction will be achieved in the presence of platinum.
Platinum acts as a catalyst, and the reaction goes to completion.

In the case of corrosive synthetic fuels, injection carburetors with diaphragms cannot be used.
Synthetic fuels corrode the diaphragms of injection carburetors.

It has been decided that National Science Foundation support will be cut back.
The NSF support will be cut back.

Condensing and pruning, however, do not always improve clarity.

The following examples are longer, but they are perhaps more clear than the condensations above. Whenever it is possible to be more clear, a writer of professional articles should always abandon a fine rhetorical effect and rephrase for the sake of clarity.

A rapid increase of power will unseat the governor. When the governor is unseated, the propeller will overspeed.

Only a catalytic effect of platinum in the presence of nitric acid permits the dissolution of cesium sulfate.

Synthetic fuels cannot be used in injection carburetors; aromatics in the fuel corrode the carburetor diaphragm.

The NSF announced that support for the study of gull sterilization by sulfur black will be cut back by 50 percent in 1968.

Brevity and restraint are more than desirable stylistic aspects; they are also economic requirements. Biological publication, for example, today costs six cents a word. It is unlikely that an editor confined to a budget will accept an article that is circular or verbose.

Most research and writing projects begin with a problem and end with a solution. The solution may be tentative or it may be conclusive, but whether the project achieves a QED or not, the work begins with facts that generate a question. The only exceptions are articles that are descriptive or enumerative.

Facts therefore exist before the question or hypothesis is formulated. Creative research organizes them into relationships which may or may not be true, but which are plausible enough to serve as a basis for investigation. When they are organized into a specific problem or hypothesis, the solution of the problem or the substantiation of the hypothesis generally determines the organization of the article. Defining the problem or stating the hypothesis, however, is the essential first step. Only when the problem has been defined can relevant data be collected.

Problem definition always precedes both research and writing, and as the definition keeps the work of a scientist at a bench relevant, so does it keep the work of the writer at a desk relevant. This is not to say that there are no blind stabs and lucky accidents made in laboratories and libraries. The work of the Curies with radium and of Fleming with penicillin are delightful examples of chance. However, the data they discovered by accident were relevant to trained scientists of their caliber, and these data became discrete bits in the solution of the problem as defined. The source of true data is unimportant; the relevance of the data is all-important.

It is apparent that the definition of a problem serves as a guideline to both research and writing, and that data are collected, selected, and arranged to solve the problem as defined. It is precisely for this reason that the definition must be made with both knowledge and care. If a problem seems easy to label and describe, it is probably not a true problem or a matter worthy of study and research. Indeed, work at the Systems Coordination Division of the Naval Research Laboratory showed that in two cases out of every five the application of logic to a definition showed a tautology or—worse still—a problem definition that contained its own solution.

All problem definitions should be formulated; that is, they should be reduced to or expressed in a formula or set forth in a definite and systematic statement. Because "a definite and systematic statement" is a description of an article or report in its entirety, it is apparent that a good definition anticipates or predicts the organization of the article or report. Further, the statement anticipates the problems of searching a library indexed by links, roles, keywords, or by any meaningful or logical system. Writing a statement that will resolve these problems in advance requires an awareness of some basic difficulties in language.

There are four areas of difficulty in all language systems—semantics, generics, syntactics, and viewpoint. Semantics involves *word meanings*. Words meaning the same thing, or seeming to mean the same thing, are often used by library indexers to file and store information. These synonyms, near-synonyms, and homographs lead to the loss or irretrievability of a significant amount of data stored in a library; for example, one index librarian will store data under the term "imperfections." Another will use the term "defects." A writer searching that library must use both terms if he is to recover all data so indexed. Only if his search statement or problem definition is adequate can he hope to do so.

Generics involves *hierarchical word families*; for example, "nickel cadmium batteries" and "nickel zinc batteries" are members of the class "nickel batteries" are members of the class "batteries." This generic tree, if allowed to branch out indefinitely, becomes a jungle of verbiage that effectively hides data.

Syntax or syntactics involves *word order*; for example, putting the word "only" anywhere in the sentence "She said that she loved me" changes that sentence. At least seven meanings are possible; all depend on the syntax of the sentence.

Viewpoint involves *individual orientation*. For example, in the nickel cadmium battery mentioned above, is the nickel a base element, an alloying agent, or a catalyst? The viewpoint of the indexer—which is not always that of the writer—can result in individual interpretations that may seem random and perverse.

Writing a definite and systematic statement which avoids the pitfalls of language and serves as both a problem definition and a search statement compatible with a library's indexing system requires a high degree of exactness and specificity. Consider the following examples.

To determine a good insecticide for houseflies.

This is obviously too broad. What kind of insecticide? What does "good" mean? Is Musca domestica what is meant by "housefly"? The statement might make an adequate title for a *popular* article, but it is meaningless to a professional.

To determine the effect of dichlorodiaphenyltrichloroethane on humans and houseflies.

This is still too broad. What concentration of DDT is involved? How is it carried? What kind of effect? All houseflies? And so forth.

To determine the physiological effect of skin penetration, inhalation, and ingestion of DDT in a 5 percent wettable powder upon humans and domestic animals.

This is better. There are still generic problems with the words "Physiological effect" and semantic problems with the words "domestic animals." One hopes that "skin penetration, inhalation, and ingestion" will resolve the former. Viewpoint and intelligence may resolve the latter. Pet parakeets, fish, and snakes are not "animals," and anything more exotic is not usually "domestic."

The last statement is adequate to guide both the writer and the searcher of literature. The writer could not digress into a discussion of the preparation and production of DDT because those areas are not relevant to his statement. The searcher of literature would be guided by the keywords in the statement. These would keep him from being sidetracked into irrelevant areas.

Ending Time:

_____

WPM: _____

Comprehension Check: Design and Approach

Directions: Complete each of the following statements by either writing in or circling the correct answer.

1.   The major purpose for this discussion of writing for professional journals is

_____

_____

_____.

2.   Because of the professional reader's "colossal self-esteem," his major reaction to any article is

  a.   "What contribution does this make to the field?"
  b.   "How does this author differ from the others?"
  c.   "What's in it for me?"

3. A major difference between professional writing and writing for general public consumption is that

   a. professional articles abandon rhetorical effect for the sake of clarity.
   b. general commercial writing follows an exact format for all written presentations.
   c. professional articles always follow a descriptive or enumerative format.

4. Pruning a sentence to its simplest form achieves

   a. style.
   b. clarity.
   c. mechanics.

5. The two types of logical reasoning that are common to professional writing and that serve as guides to the development of the presentation are

Comprehension Accuracy: _____

_____.

PRACTICING FLEXIBILITY

In Selections 4 through 10 you are not given a purpose or speed for the reading. Now you must determine your own purpose. You must also exercise flexibility in selecting your own speed. For each selection, use the following procedure:

1. Preview the article by examining the title and any subtopical headings. Decide what you want to know about the topic. Set your own purpose for the reading.
2. In the margin under "Appropriate Rate," jot down the type of speed that is most appropriate for this reading. Use one of these code initials:

   Sk   — Skimming
   Sc   — Scanning
   HPS   — very fast High-Powered Speed
   F   — Fast, but gives time to gather some facts
   E STR — Efficient Study Reading or important fact hunting speed

3. Record your beginning time.
4. Read.
5. Record your ending time.
6. Check your comprehension by answering the questions at the end of the selection.
7. Compute your reading rate and comprehension accuracy.
8. Plot these scores on the Flexibility Chart at the end of this unit.

Appropriate Rate:

_____

Beginning Time:

_____

Total Words: 682

Selection 4: The First Rebels _____

History question: Who were the first black slaves in the Americas to gain independence from their white overlords? If your answer is the Haitians, you are

SOURCE: Reprinted by permission from TIME, The Weekly Newsmagazine; Copyright Time Inc., 1976.

wrong by more than 100 years. Correct answer: the bushmen of Surinam, formerly Dutch Guiana, who escaped from their Dutch slave masters in the early 1600s, established a nation of small villages in the jungle and won a century-long guerrilla war against the European colonists and their mercenaries.

By the accounts of the time, the rebel slaves were shrewd and able people. The men raided the plantations for black women and supplies. They built their own villages at the head of river rapids (where intruders could be sighted during portage) and raised crops far from the villages so that Europeans would be unlikely to find them. English Mercenary Captain John Gabriel Stedman, who fought against the bush people from 1772 to 1777, wrote of one military maneuver: "This was certainly such a masterly trait of generalship in a savage people, whom we affected to despise, as would have done honour to any European commander, and has perhaps been seldom equalled by more civilized nations."

Tilting Coffin. The most striking aspect of the bush society is its remarkable stability. Two U.S. blacks from Harvard, Neurobiologist S. Allen Counter Jr. and Admissions Officer David L. Evans, have spent five years studying the 5,000 surviving bush people of the interior and have produced a one-hour documentary film, *The Bush Afro-Americans of Surinam and French Guiana: The Connecting Link.* Says Counter: "These people represent for all of us a historical control group. They represent to American blacks a mirror of the best example of what we would have been like if we had chosen not to live in slavery and had removed ourselves to another place."

The film shows a healthy, handsome and cheerful people organized as a matrilineal society under tribal chiefs, or "Gran Men." Their laws and customs date back to a pre-colonial Africa uninfluenced by European rulers. In one scene, a group of pallbearers carries a coffin from door to door so that the obeah, or medicine man, can ask if someone in the house was involved in the death. "Death is rarely considered natural," Actor James Earl Jones says as narrator of the film, "and certain people are divined to be responsible." If the coffin tilts toward a particular house during the ritual procession, the owner is considered guilty and must provide gifts to the survivors.

The bush people speak a language that combines Dutch, English, French, Portuguese and six West African languages. Much of their design and decoration, including sculpture, chairs and dugouts hollowed from felled trees, resembles that of West Africa. In fact, two Gran Men who recently traveled to West Africa at the expense of the Surinam government were able to recognize certain shrines and could communicate with Africans though the two cultures have had no contact for centuries.

The jungle environment helped the original bush people to re-create Africa in America. They found similar game, including monkeys to be eaten, and then celebrated in monkey dances that resemble West African gorilla dances. The bush people also retained a reverence for the silk cotton tree, which flourishes in Surinam as it does along the Niger River and they found the same white clay they had used in their homeland to decorate their bodies during rituals. One of their villages, where priests live, is called Dahomey and is barred to all whites, including government officials.

Like primitive peoples everywhere, the bush people are now threatened by creeping civilization. Highways will soon slice through the heart of their territory, and many of the young have been lured to jobs in coastal towns. Says Evans: "They know technology is coming, but they refuse to allow it to disrupt their

Ending Time:

_____

WPM: _____

lives.'' Last year, when Surinam's Premier explained that the Dutch territory would soon be independent, a bushman chief wondered: ''What is the independence you offer? We have been independent for 300 years.''

Comprehension Check: The First Rebels

Directions: Complete each of the following statements by writing in or circling the correct answer.

1.   ''The First Rebels''
   a.   is a story about southern soldiers of the Civil War period.
   b.   is a description of the colonial American rebels who defied Great Britain.
   c.   is a discussion of the first African slaves to win their freedom from white overlords.

2.   What is the significance of the existence of people like the bush Afro-Americans from Surinam?_____

   _____

   _____

   _____.

3.   Which colonial power besides the British made slaves of Africans?
   a.   the Norwegians
   b.   the Dutch
   c.   the Spanish

4.   Preservation of many ancient customs was hindered because the bushmen did not find a region similar to their homeland in Surinam.
   True   False

Comprehension Accuracy:

_____

5.   The onrush of civilization will have no effect on the bushmen of Surinam as they have survived for over 300 years without interference.
   True   False

Because information from ''The First Rebel'' is far less well-known than other information you already know about slaves, you probably used an average rate of speed to read it, thus giving yourself time to grasp unusual facts but speeding over the uninteresting portions. Such interval variation of speed is a highly desirable characteristic of flexibility. Now proceed to Selection 5.

Appropriate Rate:

Selection 5: Ideology

_____

Beginning Time:

_____

Total Words: 1145

''Ideology'' is one of the most common and slippery terms in the lexicon of public affairs. In this [essay] . . . , the term is employed to mean a ''world view'' of reality and of how to deal with that reality. The ideological environment of American public administration is a system of ideas, assumptions, beliefs, value propositions, and norms. Not a closed or consistent system, it contains contradictions and illusions. The ideological environment offers rationales regarding the nature of human beings, the role of government, the nature of change, the appropriate use of human energy, rights and obligations of citizens, relations among citizens, relations between ruler and ruled, and so on.

Americans are distinctly nontheoretical in their approach to public affairs, and they tend to be "ideological" in the sense of a rigid commitment to doctrine. Furthermore, "practical" people in public administration, as in some other fields of work and study, may protest that they are not bound or even influenced by any ideological forces in the environment. Yet, evidence seems to support the argument made many years ago by the British economist, John Maynard Keynes, that even the supposedly most practical-minded people were subject to intellectual influences. In the following paragraphs, we introduce briefly some of the major features of the ideological environment within which American public administration takes place.

Individualism

The Preamble to the Constitution of the United States begins, "We the People of the United States," but the political institutions and ideology of this country are based on the singular pronouns I, you, he, and she. There is a strong belief in this country in the importance and supreme worth of each person. We tend to be hostile toward collective identities, such as classes, even though we are quick to join forces in a variety of special-purpose groups. The prevailing orientation in the United States is toward the conviction that the individual is capable of being self-sufficient and of participating meaningfully in self-government.

The Frontier Tradition

Although the physical frontier disappeared years ago, its concepts, values, and ethics remain alive in the United States. Americans have not forgotten the forest primeval, the settling of a continent, and the building of a nation. It may seem incongruous for some Americans . . . to behave as their grandparents or great grandparents did in the wild and woolly west, but frontier attitudes toward use of land and water, local enforcement of law, neighborhood relations, and the legal powers and rights of private enterprise have not disappeared.

An important part of the frontier tradition is the continuing reverence for land. This reverence was an important influence on the settling of the North American continent. Land has historically been a root cause of much conflict and struggle in American history. Men and women faced torture, starvation, and death to secure land. An enduring consequence of the worship of land is the historical commitment in the United States to territorial representation. A great many Americans are still as much Virginians, Texans, and Californians as were their pioneer forebearers.

Optimism

One of the reasons why the social upheavals, economic instability, ecological imbalance, and energy shortages of recent years have been traumatic for the American people is that these disturbances have challenged this country's historic sense of optimism. Americans have long believed that progress and enlightenment are inevitable. Neither the Great Depression of the 1930s nor the shock of World

War II was able to quench the indomitable American conviction that tomorrow will be better than today.

The American people, Arnold Kaufman has observed, have been particularly susceptible to promises. Presidents, state governors, mayors, congressmen, state legislators, and other political people have long known that the American people are basically optimistic and want to believe the promises that are made to them. Public administrators, as the instruments through which promises are fulfilled, are highly dependent on this force of optimism in the national environment.

Pragmatism and Activism

"Democratic government does something," declared Henry James, "and waits to see who hollers." It was that sense of pragmatism that has characterized much of American politics and government. Complementing the individualism, optimism, and frontier tradition is a strong experimental orientation, a willingness to innovate, an emphasis on practicality and feasibility. The American tends to ask not, "Is it right?" but rather, "Will it work?" The worst offense that the American can commit, according to his philosophy, is to try to re-invent the wheel.

Americans are pragmatic activists. At the depth of the Great Depression in 1932, Franklin D. Roosevelt, running for president for the first time, expressed the mood in classic terms: "The country needs and, unless I mistake its temper, the country demands bold, persistent experimentation. . . . take a method and try it: If it fails, admit it frankly and try another. But above all, try something." The key words in the American lexicon are progress, change, innovation, experimentation, development, and growth. It may seem contradictory, but it can truly be said that this commitment to pragmatism and activism is an American doctrine.

The American Business Creed

In many ways, the United States is a business society. Virtue lies in values that are basically business values—competition, mechanical efficiency, productivity, the sanctity of private property, the freedom to contract and the binding quality of the contract, and the administration of affairs on the basis of personal advantage and gain. The market mechanism has influenced the structure of many public services. The corporate form of organization has influenced the organizational structure of many agencies of government—federal, state, and local. That frequent question, "Why can't government be more businesslike?" is symptomatic. Finally, the tendency to glorify bigness is an important element in the creed of American business. As already seen, it was not an accident of history that the principles of scientific management, which have been influential in the development of American public administration, found their first fulfillment in American commerce and industry.

Democracy

Here again is a most influential but slippery idea in the ideological environment of public administration. By "democracy" is meant a system which emphasizes certain substantive guarantees, such as freedom of assembly and certain procedural guarantees, such as limited government, popular control of policy makers, the individual citizen's equality and freedom in the political arena, majority rule when the people's representatives disagree, and due process in law and administration.

Closely associated with democracy in this ideology are the ideas of constitutionalism and the rule of law. Government, it is believed, should be controlled and power limited through enforcement of a system of restraints which are, in a sense, "rules of the game." They are rules that are supposed to assure fair play in politics and government. And it is through the instrument of a constitution that these rules are formulated and set down for posterity.

Constitutionalism provides for making changes in the rules themselves, such as through constitutional conventions and the amending process. In other words, no person, village dogcatcher or president of the United States, is above the law as formulated in the Constitution and interpreted by the courts. If one wants to change the system, one must do so through the system.

Ending Time:

_____

WPM: _____

Comprehension Check: Ideology

Directions: Complete each of the following statements by writing in or circling the correct answer.

1. This selection describes the underlying ideology of
    a. American religion.
    b. American race relations.
    c. American public administration.

2. Economic instability, ecological imbalance, and energy shortages are difficult issues for Americans to face because_____

    _____

    _____.

3. The American government and people's emphasis on practicality and feasibility of experimentation and willingness to innovate have resulted in a national doctrine committed to
    a. individualization.
    b. pragmatism.
    c. theology.

4. List the six factors that the author lists as being significant proof that Americans do operate within an ideological environment.

    a._____

    b._____

    c._____

    d._____

    e._____

    f._____

5. The most important function of an ideology is _____

    _____

Comprehension Accuracy:

_____

    _____

Appropriate Rate:

Beginning Time:

Total Words: 824

Selection 6: Jefferson: Taste of the Founder

The man who wrote the Declaration of Independence, made the Louisiana Purchase and dispatched the Lewis and Clark Expedition was also a multifarious taster of art, a dilettante. Lacking a theory, Thomas Jefferson was blessed with an eclectic curiosity about aesthetic experience. As architect, he drew up some of the most refined structures in all Georgian building—Monticello, the Richmond capitol and an "Academical village," the university of his native Virginia. He also had a devouring and insistent eye for detail; designs for stair rails, coffee urns, goblets and garden gates flowed from his hand. He systematically assembled a library, "not merely amassing a number of books, but distinguishing them in subordination to early art and science."

INSTRUCTIVE FIGURE. He studied landscape design and was a botanist. He was also one of the first foreigners to discern, as minister to France in the 1780s, the challenging merits of new artists like Jacques Louis David and Antonio Canova. "I do not feel an interest in any pencil but that of David," he wrote in a flush of enthusiasm. Jefferson became the first American to transcend the cultural provinciality of his own land, moving with some ease between the New World and the Old. Even if he had had no political life, he would on that ground alone have been one of the most instructive figures of the 18th century.

Jefferson's achievements and tastes are celebrated in a vast show (609 items), that runs through the summer at the National Gallery of Art in Washington, D.C. The aim of "The Eye of Thomas Jefferson" is to sketch the cultural environments through which Jefferson moved. This is a pharaonic enterprise: pushed to its limit, the subject of such an exhibit might be nothing less than the whole of aristocratic and high bourgeois culture in Georgian England, America and France. Of course, no show could encompass (or even adequately sample) all that; so what there is, in essence, is a glamorous but uneven struggle to display cultural history as saga.

Still, the exhibition is rich with detail. One realizes, with fresh interest, how cramped the visual resources of Jefferson's Virginian education must have been; his own remark on local architecture in 1781, that "the first principles of the art are unknown," is borne out in other fields by the stiff, crude society portraits of the young colony. The show traces the neoclassical ideal forming in Jefferson's ideals and tastes—the growing certainty that republicanism was a function of natural law, that a new age of civic virtue was dawning and that an art of reasoned severity and correct classical proportion was needed to embody it. As William Howard Adams writes in the show's excellent catalogue: "Jefferson envisioned a style and form based on antiquity but with a purity that left behind history's corrupting influences of rotten governments, benighted rulers and unenlightened institutions."

BENEVOLENT SQUIRES. Here he is in Paris, "violently smitten" with the geometrical volumes of the Hotel de Salm, so denuded of fripperies of rococo as to promise him a new mode of architectural thought. There he is in Nimes, entranced by the proportions of the Roman Maison Caree, ordering a model of it, which, shipped back to Virginia, became the basis of the capitol at Richmond.

Of course, there are things one does not learn from the show. The part titled

SOURCE: Reprinted by permission from TIME, The Weekly Newsmagazine; Copyright Time Inc., 1976.

"The British Connection" is merely a rehash, laid forth in paintings, of the now outmoded picture of 18th century England as an Age of Elegance, populated by enlightened lords, benevolent squires and happy forelock-tugging peasants. The whole matter of slavery is discreetly omitted from Jefferson's American experience, although neither his wealth nor the leisure he needed for self-cultivation would have been possible without slaves. (If the National Gallery wanted to be consistent in its policy of using great borrowed paintings to allude to the social and intellectual norms of Jefferson's day, it might as well have borrowed Turner's *Slave Ship*.

Moreover, there is the problem that Jefferson had actually seen few of the major works in the show. There on view is the Uffizi's Medici Venus, because Jefferson longed to install a copy of her at Monticello. Not having been to Florence, he had never seen the original, which he knew through engravings and plasters. It is pleasant to see the Towneley Vase, that once renowned Attic marble of the 1st century A.D. on which Keats based several lines of *Ode to a Grecian Urn*. But Jefferson never saw it, and (as the catalogue admits) would probably have disliked the "licentious mysticism" of its Bacchic figures.

These distortions matter because they imply that Jefferson's experience of the visual arts was much wider than it really was. He did not have the automatic overview of a modern museum goer; nor was he a kind of Yankee Kenneth Clark, mellifluously discoursing among the servants and mockingbirds of Monticello. He believed, correctly, that he was an instrument of history; but he did not imagine himself as a character in a cultural saga. Jefferson's tough, ambitious self-teaching, in all its patchiness, cannot have been the smooth inheritance of masterpieces that his show suggests. It was won, not inherited, and in that sense was profoundly American.

Ending Time:

_____

WPM: _____

Comprehension Check: Jefferson

Directions: Complete each of the following by writing in or circling the correct answer.

1. From the terms listed below, circle those that are *not* appropriate descriptions for Thomas Jefferson.

artisan	cosmopolitan	politician
author	charismatic	dictatorial
connoisseur	provincial	arrogant

2. George Washington, the first President, is considered to be the Father of Our Country. In the young colony of Virginia, Thomas Jefferson is considered to

be the progenitor of _____

_____

_____

3. Thomas Jefferson's contributions to the culture of Virginia were described as "profoundly American." To what is the author referring?

_____

4. When the art critic who evaluated the showing of "The Eye of Thomas Jefferson" referred to a part of it as the "Benevolent Squires," he was implying that

_____

5. In the critic's judgment, a weakness in the art show's depiction of the cultural environment of Jefferson

   a. is the noticeable lack of pictures of slavery, for without slave labor, he would have had no time for such things.
   b. was the inclusion of too many works totally unrelated to Jefferson's experience.
   c. came about as the result of transporting the collection of priceless objects.

The meaning of this short selection is not readily apparent, and the author used highly specialized terms throughout. Your speed probably slowed markedly.

Selection 7: Factors Determining the Quality and Quantity of Physical Activity

BELIEFS, CUSTOMS, TRADITIONS

With the possible exception of midwifery, no branch of medicine is more filled with superstition, unfounded beliefs, fads, and customs than sports medicine and its relation to training and competition. It is essential for the doctor who is in medical charge of the athlete to understand these beliefs, to support those founded on experience, and to give rational explanations that lead to the abandonment of those that may be harmful or extravagant. Many beliefs are founded on empirical experience, others on superstition, and others on discarded or misunderstood physiological and psychological theory. The main fields in which beliefs and opinions play a prominent part are

1. Training—frequency, different types.
2. Diet, including vitamins and "magic mixtures."
3. Other factors—other sports, sleep, sex.
4. Routines on the day of competition—diet, warm up, charms, and talismans.
5. Reliance on the coach and its relation to the educational standard of the athlete.
6. Reliance on the doctor, dependent on his full understanding of the sport and its special stresses.

Beliefs Concerning Training

It is a widespread belief in many sports that it is the duration of a training session that counts and not the intensity of work done in the session. Two or three

Comprehension Accuracy:

_____

Appropriate Rate:

_____

Beginning Time:

_____

Total Words: 3151

SOURCE: Reprinted with permission of Macmillan Publishing Co., Inc., from ENCYCLOPEDIA OF THE SPORT SCIENCES AND MEDICINE by Leonard A. Larson. Copyright © 1971 by Macmillan Publishing Co., Inc.

hours are spent twice a week, or worse still once a week, and no training at all is done on the remaining days. In athletic training, as in rehabilitation, it is much better to train for half an hour every day, working really hard. Many British cyclists merely "get the miles in," traveling perhaps 150 miles on a Sunday, at a steady but fairly leisurely pace. The idea of a short-duration circuit of intensive work appears revolutionary to them and is accepted only with reluctance, although swimmers, and track and field coaches, and athletes have found this most effective for over a decade.

For nearly every sport, strength, (or, more correctly, power, i.e., strength per unit time) is essential, but many male athletes in the less well-coached sports, and the majority of female athletes and coaches, regard any form of weight training with the greatest suspicion. Fears are that strength can be acquired only at the expense of flexibility, that the athlete will become "musclebound," (whatever that may mean), and that the limb contours will resemble those of the bodybuilder rather than the ballet-dancer. If, however, a good weight-training schedule is given and if proper attention is given to the maintenance of flexibility, the athlete will not become musclebound. If the weights lifted are heavy, being of a weight that can be lifted only a few times, the contractile element in the muscle will hypertrophy, rather than the connective tissue and vascular bed on which the body-builder largely depends.

Beliefs Concerning Diet

In a survey held during the VLth British Empire and Commonwealth Games in 1958, only some dozen out of 350 athletes had even an approximate idea of the calorie value of their daily diet or could give an accurate estimate of any aspect of their food intake. Most of the 350 athletes had a high protein intake, as far as could be ascertained, largely of the more expensive foods, such as grilled steak, rather than in more economical forms, still of first-class protein, such as breast of lamb or herrings. It would be helpful if dietary tables gave food values in calories per dollar as well as the more conventional calories per gram, and it would also be of great benefit to the families of impoverished athletes, who accept some undernourishment for themselves to buy luxury food for their athletic star. The resemblance of fillet steak to the muscle the athlete wants is largely sympathetic magic, though it has more justification than the horn of the rhinoceros had for the aging Chinese mandarin.

Vitamins are taken, sometimes in excessive amounts, by many athletes, not so much because they believe in their effectiveness as because they feel they cannot risk not taking them. These excesses are usually harmless though expensive, but over-dosage of calciferol (vitamin D) can lead to a general calcium imbalance, seriously endangering health. Evidence obtained at the Empire Games survey and at other times suggests that it is the less wealthy and the less well-educated people who spend the most money on dietary additives of doubtful value.

Glucose is a favorite dietary additive in nearly every sport. It is absorbed into the blood stream a little faster than other sugars but cannot exert any action for at least 15 minutes after ingestion. Sprinters have been known to swallow some glucose while assembling at the starting blocks; this cannot possibly have an effect on the immediate event, but one sprinter regarded his last-minute glucose boost as a means of giving his opponents a feeling of inferiority. As part of the normal diet, glucose is a valuable form of carbohydrate, though it is doubtful if its high cost justifies its substitution for sucrose. Although not yet investigated thoroughly, it is possible that the trained athlete has a greater capacity for liver glycogen storage than the average man; 200 grams of glucose given to an athlete after a good breakfast may show no trace in the urine yet would cause a severe glycosuria in a fasting nonathlete. Glucose taken for the sole purpose of giving an athlete an unfair advantage over his opponent may well be construed as doping.

Sometimes a doctor is requested to prescribe some special diet, of apparently magical properties, to which success in sport can be attributed and which must be kept a closely guarded secret. Provided the "foods" are composed of substances of dietary value, their use may be justified, but the addition of caffeine, dextro-amphetamine, or other "prescription only" substances is definitely doping and therefore ethically, if not legally, prohibited.

Other Factors in the Training Period

Participation in Other Sports. If an athlete is engaged predominantly in one sport, he is often most reluctant to participate in any other. It is a widespread belief that even gentle recreational swimming will have an adverse effect on a runner; cyclists are reluctant to run and swimmers to cycle. There is hardly any justification for this fear, provided that the other activity is not done to excess and that unnecessary risk of injury is not taken.

Staleness Immediately Before Competition. A strenuous pre-Olympic training schedule can, on the other had, be lightened by a change of activity; a short game of basketball or football, a day at the seaside with beach games and recreational swimming, vigorous ballroom or folk dancing—all of these, if laid on the foundations provided by the physiological benefits of training, can have a profound psychological value and may easily prevent an entire team from becoming "stale" or from "overtraining."

Sleep. At the 1958 Empire Games survey, most of the athletes questioned stated that they slept for eight or nine hours a night. With teams of adolescents, swimming teams, for example, the good team manager insists on an early curfew. The popular idea that sleep before midnight is more beneficial than a long "lie in" is supported by physiological reasoning. An early breakfast has a chance to start digestion before morning training session, there is time for the gastrocolic reflex to be invoked, and the athlete has time for a "proper" wash and shave before starting his day's work. Morale is much better in a clean and well-disciplined team. Adjustments to an altered sleep rhythm, such as when traveling a few thousand miles east or west or when going on night duty, appear to require at least a week to become established. The effects of altitude also disturb sleep for about ten days, as was found among a small group of British athletes in an experimental period at Mexico City.

Sex. Sexual problems, real or imaginary, can have an effect on an athlete's performance, and some superstitions are widespread. A gluttonous approach to life in food, drink, or sex will, of course, ruin an athlete's work output, but there is no reason the married athlete should not continue to lead a normal life. His or her own experience should be the guide as to the degree of moderation that best serves both family and competitive needs. The psychological effects of the stress of competition on the young girls may alter the normal rhythm of the menstrual cycle. In certain cases this may cause anxiety and affect their performance unless they have been adequately forewarned.

Charms and Talismans. Whether of Christian or pagan origin, charms and talismans are of great antiquity. The use of the priesthood to invoke Divine support for war was carried over into sport and is still widely practiced in the bull-ring chapels of Spain and Latin America, or even in the community hymn singing at British footballcup-final matches. Maoris usually carry their tikis at least as far as the changing room, and this custom seems to be followed by many New Zealanders of European extraction who also use a Maori war dance as a method of motivating their teams and supporters at rugby football matches. The Roman Catholic athlete may get moral support from wearing the medallion of an appropriate saint. Muslims, forbidden by the teaching of Mohammed to make effigies of animate creatures, cry "Allah!" in moments of stress. This seems to act as a strong motivating force, in weight lifting, for instance, giving a powerful psychogenic stimulus, similar to the pistol shot, and external stimuli reported by Ikai and Steinhaus.

Good-luck charms without religious significance probably date from the age of chivalry, when knights would wear an item of clothing such as a glove or kerchief, donated by a current lady love, as a token to ensure victory in jousting and immunity from wounds. By the seventeenth century, when dueling became strictly formulated, the use of amulets and nostrums to give unfair advantage over an opponent or immunity from injury was specifically prohibited (the intention of unfair advantage is reflected in our contemporary views concerning doping in sport). The modern athlete frequently uses charms, but not so obviously. He may feel that he cannot run a good race unless wearing his favorite socks, shoes, singlet, or some other article. If he is not wearing them, he may feel that his performance will be adversely affected. Teams often have their own mascots: stuffed animal effigies such as the hanged monkey of Hartlepool Rovers Rugby Football Club (which commemorates the execution of a spy in the Napoleonic Wars, before his species, let alone his nationality, was ascertained); a person in costume (such as the Magpie of Newcastle United Association Football Club); or the gaggle of glamorous drum majorettes and cheerleaders, without which no American college could ever hope to win anything!

Day of Competition. Up to the time the starting pistol is fired, superstitions and beliefs still play their part. The controversial question of the psychological and physiological benefits of warm up are discussed elsewhere, but the reasons for warming up as given by athletes are varied and interesting. At the Empire Games survey the duration of warm up varied between none and an hour and a half. Apart from the marathon runners, who did little or no warming up, the length of time and intensity of work in this period bore no relation to event, nationality, climate, or anything else. If warm up is to be beneficial in shunting blood from the splanchnic circulation to the skeletal muscles, then it must take place immediately before the event, as the physiological changes reverse within a very few minutes. Nearly 40 per cent of the athletes questioned rested for ten minutes or more after warm up and before the starting gun, and all physiological benefits must have canceled out by such a long period of recovery.

Diet on the day of competition shows some astonishing fallacies. The large plateful of steak and kidney pie before the football match is almost traditional, and the prematch "session" in which up to four pints of draught beer are consumed is not an uncommon custom in some rugby football clubs. One cross-country runner, realizing that a light diet was advisable before a run, always ate baked beans and fizzy lemonade. When the effects of gastric fundus gas pressure on the left ventricle and left lung were reduced by a change to honey and sultana sandwiches and noncarbonated lemon squash, the runner started winning races.

Belief in the Coach. The reliance an athlete places on his coach appears to vary with the educational standard of the athlete rather than with the ability and knowledge of the coach. In the Empire Games survey the educational background of each competitor was ascertained, and the results were classified according to each main class of events. . . . Track and field athletics, rowing, and fencing attracted people with a background at, respectively, a boarding or fee-paying grammar school, a university, and a teacher-training or technological college. The swimmers were mostly from a similar range of schools, but most were too young to have reached the age of postschool education. In these four sports, the advice from coaches was in general listened to but not followed blindly. Coaches were respected for their knowledge rather than for their personality (if it was not backed by sound technical ability).

Cycling, boxing, wrestling, and marathon running tended to be "working-class sports"; none of the athletes had had a university education and few had had even part-time technical college training. In these events the influence of the coach could have been immense. However, as the coach was usually from an educational background similar to that of his athletes, his knowledge often tended to be empirical, based on his own personal experience and supported by ill-understood theoretical concepts. Few of these coaches were physical educationists. There were, however, some from the armed forces who were excellent.

The lack of a scientific background in a coach leads to some extraordinary beliefs among his charges. In a survey of training methods of leading cyclists carried out recently by Thomas and Madgett and Brooke, a reason given by one cyclist for shaving his legs was "so that the poison won't get in by the roots." Another cyclist, refusing to undertake specific strength training, stated that "cycling muscles should not be strong—strong muscles are slow"; and yet another said that "if riding the bike doesn't develop the muscles, then I don't need those particular muscles."

Empiricism and prejudice among coaches is by no means confined to those in the working-class sports. It is found in all sports, including rowing, even though the coach is more likely to be a dignitary of the church or a university rather than a factory foreman. Those men can be equally ignorant of, say, dietetics and the physiological basis of exercise and training.

Reliance on the Doctor. The correct relationship between the athlete and the doctor is not easy to define. Most athletes feel that a doctor who understands their event and its special stresses can help them a great deal, but it is difficult to get the athlete to state precisely what he wants, how he would like the doctor to help him, and how he would like to receive the assistance he really needs. As a substitute for the hard training that brings success, the less well-educated athlete may ask for the magic tonic, the secret dietary regime, or the innovation that will enable him to perform better. If injured, he expects the same magic to keep him in competition: the injection of local analgesics, massage, manipulation, adhesive strapping, or some undefined secret formula. He likes to have qualified medical approval for all his training fads and like most people is only too ready to follow the advice that suits him and to go around seeking other opinions if the advice given is not to his liking. This seeking for advice can be regarded as a nuisance, the advice usually being sought for out of office hours, in a bar, on the golf course, or wherever the athlete meets a doctor whose opinions he has not tapped before. This gives doctors the impression that all athletes are hopeless neurotics; and in studies into the personality of athletes, based on psychologists' questions, athletes generally score highly in both neuroticism and extraversion. It is very necessary for an athlete to understand and care for his body—as necessary as it is for a racing driver to care for his car or a rodeo rider for his horse—but to the psychometrist this constitutes neuroticism.

Many athletes feel, not entirely without justification, that the average general practitioner or hospital specialist without sports medicine experience is not well qualified to treat their soft-tissue injuries or even to advise them regarding exercise vs. rest in the aftertreatment of any condition. The athlete too frequently demands a specific remedy for his specific sports injury—"shin splints," "Charley horse," or "jumper's heel"—and is resentful if he does not get the same treatment as his teammate, even though his simple self-diagnosis does not take into account the dozen or so pathological processes that may underlie a painful heel in a triple jumper or the nine or ten processes that might cause pain in the anterior tibial musculofascial compartment or bone or periosteum of a sprinter. The doctor must not only make an accurate diagnosis of a sports injury but must be able to explain its etiology, pathology, and prognosis so that the athlete will understand the reasons for his treatment and cooperate in it.

In a pilot investigation into the nature and frequency of sports injuries, the answers to a question on why some athletes did *not* consult their doctors about their injuries were interesting and alarming: "My doctor is all right for signing certificates and treating old people, but is quite uninterested in sports injuries"; "My doctor knows all about children and the elderly, but nothing about the active sportsman"; "He regards sports injuries as of little importance compared with his seriously ill patients"; "It is no good my seeing my own doctor; he will not really examine me but will just tell me to rest or to give up sport." Other criticisms are even more outspoken.

It is essential that the good team doctor be a member of the team; he should work with its members, eating and living with them, and not be isolated in a luxury hotel several miles away, paying his daily visit for a routine inspection, and so just qualifying for his free ticket in the grandstand. He must be available to the athletes at all times to relieve their fears, whether serious or trivial and groundless. He must know something about the techniques of the events and their training methods. He must speak the athletes' language, technical and slang, and be able to give rational explanations for his specific and general advice, to rationalize the training scheduled (without interfering with the duties of the coach or team manager), and to give a factual basis to routines for the athletes to follow with knowledge and insight instead of allowing them to depend on the blind observance of schedules they do not understand.

Ending Time:

WPM: _____

Comprehension Check: Factors Determining. . . .

Directions: Complete each of the following statements by writing in or circling the correct answer.

1. The nationality of this sports medicine writer is
    a.   American from the United States.
    b.   British.
    c.   Communist from Russia.

2. The author feels that, when athletes are injured and need treatment, doctors and coaches are replacing superstitions, fads, and customs with a scientific medical approach.

    True   False

3. The medical doctor's role when working with athletes is best fulfilled if

    _____

    _____.

4. Athletes from the less well-coached sports tend to have more misconceptions about the care and treatment of their bodies.

    True   False

5. The Empire Games survey revealed that the athlete's belief in his coach's advice was largely determined

    a.   by his geographical region.
    b.   by his educational standard.
    c.   by his coach's personality.

Comprehension Accuracy:

_____

An average rate of speed would be effective for Selection 7.

Appropriate Rate:

_____

Beginning Time:

_____

Total Words: 1459

Selection 8: How to Cope With Being Out of Work _____

One recent Monday morning, Ben Ferris awoke to the jangling of his alarm and stumbled bleary-eyed from bed to get ready for another week at the huge Grumman plant on Long Island, where he was employed as an aerospace technician. Moments later, with one foot in his pants, the truth suddenly pierced his sleep-fogged brain—there was no job any more. He'd been laid off Friday afternoon.

Ben is one of the 23,600 jobless in Suffolk County, N.Y. where conditions are so serious that Labor Commissioner Lou Tempora labels the entire county an "economic disaster area."

Suffolk is not alone. The chill-laden fact is that all across the nation millions of men—many of them young, energetic and highly trained—are facing possible unemployment. And all indications point to continued—and possibly rising—joblessness all through this year.

It is a scary situation for growing numbers of Americans, white or blue

SOURCE: Reprinted from *Mechanix Illustrated Magazine*. Copyright 1971 by CBS Publications, Inc.

collar. In Pittsburgh, an import manager out of work eight months applied for a position as hash-house counterman and was too late . . . an unemployed manufacturing engineer got there first. In Seattle, Wash., aircraft workers never know when they get to work if they'll be greeted with a layoff notice. Boeing employees (or ex-employees) have a wry joke: "An optimist is a guy who brings his lunch to work."

Already 35 major areas around the U.S. are on the Government's list of sections suffering from "substantial unemployment," meaning over 6 per cent of the work force. By the time you read this, there will be many more.

What does a man do when the axe falls? How does he protect himself and his family? Where does he go for help? How does he get a new post? The questions are relevant, indeed crucial, as the realities of joblessness come to more and more Americans.

From interviews with labor experts, job counselors and money-management specialists, MI developed an action plan for the unemployed in the current recession. We sought out nuts-and-bolts facts that anyone who finds himself out of work for any reason—layoff, outright firing, a strike or quitting—should know. Heed closely, because what follows could prove a life preserver in the prevailing economic weather.

The first impulse is to start beating the bushes as quickly as possible to start the money flowing again. Resist it. Forget about other work till you review your financial setup and make the necessary changes to fit your altered circumstances.

If another job appears a virtual certainty or if you're assured that the layoff is for a limited time, little change is needed. But if you look down the road and conclude that you're in for a lengthy siege, tighten ship at once.

Your first step: Know precisely how much money is coming in regularly. Add up everything you can count on, including severance pay, unused vacation pay, your wife's income, if any, and even the kids' after-school job pay. Why not? They're a part of the family and must learn to help out when the chips are down. At the same time, make a careful list of your assets so you know where you can put your hands on more cash if needed. Include anything that's convertible into money— bank accounts, stocks and other investments. Also, find out how much cash value has accumulated on life-insurance policies. Many people forget that these dollars are there for crisis situations such as this.

We left for last your one big item of regular income—unemployment insurance. Get going on this immediately. The Division of Employment of New York State Department of Labor reports that many men lose cash coming to them because they let weeks pass before applying. In the typical instance, an upholsterer lost his job May 1 and found another one 12 weeks later. He was entitled to 11 weeks jobless pay as there's a one-week waiting period, but only collected seven because he was tardy in applying.

If being out of work is a novel experience, understand that this pay is not charity but protection for the person who's out of work through no fault of his own. Your employer paid for it over the years and you earned you share through your work. In a few states, the worker also contributes to the fund.

Provisions differ widely in the various states but you generally receive benefits for up to 26 weeks. Under recently enacted legislation, several states extend payments an extra 13 weeks for a total of 39 if the unemployment rate reaches a certain percentage of the work force. Cash payments range from $40 to

$90 a week, and are based on the number of dependents in a family. Most states require a waiting period of a week before checks are authorized.

To start payments flowing, you must file a claim in person at your state unemployment office. Bring your Social Security card and any records showing where and for whom you have worked in the previous year. The vast majority of jobs are covered.

You can't qualify if you've been involved in a labor dispute. In addition, you must be willing to work, meaning you must actively try to get another job while collecting benefits, and accept a job offered to you provided it is in your field, pays comparable wages and is suited to your training and experience.

Other sources of income include strike benefits for those out because of labor dispute and severance pay if you've been fired. Still another is supplemental unemployment insurance paid by several labor unions. In some instances these benefits, when added to regular jobless pay, will total to 80 or 90 per cent of a man's income when employed. The plans vary enormously.

After you've touched all bases and know to the dime what's coming in, do everything you can to make it last. This means a thorough overhauling of every expense item in the household budget.

Make it a backyard vacation this year, or borrow gear and go hiking and camping over the nation's elaborate network of wilderness trails. Biking vacations are also inexpensive and increasingly popular.

Everything goes austerity. The kids' allowances get cut to the bare minimum. Eating out means hot dogs on the patio. Entertainment will be reading or songs around the piano. Make do with last year's clothes, car, etc.

Expenses that cannot be slashed can be deferred. For example:

The Mortgage. Call your bank or lending agency and lay the problem on the line. If your credit has been good and other debts not too bad, you can probably get a three-month extension.

If you've already paid off a healthy chunk and have a sizable equity in the house, you might get as long as a year.

Insurance Payments. You're better fixed than you thought. First, you've got a month's time to pay up after the final payment due date without losing a thing. Next, most policies now have a life-saving premium loan feature for just this kind of problem. It automatically takes care of any premium not paid when due, the money coming from the accumulated cash value of your policy. Of course, when the cash value is gone, the policy lapses. But note that term insurance doesn't have cash values.

Those Bills. Gas, electricity, fuel, water, telephone, doctor, dentist, charge accounts—all can be deferred for a reasonable interval provided you inform your creditors in advance. Most companies and probably individuals will go along.

Next to housing, food is probably the biggest item in your budget. You can save almost 40 per cent by smart buying.

Shop the food specials offered daily by the supermarkets. These items, with prices, are advertised in local newspapers, on flyers stuffed in mailboxes and are plastered all over the store windows. (Sometimes you have to hunt hard for the bargains, though, as recounted in How To Shop Aggressively and Save, January MI.)

When all economies and deferments have been made and outgo still exceeds income, borrow—but judiciously. Tap relatives and friends first, as no or low interest will be charged. Next, borrow on your life insurance if there's cash value, since interest here is the lowest you can get. Savings banks offer *passbook* loans. You can borrow on the amount you have on deposit. Of course, you pay interest on the loan but at the same time you continue to collect interest on the full sum you've got in the bank.

Try for a free loan. Surprisingly, there are some organizations, particularly religious ones, that object strongly to the interest system of lending and offer loans gratis to qualified persons. Hit banks and other commercial lenders last because here the interest is highest.

With the money situation stabilized, you're in a far better frame of mind to go job-hunting. Where to start? The New York State Employment Service says these are the six best sources:

• Your state employment office, which has the facts about job opportunities in your community, plus free counseling and aptitude tests.

• Check relatives, friends and neighbors. You've probably known from your own experience that most employers rely on recommendations from their own friends and workers to fill openings.

• Keep in touch with the job placement office of your school or college.

• Study the want ads in newspapers and trade journals.

• Comb the classified phone book and industrial directories for the names of companies hiring workers in your field. Apply in person or by mail.

• Hunt up non-profit agencies such as the YMCA in your town. Most have job placement bureaus.

Ending Time:

_____

WPM: _____

Comprehension Check: How to Cope. . . .

Directions: Complete each of the following questions by writing in or circling the correct answer.

1. The advice offered by the author applies only to the jobless workers of New York State.

   True   False

2. At the time of writing, _____ were most frequently found in the ranks of the jobless.

3. Unemployment insurance should be viewed as _____

   _____

   _____

4. The author suggests that you "beat the bushes" first when you learn that you are jobless.

   True   False

5. List three ways that unemployed and their families can conserve the money they have at the time the job was lost.

   a. _____

   b. _____   Comprehension Accuracy:

   c. _____   _____

A moderate to fast speed would have been appropriate for Selection 8.

Flexibility in choice of rate means that you deliberately choose the speed at which you will read. This is determined by the purpose you consciously set for yourself. Selections 9 and 10 contain specific guides to help you set purposes as you read. Glance over these two articles. Notice how the subtopics guide your search and suggest the ideas to be discussed. How familiar are you with these terms? If your knowledge of these is vague, quickly scan the lines for any unfamiliar vocabulary. Mark these and speed onward. When you read the selection, be especially careful that the paragraph containing the unknown word suggests the overall meaning to you. Then continue your reading. If, when you finish and check comprehension, you find that your knowledge of the topic was spotty, take time to locate these words in the dictionary. Then quickly skim the selection again. The comprehension questions should mean more at this point. When you are finished, record your reading rate and comprehension scores in the Flexibility Chart at the end of this unit.

Now continue your reading.

Selection 9: The Swiss Way of Life

Appropriate Rate:

_____

Beginning Time:

_____

Total Words: 3088

With such diversity in the Swiss scene—four national languages, twenty-two Catholic and Protestant member states—it is astonishing that there should be a Swiss way of life. And yet there is one, which might perhaps be better defined as an outlook, an attitude to the outside world that has been shaped, not by history, but by economic and political necessity.

Switzerland is a very small country indeed. Nature has been lavish only in the bestowal of beauty. Everything the Swiss possess they have had to work hard to obtain. The prosperity they enjoy is due to the foresight, orderly planning, business and political acumen of the federal and cantonal governments, of executives engaged in private enterprise, and also to the discipline and thrift of the nation.

Thoroughness. The struggle to win and maintain political and economic independence has undoubtedly colored the national character. The Swiss are cautious, extremely prudent in the acceptance of new theories, new methods, ideas or commodities. Their ancestors could not afford to buy a pig in a poke and, at many turning points in Swiss history, a slight error of judgment might have spelled disaster.

The blend of German and Latin cultures has resulted everywhere in a love of orderliness and cleanliness, a keen appreciation of thoroughness. What the Swiss do, they do well. They may take a long time to decide on a course of action or an undertaking of any kind, but once the decision has been made, no detail is overlooked. Their new hospitals, such as Basel-Burgerspital, Zurich-Triemli or Bern-Insel, or the surgical department of the Lausanne cantonal hospits, took a long time to build, but they are models of their kind. This trait is expressed even in the field of sport. Skiing, for example, was introduced from Scandinavia some sixty years ago and did not become really popular until a year or two before World War I. Now it is the national sport, and all enthusiasts are equipped with the finest possible kit, from boots to caps, all craftmade in Switzerland.

SOURCE: Reprinted with permission from FODOR'S SWITZERLAND by Eugene Fodor, ed. Copyright 1977. Published by Fodor's Modern Guides.

Love of quality. Closely linked to this characteristic is an appreciation of quality. There is no market in Switzerland for cheap and slovenly merchandise. Poor workmanship is generally considered a disgrace. In a typical Swiss home, even the most modest, you will find well-made—though not necessarily beautiful— furniture. Newlyweds with only a one-room apartment will spend the utmost on a handsome bedroom suite. Brides-to-be of all classes take pride in their trousseaus, cherish and embroider fine linens, even though it may strain their budget to do so. In central and eastern Switzerland, the general trend of taste is for all that is heavy and rather massive in line. In the western cantons, a certain Latin love of more refined elegance prevails. There is, nevertheless, everywhere, an intense love of fine craftsmanship and good quality.

It is hardly necessary to point out that this national trait has won for the Swiss a worldwide reputation for the production of high-quality goods. It is richly illustrated in their daily lives. Their stores, tearooms, restaurants, for example, are luxuriously appointed and furnished with handsome, craftmade equipment. Note the details in a city tearoom: chairs, tables, lamps, soft furnishings, all planned with careful art. One may not always appreciate the style, but there is nothing slovenly.

Craftsmanship. Thoroughness and love of quality have also directed the strict control of trades and skill. One cannot, in Switzerland, set up a shop or open a business at random. To be a hairdresser, an electrician, a plumber, a garageman, a stenographer, or what have you, one must produce a diploma of apprenticeship or a certificate of mastership. For this reason, craft work is of the highest order. Fine millinery, clothes, footwear, jewelry, lingerie, furniture are made and sold by professionally competent tradespeople. Mass-produced articles are, of course, available in the large stores but if they are of poor quality or bad workmanship, not many Swiss will buy them.

No castles in Spain. The necessity for prudence has made the Swiss adopt a fairly materialistic or rather concrete outook. Your typical Swiss does not day-dream, or wander through life with his head in the clouds. He is put to work early and made to understand that "Life is earnest." School-leaving age is fifteen or sixteen and, after a three- or four-year term of apprenticeship, the young boy or girl goes into father's business (if there is one) or seeks to perfect his knowledge in his chosen trade. Safe government jobs are in great demand, for they mean security, a cosy home, and a pension. It is estimated that there is one civil servant (including officials of the state railroads, police, etc.) for every five people. Training for the professions is equally thorough, and Swiss universities set a high standard of scholarship.

Independence. Seven hundred years of democracy have given the Swiss nation a great love of freedom that, paradoxically, is contradicted by the extraordinary number of rules, regulations, and restrictions that overshadow the individual. Application forms, legal documents, statistics have grown and multiplied, since the war years especially, but the citizen does not pay undue attention to them. He is not really aware of the "Do not spit," "Do not walk on the grass," "Do not shout," "Do not" this and "Do not" that strewn across his path by order-loving officials. He proves his independence of spirit at the polls, in the cafes, where he grumbles freely, and by occasional sturdy refusals to comply with a municipal, cantonal, or federal order.

DIVERSITY BUT UNITY

Diversity. It is often said, "There are no Swiss. There are Bernese, Genevans, and so on . . . in fact, twenty-two different nations, but no typical Swiss!"

That is, to a certain extent, true. A Vaudois will fume at and criticize a Bernese. A Genevan will say of the people of Zurich that they are greedy, materialistic. The population of each canton supposedly has at least one outstanding "national" shortcoming. And yet, when it comes to the push, when a national emergency arises, there are no cantons, only Switzerland.

There are three official languages—German, French, and Italian—and a fourth "national" language, Romansch. Each language group has identical rights, and all official government communications must be in the three official tongues, so as not to favor one over another. You could, if you wished, speak only one language all your life if you were Swiss . . . but, being a good democrat and eager to protect the other language groups' rights as your own, you would probably learn at least one other language.

Unity. Despite their racial and linguistic differences, the people of Switzerland are one in their love of the soil. The Alps and their brown chalets, the quiet lakes and forests, have cast a spell over them, and maybe even helped to give unity to a strange medley of what might otherwise have been a very disunited people. Nevertheless, the cantons cleave to their independence, and there is frequently healthy disagreement by cantons and voters with the federal government in Bern. But in its militia Switzerland has found a remarkable smoother-over of difficulties; an infallible sponsor of enforced good fellowship. "My buddy in the army" may come from Geneva, Bern, Thrugau, or Solothurn; he may speak only broken French, German, or Italian, but four months of grueling military training at the age of twenty, and refresher courses every year after that, are most conducive to true human understanding among men.

Democracy. And perhaps, too, the Swiss militia system has served yet another purpose: the establishment of a true sense of democracy among the people. During the formative years, young men of every walk of life, of every class, are submitted to the same treatment, to the same pitiless commands. The effect is not forgotten in the course of years, because until the age of thirty-six there are the regular three-week terms of service and, thereafter, incorporation in the *Landwehr* and *Landsturm*. Young men who are unfit for the military must enlist in auxiliary services.

Atmosphere. The diversity of Switzerland is much a question of atmosphere. In the German-speaking cantons, in the large cities of Zurich, Bern, and Basel, one senses an earnest purposefulness, a certain rather unsmiling sternness. Life and the sustenance of life by hard work, the acquiring of security by money in the bank, are very real here. Swiss-German businessmen are efficient; they divide their time neatly and tidily into working days (and the office) and rest days (and the family).

It is significant that many German-Swiss girls of all but the top-bracket income classes are sent, immediately on leaving school, to serve as maids-of-all-work with families in French-speaking countries as well as in Britain. As they are often paid a mere pittance and work hard, life is far from easy. This is picturesquely called *manger de la vache enragee* ("eating humble pie") and is considered an excellent and cheap way of introducing girls to the cold realities of life and work; of giving them a practical illustration of the ''Life is earnest'' concept. Few French-Swiss girls are subjected to this system.

Parenthetically, it is appropriate to mention that this is far from being a one-way traffic. From Britain in particular there is a steady flow of girls going to work with Swiss families, to say nothing of with hotels, restaurants, and suchlike. Less appropriate here, but still worthy of mention, is the considerable number of young people of many nationalities—and especially from the United States—who go to Swiss universities and other educational establishments, sometimes for degree courses of several years, sometimes for summer courses of only a few weeks.

In the western cantons, in Geneva and Vaud especially, a strong Latin influence is prevalent. Life is taken more lightly; thrift is not so much the order of the day. The Germanic Grundlichkeit (thoroughness) prevails but it is alleviated and made more joyful by a certain graciousness and a latent sense of *manana*. ''There are more days to come from behind the mountains,'' say Lausannites and Genevans. That does not mean to say that people work less hard. On the contrary, they work very hard indeed, but they also play hard. The entertainment trades— cinema, theaters, nightclubs, and so on—are prosperous in this region of Switzerland and patronized not only by visitors from abroad, but by the Swiss themselves.

To arrive in the Ticino, Switzerland's Italian-speaking and southernmost canton, from, say Zurich, is almost like entering another country. Here is a different climate and Mediterranean warmth. And south of the Gotthard massif the luxuriant vegetation at lower levels is obvious even to the most myopic traveler. The Ticinesi are different, too: hardworking like most Swiss, but largely of Lombard stock so that their mannerisms and appearance, as well as their language, are inescapable reminders of Italy.

With the coming of railways and good roads, and the growth of easy and rapid travel for all, especially over or through mountain barriers which had hitherto deterred all but the brave and hardy, the previous virtual isolation of many Swiss communities was brought to an end. Inhabitants began to move from one part of Switzerland to another, and intermarriage took place, so that many local traits and characteristics gradually became toned down or modified. Particularly noticeable was the movement of German-speaking Swiss across language borders to other parts of the country where they rapidly adapted themselves to life, and successfully established businesses.

WOMEN AND THE HOME

The Swiss Home. There are many kinds of homes in Switzerland, rich and poor, plain and beautiful, farmsteads, apartments, houses in garden suburbs, but in the great majority of them is an excellent housewife. Although, during World War II, she and her sisters remained inglorious on the home front while their menfolk stood guarding the frontiers, they accomplished miracles of skill in eking out meager rations; their untiring work contributed in no small measure to the solving of the national food problem.

The art of homemaking is the supreme seal of womanhood in Switzerland. Beautiful household linen, a fine kitchen, spotless cleanliness, and sleek tidiness are the Swiss woman's pride. Shining rows of bottled fruit and homemade jams testify to her skill.

Servants are rare and expensive in Switzerland. Even upper middleclass housewives are usually saddled with a fair burden of housework.

Swiss women only recently gained the right to vote but they are increasingly interested in politics although many still consider this to be essentially a masculine headache. Although women doctors, dentists and lawyers are excellent, until a few years ago the true career woman was virtually unknown in Switzerland. She had a hard time being taken seriously, society tending to feel that she was merely filling in time before marriage. She stood little chance of finding a niche in big business, committee work, or administration. These executive jobs were the preserves of men. But the situation is changing, and changing rapidly.

In the lower income brackets there is a rather different attitude, most young wives adding to the family income by continuing work at least until the children arrive.

Hospitality. British and American visitors to Switzerland may be struck by the apparent lack of homely hospitality (although a number of Tourist Offices operate an excellent "Meet the Swiss" scheme designed specifically to enable foreigners to visit the Swiss in their homes). The reason for this is not very clear as the Swiss themselves are anything but an unfriendly people. It is probably due to the fact that here, as in many parts of the Continent, life is lived to a great extent in public. The Swiss, too, seem to experience a certain reserve or shyness towards strangers, due perhaps to the great emphasis laid on the family as a unit. Distant family connections are maintained to the nth degree, while relations with the outside world remain on a conventional footing.

Not so many years ago it was the custom for Swiss men of forty and over to spend their Sunday afternoons playing cards in cafes with their buddies, possibly to be joined by their wives after tea. But in Switzerland, as elsewhere, times change customs. Nowadays, a growing number spend Sunday afternoons in front of the television set, or out in the family car.

Generosity. Despite their rather shy reticence and marked dislike of expressing deep emotion—a Swiss audience almost seems cold and sparing of rapturous applause—the Swiss are a most kindly people, secretly warmhearted. The nation as a whole feels a deep sense of gratitude for the peace it has enjoyed for over one hundred years and this thankfulness is shown by a great generosity towards the war-stricken populations of Europe. Children have been the special object of their attention. Thousands were brought into Switzerland in the few years immediately after the war. Placed in charge of foster parents for periods of three months, they blossomed into health and happiness. The love and care lavished on them, the parcels of warm clothing and toys they carried away with them at the end of their stay, testified to the sincerity of the welcome they received.

Towards the end of the war, the "Don Suisse" was instituted to provide, by voluntary, national subscription, material aid to war-striken areas; trainloads of furniture, clothing, food, and hospital equipment were sent out of the country. A similar institution, "Caritas," was organized by the Catholic communities of Switzerland and still sends food and clothing to less fortunate people abroad.

Immediately after the collapse of the Mussolini government in 1944, thousands upon thousands of refugees came pouring over the southern border to escape Nazi persecutors. Old people and young children, men and women of military age who had reason to fear retaliation—the tide could not be held back. The rural population in the Ticino took matters into their own hands. Along the roads leading from the frontiers, they posted women and children with large baskets heaped with fruit, bread, and other food, shoes, and clothing. To the weary traveler, these gifts were given with a kindly word and a smile.

Some years later, the Swiss led in organizing relief for the flood of refugees that began streaming out of Hungary in the autumn of 1956 and out of Czechoslovakia in 1968. Not only did they spontaneously contribute clothing, medicine, and food, but the government welcomed many thousands of homeless families to Switzerland as permanent immigrants, finding them places to live, work to do, and new starts in life. Nor were the needs of the spirit forgotten in the flood of material assistance. Zurich's newspapers banded together to publish a newspaper in Hungarian for free distribution among the refugee camps in Austria.

Sports. In the last thirty years, the Swiss have become very sportsminded. Foremost, of course, is skiing. On winter Saturday afternoons a forest of skis waves through all the main stations of the country, en route for the snowfields. In summer, water sports predominate. Sunbathing at the innumerable lake and river beaches is practiced with extraordinary enthusiasm. In the cities, a pale face attracts attention. Physical fitness and a look of health have become almost a fetish with the younger set, and girls and women sport off-the-shoulder fashions that stress cherished tans.

. . . Next to Godliness. Relatively few Swiss are indecently wealthy, and there are even fewer of the much publicized "gnomes" who, with phone in hand, make fortunes out of buying and selling currencies they neither see nor own. Like every country Switzerland has its poor, but there are no slums—at least in the sense that a Briton or American understands the word. And of course, the Swiss are exceptionally lucky in that no area of their country—not even Zurich, Basel and other industrial centers—lies more than half an hour from mountains, country-side, lake or river. Everywhere, within easy reach, are fields and forests.

True, in the cities heavy traffic fills the air with noise and fumes, but smoking factory chimneys are a rarity seen by few tourists anywhere in Switzer-land. Cleanliness throughout the country, not least in the towns, is a matter in which the authorities and the people may have a subconscious pride, but certainly seem to accept as something no more than natural. Where else but in Switzerland would you see a post office official, armed with dusters and all the necessary materials, carefully cleaning and polishing a letter box in a busy city street? If cleanliness is next to godliness, Switzerland must be nearer to heaven than most.

Ending Time:

_____

WPM: _____

Comprehension Check: The Swiss Way. . . .

Directions: Complete each of the following statements by writing in or circling the correct answer.

1. The phrase that most accurately describes the Swiss way of life is
    a. hospitality
    b. love of quality.
    c. diversity but unity.

2. The author called Switzerland's love of democracy a paradox because

_____

_____.

3. The geography of Switzerland has little effect on the attitudes and atmosphere one finds among its peoples.

   True   False

4. Skiing is a relatively new sport in Switzerland since _____

   _____

   _____.

5. Since the German-Swiss feel very strongly about life's seriousness and hard work, they practice what seems to be a harsh method of impressing young women with this fact. The girls actually

   _____

   _____.

Comprehension Accuracy:

_____

A moderately slow to average speed was probably most appropriate for this selection.

Appropriate Rate:

_____

Beginning Time:

_____

Total Words: 1706

Selection 10: The Struggle Over Nuclear Power _____

Like an infantry platoon under an artillery bombardment, the power industry has spent most of the past year hunkered down in the trenches as its opponents pounded away with questions and criticism. But now, in a campaign that could well determine the future of nuclear power, pro-nuclear forces are on the offensive. Around the nation, power-company officials at press conferences and on podiums have been presenting figures to show that nuclear energy is more practical than other alternatives to oil. In Washington last week, a parade of executives, engineers and federal officials trooped before a joint congressional committee to rebut charges that their installations are unsafe and to convince an increasingly anxious American public that nuclear power plants are necessary.

One reason for the campaign is that on June 8 Californians will go to the polls not only to choose among presidential candidates but to vote on a nuclear referendum. Proposition 15 on the ballot is not, as some opponents have charged, a proposal to outlaw nuclear power plants. Yet, if enacted, the measure could accomplish exactly that. The California initiative would ban the construction of 28 new plants planned for the state over the next two decades unless they met stringent safety standards and won approval by a two-thirds vote in both houses of the state's legislature.

RECENT THREAT. Proposition 15 could also force the closing of the three nuclear plants now operating in California. It would forbid existing plants to operate at more than 60% of capacity unless federal limits on liability in case of an accident are raised above the recently extended $560 million ceiling. It would also further reduce power output by 10% a year unless two-thirds of the state's legislators endorsed waste-disposal and safety measures. Many believe that the two-thirds approval required in the legislature constitutes an impassable barrier.

The anti-nuclear drive is not unique to California. At least 17 states are now

SOURCE: Reprinted by permission from TIME, The Weekly Newsmagazine; Copyright Time Inc., 1976.

considering various measures to curtail nuclear power. Passage of Proposition 15 in California could thus have far-reaching effects on the power debate in these states.

The threat is relatively recent. In polls conducted last year, over 70% of Californians and 60% of the public nationwide approved of the expansion of nuclear power; no more than a handful of those with reservations about atomic plants seemed concerned enough to try to do something about them. But the anti-nuclear forces seem to be gathering momentum. Last month a trio of middle-level engineers at GE's nuclear-energy division in San Jose, Calif., suddenly resigned their jobs in protest. The trio, Dale Bridenbaugh, 44, Gregory Minor, 38, and Richard Hubbard, 38, announced that they would instead work full time for Project Survival, the organization coordinating the anti-nuclear referendum drive in California. Another engineer, Robert Pollard, 36, quit his job with the federal Nuclear Regulatory Commission in protest over conditions at Consolidated Edison's Indian Point nuclear power plants in Buchanan, N.Y.

HORROR TALE. All four cited the same basic reasons for their resignations: inadequate protection of the public from nuclear hazards. The public, said the San Jose Three in a statement to the Congressional Joint Committee on Atomic Energy, "has a right to know that an electrical appliance, such as a toaster or hair dryer, has more stringent safety checks than the electrical instruments that control a nuclear plant."

What concerns these nuclear engineers—and many of their fellow protesters—is not any possibility that a conventional nuclear plant will blow up in a mushroom cloud and wipe out a city. All but a few ignorant hysterics recognize that that is impossible. What they do fear, however, is a "meltdown," which can occur if a reactor loses the water used to control the temperature of its uranium core. The four claim that safety systems designed to prevent accidents have not undergone enough testing. If they failed in a crisis, say the four, the results could be disastrous.

They could indeed. An uncooled core would build up heat, melt and drop to the bottom of its container. Its heat would vaporize whatever water remained and the pressure of the resulting steam could burst the containment vessel and rupture the outer reactor container as well. This could release a radioactive cloud that would drift wherever the wind blew it. Depending on the location of the plant, such an accident could result in numerous immediate deaths from radiation and even more later from radiation-induced cancers. Far from being a horror tale, insists the nuclear opposition, such a mishap could well occur if nuclear plants are allowed to proliferate.

Nuclear power opponents are jubilant over the resignations and the safety issues thus spotlighted. The anti-nuclear movement has been searching for just such an event to convert the public. The resignations, said Richard Sextro, the Sierra Club's coordinator for passage of Proposition 15, "renewed people's concern that individuals and companies in technology are split."

Just what effect the resignations will have on the California initiative is uncertain. Project Survival President James Burch, who helped arrange the defection of the three GE engineers, is not overly optimistic about the impact on the initiative. But others feel that the resignations, with a few more expected, can only help the anti-nuclear movement in California and other states.

OLD QUESTIONS. In public at least, nuclear industry officials have tended to play down the political effect of the resignations. "Speaking in radiation terms, how long a half-life will the issue have?" asked one GE spokesman. "I doubt it will last significantly for the next four months." Some of the San Jose Three's quondam colleagues have attempted to portray them as unrealistic idealists because they are members of a self-improvement group called the Creative Initiative Foundation. Others are trying to offset the resignations with strongly pro-nuclear statements.

The industry has taken pains to respond to the defectors on the safety issue. George Stathakis, vice president and general manager of GE's Nuclear Energy Programs division, told the congressional committee that the charges raised by the former GE engineers were old and had either already been answered or were in the process of being dealt with. Con Edison Spokesman John Conway insisted that the Indian Point plants were safe. Said he: "None of these plants constitutes an unreasonable risk to the health and safety of our own personnel or to the public at large."

From within the Government, Nuclear Regulatory Commission Chairman William Anders said that nothing in the defectors' claims would require his agency to take drastic action. Others insisted that nuclear power risks are reasonable. Said NRC Commissioner Edward Mason: "There is not enough money in the U.S. to raise man's other activities to the safety level already achieved by nuclear power plants."

The nuclear safety record to date is impressive. No member of the public has been injured as a result of a reactor accident since the first U.S. nuclear power plant was brought on line in 1957. The odds against future injury are enormous. A controversial study directed by Nuclear Physicist Norman Rasmussen of the Massachusetts Institute of Technology concludes that nuclear plants are thousands of times less apt to produce fatal accidents than fires, non-nuclear explosions, toxic chemical releases, dam failures, airplane crashes and earthquakes. Even with 100 reactors operating (there are now 59 licensed), says Rasmussen, the odds that an individual will be killed by a reactor accident are only 1 in 5 billion per year.

For all these odds and all the safeguards, there has been at least one close call. Last March the world's largest nuclear plant, located at Brown's Ferry, Ala., was well into the chain of events that could lead to a meltdown after human error caused failure of several key safety systems. On a lesser level, a Northeast Utilities plant in Waterford, Conn., spilled radiation outside the plant when a steam condenser ruptured. Other nuclear power plants have had to suspend operations for anywhere from weeks to several months as a result of equipment failures. But most nuclear proponents insist that this record is remarkably good and see no unreasonable hazard in stepping up nuclear power plant construction to meet about a third of U.S. energy needs by 1999.

A study sponsored by the American Physical Society suggests some reservations, however. The report issued last spring concluded that the nuclear power Establishment has underestimated the consequences of nuclear accidents and may well have overestimated the effectiveness of its safety systems. "There is," said the report, "a lack of well-quantified understanding of the performance of some of these special systems under some severe accident conditions." To develop that understanding, the study advised, the reactor safety program should be improved and expanded.

Nuclear plants also raise other questions and fears. One is that expansion of the nuclear power industry would make it easy for terrorists to steal fissionable materials for homemade bombs. That is probably exaggerated. Stringent security can keep nuclear materials from falling into the wrong hands.

RADIOACTIVE LEGACY. A major concern is nuclear wastes, one of which, plutonium, has a half-life of over 24,000 years. Safeguarding wastes alone, says Biologist Barry Commoner, would require the creation of a kind of permanent "nuclear priesthood," to watch over the radioactive legacy each generation of Americans handed down to its successors.

Meanwhile, where and at what price is the U.S. to get the energy it needs? The pro-nuclear argument is a strong one. With oil reserves finite and access to foreign supplies dependent upon OPEC's whims, the U.S. must find alternate sources of power. But the clear and present choices are anything but promising. Harnessing wind and wave power is today and for the near term little more than an engineer's pipedream. Solar energy will probably not become practicable on a large scale for several decades. Coal, which the U.S. has in abundance, does not seem to be the only answer. Deep mining is expensive and dangerous and stripmining scars the land, especially in the semiarid West. Coal-fired plants are also far from clean.

Even with rising construction costs, nuclear power plants, which are clean, are considered by many experts to be the best and most economical answer to the nation's short-term alternate energy needs. That is all the more reason to ensure that they are as safe as human ingenuity and diligence can make them. Critics who can help in that process are welcome regardless of which side of the nuclear argument they are on. Whatever the odds, the reality of a serious nuclear accident would be catastrophic. It might take only one such mishap to force an indefinite shutdown of the entire nuclear power industry. The U.S. needs nuclear plants and can afford the costs of making them safe; what it cannot afford is a major accident.

Ending Time:

_____

WPM: _____

Comprehension Check: The Struggle Over Nuclear Power

Directions: Complete each of the following statements by writing in or circling the correct answer.

1. The author compared the power industry to a besieged army. Why was this comparison drawn?_____

    _____

    _____

    _____

2. What is the significance of "Proposition 15" as proposed in California?

    _____

    _____

    _____

    _____.

3. The anti-nuclear power movement gained momentum when

    a. a catastrophic accident occured at the Oak Ridge, Tennessee facility.
    b. three nuclear engineers resigned their positions because of alleged unsafe practices that could lead to public harm.
    c. the Atomic Energy Commission voted unanimously to waive certain inspection standards.

4. The legacy of the nuclear power industry to future generations of Americans will be _____

    _____

    _____.

Comprehension Accuracy:

_____

5. The most serious type of accident that can occur in a nuclear facility is

    a. a violent explosion resulting in a mushroom cloud.
    b. the improper operation of the reactor itself.
    c. a "meltdown" of the uranium core.

Average to fast speeds are appropriate for Selection 10.

EVALUATING YOUR PROGRESS

High-Powered Speed Rate

You can now evaluate your overall progress in achieving flexibility of speed. Follow this procedure to calculate your average high-powered rate:

1. Find the five high-powered speed scores for the selections in this unit (Selections 1, 2, 4, 8, and 10). Add your scores. Divide your total by five to find your average high-powered rate of speed.
    How does this compare with the goals you established in Unit 1? Compare your average high-powered rate with the goal you recorded on p. 6.
2. Add the comprehension percentage scores for these same selections. Divide your total by five to find your average comprehension accuracy score during high-powered speed reading. Congratulations! Increasing your speed brings with it increased efficiency and better comprehension. If you have not yet reached your overall goal, continue applying your high-powered speed skills during daily home practice sessions. In time you will achieve your goals.

Study Reading Rate

Now compute the same scores for your study reading in Selections 3, 5, 6, 7, and 9.

1. Add your scores. Divide by five to find your average study reading speed.
    How does this compare with the goals you established in Unit 1? Compare your average study reading rate with the goal you recorded on p. 6.

2. Add the comprehension percentage scores for these same selections. Divide your total by five to find your average comprehension accuracy score during study reading.

Maintaining a high level of comprehension should be your goal when you increase your study-reading reading rate. You are doing well if you have used faster reading speeds and have maintained or increased your levels of comprehension. You may continue working toward increasingly faster study speeds. Remember, though, that you should read no faster than you can remember. If your comprehension levels have dropped, then decrease your speed and continue applying skills such as previewing, phrase reading and paragraph reading techniques for every new selection you read. Eventually you will achieve a more rapid reading speed.

Epilogue

Now that flexibility training has made you aware of more efficient reading techniques and you have acquired such skills, a warning is appropriate: *you must use these skills or you will rapidly lose them.* It is important that whenever you read—whether you choose magazines, newspapers, or textbooks—you must consciously apply a reading strategy. In other words, *establish a set procedure that you can follow each time you read.* For everything you read, apply these principles:

1. **Select a purpose for your reading.** Ask yourself, ''Why am I reading this? How much do I want to know when I finish?'' This will help you determine which reading speed is most appropriate to use.

2. **Scan the material to identify any unfamiliar words.** Try to grasp the meaning of the word from its context in the selection. If this doesn't work, look up the word in a dictionary or in the glossary of the text. By doing this *before* you actually begin reading, you clear away one barrier that can slow your reading.

3. **Preview the material.** Before you begin to read, familiarize yourself with the main ideas and supporting details within the selection. Jot down a sketch outline as you preview, two or three words per point. Such an outline will take no more than a few minutes. When it is complete, you should be aware of the ideas to be presented.

4. **Decide which speed you will use to read.** This speed should be based on your purpose and your preview.
   a. Will you **skim** to get the main ideas only?
   b. Will you **scan** for a specific piece of information?
   c. Will you use **high-powered speed** for pleasure reading?
   d. Will you use slower, **efficient study reading** for more difficult material?

5. **Read.** After deciding on an appropriate speed, ignore all intrusions. Concentrate fully on the material. Remember to identify major supporting points, paragraph by paragraph, relating each to the main idea.
   a. Use your **phrase reading** skills to identify main ideas and supporting details.
   b. If you are reading a newspaper column or magazine article, complete your reading and then mentally **outline** what you have learned.
   c. If you are reading a textbook, stop to **outline** each major subtopic as you come to it. When you have finished, you will have constructed a complete outline of all the information contained in the selection. This outline can be invaluable as a study tool for taking a test on the material on for writing an essay about it.

If you follow these procedures for each selection you read, you will never again be tempted to fall back into the habit of reading everything at the same speed. Your reading efficiency and flexibility will increase and your concentration and comprehension will improve. You will be a strong speed reader.

Flexibility Chart

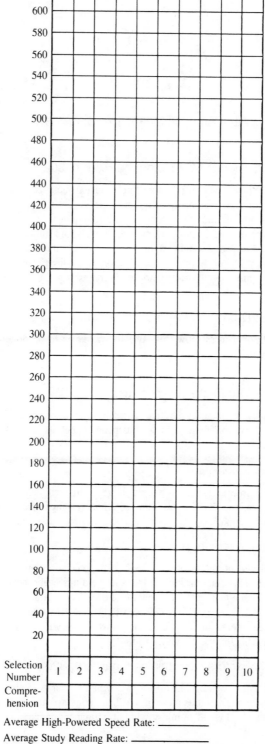

Selection Number	1	2	3	4	5	6	7	8	9	10
Comprehension										

Average High-Powered Speed Rate: _____

Average Study Reading Rate: _____

Answer Key:
Unit 7

Selection 1: What America Means to Me, p. 301

1. a **2.** b **3.** a **4.** a **5.** b

Selection 2: There's No Fleeing the Flea, p. 302

1. humor combined with very interesting, unusual facts **2.** List any five of these: **a.** lived a long time **b.** many different kinds **c.** flat with claws on feet **d.** adults suck blood with siphon **e.** don't thrive in extreme cold or heat. **f.** not especially fertile **g.** fleas have own parasites **h.** cause irritation in animals and humans by injecting proteins into wounds **3.** "Moral turpitude" means: wicked or evil in character; weakness **a.** children watching trashy TV, or **b.** having cavities, or **c.** having rickets **4.** training fleas for entertainment purposes **5.** Choose any phrase relating to the flea's ability to survive or afflict men.

Selection 3: Design and Approach, p. 306

1. to describe in general how this style of writing is to be done, not to give a 1, 2, 3, pattern for actually writing the article. **2.** c **3.** a **4.** b **5.** inductive and deductive reasoning.

Selection 4: The First Rebels, p. 312

1. c **2.** They demonstrate that Africans can develop a very effective governing system and thrive on their own as independent people. **3.** b **4.** False **5.** False

Selection 5: Ideology, p. 314

1. c **2.** Americans as a people have a historic sense of optimism **3.** b **4.** individualization, frontier tradition, optimism, pragmatism and activism, American business creed, democracy **5.** it provides rationales for explaining reality.

Selection 6: Jefferson, p. 318

1. provincial, dictatorial, arrogant **2.** art appreciation, architecture, botany, landscape design **3.** His cultural knowledge and holdings were not inherited. He was self-taught, a self-made man. **4.** That the show was a mixture of what Jefferson really saw and did, but included a generous number of classical art works that Jefferson never saw but had only read about. In his view, the show was trying to show all of classical art's development with Jefferson's views added.

Selection 7: Factors Determining Quality, p. 320

1. b **2.** False **3.** The doctor lives with his charges, knows their language, beliefs, etc. because he must know these if he is to convince the athlete to use the scientific approach which will result in injury without permanent damage. **4.** True **5.** b

Selection 8: How to Cope With Being Out of Work, p. 326

1. False.   **2.** Males   **3.** your earned right, not charity; something to be secured immediately after losing your job   **4.** False   **5.** Choose any three: **a.** vacation at home, backpack or bike **b.** cut food costs, buy on sale **c.** defer mortgage payments on home **d.** tap insurance and other savings **e.** borrow carefully

Selection 9: The Swiss Way of Life, p. 330

1. c   **2.** many rules are imposed on the Swiss   **3.** False   **4.** It was only introduced 60 years ago and became popular just before World War I.   **5.** work as servants in French-speaking or British homes

Selection 10: The Struggle Over Nuclear Power, p. 336

1. The power industry was under severe criticism, especially for the safety of its nuclear power plants.   **2.** It requires nuclear plants to observe very stringent safety rules and almost surely would block construction of any new plants in California. This could also produce an anti-nuclear revolt nationwide.   **3.** b   **4.** the disposal and careful monitoring of radioactive wastes.   **5.** c

Bibliography

Adams, Royce W. *Developing Reading Versatility*. New York, N.Y.: Holt, Rinehart and Winston, Inc., 1973.

Bracy, Jane and Miriam McClintock. *Read to Succeed*. New York, N.Y.: McGraw-Hill Book Company, 1975.

Johnson, Ben E. *Learn to RAPID-READ*. Indianapolis, IN.: Howard W. Sams & Co., Inc., 1977.

Robinson, H. Alan and Ellen Lamar Thomas. *Improving Reading in Every Class*. Boston: Allyn and Bacon, Inc., 1977.

Smith, Nila Banton. *Read Faster and Get More From Your Reading*. Englewood Cliffs, N.J.: Prentice-Hall, Inc., 1958.

Spache, George D. and Paul C. Berg. *The Art of Efficient Reading*. New York, N.Y.: Macmillan Publishing Company, 1978.

Walcutt, Charles C., et al. *Teaching Reading, A Phonic/Linguistic Approach to Developmental Reading*. New York, N.Y. Macmillan Publishing Company, 1974.

Acknowledgments

Adams, W. Royce. Excerpts from *Developing Reading Versatility,* Second Edition. Copyright © 1977, 1973 by Holt, Rinehart and Winston. Reprinted by permission of Holt, Rinehart and Winston.

Allard, William A. Excerpts from "Chinatown, the Gilded Ghetto." *National Geographic,* 148 (May 1970), p. 637. Copyright © 1970 by The National Geographic Society. Reprinted by permission.

Allen, Ken. "Playboy Visits Down Home to Find 'Girl Next Door'." *The Charlotte Observer,* Charlotte, N.C., 26 Mar. 1978, Sec. A, p. 14. Reprinted with permission.

Ashe, Arthur. "What America Mean to Me." *Reader's Digest,* 108 (Jan. 1976) pp. 119–20. Copyright © 1976, by The Reader's Digest Association, Inc. Pleasantville, N.Y. Reprinted with permission.

Burner, Marcus, Rosenberg. *AMERICA: A Portrait in History, Volume I/A New People,* © 1974, pp. 42, 81, 99, 184, 186, 300, 304. Reprinted by permission of Prentice-Hall, Inc., Englewood Cliffs, N.J.

Capotosto, Rosario. "The ABC's of Veneering in Easy Photo Steps." Reprinted from *Mechanix Illustrated Magazine,* 73 (March 1977), p. 118. Copyright © March 1977 by CBS Publications, Inc.

Chan, Janet. "Teaching Your Body to Work Better." *McCall's,* (Dec. 1978). Copyright © 1978 by The McCall Publishing Company. Reprinted by permission.

Collins, Myrtle T. and Dwayne R. Collins. Excerpts from *Survival Kit for Teachers,* pp. 35, 60, 85–86. Copyright © 1975 by Goodyear Publishing Company, Inc. Reprinted by permission.

Conger, Dean. Excerpts from "Siberia: Russia's Frozen Northland." *National Geographic,* 131 (March 1967), pp. 341, 344. Copyright © 1967 by The National Geographic Society. Reprinted by permission.

"Congress Where The People Speak." *U.S. News and World Report,* 82 (May 1977), pp. 49–51. Copyright © 1977 The *U.S. News and World Report.* Reprinted by permission.

Conlin, David A. et al. Excerpts from *Our Language Today—8.* Copyright © 1966 American Book Company. Reprinted by permission.

Cooper, Mildred and Kenneth H. Cooper, M.D. "One Woman's Liberation From Fat, Fatigue and Apathy," from *Aerobics for Women.* Copyright © 1972 by Mildred Cooper and Kenneth Cooper, M.D. Reprinted by permission of the publisher, M. Evans and Company, Inc., New York, N.Y. 10017.

Cramer, Ronald L. "Nativist Theory," from *Children's Writing and Language Growth,* Columbus, OH: Charles E. Merrill Publishing Co., 1979, pp. 11–12.

David, Lester. "How to Cope With Being Out of Work." *Mechanix Illustrated,* 67 (March 1971), pp. 53–55, 152. Reprinted from *Mechanix Illustrated* magazine. Copyright © 1971, by CBS Publications, Inc.

Dechant, Emerald V. and Henry P. Smith. PSYCHOLOGY IN TEACHING READING, 2nd ed., Copyright © 1977, pp. 38–39, 93, 138. Reprinted by permission of Prentice-Hall, Inc., Englewood Cliffs, N.J.

De La Haba, Louis and Long, Michael E. Excerpts from "Belize: The Awakening Land," *National Geographic,* 141 (Jan. 1972), Copyright © 1972, The National Geographic Society. Reprinted by permission.

Earle, Sylvia A. Excerpts from "All Girl Team Tests the Habitat," *National Geographic,* 140 (Aug. 1971), p. 291. Copyright © 1971 by The National Geographic Society. Reprinted by permission.

Fell, Derek. "Daffodils go au naturel. Grow ones that spread in drifts and clumps." From *Plant's Alive,* 6 (Oct. 1978), pp. 26–27. Copyright © 1978 *Plant's Alive.* Reprinted by permission.

Fellows, Brian H. Excerpts from *The Discrimination Process and Development.* Copyright © 1968 Pergamon Press, Ltd. Reprinted by permission.

Fest, Joachim C. "Contents" from HITLER, pp. vi and vii. Copyright © 1973 by Verlag Ullstein; English translation by Richard and Clara Winston, Copyright © 1974 by, and reprinted with permission of, Harcourt Brace Jovanovich, Inc.

"The First Rebels," TIME, 108 (12 July 1976), p. 34. Reprinted by permission from TIME, The Weekly Newsmagazine; Copyright Time Inc. 1976.

Fodor, Eugene, Ed. Selections from *Fodor's Switzerland*. Copyright © 1977 by Fodor's Modern Guides. Reprinted by permission.

Fox, Michael W. "How To Choose A Dog." *McCall's* (Aug. 1978), pp. 104, 106, 210. Copyright © 1978 by The McCall Publishing Company. Reprinted by permission.

Friedman, Myra. "How I Learned to Sleep." *McCall's*, 106 (Nov. 1978), Copyright © 1978 by The McCall Publishing Company. Reprinted by permission.

"Gardeners Find Greenhouse Can Increase Delights of Horticulture," *The Charlotte Observer*, Charlotte, N.C., 26 Mar. 1978, Sec. G, p. 9. Reprinted by permission.

Gaspar, Radomir and Dalid Brown. From PERCEPTUAL PROCESSES IN READING. Copyright © 1973 Hutchinson Educational Books, Ltd. Reprinted by permission.

Goldman, Eric F. from THE CRUCIAL DECADE. Copyright © 1956 by Eric Goldman. Reprinted by permission of Alfred A. Knopf, Inc.

Graf, A.B. Excerpts from *Exotic Plant Manual: Fascinating Plants to Live With—Their Requirements, Propagation, and Use*, 2nd ed. Copyright © 1970 by Roehrs Company. Reprinted by permission.

"Grasshoppers: They're Kinky, Really Kinky." *The Charlotte Observer*, Charlotte, N.C., 26 Mar. 1978, Sec A, p. 12. Reprinted by permission.

Hannon, Leslie F., ed. "Nineteenth Century Niagra," MACLEANS CANADA. Copyright © 1960 by McClelland Stewart Limited. Reprinted by permission of Hawthorn Properties (Elsevier-Dutton Publishing Co., Inc.)

Hobbs, Jack A. Selection from ART IN CONTEXT, pp. 81–85. Copyright © 1975 by Harcourt, Brace, Jovanovich, Inc. Reprinted by permission of the publisher.

Holmes, Marjorie. "Look Out—Your Punctuation Is Showing," from LOVE AND LAUGHTER, pp. 182–84. Copyright © 1959, 1967 by Marjorie Holmes Mighell. Reprinted by permission of Doubleday & Company, Inc.

Holmes, Parker M. et al. (Eds.) "Anthropology's Contributions to Marketing." *Readings in Marketing*. Columbus, OH: Charles E. Merrill Publishing Co., 1963, pp. 144–51.

Howe, Louise Kapp. "Secretaries: Are Bosses Getting Their Message?" *McCall's*, 105 (Sept. 1978) pp. 93–96. Copyright © 1978 by The McCall's Publishing Company. Reprinted by permission.

Janson, H.W. and Dora H. Janson. Selection from *The Story of Painting From Cave Painting to Modern Times* by H.W. Janson and Dora H. Janson. Copyright © 1963 by Harry N. Abrams, Inc. Reprinted by permission.

"Jefferson: Taste of the Founders." *Time*, 108 (12 July 1976), p. 51. Reprinted by permission from TIME, The Weekly Newsmagazine, Copyright Time, Inc. 1976.

"The Jogging-shoe Race Heats Up." Reprinted from the April 9, 1979 issue of *Business Week* by special permission. Copyright © 1979 by McGraw-Hill, Inc., New York. 10020. All rights reserved.

Jolna, Stacy. "Business, Labor Join to Battle Alcoholism." *The Washington Post*, 5 Feb. 1978. Copyright © 1978 *The Washington Post*. Reprinted by permission.

Jordan, Thomas E. Excerpts from *The Exceptional Child*. Copyright © 1962 Charles E. Merrill Publishing Company. Reprinted by permission.

King, Peter H. "Chinese Greet Year of Horse." *The Daily Reflector*, 7 Feb. 1978. Copyright © 1978 The Associated Press. Reprinted by permission.

La Grand, Louis E. Excerpts from the book DISCIPLINE IN THE SECONDARY SCHOOL. Copyright © 1969 by Parker Publishing Co., Inc. Published by Parker Publishing Co., Inc., West Nyack, New York 10994.

Li, David H. "Accounting as a Tool of Management," *Accounting for Management Analysis*. Columbus, OH: Charles E. Merrill Publishing Co., 1964, pp. 2–8.

Lidster, Douglas. "Car Rentals." *Better Homes and Gardens*, 54 (Jan. 1976) p. 26. Copyright © Meredith Corp. 1976. All rights reserved.

Mitchell, John M. "Design and Approach," from WRITING FOR PROFESSIONAL AND TECHNICAL JOURNALS. Copyright © 1968 John Wiley and Sons, Inc. Reprinted by permission.

Molstad-Anderson, Oystein. "Only One Came Back." *Reader's Digest*, 108 (March 1976) pp. 64–68.

Copyright © 1976, by The Reader's Digest Association, Inc. Pleasantville, N.Y. Reprinted with permission.

"Monday Television." *The News and Observer*, Raleigh, N.C., 1 June 1981, p. 16. Reprinted with permission.

Mydans, Seth. "Pop Eyed in Moscow." *The Washington Post*, 5 Feb. 1978. Copyright © 1978. Reprinted by permission of The Associated Press.

"Namibia: A Wealth of Minerals Waiting to be Tapped." Reprinted from the December 4, 1978 issue of *Business Week* by special permission, Copyright © 1978 by McGraw-Hill, Inc., New York, N.Y. 10020. All rights reserved.

"Narrow Guage in Italy." *The New York Times*, Oct. 1980. Copyright © 1980 *The New York Times*. Reprinted by permission.

"National Autofinders, Inc." Advertisement. *The News and Observer*, Raleigh, N.C., 1 June 1981, p. 8.

"Nixon's Embarrassing Road Show." TIME, 107 (8 Mar. 1976) pp. 22–25. Reprinted by permission from TIME, The Weekly Newsmagazine. Copyright Time Inc. 1976.

"Oil Spill Is No Holiday for Resorts." *The Charlotte Observer*, Charlotte, N.C. 26 Mar. 1978, Sec. A, p. 8. Reprinted by permission.

"Pack Up Your Ski Togs; Time to Hit the Beach." *The Charlotte Observer*, Charlotte, N.C. 26 Mar. 1978, Sec. E, p. 1. Reprinted by permission.

Petrovich, Michael B. and Philip D. Curtin. Excerpts from INDIA AND SOUTHEAST ASIA. Copyright © 1970 Silver Burdette Company. Reprinted by permission.

The Phone Book. Copyright © 1979. Carolina Telephone & Telegraph Company. Reprinted by permission.

Pines, Maya. "Modern Bioengineers Reinvent Human Anatomy Using Spare Parts." *The Smithsonian*, 9 (Nov. 1978), pp. 50–56. Reprinted by permission of the author.

Pitcher, Evelyn Goodenough. "Male and Female." *Atlantic Monthly*. Copyright © 1963, by The Atlantic Monthly Company, Boston, Mass. Reprinted by permission.

"Praise Julia, Pass the Haute Cuisine." *The Charlotte Observer*, Charlotte, N.C. 26 March 1978, Sec. E, p. 4. Reprinted by permission.

PSYCHOLOGY FOR TEACHING, A BEAR ALWAYS USUALLY FACES THE FRONT, Second Edition, by Guy R. Lefrancois. Copyright © 1975 by Wadsworth Publishing Company, Inc. Reprinted by permission of Wadsworth Publishing Company, Belmont, California 94002.

Richardson, Ivan L. and Baldwin, Sidney. "Ideology," *Public Administration: Government in Action*. Columbus, OH: Charles E. Merrill Publishing Co., 1976.

Robinson, Edward J. "Public Relations." From *Communication and Public Relations*. Columbus, OH: Charles E. Merrill Publishing Co., 1966, pp. 40–55. Reprinted by permission.

Robson, H. Evans, "Beliefs, Customs, Traditions," pp. 13–17 from *Encyclopedia of Sport Sciences and Medicine*, Leonard A. Larson, Ed. Copyright © 1971 by Macmillan Publishing Co., Inc. Reprinted by permission of Macmillan Publishing Co., Inc.

"Roses Prized for Ages as Medicine and Food." *The Charlotte Observer*, Charlotte, N.C., 26 Mar. 1978, Sec. G, p. 7. Reprinted by permission.

"Run the Gamut to Jogging Comfort." *The Charlotte Observer*, Charlotte, N.C., 26 March 1978, Sec. E, p. 6. Copyright © 1978 *The Charlotte Observer*. Reprinted by permission.

Ryan, Peter and Ludeh Pesek. Excerpts from UFO's AND OTHER WORLDS. London: Penguin Books, 1975, p. 41. Copyright © 1975 Penguin Books, Ltd. Reprinted by permission.

Schein, Jerome D. and Marcus Delk, Jr. Excerpts from THE DEAF POPULATION OF THE U.S. Copyright © 1974 National Association of the Deaf. Reprinted by permission.

Sessoms, H. Douglas. "Biases, Prejudices, Tolerance," pp. 18–19. From the ENCYCLOPEDIA OF SPORT SCIENCES AND MEDICINE, Leonard Larson, Ed. Copyright © 1971 by Macmillan Publishing Co., Inc. Reprinted with permission of Macmillan Publishing Co., Inc.

"The Shot Heard Round the World." *U.S. News and World Report*, 14 Apr. 1975 pp. 57–59. Copyright © 1975 U.S. News & World Report, Inc. Reprinted with permission.

Smith, H. Allen and Ira L. Smith. Excerpts from *Low and Inside, A Book of Baseball Anecdotes, Oddities, and Curiosities*. Copyright © 1949 by H. Allen Smith and Ira L. Smith. Copyright © renewed 1976 by H. Allen Smith and Ira L. Smith. Reprinted by permission of the Harold Matson Company, Inc.

Smith, Nila Banton. Excerpts from READ FASTER AND GET MORE FROM YOUR READING.

Copyright © 1958 by Prentice-Hall, Inc., Published by Prentice-Hall, Inc., Englewood Cliffs, New Jersey 07632.

Smith, Susan J. "Dictionary Documents Dialects." *The Daily Reflector*, 26 Oct. 1980. p. C–8. Reprinted by permission of The Associated Press.

Excerpts from Snell, Martha. *Systematic Instruction of the Moderately and Severely Handicapped.* Columbus, OH: Charles E. Merrill Publishing Co., 1978, pp. 3, 9.

Stauffer, Russell G. et al. "Index." DIAGNOSIS, CORRECTION, AND PREVENTION OF READING DISABILITIES. Copyright © 1978, Harper & Row Publishers, Inc. Reprinted by permission.

"The Struggle Over Nuclear Power." TIME, 107 (8 Mar. 1976), pp. 69–70. Reprinted by permission from TIME, The Weekly Newsmagazine. Copyright Time, Inc. 1976.

Sturm, Paul W. Excerpt from "German Autos: Small Is Beautiful," FORBES, 123 (March 1979), p. 40. Copyright © 1979 by FORBES MAGAZINE. Reprinted by permission.

Texas Instruments Learning Center. Excerpts from *The Great International Math on Keys Book.* Copyright © 1976 Texas Instruments, Inc. Reprinted by permission.

"There's No Fleeing the Flea." *Reader's Digest,* 112 (Jan. 1978), pp. 11–16. Copyright © 1978, The Reader's Digest Association, Inc., Pleasantville, N.Y. Reprinted by permission.

Thomas, Dian. From ROUGHING IT EASY. Copyright © 1974, by Brigham Young University Press, Provo, Utah. Reprinted by permission.

Thomas, Ellen Lamar and Robinson, H. Alan. Excerpts from IMPROVING READING IN EVERY CLASS, Second Edition. Copyright © 1977 by Allyn and Bacon, Inc., Boston, Mass. Reprinted by permission.

Thurston, Hazel. "History." *The Travellers' Guide to the Balearics: Majorca, Minorca, Ibize & Formentera.* Copyright © 1979 Jonathan Cape Ltd. Reprinted by permission.

Truslow, Frederick K. Excerpt from "Businessmen in the Bush," *National Geographic,* 137 (May 1970), p. 650. Copyright © 1970 by The National Geographic Society. Reprinted by permission.

"Tips for Cold Weather Driving." Reprinted from the February 1980 issue of *Family Circle Magazine.* Copyright © 1980 The Family Circle, Inc. All rights reserved.

"Udderly and Odderly, the Otters." *The Daily Reflector.* 9 Apr. 1978. Copyright © 1978 by The Associated Press. Reprinted by permission.

Valente, William D. "Racial and Ethnic Discrimination." *Law in the Schools.* Columbus, OH: Charles E. Merrill Publishing Co., 1980. Reprinted by permission.

Van Lawick-Goodall, Baroness Jane. Excerpts from "Tool-using Bird: The Egyptian Vulture" *National Geographic,* 133 (May 1968), pp. 631–41. Copyright © 1968 by The National Geographic Society. Reprinted by permission.

Waldman, John. Excerpts from READING WITH SPEED AND CONFIDENCE. Copyright © 1972 Random House, Inc. Reprinted by permission.

"Want Ads." Classification Index. *The News and Observer,* Raleigh, N.C., 8 Apr. 1978, p. 33. Reprinted by permission.

"Want to Buy A Nice Swimming Pool? Then Don't Let Yourself Get Soaked." *The Charlotte Observer,* Charlotte, N.C., 26 Mar. 1978, Sec. G, p. 2. Reprinted by permission.

"Wife-selling in England." *The Daily Reflector,* 9 Apr. 1978. Copyright © 1978 by The Associated Press. Reprinted by permission.

"Will Pollution Controls Boost Electric Bills?" *Environmental Protection Agency Journal* (June 1977). Reprinted by permission of the publisher.

"Women Become Farm Managers." *The Daily Reflector,* 8 Jan. 1977. Copyright © 1977 by The Associated Press. Reprinted by permission.

Wood, Dorothy A. Excerpt from *Test Construction.* Copyright © 1961 Charles E. Merrill Publishing Co. Reprinted by permission.

Yates, Brock. "The Best Small Cars." *Family Circle Magazine,* 92 (20 Nov. 1979), pp. 31, 32, and 62. Reprinted by permission.

Zahl. Paul A. "Scallops See With a Hundred Eyes," from "The Magic Lure of Sea Shells," *National Geographic,* 135 (March 1969), p. 396. Copyright © 1969 by The National Geographic Society. Reprinted by permission.